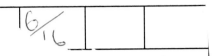

POLES IN DEFENCE OF
GREAT BRITAIN

Poles in Defence of Great Britain

July 1940 – June 1941

by Robert Gretzyngier

in association with Wojtek Matusiak

GRUB STREET · LONDON

First published in 2001 by
Grub Street
4 Rainham Close
London SW11 6SS

Copyright © 2001 Grub Street, London
Text copyright © Robert Gretzyngier

This 75th Anniversary Edition first published 2016

British Library Cataloguing in Publication Data
   A CIP record for this title is available from the British Library

ISBN 978-1-910690-15-4

Typeset by Pearl Graphics, Hemel Hempstead

Printed and bound in India by Replika Press Pvt. Ltd.

CONTENTS

ACKNOWLEDGEMENTS

This book could not have been compiled without the generous assistance of many Polish Air Force airmen, veterans of WWII. I am particularly indebted to Jerzy B. Cynk, G/Cpt Stanisław Wandzilak and Roman Kulik, who supported me and my friend Wojtek Matusiak in our endless research in London archives. Their priceless help in surviving our yearly expeditions to the Last Hope Island are inestimable. I would like to thank Stanisław Bochniak, Jan Budziński, Michał Cwynar, Edward Jaworski, Ludwik Martel, and many others for their anecdotes, details of service of the Polish personnel in the RAF, as well as hours of discussions.

Special thanks go to Andrzej Suchcitz, Wacław Milewski and Krzysztof Barbarski from the Polish Institute and Sikorski Museum in London, as well as to the staff of the RAF Museum, Hendon, the Public Records Office at Kew for their patience, and to Christopher Shores for his excellent foreword.

Among those who kindly provided information and photographs were: Peter Arnold, Bartłomiej Belcarz, Krzysztof Chołoniewski, Stefan Czmur, Tomasz Drecki, Mrs. Gabszewicz and Stefan Gabszewicz, Kazimierz Gardzina, Franciszek Xawery Grabowski, Jerzy Janaszewski, Dr Jan P. Koniarek, Tomek Kopański, Leszek A. Kosiński, Michał Mucha, Jiři Rajlich, Andrew Różycki, Paweł Sembrat, Grzegorz Śliżewski, Olivier Tyrbas de Chamberet, Simon Watson, Piotr Wiśniewski, and Józef Zieliński.

My final thanks always go to my wife who supported my interest in the Polish Air Force history for the last decade, continuously asking 'when are you going to finish your work?'

PREFACE

By the time I and my friends arrived in Britain in 1940, we had travelled around the whole of Europe, spurred by the will to fight for our oppressed homeland. My desire to fight was finally fulfilled when I was posted to a fighter squadron of the RAF. Far from officialdom, among my British colleagues, I felt really happy. Luck was with me during those months – it was with me when I shot down an enemy plane, and it did not abandon me when I was badly hit myself.

The latter fact is more and more often brought to my attention – both by my old bones, and by people who have researched the Battle of Britain. For some time now they have not only been British historians, but also young men from Poland, who persistently bother me and my aged friends with detailed questions about what happened sixty years ago. Unfortunately, they are not always satisfied with my answers, while my memory does not serve me as it used to . . .

Attending Battle of Britain meetings every year, I notice fewer and fewer of the familiar faces, and the number of surviving Polish participants of that great air battle has long since become a single-digit one. More and more often we mourn yet another Polish pilot who at one time flew in defence of Britain. If not for the commemorative plaques, monuments, and memorials, erected by the Polish Air Force Association as well as by our British friends, any trace of the Polish Air Force on British soil would soon be gone.

When we came to this Island of Last Hope, nobody promised things would be easy. We fought on, knowing that a good life is seldom an easy one. Today, it is not easy, too, when we fight to preserve the memory of that great effort and great sacrifice of so many young lives. I see this book about Poles who fought in defence of Britain as a homage to the lost generation and to all my colleagues, even if I no longer remember their names.

Ludwik Martel

AUTHOR'S PREFACE

This work was initiated during one of the last Polish Air Force Association congresses by discussions between members of the PAFA and young history enthusiasts. For many years historians from my country were cut off from the historical sources of the Polish Air Force, located mostly in London. All information about the PAF history and people who served in its units came from the books published in Poland, written by several pilots who survived the war and the communists' repressions. In fact my interest in the Polish airmen serving in the RAF during WWII was aroused when I read the exciting stories of those fighter pilots. Many years later I was able to meet and talk to Witold Łokuciewski, Bolesław Gładych, Witold Urbanowicz, Stanisław Skalski, and other top scoring aces of the famous Polish squadrons, and then I realised how little we knew about the birth of the Polish Air Force in Britain and the first year of fighting against the Germans alongside the RAF. Every child in Poland knows about 303 Squadron and its heroes, but the knowledge about other units is almost nil. Also English speaking readers associate the famous *Kościuszko* Squadron with its victories during the Battle of Britain, but who knows of the Polish airmen serving in many of the RAF squadrons? The rest of the Polish Air Force is left somewhere in the shadow of the most famous unit and its pilots.

It is hard to describe the feelings of all the people who in September 1939 left their homeland and answered the appeals of their commanders to continue their fight. Left only with shabby uniforms, they made the long journey through European and North African countries to reform the Polish Air Force, first in France and finally in Britain. To show the hard days of the Polish soldiers I decided to use their original memoirs and diaries written during the war, as often as it was possible. Now, their stories provide a colourful addition to the documents preserved in archives and museums, which show only dates, figures and names of what then was their entire life.

This work is dedicated to those who sacrificed their lives in wartime.

FOREWORD

By the end of August Fighter Command had been fighting a series of increasingly desperate combats since the Dunkirk evacuation, three months earlier. During this period many of the long serving, experienced career pilots had been killed, wounded, or were close to exhaustion. Others – particularly those who had been involved in the fighting over France during the weeks of the 'Blitzkreig', had already been rested and sent to the new Operation Training Units in order that they might pass on at least a fraction of the experience they had gained to those now being rushed through the training process to get them into the front line units as replacements and reinforcements.

In the situation in which the Command found itself, there were simply insufficient pilots and insufficient time to train those that were available, before they had to be thrown into the fray. The brilliant initiative that had set up the RAF Volunteer Reserve had provided at least a 'nursery' of partly trained personnel when war broke out, but now these young acolytes, and indeed, many pilots from other Commands who now volunteered to transfer to fighters, were being provided with so brief an introduction to operational flying, as to be little more than nothing. Whereas later in the war the period spent at OTUs would stretch for weeks, at this time no more than a few days could be provided, so great was the call for replacements. Many young pilots arrived on their first squadrons with only a few hours of experience of flying a Hurricane or Spitfire – barely enough to allow them to take off, hold formation, and land again. Indepth training in aerial gunnery simply was not available.

In consequence numerous squadrons – both newly-formed or withdrawn after suffering heavy casualties – were little more than advanced training units. Steadily, the quality of the defence offered to the depredations of the experienced units of the Luftwaffe, was declining.

Against this background, and at this crucial moment, three squadrons of Polish and Czech pilots entered the battle. The majority of their pilots were highly-trained, experienced prewar personnel, many of whom had already fought the Luftwaffe over Poland or France – or in some cases, over both countries. Although there was some initial difficulty in adapting to the advanced defensive methods then employed by Fighter Command, which required direct control by radio, and whilst there were some problems with the controls and instrumentation of the British fighters which they now had to fly – particularly with the throttles, which operated in the opposite direction to those on the machines which they had previously flown – these were soon overcome. Essentially, these units contained relevant experience that was of an incomparably greater level than that of other new units which were being sent into action at the very height of the Battle of Britain. Above all, these Polish and Czech pilots knew how to shoot – and were deeply motivated to do so.

Some of their fellow nationals had already joined British units where they had rapidly demonstrated their prowess. Some would now join their own countrymen to add the extra experience which they had so recently gained, whilst others continued to serve alongside their British and Commonwealth colleagues.

For the reasons set out, the immediate impact of the arrival in 11 Group of 303 Squadron proved quite disproportionate to the numbers involved, and the unit rapidly achieved extraordinary results and a tremendous reputation, soon becoming one of the very highest-scorers of the Battle. Some may ask why their fellow Poles on 302 Squadron and the Czechs of 310 Squadron did not at one achieve similar results and fame. This book soon makes the reason clear – while 303 was in the front line with 11 Group, the other two units were retained initially in 12 Group, with many fewer opportunities to engage in the heart of the fighting until later in the year, when the pace of the air war changed anyway.

The efforts of the Polish pilots and the contribution they made to the later stages of the Battle of Britain were exemplary and were of the highest possible value to the Allied war effort. They gained for themselves a place of deep affection and gratitude in the hearts of the British people at the time, and hopefully history will not come to forget their achievements. It is my privilege and a great honour to be able to salute them by writing the foreword to this book.

Herein will be found the full story of what they did during 1940 and into the Spring of 1941 – and I mean the full story. Every victory, every loss, indeed, virtually every posting, is recorded here. But the story also tells the oft-neglected non-operational tale, recording as it does all the tragic losses and embarrassing accidents that occurred during the dangerous business of flying aircraft, even when no enemy was about. When the reader has read this book, he will know everything about the involvement of the Polish fighter pilots during the period under review.

Having introduced Robert Gretzyngier and his manuscript to Grub Street, it was both a pleasure and a satisfaction to be asked both to edit the book, and to write this foreword to it. A word about the editing; whilst I set out to Anglicise the text which Robert had prepared, I have sought to make no change to the words of the pilots themselves, recorded as they were at or near the time in question. These excerpts from combat reports, diaries, subsequent accounts and unit record books have been included just as they were written. Identifications of aircraft types, ranks, units, etc., have not been edited for conformity or "house style". The grammar and terminology has not been corrected at all, however quaint some wording may seem to the English-speaking reader. This, I believe, gives a greater flavour of the time and the events recorded.

Only the linking text was modified to being it in line with other Grub Street campaign histories.

Christopher Shores
Hendon, June 2000

INTRODUCTION

LONG WAY TO THE LAST HOPE ISLAND

Almost all youngsters in the Poland of the late twenties were fascinated by technological innovations and modern vehicles. Overseas travels were inspired by the *Liga Morska i Kolonialna* (Maritime and Colonial League), while aeroplane and glider flying was widely popularised by *Liga Obrony Powietrznej i Przeciwgazowej* (Air and Anti-Gas Defence League). Aircraft became a challenge for the traditional gallant cavalry. An image of a winged rider, as well as that of a cavalryman, was then very attractive to young men.

Successes of Polish engineers and pilots in the Challenge of Tourists' Aeroplanes competitions at the beginning of the thirties, and the growing aeronautical industry gave good background to the training of military pilots. However, the possibility of expansion, or even recognition of the air force's potential, still under the strong influence of army staff officers, was rather limited.

1 September 1939 was the most tragic date for every Pole who could remember it. After twenty-one years of independence, the entire country and its military power collapsed before the eyes of its allies in just a few weeks.

Well organised air defence of the capital city led by płk. Stefan Pawlikowski proved the value of Polish airmen during the first week of the campaign. A system generally similar to that which saved Britain almost a year later, but fully dependent on observation posts rather than radar, lost its operational value the day the front collapsed and the Polish Army began its retreat. That day the OC of the *Brygada Pościgowa* (Pursuit Brigade) had many more skilled pilots than serviceable aircraft. All younger officers and soldiers believed help would come from France and Britain, which both declared war against Germany on 3 September. Until the day the Soviet Union invaded the eastern part of Poland on 17 September, almost all airmen trusted that French units would come to join the fight, and the promises of aircraft deliveries seemed very real. The myth of English and French aircraft awaiting delivery in Constanta docks in Rumania was in many cases the only reason for the younger flying personnel to head south. Had they known the truth, those young Polish Air Force cadets, eager to fight and well trained, would have joined up and taken part in combat against the aggressor on the ground, unable to fight in the air due to the shortage of serviceable aircraft. Fortunately, many of them, led by instructors of the Air Force College or unit commanders who understood the value of well trained young pilots, reached Rumania. There they soon realised that none of the modern aircraft had arrived, the Allies had failed to fulfil their promises, and Poland was left alone in its fight. Many officers decided to go back home, to fight in the underground resistance movement, while others answered Gen. Sikorski's appeal, and would go to France to form new Polish units. As the Rumanian authorities did their best to force Polish military personnel into internment, officers and men were quickly transformed into 'tourists', 'artists', 'students', 'teachers', 'businessmen' etc., which brought them the collective nickname of 'Sikorski's tourists'. With new documents, avoiding security checks inspired by German secret services, those 'tourists' headed for Rumanian ports.

> "Foreigners, when talking to us about the 1939 Campaign, would nod their heads with pity, using uncertain arguments about our inefficiency. Shame would burn our faces, and why . . . Later on they would realise, change their opinions, but it would be too late, the wrong they did at that time, has its evil consequences to date. I was overwhelmed by all that, and when my friends and colleagues started to describe how unprepared France was for the war, this would take away any wish to think about the future."[1]

These words came from the personal diary of Maj Jakub Kosiński, one of the officers involved in transferring the Polish 'tourists' to France. In a few weeks, a well established chain to transport them to France was organised, and soon the Training Centre at Lyon-Bron was set up. The most experienced fighter pilots formed the backbone of the training staff, and quickly converted from obsolete monoplanes to modern French aircraft. The training process was in full swing when Germany invaded France. Meanwhile, the idea of forming some Polish units in the British Isles became a reality. The witness of those days, Maj Kosiński, wrote at the end of 1939:

> "Recruitment of airmen, both flying and ground personnel, for the air units formed in England has started. Special English commissions selected the people who were later sent for training in England. Initially there were too many candidates, so only those who volunteered and were accepted by the English Commission were recruited. Obviously, the English selected the best candidates, both in terms of health, and combat experience from the Polish campaign. This question was assessed by the English with great reserve, as they did not know the Polish character, while our momentary moods, and lack of discipline amongst us, did not give the English a good opinion of us. What was more, enemy propaganda did their best to discourage the English towards us, maintaining that no army in history, after a total military defeat, had been able to re-create itself without fresh force from outside in order to present any significant military value. But our friends held to their opinions. England agreed to an experiment which in that country's critical moment proved its value. Forming our air force in England was obviously not without snags and problems, caused by our people. Some of the difficulties brought the whole enterprise close to cancellation. Those difficulties stemmed from the oath to the King of Britain. Some 'gung-ho patriotic' cadet-

---

[1] Maj Jakub Kosiński wrote his wartime memoirs in the form of a letter to his son, Leszek, whom he had left at the age of 10 in occupied Poland. These unpublished diaries were kept by his son for a long time before he decided to show them to persons interested in the history of the Polish Air Force in Britain. These memoirs gave a very detailed personal account of the formation stage of the PAF in the West, the less known part of its history.

officers refused to take the oath, saying they were soldiers of Poland and would not swear loyalty to a foreign king. The whole matter was eventually settled, and those most excitable were sent back to France. The rest took the oath.[2]

"The cadre of the future entire Polish Air Force started its work in Britain."

In the meantime Polish airmen, split among fighter units, took part in the Battle of France. The only complete Polish-manned unit flew Caudron CR 714 Cyclone modified racing aircraft, and claimed some victories, even though most of the pilots of that unit stated that the Caudron was very pleasant to fly, but useless for combat. Several fighter sections attached to French front-line units also claimed victories.

The disorder in the French army and reluctance to continue the war among the French population brought the armistice and forced the Polish forces to withdraw their units to Britain. Again, the most valuable element of the reborn Polish Air Force had to be moved in a hurry to its new destination. Maj. Kosiński described the arrival to Britain:

"We arrived in Britain. That night an air raid sounded. Artillery fired somewhere inland. But the Germans did not bomb, as they only laid mines in the water. On the morning of 16 July everything alive came up to the main deck, looking at the docks and the city, located on both sides of the river. Of the entire convoy, only our ship entered Liverpool. The rest of the ships steamed north during the night. People ferrying across the river waved in a friendly manner at our ship anchored in the middle of the river Mersey. This very first contact with the local population proved that these people felt friendly towards us, a good omen. I was afraid, though, that our soldiers should not spoil it with their actions. Our soldiers, having put their clothes in order, washed and shaved as much as was possible, looked quite well in the shining sun. They showed no trace of the recent events, the difficult journey in less than primitive conditions. The contentious and irritable attitude disappeared, replaced by kindness and helpfulness. May this be a good omen for the many, many hard days ahead of us. Looking at the docks and the city from the deck, I felt a strange calmness engulf me. Huge buildings towered around, shining in the sun, full of solemn, calm, and wealthy appeal. My thoughts then flew far away, to my home country. Not long ago a foreigner would have got a similar impression in our beloved Gdynia and so, so many other Polish cities, that now lay in ruins.

"The sound of the raised anchor interrupted my reflections. We were going to berth and disembark. An English officer with a civilian came on board, asked płk. Luziński if he knew everybody who arrived with him, and upon receiving an affirmative answer he informed us that we would disembark directly into a train that awaited us at the harbour station. I was appointed the disembarking officer. I was responsible for the disembarking and loading onto the train. I was given an interpreter for assistance. I disembarked and stepped onto English soil. Through a tunnel under a harbour building the interpreter and I went to the railway station, where at Platform 1 there was a train for us, that included 1st and 3rd class carriages, which at first sight only differed in the signs of the I or III

---

[2] One of the protesting pilots later wrote: "The Nation that bears the slogan 'for our freedom and yours' needs no oath".

class. Both classes had soft seats. The only difference was that a compartment in 1st class had six seats, while a compartment in 3rd class, eight seats. English railways have no 2nd class cars, and they are a private enterprise, not state-owned like ours in Europe. We started disembarking and loading onto the train immediately, and soon completed it. I went back to the ship to take my belongings and say goodbye to the Captain of the ship. At the farewell, which seemed pretty cordial for a cold-blooded Englishman, I handed him a small Belgian pistol as a souvenir from myself, in recognition of his kindness on the ship. This small gift delighted the Englishman, who asked me to pay him a visit in Central England, where he lived with his family. Unfortunately, we have never met again, as this ship was soon sunk by the Germans, and the Captain went down with it. We left our 'Cidonia' (the name of our ship) with a sentimental feeling and gratefulness for bringing us safely to England. Soon our train departed. We did not know where we were being taken to. We carried on without stopping at stations, their names unknown to us as they were all overpainted. About 6 pm our train stopped at a small station, where we were told to get off. At the station we were met by three English officers from the RAF and a couple of trucks. Our belongings were loaded onto these trucks, and the troops, led by the officers, marched on foot. Having marched for some two km, we arrived at an RAF camp, where we were placed in a large hall on straw or straw mattresses on the floor. We were given an apology for having to spend the night like that, but they could not allow us into the huts without medical examination and showers for fear of disease or insect infestations. It turned out that we were in an RAF camp some three km from the city of Gloucester, located on the Bristol Channel on the west coast of England. Since our airmen from previous transports had already been in that camp, in a short while we knew the camp thoroughly. Naturally, I did not sleep in the hall, as my friends took me to one of the huts where I was given a good spring bed with snow-white sheets. Before that I was taken to the mess, where I had my supper, and then to the shower hut, where I had a good bath. You have no idea, Leszek, what a joy it was to lie down in a decent bed after so many nights of misery. I learnt from my friends who had been here for a couple of days or more, that they did not know what would happen to us, or what plans the English had towards us. Apparently in the city of Blackpool some centre for our air force was being organised, our officers and men being sent there in parties. Before that, though, we had to undergo some formalities, such as medical examination, 'R.A.F. Intelligence Service' check, photographs, fingerprints etc. I did not care about all that, what mattered was that I was in a bed, and I fell asleep as they were explaining it. We spent the next few days going through the various formalities related to verification of our identities. I was assigned to assist the English officer of the Intelligence Service who, fortunately, spoke fluent French and German, in order to help him identify our men. This took several days. We ate in one of the huts, food was in good supply, but mostly canned, all in one and the same taste. In the evenings a few of us would take leave to go for a walk towards the city of Gloucester, some three-four km from the camp. All the officers from our ship lived together in one hut, where I moved, too, and together with Major Skorobohaty we had, to ourselves, a separate room, so small that when one of us got off his bed, the other had to lie down on his, as there would be no place to move. Nevertheless that was better than sleeping in the main hall. German aircraft flew over our camp every day, both in daytime and at night, but our camp was not bombed. AA artillery was in action nearly all the time. This was annoying, especially at night when the noise from the guns would not allow us to sleep in peace. Many of our soldiers, after their recent experiences, could not stand the continuous alerts, and they ran through the camp across the fence to the woods nearby. This was rather sad, as the English soldiers stayed calmly in their huts at the same time. But they would not know, so far, what being bombed was really like. Clumsy barrage balloons, resembling elephants, hang over Gloucester and the nearby industrial settlements. Once every two or three days a party of our soldiers would leave the camp to the Air Force Centre, where all of us would apparently go soon. Our Air Force HQ was in London now, brought there from Paris. The Polish-English agreement about the restitution of our armed forces in England was being prepared there. Meanwhile, officers were paid five pounds sterling each, and the ranks, one pound each from the Polish funds brought to the camp from London. Walking around the camp I saw the suburbs of Gloucester and the local villages. I had not seen such a high standard of living in any other European country. Fortunate land. People in rich clothes, wealthy housing, extremely joyful and kind."

As described above, the first Polish airmen arrived at the Last Hope Island at the beginning of 1940. Many of them underwent training at OTUs and converted to the fighter role according to British rules. In general, almost all flying instructors of the pre-war Polish Air Force College at Dęblin[3] who reached Britain, later joined RAF fighter units. Their first contacts with the RAF training system proved surprising for both sides. British instructors had not expected to have experienced flying instructors as pupils. A few dual flights would be followed by solos, and that concluded the training course in a short time. The main Operational Training Units where the Poles converted onto modern types were Aston Down (5 OTU) and Sutton Bridge (6 OTU). Fighter training course lasted between three and six weeks, and consisted mainly of individual and formation flights, tactics and R/T communication.

AOC Fighter Command, ACM Sir Hugh C. T. Dowding later said: "It is necessary to start the flying training of a pilot about a year before he is ready to engage Enemy Fighters . . ." Some Polish airmen already had about one year of fighter combat experience, having taken part in the Polish and French campaigns. Their new comrades did not initially trust the combat skills of the Polish Air Force personnel. Although they had already survived combats with a technologically advanced enemy, being shot down in the air and bombed on the ground, and had gone through the chaos of evacuation in two campaigns, they were considered inferior to the exhausted RAF flyers coming back from the other side of the Channel in June 1940. Only a proportion of them took part in the second part of the Battle of Britain. The new procedures of training were sometimes difficult for older pilots. After damaging an aeroplane on 22 July 1940 P/O Władysław Różycki wrote in his diary:

"This day a very sorry and unpleasant thing happened to me. I have damaged a machine, for the first time in my eleven years of flying! Even more painful, as it happened on foreign soil."

---

[3] The full title was *Centrum Wyszkolenia Lotnictwa nr 1* (No. 1 Air Force Training Centre) and it included the *Szkoła Podchorążych Lotnictwa* (Air Force Cadet Officers' School) which trained the vast majority of Polish officer pilots.

The main trouble for the Poles was the language. More then half of the officers before the war spoke French or German, which allowed them to contact and visit military allies like Bulgaria, Rumania, Yugoslavia, or France. The first English-speaking Polish fighter pilots reached RAF units in March 1940 but would not take part in operational sorties until July 1940. Most of them learned English procedures very quickly and flew together with the British, who found their experience and knowledge of fighter tactics surprisingly good. Eventually, during that difficult period almost 100 Polish pilots flew with some 30 RAF fighter squadrons.

Those who established the first Polish-manned fighter units also had to learn the language of their hosts. One of 303 Squadron's pilots, P/O Jan Zumbach later wrote:

> "First we had to go back to school. Every morning a bus took us the ten miles to Uxbridge to learn the basic vocabulary which could be coming over our earphones. We also had to be able to count up to twelve in English, so as to use the clock-face system of giving bearings. Then came the simple code words – Angels for thousands of feet altitude, pancake for landing, bandits for enemy planes and so on."[4]

On 19 June 1940 Winston Churchill had said to Gen. Władysław Sikorski, C-in-C Polish Armed Forces: "We are now united for better or for worse". A month later this became real, when the first Polish fighter pilots were posted to RAF squadrons. On 16 July 1940 F/O Antoni Ostowicz and F/Lt Wilhelm Pankratz joined Tangmere-based 145 Squadron. Three days later one of them shot down a German aircraft. At long last the Poles were able to fight on equal terms against the Third Reich . . .

---

[4] Jan Zumbach, *On wings of war – My Life as a Pilot Adventurer*, Corgi Books, London.

Chapter One

FIRST KILL, FIRST LOSS

19 July – 18 August 1940

"After the French collapse Novi and Osti and several thousand more of their indomitable countrymen escaped once more from a ravaged country and came over to England. It is easy to imagine their pleasure at finding themselves in a really good squadron, efficiently run, and with first-class equipment. They could now fly the finest fighters in the world, and meet their persecutors on equal terms.

"They certainly made the most of their opportunities, and their delight when they shot down a 'bloody German' was marvellous to see.

"They were both very quiet, possessed beautiful manners, were very good pilots, and intensely keen to learn our ways and methods. Their hatred of the Germans was quieter and more deadly than I have ever seen before.

"They had undergone so much suffering and hardship, and had lost almost everything in life that mattered to them – homes, families, money – that I think the only thing that concerned them now was to get their revenge and kill as many Germans as possible.

"They were certainly two of the bravest people I ever knew, and yet they were not exceptional in this respect when compared with other Poles in the R.A.F.

"All the squadrons that had Polish pilots posted to them formed an equally high opinion of them, and the feats of the Polish Squadron, who in five days' fighting over London destroyed at least forty-four German machines, as well as probably destroying and damaging many more, must rank as one of the best shows of the whole summer.

"Such indomitable courage and determination cannot go unrewarded, and when this war is won we must see that Poland is again restored to her former liberty and freedom, which her sons fought so valiantly to maintain."

F/Lt D. M. Crook DFC *Spitfire Pilot*

13 July 1940
On 13 July 302 (Polish) Squadron was formed at Leconfield. British personnel, led by S/Ldr W. A. J. Satchell with Flight Lieutenants J. A. Thomson, W. Riley and J. N. W. Farmer, welcomed the first Polish pilots on 17 July.

18 July 1940
The very first accident report of a Polish pilot which was preserved in British archives gives a very clear picture of troubles with Poles. LAC Zbigniew Urbańczyk who was

flying at 6 OTU Sutton Bridge damaged Hurricane N2616 during landing. His Station commander wrote "Ballooned, when holding off pulled control column back sharply, a/c stalled, hit ground owing to pilot's lack of knowledge of English and inability to fly Hurricanes successfully. Recommended to be posted for further preliminary training. Should not be sent to OTU's until they have at least some knowledge of English language." Later the unfortunate pilot became a ferry pilot and fought in 1942 with 112 Shark Squadron over the Western Desert flying Kittyhawks.

19 July 1940

The first aerial victory by a Polish pilot in the RAF took place on 19 July 1940 when F/O Antoni Ostowicz of 145 Sqn participated in shooting down a He 111. "Red Section" of 145 Squadron was scrambled to pursue a He 111 heading south towards France. This section was as follows:

F/Lt Roy Gilbert Dutton	P3155	Red 1
P/O Michael Allan Newling	P2270	Red 2
F/O Antoni Ostowicz	N2496	Red 3

The Polish pilot, an ex-bomber navigator, described that event in his personal combat report:

"I was No. 3 Red Section, 145 Sqn. We took off Tangmere at 17.50 with orders to patrol Brighton at 10 000 ft. After one circuit over Brighton above cloud we were ordered to go down to 2000 ft on a Westerly course along coast. Shortly afterwards we turned slightly South to sea, and in a few minutes sighted an aircraft flying SSE at approx. 3000 ft. I followed Red 1 and Red 2 apparently was unable to keep up with us, so I took his place as he fell back behind me. The a/c was identified as a He 111. We closed to within 300 yards of e/a and after Red 1 had fired at him the e/a turned slightly right and I was able to fire a burst at him. Smoke then issued from his starboard engine. I noticed flashes from each side of both engine nacelles below wings which I took to be two pairs of fixed M.G.'s firing backwards. A few moments later I fired another burst and broke away downward to the right. At the same time I looked to see what Red 2 was doing and saw him turning to the north with black smoke coming from his plane. I then saw the e/a turning further to the right and it went into a glide, and subsequently landed on the sea. It sank in about three minutes and I saw four of the crew in the water. I circled for five or ten minutes and was then ordered to pancake. I landed Tangmere 18.40."

The pilots of 145 Squadron probably caught the He 111P of 7./KG 55 (G1+AR) which a few minutes earlier had managed to escape the Hurricanes of 1 Squadron, RAF. The shot-up He 111 became the prey of Dutton and Ostowicz, but officially this claim is shared between all three pilots of the Red Section. After this attack Newling crash-landed at Shoreham. Meanwhile the Hurricane P3471 of 1 Squadron RAF also crashed, badly shot-up by the Heinkel's rear gunner.

29 July 1940

P/O Marian Łukaszewicz of 302 Squadron crashed Hurricane P3217 during his first solo on this type. The pilot escaped without injuries, but was posted back to an OTU.

This occured six days after this first Polish fighter unit began flying training.

31 July 1940

A dozen days after his first successful combat, on 31 July 1940, F/O Antoni Ostowicz again had an opportunity to shoot at a German bomber. The weather this morning was hazy with clouds. Ostowicz attacked the bomber without apparent effect. Back at Tangmere, he reported damaging a Do 215:

> "I was No 2 of Red Section which was patrolling over clouds in Bembridge area. We sighted a Do 215 below us. We followed and I caught sight of him (below cloud) circling above some small ships. I attacked at 400 yards and he went into cloud. I attacked twice more with short bursts, but after the third attack he disappeared completely in cloud and I never saw him again. I circled round the four small ships, hoping that the Do would return, but he did not do so. After about 10 minutes I got orders to pancake."

6 August 1940

P/O Jan Pfeiffer posted to 32 Squadron failed to get up Hurricane V7205 and went through a fence and into a wood. Accident was caused due to mishandling the throttle in reverse, a common Polish error. The detailed note about Pfeiffer on the accident card said "Sent back to OTU for further assessment of suitability for flying fighter aircraft. Was posted to 257 Squadron from OTU and involved in another accident and in consequence posted to BrG School."

8 August 1940

8 August was very busy for 234 Squadron. The unit had nine available aircraft and made three interception scrambles that day. During one such early in the morning, Yellow Section had trouble reaching home base. Yellow 1 (P/O Hardy N3277) and Yellow 2 (P/O Parker N3283) landed at Roborough due to shortage of fuel. Yellow 3, a Polish pilot, made a forced landing at Pensilva. Sgt Józef Szlagowski's Spitfire I N3278 was slightly damaged and the pilot escaped without wounds. Fortunately, the next day would be luckier for this airman.

Sgt Józef Szlagowski had been posted to 234 Squadron, based at St Eval, on 3 August 1940 together with Sgt Zygmunt Klein, and they went into action very quickly. Both were well-experienced pilots. Sgt Szlagowski had been a flying instructor at Dęblin (Polish Air Force College) before the war. Sgt Klein had flown with 142 *Eskadra Myśliwska* in September 1939 and managed to damage a Hs 126 during combat on 3 September 1939. In the coming summer days 234 Squadron would have to make a few interception scrambles each day, just as had the Polish *Eskadras* the previous summer.

Similarly intensive patrols were flown on 8 August by other units where Poles served. Almost at the same time as the pilots of 234 Squadron were landing at Roborough, Hurricanes of 145 Squadron were directed to meet a large formation of German aircraft. F/O Antoni Ostowicz, now flying Hurricane I P3319, identified his victim as a "He 113":

> "I was flying No 2 Red Section. We took off from West Hampnett at 08.31 and at about 09.00 ran into a very large formation of Ju 87 bombers with escort of Me 109 and a few He 113. I was attacked by three He 113 which were working to a plan.

One was above and the other two worked as a pair. If I attacked the single one the pair attacked me astern, if I turned to attack one of the pair the single one got on my tail. Eventually I damaged the single one severely and he left smoking hard. I did not get into contact with any other e/a and returned to my base at 09.30 hours."

In all, 145 Squadron claimed two destroyed, nine probable and five damaged aircraft for the cost of two wounded pilots and destruction of their Hurricanes. An all-day combat over convoy CW9 (codename "PEEWIT") off the Isle of Wight had begun.

About midday 238 Squadron took off from Middle Wallop. There were two Poles – Sgt Marian Domagała and F/O Michał Jan Stęborowski – among the unit's pilots. Both would claim enemy aircraft shot down during this mission.

F/O Michał Stęborowski, who was flying Hurricane I P3819, described his fight against a Bf 110:

> "I was Blue 2 and the section was ordered to intercept raid on convoy approx. 6 mile south of Needles. Blue leader on sighting E/A put section into line astern at 18 000 ft. The E/A was approx. 10 000 ft. I followed the Blue Leader down but when I pulled out I had a black out. When I recovered I saw a Me 110 and got on his tail and then the rear gunner shot at me with tracer which went over my head. I began to fire at about 250 yards from astern (about 5 short bursts of 2-3 second each) and I saw the bullets go into the E/A. I think the first burst killed the rear gunner as I received no return fire. After this the E/A turned right and left very slowly and went down in a dive. I saw another E/A above me then, and I did not see the first E/A again. There was no smoke or flames from the E/A and I did not have time to watch it go into the sea but I think the E/A was out of control. I evaded the E/A above after trying to fire and made for home to re-arm. Landed at Middle Wallop 13.10. Number of rounds fired 2400."

Sgt Marian Domagała, flying Hurricane I P2989 far ahead of Stęborowski's section, had opportunities to shoot at a Bf 109 and a Bf 110:

> "I was Yellow 2 and the section was ordered (with the remainder of 238 Squadron) to intercept raid on convoy. Took off 12.09 and arrived over convoy at approx. 12.35 hours. Yellow leader ordered line astern. I saw a Me 109 ahead and went for him but he was very speedy and I could not catch up. I saw another Me 109 which was in a bank and I do not think he saw me and I fired from astern two one sec. bursts from about 100 yards. I closed on him and fired another very short burst from 50 yards and I broke away to avoid over-shooting. The E/A did a stall turn and went straight down, smoking and then caught fire. I then saw it go into the sea. I then climbed and I saw many E/A and when I got near I recognised them as 110's. I saw 1 E/A go away and chased him. I was in a very good position almost astern. I got closer and below slight and fired from approx. 150 yards one short burst, at slight deflection. I don't think there was a gunner in the Me 110 as I did not see any return fire. I then followed the e/a which went into a dive doing slight aileron turns. I did not see any smoke or flames, but I saw the bullets (trace) going into the E/A. I think the gunner must have been killed. I saw E/A behind me so I broke off and climbed and did not see any more. I saw one man on a parachute but do not know where he came from. I feel sure the E/A was out of

control, but did not see it go into the sea. Landed at Middle Wallop 14.40. No. of rounds fired 800."

In all, 238 Squadron claimed four enemy aircraft shot down and five probables. LG 1 lost only one Messerschmitt 110, but five more returned to bases in France badly damaged. Domagała's and Stęborowski's victims, claimed as destroyed, seem certainly to have been amongst them.

In the afternoon 145 Squadron was again scrambled to defend "PEEWIT". F/O Ostowicz took part in the unit's last combat of that day. His section took off at 16.00:

F/Lt Roy Gilbert Dutton	P3521	Red 1
P/O Ernest C. J. Wakeham	P2957	Red 2
F/O Antoni Ostowicz	N2496	Red 3

After return, Red 3 wrote his combat report:

"I was No 3 of Red Section, when the squadron took off at 12 000 ft. We reached convoy and encountered large forces of E/A. I saw two E/A break away to South and one Hurricane follow them. I therefore joined in. The first Hurricane shot down his opponent into the sea and I saw him crash. I attacked the second E/A, which turned out to be a Me 109, and gave him one burst at a long range of 300 yards or over. I had hardly started firing when black smoke belched out and he shot straight into the sea. My very first bullets must have got him for I hardly pressed the button for even a full second. Later I returned to the convoy but the fight had moved on by then and I was not able to find any other E/A, so after searching, I returned to base at about 16.30."

This encounter with F/O Ostowicz in fact probably ended for a JG 27 Messerschmitt Bf 109 in a successful landing on the opposite side of the Channel. Many reports written by excited fighter pilots (who had no, or little, experience in actually shooting down enemy fighters) suggest destroying a Messerschmitt but without seeing it crash. However, it should be remembered that, due to the poor diving performance of British fighters, the best chance of escape for a German fighter under attack was to dive at full throttle. During this manoeuvre the Messerschmitt would often look as if it has been hit, emitting black smoke from its exhausts.

Officially, two other Polish pilots achieved their first successes at the same time: F/O Witold Urbanowicz and Sgt Józef Kwieciński reported downing a Bf 110 and a Bf 109 respectively. Their claims were subsequently approved by the special Committee of the Polish Air Force that verified 'Polish Fighter Pilots' Achievements During the Second World War', and now this is the only official source of information about these two victories. The claims of Urbanowicz and Kwieciński seem rather odd however: both pilots flew on that day with 601 Squadron, but in the statistics table set up by the Polish Liaison Officer to HQ Fighter Command, dated 11 February 1943, both credits were listed under 145 Squadron. In fact both pilots undertook no operational sorties in 145 Squadron until 11 August, so this is the probable date of the first victories of F/O Urbanowicz and Sgt Kwieciński. 145 Squadron Operations Record Book recorded nothing about other Poles than Ostowicz taking part in the afternoon combat on 8 August. As both Urbanowicz and

Kwieciński flew in 601 Sqn before moving to 145 Sqn, it was believed for a while that their first victories of 8 August were gained whilst with that former unit. Alas, in the 601 Operations Record Book, under the date of 8 August, the flight of F/O Urbanowicz was listed as 'cancelled' and Sgt Kwieciński did 'Local flying' late afternoon, about 6 pm.

Also there is no evidence of these events in Personal Combat Reports preserved at Public Records Office at Kew nor at the Polish Institute and Sikorski Museum in London. These mysterious victories still wait to be resolved.

The fact worth noting is that between 8 and 10 August 145 Squadron pilots were frequent visitors at Tangmere. They collected new Hurricanes and flew these to Westhampnett, so it is possible that Poles officially attached to 601 Squadron flew 145 Squadron Hurricanes.

The sorties flown by F/O Witold Urbanowicz in August 1940 with 601 and 145 Squadrons (as listed in the respective Operations Record Books) were:

Date	Aircraft no.	Duty
601 Squadron		
7 Aug.	L1819	
7 Aug.	N2602	
8 Aug.	L1819	CANCELLED
145 Squadron		
11 Aug.	R4177	1) Patrol
		2) From Tangmere
12 Aug.	R4177	1) Patrol
		2) Patrol
13 Aug.	P3521	Patrol
13 Aug.	V7251	Patrol
14 Aug.	R4177	Westhampnett to Drem
16 Aug.	R4177	Drem to Turnhouse
17 Aug.	R4177	Sector Rec.
18 Aug.	R4177	Interception and attacks
19 Aug.	R4177	1) Squadron formation;
		2) Sector Rec.
20 Aug.	R4177	Turnhouse to Drem and back

9 August 1940

On this day F/O Ludwik Paszkiewicz damaged the airscrew of his Hurricane while taxiing at Northolt. This damage to Hurricane P3645/RF-R ended a series of events during 303 Squadron training. First Polish personnel of this unit arrived at Northolt on 2 August, and between 3 and 7 August they were flying Miles Master (N7888, N7748) and Magister (T9808[5]) trainers. One of the P/Os, Jan Zumbach, later described his first date with the Hurricane:

"Finally we were introduced to the Hurricanes we would be flying. The cockpit drill

---

[5] This Magister I would serve in many Polish squadrons: nos. 306, 315, 308 and be eventually written off on 19 February 1945 with 315 Squadron.

had us baffled at first. By comparison with every other type of plane we'd ever flown, everything here was back to front. In Poland and France when you wanted to open the throttle you pulled; here, you pushed. We had to reverse all our reflexes."[6]

On 8 August Sgt Marian Bełc landed with undercarriage up, damaging Hurricane R4100/RF-N. The same error was repeated by Sgt Josef František, a Czech, in V7235/RF-M. Their British commanders must have experienced many a hardship as F/Lt John A. Kent wrote in his memoirs:

> "Some of the pilots had never flown aircraft with retractable undercarriages and, both in Poland and in France, they had been used to opening the throttle by pulling it back instead of pushing it forward. As can be imagined these differences caused confusion and we had several of the aircraft landed with their undercarriages retracted. One of these was put down by a Sergeant Frantisek and I tore him off a first class strip – he didn't know what I was saying but knew he had to answer in a foreign tongue and kept repeating: 'Oui, mon commandant', over and over . . ."[7]

The same day one of the Polish Spitfire pilots, Sgt Józef Szlagowski of 234 Squadron, had his first opportunity to fight the enemy in the air. This happened during one of eight interceptions made by nine available Spitfires of 234 Squadron that day. A section comprising P/O Mortimer-Rose, P/O Hardy and Sgt Szlagowski intercepted a Do 215 over Falmouth. On returning to base the Polish pilot claimed the Dornier damaged.

11 August 1940
During the last three relatively quiet days 145 Squadron's A Flight ferried new aeroplanes for the unit from Tangmere. At least five of them were brought by F/O Ostowicz and Sgt Kwieciński.

On 11 August the Luftwaffe put into action more than 100 aircraft in a big raid on Portland. 145 Squadron was among eight units sent up to stop the bombers. Witold Urbanowicz, who took part in this mission, described it in his report:

> "I was flying in the box of Red Section when we ran into many enemy aircraft South of Isle of Wight. One section of three Me 109 came in on the beam of my Section, so I headed them off and they left us. Then one smoking enemy aircraft appeared on my left and another Me 109 followed him. I gave chase to the last Me 109 and he continued to follow the smoking machine towards the South. Soon after I found about 15-17 Me 109 above me: they did not attack me and I dared not disclose my identity by attacking the Me 109 in front of me, so I followed him without firing for 4-5 minutes. Then when I saw it was safe I gained on him and gave him some bursts upon which he went straight into the sea. He was a Me 109. He never fired at me at all. I then turned round and flew back close to the water. As I was running short of fuel I landed at Tangmere to refuel and then reached Westhampnett at 12.40 hours"

---

[6] Jan Zumbach, *On wings of war . . . .*
[7] John A. Kent, *One of the Few*, Kimber, 1971.

While Urbanowicz claimed the Bf 109, another Pole, F/O Antoni Ostowicz, was killed during the same combat. His Hurricane V7294 crashed, probably on the Isle of Wight. This was the first loss among Polish Air Force fighter pilots attached to RAF Squadrons. But he was not the only Polish loss during this afternoon.

238 Squadron also took part in this event. Pilots of this unit, including Sgt Domagała, claimed four enemy aircraft shot down and one probably destroyed. Domagała, flying Hurricane I P2989, shot down a Messerschmitt Bf 109, but that was not his only victim . . .

> "I was Yellow 2 and A Flight was ordered to Portland at 20 000 ft. Yellow 1 gave line astern but I broke away to the right and engaged a Me 109. Just as I opened fire at the enemy aircraft a Hurricane appeared in my line of sight between the enemy aircraft and myself and got the tail end of the burst which was a very short burst of 2 secs. at range of 50 yards quarter attack. My burst went into the left wing of the Hurricane which was smoking and the pilot baled out. I watched him down and then attacked another Me after climbing. I fired a very short burst at 150 yards from astern but aircraft dived and I followed it down, and as he weaved I fired each time (about 8 times) from quarter deflection very close range about 100 yards. The aircraft climbed slightly and then fell into the sea with a splash. I had fired all my ammunition so returned to base after several attacks had been made on me by several enemy aircraft which I evaded, landed at Warmwell first, rearmed and went back on patrol. Landed at Middle Wallop 11.35. Number of rounds fired 2400 and 80 after rearming."

The victories claimed by 238 Squadron were paid for by the loss of four pilots. It is probable that one of those lost in the battle went under the guns of the Polish Sergeant. They included F/Lt S. C. Walch, an Australian with three and a half victories claimed during the Battle, and another Pole, F/O Michał Stęborowski. The latter, like Sgt Szlagowski and F/O Urbanowicz, had been a flying instructor at the Polish Air Force College before the war. Aged 31, he was a skilled airman, very popular with his pupils.

12 August 1940

On 12 August 1940 about noon F/O Witold Urbanowicz, flying Hurricane I R4177 on patrol, was directed to encounter a large force of He 111s and Ju 88s; these bombers approached the Isle of Wight with orders to destroy radar installations in that area. The section of 145 Squadron Hurricanes met a Ju 88 from KG 51 near Ventnor and F/O Urbanowicz shot it down into the sea:

> "I was flying Red 2 of No 145 Sqn. when ordered at 12.10 hours to patrol Selsey Bill-Bembridge. As soon as I became airborne I saw enemy aircraft over Portsmouth going South. I followed Red 1 to attack an enemy aircraft near his, but failed to catch this aircraft. I saw the enemy aircraft attacked by Red 1 dive into the sea. I then saw a Ju 88 by itself at 1700 ft and delivered a beam attack. After this attack the enemy aircraft dived vertically into the sea. The enemy aircraft appeared to have been attacking a small coastal vessel, but did no damage. I returned to base and landed by A.A., first, for it was smoking slightly and flying slowly."

Unfortunately, during this engagement another Pole, Sgt Józef Kwieciński, was shot down and killed when his Hurricane P3391 fell into the sea, and F/Lt Wilhelm Pankratz in R4176 was lost after combat with enemy fighters south of the Isle of Wight. At "B" Flight's dispersal the latter had left a Polish national flag which was usually laid out in front of the hut when Polish pilots were at readiness.

Some light on the last battle of F/Lt W. Pankratz, P/O J. Harrison and Sgt J. Kwieciński is thrown by the chronicle of JG 53, the opponents of 145 Squadron on this occasion. Pilots of 1./JG 53 witnessed an attack by a Hurricane section (now believed to be that of F/Lt Wilhelm Pankratz) upon a Messerschmitt Bf 110 of I./ZG 2, the latter finally being shot down into the sea. This claim was never mentioned in the RAF Fighter Command reports, because none of the three participants in this victory survived the combat. The sight of the Messerschmitt 110 (piloted by Oblt. Blume) falling absorbed the attention of the Hurricane pilots to such an extent that they did not notice when Messerschmitt 109s of 1./JG 53 appeared on their tails. The *Jägern* came too late to rescue the *Zerstörer* crew, but managed to shoot down all three RAF fighters. Hptm. H. K. Mayer, the *Staffelkapitän*, shot down F/Lt Pankratz's No. 2 while Uffz. Heinrich Rühl downed his No. 3. The rest of the 1. *Staffel* tried to shoot down the aircraft flown by F/Lt Pankratz, but got in each other's way. Finally, Hptm. Mayer got onto the tail of the Hurricane and shot it down into the sea. These were the 10th and 11th victories of this German pilot, but his own aircraft was also shot-up.

Another squadron where Polish pilots with pre-war careers as flying instructors were posted was the Auxiliary, 501. This unit suffered severely during the defence of the PEEWIT convoy, so fresh blood was needed. The first meeting with the new ally was described P/O K. W. MacKenzie in his memoirs:

> "The Squadron was made up of regulars and VR pilots, officers and sergeants with a generous sprinkling of Poles who were irrepressible, irresponsible in some respects and laugh a minute at times. We were glad of them as they had mostly received a sound blooding when their country was invaded and had made their way to England by devious ways and means to fight again. Their deep hatred of the Germans was infectious."[8]

The first to arrive in the County of Gloucester Squadron, on 5 August, were F/O Stefan Witorzeńć and Sgt Antoni Głowacki. A few days later they were joined by P/O Kazimierz Łukaszewicz, P/O Franciszek Kozłowski and P/O Paweł Zenker.

Early in the morning on 12 August the squadron moved its aircraft to Hawkinge. The first scrambles were in answer to bomber formations trying to bomb airfields. During one of the first such engagements F/O Stefan Witorzeńć, flying V7230/SD-H, damaged a Bf 110.

> "I was No. 2 in Red Section when the Squadron was ordered to patrol Dover at 7000 ft and was vectored North over land to Manston. I sighted E/A when South East of Manston at 4000 ft flying West towards Manston. The Me 110 turned and dropped bombs on the aerodrome and turned South East for Home. I attacked one of them on the South East side of the aerodrome opening fire at 150 yards closing at 100 yards with 2 short bursts from the port side. The E/A emitted white

[8] W/Cdr K. W. MacKenzie DFC, AFC, AE, *Hurricane Combat – The Nine Lives of a Fighter Pilot*, Grenville Publishing Company Ltd. London 1990.

smoke from the port engine and dived into cloud. I then turned and attacked another to the left from slightly below and gave it two short bursts from 200 yards. This climbed into clouds to join other German machines, I followed them 15 miles over Channel before returning to base."

Meanwhile, west of Ramsgate, P/O Kazimierz Łukaszewicz of 501 Squadron was bounced by Bf 109s and shot down. His Hurricane P3803/SD-Z fell into the sea with its pilot. He had been another skilled instructor of the PAF College at Dęblin before the outbreak of the war. For another ex-instructor, this combat proved successful. P/O Paweł Zenker claimed the destruction of a Ju 87.

"I was No 2 in Blue Section, when the Squadron was ordered to patrol Hawkinge at 7000 ft. We flew North after patrolling off Dover, and when over Ramsgate at 9000 ft, I saw on the horizon about 35 Ju 87B's in section of threes, stepped up in layers. They were flying South West over the Thames Estuary, coming from the sea. We turned over Margate and cut to sea flying North West. As we approached the formation it dived, turning West to bomb a ship, which I think was hit. Just as one of the Ju 87's dived to bomb the ship, I followed him down, firing one long burst from 150 yards closing to fifty. I then overshot and turned to the right. There I saw 3 Ju 87's low over the sea at 150 yards flying North East in the direction of the Dutch coast and I attacked one on the right and fired three long bursts from 200 to 150 yards, and a third burst caused a fire in the fuselage of the E/A, which turned right and disappeared. Then I caught up the third, after climbing a little and turning left, attacked from astern. I was only able to fire a short burst as my ammunition was exhausted. I am not certain whether the third Ju 87 was damaged."

An interesting note about Polish pilots can be found in the 54 Squadron ORB under 12 August:

"The 54 Squadron engaged enemy twice during the day, once in the morning and again in the evening when F/Lt Deere added still further to his personal score with one Me 109 and one Me 110 both destroyed. One of our Polish Sergeants – Sgt. Kloziński – vented his wrath on the Hun to the extent of one certain Me 109 and one probable Me 109. Our losses were P/O Turley-George and P/O Kemp both injured."

Sgt. Wojciech Kloziński's opponents were attacked five miles south of Dungeness at about 17.40, and the pilot reported this event:

"I was Red 3, on receiving orders to break formation as we encountered enemy in various layers from 30,000 ft downwards. I manouvered and got on the tail of 1 Me 109, gave 3 bursts of 3 seconds each and saw it go down in flames. Breaking away I attacked a second Me 109 and gave two bursts which sent him spinning and followed him to 1000 ft, when I broke away and returned to base. I had followed him for 10,000 ft and he was obviously out of control."

During the same engagement P/O Pniak of 32 Squadron, flying Hurricane I R4106, also claimed to have shot down a Bf 109.

> "I was flying behind Red 1 section, when at 14 000 ft we met a formation of Do
> 215 in lines of three behind each other (about) 50, escorted by 109's above. I
> attacked a Dornier 215 and got in a few short bursts at 100 yards with ¼
> deflection. I then broke away, a dog fight with Me 109 then ensued and I was
> attacked from above by a Me 109. I turned inside him and got on his tail, he
> spiraled down and got in 3 or 3½ secs. bursts. In a short time I saw much smoke
> coming from the fuselage. I wanted to make sure of him, so again pressed my m/g
> trigger but had finished my ammunition. I followed him down to 3000 ft and last
> saw him in a very tight vertical spiral, still smoking hard. The time was 17.30 and
> this combat took place about ½ way between Hawkinge and Manston."

At that time 32 Squadron, based at Biggin Hill, had more than one Polish pilot. Since
8 August 1940, there were three of them – P/O Jan Piotr Pfeiffer, P/O Karol Pniak
and P/O Bolesław Andrzej Własnowolski. Because of their strange and hardly-
pronounceable names all were nicknamed by their British colleagues, and became
simply: Fifi, Cognac and Vodka, respectively. First flights on the Hurricanes of this
unit remained unforgettable for the Poles, as well as for P/O John "Polly" Flinders,
who was responsible for their quick conversion. P/O Własnowolski finished his first
flight by bouncing over a fence and making a smooth landing in someone's garden.
P/O Pniak, who was the first to reach the unfortunate pilot, reproached him for this
event. Fortunately, the aircraft and pilot remained unscathed.

Later on Własnowolski proved to be a talented fighter pilot, claiming five victories
during the coming two months.

Sgt Paweł Gallus of 303 Squadron ended his familiarisation flight damaging
Hurricane P3890/RF-N while landing at Northolt. This incident ended his career in
this Polish squadron also, and he moved back to 5 OTU.

13 August 1940

Early on 13 August no-one in Britain was anticipating the most intense Luftwaffe
activity since the Battle of France. The *Adler Tag* began about 5.30 a.m., when
incoming bomber formations were plotted while still over France. 12 Spitfires of 74
Squadron took off at 5.55 am with orders to cover Manston airfield. Among the pilots
of this unit were two Poles. The first of them, F/Lt Stanisław Brzezina, flying Spitfire
I N3091, claimed a Do 17 of KG 2 shot down near Whitstable, and then saved his
life by a parachute jump.

> "I followed the Squadron Leader in the attack against enemy bombers in the
> Estuary. We attacked the third of three formations of bombers in line astern and
> were about to engage when we noticed a fourth section closing in on our tails. We
> broke away and came round to attack this last formation. I attacked No. 2 and gave
> him a long burst and saw him gliding down towards the sea with smoke coming
> from the engine. I did not see him go into the water. I then attacked No. 3 of the
> formation and must have got to within fifty yards when there was a sudden
> explosion in my cockpit and I found myself falling fast.
>
> "I managed to get out of the machine at about 2,000 ft and made a successful
> parachute landing. I did not see what happened to this Do 17 but I was at such

close range that it must have been severely damaged.

"It has since been confirmed by an eye witness at a search light post that the Do 17 crashed South of their post."

Another Pole, F/O Henryk Szczęsny, in Spitfire I K9871/ZP-O, also claimed a Do 17 of KG 2 near Whitstable. His combat ended at West Malling, where he "overshot forced landing while lost, and tipped up".

"I saw three Do 17s in front of me. I went to attack No. 3 of the formation when he swung round to the right. I broke away to the left and came round behind the Dos. and on their tails. One of the machines was out of formation and I attacked it from astern. At this point the Do. dropped several bombs in the sea. I got a good burst in from very close range and the Do. started to dive towards the sea. He tried to land there but as he flattened out he burst into flames and toppled straight into the water. This must be somewhere in the Estuary East of the Isle of Sheppey. I did not know where I was and managed to force land at Maidstone with my undercarriage up, as I could not get it down."

Both Brzezina and Szczęsny had been posted to 74 Squadron on 5 August 1940, and were soon dubbed Breezy and Sneezy, respectively. Szczęsny (also known as Henry the Pole) would continue to fly with the Tigers till mid-December.

Polish pilots of another Spitfire unit taking part in combat this day, 609 Squadron, achieved no success until the afternoon raid, when a patrol from this unit met a formation of Ju 87s with Bf 109 cover over The Solent. F/O Tadeusz Nowierski, flying Spitfire I L1082/PR-A, described his attack on Messerschmitt Bf 109s of JG 53 over Weymouth.

"I was Green 2 and we sighted a large number of enemy aircraft coming from the South. We circled above them and Green 1 dived to attack. At that moment I saw one Me 109 above me and ahead. I climbed up behind him and fired three bursts at fairly close range and dead astern. White smoke appeared from his fuselage and he turned over and started to dive. Some large object, probably the cockpit door or roof flew away and the pilot got out and opened the parachute. I then saw 2 Me 109s behind me and I dived and pulled out in a violent left hand turn and 'blacked out'. Ten minutes later I saw another Me 109 ahead and approached him from behind and gave him a good burst at very close range. White smoke appeared from the fuselage and he dived steeply into a cloud and disappeared. I dived through the cloud and a minute or so later saw another aircraft dive into the sea. This occurred too late for it to have been my victim. Before attacking my first 109 I saw a Spitfire attack and shoot down a Me 109. This was probably P/O Crook."

It is probable that Nowierski's opponent was Fw. Pfannschmidt in Bf 109E 'Black 9' who became a prisoner of war. What is noteworthy, is that this was the first fighter combat for the Polish pilot in his entire career! He had been a bomber pilot in Poland before the war and during the 1939 campaign. He then volunteered when the opportunity arose for Poles to join RAF fighter squadrons in 1940, and went on to become one of the Polish aces and top fighter leaders of the war.

Another Polish pilot involved in this engagement was P/O Piotr Ostaszewski-Ostoja (an advanced flying instructor before the war). Five miles west of Dorchester his section attacked dive bombers of StG 2 with considerable success, Ostaszewski's being credited with two probables.

"I took off as No. 2 Blue section. At 20,000 ft. we sighted the enemy. I followed my leader into the attack on a formation of Ju 87s. I fired a burst of two seconds at about 400 yards from the beam. No effects were observed. I broke away and turned right and attacked another Ju 87 from astern with burst of about 3 seconds opening at 400 yards and closing to 200 yards. No effect observed and return fire experienced. After breaking away from this attack I was not engaged again."

Both Nowierski (known to his squadron mates as Novi) and Ostaszewski (Osti or Post) had undergone conversion training at 5 OTU, and been posted to 609 Sqn on 5 August. According to the squadron Operations Record Book:

"neither could speak much English at the time, but both rapidly acquired efficiency on Spitfires".

Apparently the language problem was simply cured by the unit OC, S/Ldr H. S. Darley, who warned the Polish pilots that if he overheard them speaking Polish over the R/T, they would be grounded immediately. This improved their command of English within days. As for the "efficiency on Spitfires", the results of 13 August spoke for themselves.

14 August 1940
The second day of the offensive brought no success for Polish fighters, and bad weather limited the action of German aircraft over Britain. About noon one big raid was intercepted by two squadrons of Spitfires and two of Hurricanes in the Dover area. These included 32 Squadron Hurricanes, which had an encounter with JG 26 Messerschmitts covering Ju 87s. The melee of more than 100 fighter aircraft lasted an hour and British fighters suffered heavy losses. Three of 32 Squadron aircraft were shot down. Amongst these was P/O Bolesław Własnowolski, for whom it was his first combat sortie over Britain. He was shot down by a Messerschmitt 109 and force landed near Dover. He left his damaged Hurricane V7223 and came back to the unit, as did two other members of the unit, including the only victorious pilot, P/O R. F. Smythe. The latter managed to shoot down a German Messerschmitt, making Uffz. Gerhard Kemen a prisoner of war and the only loss of JG 26 that day.

15 August 1940
"By now the order 'patrol behind Dover and engage Enemy Fighters' is becoming as familiar as the old convoy patrols."

– stated the 54 Squadron Operations Record Book. Four patrols by Spitfires from this unit during the day resulted in two clashes with the enemy. About 11.20:

"large formations of Me 109's scattered before the Squadron's approach over Dover, proceeding to Hawkinge further He 113's were met, their tactics of 'milling' and 'circling' did not bring our pilots into the trap set for them. Sgt. Lawrence showed his genuine hatred for the Ju 87 by shooting down three of them in flames before himself falling a victim to an enemy fighter. He had a fortunate escape when his machine crashed in the sea, taking him down with it. Rescued by the Navy he is now in Dover Hospital suffering from shock. Sgt. Klozensky [*sic!*], our other casualty, was shot down near Ashford, but is making progress in hospital there. For those losses we claim 4 enemy aircraft destroyed (including a new type (Ju 87) to our list) and three damaged."

Sgt Wojciech Kloziński (the more correct spelling) had been flying Spitfire IA R7015.

15 August, later called *Schwarzer Donnerstag* ("Black Thursday") by the Germans, proved to be a victorious day for Sgt Antoni Głowacki of 501 Squadron, one of the future fighter aces of the Polish Air Force. He recalled that day in his memoirs (originally in Polish):

"I have been in the first line for 10 days, and I have not seen the Jerries yet. I have had some 50 hours flown in Hurricanes. I know these are marvellous machines, fast, manoeuvrable, perfect in aerobatics, and what is most important they are armed with 8 machine guns. I would like so much to test them at last on the Jerries, and still I have to wait and wait. Suddenly three rings of the phone . . . That's for us! Duty phone operator listens for a moment, and then shouts 'Mandril Squadron Scramble! 15 thousands over base' . . .

"Two minutes later the whole squadron is already airborne. We gain height in a great spiral over the aerodrome. I am in the last sections and look out for the enemy. My eyes turn misty, I look so intensely to the South where we expect the Jerries. The radio says: 'Large formation of Bandits approaching from the South, Mandril Leader steer one seven zero'.

"I look South. There are aircraft! Far, a swarm of tiny dots, they grow, get their wings, landing gear . . . They are Junkers 87 'Stukas'. They fly towards Dover and probably to our aerodrome.

"I count – thirty machines and very high a swarm of little flies, that must be the fighter escort, Messerschmitts. But that is nothing, we are going to be the first at the bombers before the escort starts to defend them.

"We loosen our formation, I check my gunsight, arm the machine guns. First sections are attacking already, I can see traces of incendiary rounds. We get into the firing distance. First sections have already broken among the bombers and are already in combat. The Germans have run in all directions, they failed to withstand the blow and made a great melee. Swastikas and crosses, red-white-blue rings and crosses again. All this is circling at great speed and spitting fire."

F/O Stefan Witorzeńć, flying his Hurricane V7230/SD-H, was one of the first of 501 Squadron's fighters to run into the dive bomber formation:

"Red 1 attacked the left aircraft of an enemy section and I attacked one of the right from dead astern, after which enemy formation broke up. After firing 3 long bursts, I saw the enemy plane diving steeply to the ground with smoke coming out of the fuselage. This was subsequently confirmed. After this I saw a Ju 87 dropping a bomb on the aerodrome and return for home. I followed him and fired two bursts from dead astern after coming up with him over the sea. The rear gunner fired at me but ceased. White smoke came from enemy plane which dived at an angle into the sea. My plane was slightly damaged and I landed at Hawkinge. My claims are confirmed by F/L Stoney and others."

At the same time Sgt Antoni Głowacki attacked the bombers. The original combat report of Sgt Głowacki gave some details of the exchange at 11.30 am:

"The Squadron turned from North of Folkestone and intercepted a force of some 20 Ju 87's off Folkestone, attacking them in formation 'A' Flight Leading. I attacked a Ju 87 which was diving and fired one short burst and saw the rear gunner bale out turning over before my aircraft. I saw the enemy aircraft dive vertically into the sea. Then I climbed over Hawkinge and attacked a Ju 87 diving into a hangar from astern but did not see what happened to it. After this I climbed and attacked an He 113 with a beam attack (90 deg.) deflection and the enemy aircraft climbed quickly out of sight. Then I turned to attack two Ju 87's over Folkestone from astern but my ammunition gave out after firing one short burst at one of them. I returned and landed at base."

After this combat Sgt Antoni Głowacki reported one Ju 87 Destroyed but his log-book also lists one not confirmed Probable. Some interesting details of this mystery could be resolved reading Głowacki's memoirs.

"I catch the nearest machine and press the trigger from a distance of 200 metres. The Junkers makes a sudden turn right, I let him go, I pull up above him and attack him again from a wingover. Short burst from vertical. I can feel the recoil of 8 machine guns brake the speed of my machine.

"He's got it! The Junkers goes vertically down. Black smoke from the engine. An object falls apart from the Junkers. Spinning and cartwheeling, closer and closer. I fire another burst to the Junkers through that object. The distance shrinks, mere 100 metres. I fire again. Suddenly the object spinning between me and the Junkers opens up. I can see arms and legs.

"By God! That's a man! Probably a tail gunner who bailed out of the shot down Junkers. I can see clearly the brown flying suit, parachute on the back, yellow life vest. I pull sideways, no more than 20 metres from him. A moment later, and I would have rammed him. I feel hot suddenly. I circle round the falling machine, and see the moment when it splashes into the water. A moment later the gunner hits the water.

"I pull up. Above me a true dog-fight. Duels in all directions. To the left, a little above, I can see two white umbrellas. Somebody is hanging on a parachute already. I catch another Junkers that dives to bomb the port of Dover. Distance between us some 300 metres; I give full throttle and come closer at an angle. I get on his tail, and this moment I can see a great bomb fall off. He starts to pull up. I set a short deflection in front of the Junkers' nose and push the trigger. I fire a long burst. I can feel the guns recoil again. I fire until fifty metres and pull up above him, in order to avoid collision, as my speed is much greater. I pull the control stick with all power, I black out, red flakes float in my eyes. I did it! I pulled up, and down there, right at the entrance to the port I can see a bomb blast. A great geyser of water and a large white spot. Suddenly another blast, right by the first one. My Junkers vertically hits the water, right by his bomb. Perhaps the pilot was killed and failed to recover from the dive. Out of the corner of my eye I spot a trio of Messerschmitts – they want to cut through my path. Very well. I make a sharp turn and here I go head-on to the section leader . . . I fire! The Germans have pulled up in a fan-shape. Refused to accept the combat. Suddenly I can feel the emotion, sweating I shudder. My arms and legs shudder strangely. And I am glad, I shout in joy . . .

"I fly towards the aerodrome, where I can see smoke and artillery bursts from a distance. I can also see a swarm of small aircraft. I still have some ammunition, it needs to be spent. I pass Dover and get over the land. Only now I can see that some of the Junkers have survived the defence and attack the aerodrome. Hangars demolished, petrol tanks on fire and a column of black smoke is standing over the aerodrome like a huge club. Immediately above the aerodrome I can see a lone Junkers strafing the buildings. Just you wait, bastard, you're mine already. I dive on him and catch him in my sights. I fire. The tail gunner returns my fire. I can feel his rounds strike the wings of my Hurricane. But that is nothing. He has only two guns, I have eight. Distance 200 metres, right under the tail of the Junkers. I fire. I got the gunner, I can see how the barrels of his guns went up, he must have fallen down into his cockpit.

"That moment the Junkers reached the edge of the cliff on which our aerodrome, Hawkinge, was located, and dived down onto the town of Folkestone at the base of the hill. I dive after him, but do not fire. I can see him clearly. The Junkers pilot is trying to fly very low, right above the roofs. Suddenly he strikes a roof with his wheels. I can see pieces of the machine fly away as it crashes into another house, tanks explode. Pieces of the machine and its wings fly in all directions, the whole building collapses in a cloud of smoke, flame and dust.

"I circle the town. Fire brigade vehicles are rushing along the streets towards the fire started by the Junkers. I have nothing to do here, so I return to the aerodrome. Some other Hurricanes are circling it, waiting to land.

"And the aerodrome is covered with bomb craters. It has only been a dozen minutes from the Junkers raid, and herds of English soldiers fill the craters, to make landing possible for us. The machines finely land at the undamaged portion of the aerodrome. Finally comes my turn. I land, then taxi to the place where the pilots' tent was. It was blown away by a nearby bomb blast. I switch off the engine and sweating and tired I leave the machine. I'm on my last legs. My fitters run and hug me. The cool and phlegmatic Englishmen are crazy with joy. They had a wonderful show, and even saw me fire at the last Junkers. So I make my report and wait for the rest of the pilots to come back."

The first Junkers attacked by him crashed into the sea and the crew baled out. His later victim, claimed as a probable and never credited, which fell in Folkestone, was the Ju 87B of 10./LG 1 flown by Uffz. Weber. This was the only Stuka which crashed in an urban area that day, and details of the crash site visible in photographs match the story told by the Polish pilot. The chase was not one to be easily forgotten, but Uffz. Weber's Ju 87 was not lost until 5.30 pm. Yet, there is no trace of this chase in any official RAF documents related to 501 Squadron or Sgt Głowacki.

The other victorious Pole, F/O Stefan Witorzeńć, came back to base in a damaged

Hurricane, but claimed two Ju 87s destroyed. This was not the end of Polish victories for that day however. 501 Squadron was airborne four times and during a patrol over Chatham about 3.30 pm Sgt Głowacki damaged a Do 17.

"I was No 2 in Blue Section when the squadron consisting of 7 aircraft was ordered to take off to intercept enemy raid behind Dover at 8,000 ft. Over the R/T we were told that enemy aircraft were at 5,000 ft and we dived down over Dover. While diving I sighted wave of Do 17 and Do 215 at 12,000 ft approximately crossing the coast from South East near Folkestone. Red leader led the Squadron round to South East and then North West parallel with the enemy and then we climbed to attack. Red 1 attacked the second wave of bombers and from astern at the same height I attacked the third section while my leader Blue 1 attacked the fifth. They broke up and I attacked a Do 215[9] with a beam attack from third quarter using full deflection. The enemy aircraft dived emitting white smoke and turned over as it dived. I attacked a second aircraft from astern with a long burst breaking off when my ammunition was finished. I did not see what happened to it. I dived to 3,000 ft and could see Rochester being bombed. I then turned to base."

At the same time, further west, P/O Bolesław Własnowolski managed to shoot down his first enemy aircraft in the British sky. 32 Squadron were scrambled to intercept a large bomber formation heading for Martlesham Heath. Soon these Hurricanes were joined by others from 1 Squadron, based at Northolt, and 17 Squadron from Debden. A formation of Messerschmitt Bf 110s from ErpGr 210, covered by Bf 109s, were spotted near Harwich. The fighter cover engaged the incoming Hurricanes, and the *Zerstörern* led by Hauptmann Walter Rubensdorffer reached their target. Bombs that fell on Martlesham Heath caused the total destruction of two hangars and some minor equipment of 25 (Night Fighter) Squadron. A direct hit was gained on a fully loaded Fairey Battle, and the explosion of its 100 lb bombs caused the greatest damage. Meanwhile, in the fighter melee, P/O Własnowolski shot down a Messerschmitt Bf 109E-4 with "Black 2" on the fuselage, piloted by Fw. Stiegenberger; this aeroplane crashed into the sea near Margate. The pilot from 5./JG 51 was rescued by an MTB and taken prisoner.

32 Squadron lost Hurricane P3891/GZ-C in this combat. The pilot, P/O Douglas Hamilton Grice, baled out and was also rescued by MTB. Własnowolski's Hurricane I N2671 was shot-up, too, and suffered a glycol leak. The Polish pilot was forced to land in a field in the Harwich area about 3.35 pm. Własnowolski reported the combat and crash landing:

"I was flying 3 of the Red Section, when I saw nine Me 109's above me in vic formation. I climbed up and attacked one of the Me 109's from astern, we circled round each other then the Me 109 dived away. I got in a good burst and the Me 109 burst into flames and dived down towards the sea. I turned towards the other Me 109 but could not catch them. My glycol temp. was too hot so I force landed in Essex. The machine is temporarily unserviceable as my undercarriage was smashed owing to bad surface of landing field."

---

[9] Throughout 1940 the Dornier Do 17Z bomber was frequently identified by RAF pilots, British and Polish as "Do 215". The latter was in fact a small-production reconnaisance aircraft. In the vast majority of cases, claims against "Do 215s" in fact related to Do 17Z.

Two hours later 32 Squadron joined other fighters sent up to intercept more incoming bombers, and a combat took place near Croydon. This time P/O Karol Pniak, flying Hurricane I N2524, had more luck:

> "I attacked a Do 17 at 11 000 ft which turned over Croydon. I opened fire from 200 yards, I fired several short bursts from astern, the Do 17 began to smoke. I saw him glide down, with much black smoke coming from him. When I climbed up I saw a Me 109 which was attacking another Hurricane. I attacked him from astern opening fire from 250 yards. I fired several short bursts, he planed zig zagging with thick black smoke coming from him. I broke away and when I climbed, I was attacked by another Me 109 from head on. I pressed my trigger, but found I had run out of ammunition."

The Operations Record Book of 151 Squadron (flying Hurricanes) mentions a success and a loss of one Polish pilot during this day:

> "Today the Squadron had a busy day. At 14.45 hours the squadron took off from Rochford and ran into a formation of Me 109's a few miles West of Dover. P/O Debenham followed one Me 109 and it crashed in France. P/O Ellacombe and P/O Rozwadowski both shot one down, P/O Ellacombe's in flames and the other into the sea. F/O Milne also succeeded in bringing one down. Shortly afterwards about 50 Do 215's and Me 110's escorted by Me 109's in large numbers made their appearance. F/O Blair and P/O Smith made one attack on the bombers but were unsuccessful owing to the unwelcome attention of the 109's. There were no casualties but P/O Debenham's aircraft was shot up a bit. At 6.45 pm the squadron again took off to intercept enemy aircraft West of Dover. A large force of Me 109's were again encountered. In this action we faired badly, P/O Johnson, Sub/Lt Beggs, P/O Ellacombe and P/O Rozwadowski being shot down. P/O Johnson was later picked up in the sea but he was dead. Sub/Lt Beggs and P/O Ellacombe are in hospital but are not seriously injured. P/O Rozwadowski is at the moment missing. S/Ldr Gordon was peppered with shrapnel from a cannon shell and was slightly wounded in the back of the head and leg. He is however, quite OK. P/O Smith is certain he got a 109 as it was spinning at something over 400 mph at about 5000' when he broke off the engagement, having run out of ammunition."

The losses to 151 Squadron taking part in this engagement were as follows:

S/Ldr Gordon	P3940
F/O Blair	P3309
P/O Smith	V7411
S/Lt Beggs	P3065
P/O Rozwadowski (Polish)	V7410
P/O Ellacombe	L1975
P/O Johnson	P3941

151 Squadron was one of the units which received a large number of Polish pilots. On 8 August P/O Mieczysław Rozwadowski and P/O Tadeusz Wilhelm Kawalecki had arrived at North Weald. By the end of August this unit was also joined by P/O

Franciszek Surma, P/O Jerzy Solak, P/O Wilhelm Szafraniec, P/O Gustaw Radwański, Sgt Feliks Gmur and P/O Franciszek Czajkowski.

On 14 and 15 August 234 Squadron moved to Middle Wallop from St Eval. After all the AZ-coded Spitfires had reached the new landing ground in the afternoon of 15th, a big German raid approached Swanage. Thirteen Spitfires were scrambled to intercept the bombers, but four of these and three pilots of the Squadron were lost[10]. Polish pilot, Sgt Zygmunt Klein, flying Spitfire IA P9363, was shot down, but survived the crash and returned to the unit. Among the unit's victorious pilots was another Pole, P/O Janusz Żurakowski (flying Spitfire I X4016) who described his combat in these words:

"I attacked circle of Me 110 from above and behind last aircraft, enemy dived down to ground. The rear gunner ceased to fire. On the way down a second Spitfire from 609 Squadron attacked but when it broke away I engaged five more times, e/a eventually crashed in Isle of Wight."

The Spitfire of 609 Squadron encountered by Żurakowski behind this tail of the Messerschmitt Bf 110C of 6./ZG 76 (coded M8+BP) was also flown by a Polish pilot, F/O Piotr Ostaszewski. From his point of view finishing off the Messerschmitt happened like this:

"While flying at 10,000 ft I was alone having taken off independently of my section. I saw a circus of about seven Me 110's doing left hand circuit. I turned and made a circuit right handed outside them. One machine broke away from the circus to try to engage me. I turned inside him and opened fire from the quarter at about 300 yards. I gave him a 2 or 3 second burst and the e/a dived steeply making S turns. I followed him down, we went through the balloon barrage at Southampton. He pulled out just above the ground and started hedge hopping. I gave him several short bursts closing from 300 yards to 100 yards. The e/a flew low across Southampton Solent and onto the Isle of Wight. I saw another Spitfire, which was chasing him too and firing at him. After other several short bursts I noticed both engines smoking and then stop. The e/a then made a crash landing and burst into flames. The Me 110 struck the side of a road, skidded across it and came to rest, burning on the other side of the road. He crashed on the South side of the Isle of Wight a few hundred yards from the sea."

Only the gunner, Uffz. Max Guschewski (also with a Polish-sounding name!) from the Messerschmitt survived the battle; the pilot, Fw. Jakob Birndorfer was killed in the crash. This combat must have been a memorable event for the whole Squadron, as F/Lt Crook described it in his memoirs:

"Osti distinguished himself in this action. He chased an Me.110 which in its efforts to shake him off dived to ground level and dodged all over the countryside at over 300 m.p.h., even turning round a church steeple. But Osti stuck to him and refused to be shaken off, and finally the German, as a last desperate resort, flew

---

[10] One was killed and two taken PoW by the Germans. One of the latter was P/O R. Hardy, who landed his Spitfire N3277/AZ-H at Cherbourg.

right through the Southampton balloon barrage. Osti went through after him, caught him up over Solent, and shot him down in the Isle of Wight."[11]

The same engagement brought some excitement to another Polish Spitfire pilot of 609 Squadron. Nowierski's report states:

"I was Blue 2. Leader was manoeuvring into position to attack and as we turned to attack I saw on my right at the same height five enemy aircraft coming towards me. I turned towards them. They were Ju 88's. I passed them and turned to attack. Just as I got into range they turned into the sun right across my path and flick rolled. I blacked out, came to and by then I had lost sight of the enemy aircraft. I climbed up again to approximately 10,000 ft and saw one enemy aircraft going in a southerly direction. I climbed above him into the sun, I attacked and gave him a burst from the quarter. He turned into the sun, I followed, overtaking very fast in bad line astern. I throttled back so as not to overtake, I could not see well because of the sun. He turned left out of the sun and I opened fire. But I had the throttle back and he drew away. I had no more ammunition so I went back to base."

16 August 1940

Interception scrambles made at about 10.30 and 13.00 were inconclusive. Around 5 pm twelve aircraft of 234 Squadron were sent against an approaching raid. They met Messerschmitt 109s over Portsmouth and claimed five of them for the loss of two Spitfires. One of the Messerschmitts fell victim to Sgt Zygmunt Klein (flying Spitfire I P9460) of Red Section with F/Lt Hughes (R6896) and P/O Mortimer-Rose (N3283). The attack on the JG 53 Bf 109 was later described as follows by the Polish fighter:

"I was Red 2 & in the middle of a dog fight. I got my sights on one Me.109 at the top of a loop. I was turning outside or above him. He went straight down. I followed him down to 10,000 feet giving him several short bursts till he went into a cloud. I went round the cloud & below. I saw a man on a parachute & saw nothing more of the machine."

The parachutist, who fell south of the Isle of Wight, was probably Fw. Hansen, who was taken prisoner.

17 August 1940

The "teething period" for 302 Squadron (as well as for 303) brought accidents which prevented a few pilots from taking part in the Battle. One of them, P/O Czesław Głowczyński, the future ace (who had already claimed victories over Poland and France) had to save his life in dramatic circumstances. During a training flight his Hurricane P3927/WX-E caught fire and he had to make an emergency landing. He was badly burnt and would not resume operational flying until April 1941.

18 August 1940

On 18 August at about 8.30 am all available aeroplanes of 501 Squadron moved to Hawkinge where they were placed at 15-minute readiness. Soon afterwards they were

[11] F/Lt D. M. Crook DFC, *Spitfire Pilot*, Faber & Faber 1942.

scrambled to meet the enemy over Canterbury. A little haze and clouds placed the squadron at a disadvantage however, allowing Bf 109s to initiate a surprise "bounce". This attack caused considerable casualties to the unit. Oblt. G. Schöpfel of JG 26, who led his fighters in this combat, said:

> "I saw a *Staffel* of Hurricanes below. They were using the English tactics of flying close formation of three and climbing in a wide spiral. Being about 1000 metres above them I turned with them and managed to get behind the two weavers. I waited until they were once more heading away from Folkestone and then dived out of the sun, and attacked from below."

During this surprise attack 501 Squadron lost four Hurricanes destroyed and one pilot killed; three pilots managed to bale out. The only Polish loss to Oblt. Schöpfel's attack was P/O Franciszek Kozłowski. His aircraft crashed in flames at Rayhams Farm near Whitstable. The wounded pilot was sent to hospital with the two other survivors. Another Pole engaged in this clash, P/O Paweł Zenker, wrote:

> "I was No 2 in Green Section, when the Squadron was patrolling in the vicinity of Canterbury and was acting as rear-guard. While the rest of the squadron was engaged in a general dog-fight with twenty plus Me 110 and 109's I saw one Me 109 straggling below me. Then I approached and noticed three Me 109's on my tail. I took evasive action and I attacked one of them with a short burst from quarter at 50 yards range. Then I saw one under me which was diving about 300 yards away. I chased him and from 250 yards I gave him two or three bursts until my ammunition was gone and saw black smoke coming from the side of his fuselage. I did not see what happened to him."

During a pursuit of the next wave of bombers to approach at about 1.30 pm, a Polish fighter pilot of 32 Squadron claimed to have shot down two enemy aircraft. 32 Squadron, sent to intercept one of three main formations that headed for airfields at Biggin Hill, West Malling, Croydon and Kenley, met bombers from KG 76. F/Lt Peter Malam Brothers and P/O Własnowolski (P3679) attacked a Junkers Ju 88 of KG 76. Although both pilots of 32 Squadron identified their victim as a Ju 88, most sources credit them with downing a Do 215. One of the Dorniers shot down by 32 Squadron which crashed near Kenley was the Do 17Z F1+1H (Werk Nr. 2504) of 1./KG 76 and possibly this one fell to the Brothers-Własnowolski team. On the other hand, one of the Junkers bombers of 5./KG 76 (with the crew of Oberfw. Eichhorn, Oberfw. Vetter, Fw. Geier and Gefr. Skuthan) was attacked by 32 Squadron Hurricanes and 64 Squadron Spitfires, and finally crashed with all the crew on board. Thus, the identity of the victim is hard to trace with absolute precision because KG 76 lost two Junkers 88s and seven Dornier 17Zs in this battle. Three of the latter were claimed by 111 Squadron, and one by the pilots of 1 Squadron. Three others have not been matched specifically with RAF claims.

During the late afternoon battle over Canterbury the same team of Brothers-Własnowolski proved its value again, downing a Messerschmitt Bf 109E-1 of 7./JG 26. The combat against Lt. Müller-Duhe's aeroplane was described by Własnowolski in his report:

"I was flying with the squadron next to F/Lt Brothers when I saw a Me 109 behind and at the same height. I turned and attacked him, he turned away towards the ground. I followed, firing several short bursts, he dived into the ground and went up in flames. I circled round and saw two aircraft on fire on the ground. The Me 109 had yellow wingtips. The place was near Chatham."

The Polish pilot had shot it down with just three short bursts, using only 600 rounds of ammunition. In the same combat another Pole of 32 Squadron, together with P/O Alan Francis Eckford (P3936), shot at the Messerschmitt Bf 109E-4 of Maj. Blume of 7./JG 26. P/O Karol Pniak (flying N2542) reported:

"I flew in Blue Section as No 2. To our right I saw at the same height two Me 109's. I attacked the one which was nearer me from a distance of 250 yards. I gave him a short burst at first. He was quite surprised, I drew nearer and gave him two (2 sec) bursts and just after I saw an Me 109 in black smoke and flames. He was diving in SE direction. I climbed to a height of 13 000 ft and saw 2 Hurricanes which were fighting with 5 Me 109's and I attacked one which was near to the back of one Hurricane. He saw me because I attacked ¾ from front above. At once he turned in my direction and began to dive. I turned in his direction and after several seconds I was near him. I gave the first burst from 300 yards. After several bursts he was burning. I left him at a height of 7 000 ft. He was travelling in a southerly direction. When I came back I saw some Me 109's who were diving in the same direction but they were too far away. I came home."

Pniak's victim crashed at Elmstead Court, Barnham.

At the same time that these Polish-British teams were gaining their successes, F/O Franciszek Gruszka and P/O Szulkowski, flying Spitfires of 65 Squadron, were also involved in combat with Messerschmitts. After the unit returned home it was found that Gruszka was missing. An eyewitness of this fight later described seeing a single Spitfire dog-fighting Messerschmitts between Canterbury and Manston. It is believed that during this chase Gruszka shot down his opponent before being killed himself. He was listed missing until 1971, when remnants of his aeroplane were excavated by aviation archaeologists. The Spitfire R6713 had been buried deep in the Grove Marsh with the body of Gruszka still at the controls.

Jeffrey Quill recalls his meeting with the Poles who served in 65 Squadron:

"[...] as soon as I got there [to 65 Sqn – author] I was asked to lead three recently joined pilots up to Sutton Bridge for more air firing [...] These new pilots comprised a nineteen year-old fresh-faced young Pilot Officer straight from OTU called Derek Glaser whom I had known as a boy, and two Polish pilots, Szulkowski and Gruszka. According to my diary notes at the time, they did their air-to-ground firing and we had some tea in the Mess and flew back to Rochford. [...] While we were having tea in the Mess at Sutton Bridge I had the chance to ask the two Poles about their escapes from their country, but their English was limited and they were obviously confused by the trauma of their recent lives, culminating in being trained to fly Spitfires in a foreign land and in a foreign tongue and then pitched into the strange environment of a Royal Air Force fighter squadron. I wondered how they would ever understand anything over the R/T, for in those days we still had old TR9D H/F sets whose sound quality was so poor I had difficulty enough myself in hearing distinctly. Young Glaser was extremely good with them, and they seemed to feel at ease with him, as they had joined the squadron together. Until the day that Gruszka was shot down and Szulkowski became inconsolable and silent, they spent hours poring over an English dictionary. [...]

"[...] (18 August) Gruszka the Pole failed to return from a sortie. It had been a very active day and those two Poles of ours, both very aggressive, were also much inclined to go off on their own once anything began to happen and we assumed that Gruszka must have been shot down into the sea as there were no reports of crashed Spitfires inland which could have been his. Needless to say the unfortunate Szulkowski was terribly upset but could shed no light on the matter. (In 1975 Gruszka's Spitfire was discovered in Kent with his body still in the cockpit. He was buried with full military honours at Northwood cemetery in the presence of many members of the Polish community in London. Dave Glaser and I also attended.)[12]"

Almost at the same time when the 32 Squadron Hurricanes and 65 Squadron Spitfires were engaged over Kent, at about 5.40 pm seven Hurricanes of 501 Squadron were scrambled to intercept about 50 Messerschmitt Bf 110s and Bf 109s. This engagement ended with the loss of F/Lt Stoney, while two JG 51 Messerschmitt 109s were claimed. Both fell victim to Polish pilots. P/O Paweł Zenker claimed one:

"I was No 2 in Green Section when the squadron consisting of 7 Hurricanes, left Gravesend to patrol forward base. When flying North East near Westgate, I saw on my left about 50 Do's in formation flying East off the coast and behind them at about 14 000 ft 25 to 30 Me 109's not flying in ordinary but in search formation. Flight Lieutenant leading the squadron turned left to attack Do from the beam and I with Green 1 went straight to the fighters and engaged one of them. He turned back towards France and I chased him as he climbed firing from 300 and closer ranges and about 10 miles over the sea I saw smoke and fire come from the fuselage and he rapidly lost height. The Me 109 did not adopt evasive action but flew straight on until it crashed into the water somewhere near the North Goodwin Lightship."

In the same combat F/O Stefan Witorzeńć, flying Hurricane I L1868/SD-D, claimed another Messerschmitt:

"I was No 2 in Red when the Squadron was patrolling in the East Kent Area at approximately 17.40 hours, we sighted large force of Do about 50, flying East over and parallel with the coast, and behind them a large escort of Me 109's. Red 1 (F/L Stoney) attacked the bombers from the beam and quarter to break up the formation. I followed him in but noticed about two Me 109's behind approaching from the third quarter and from above and firing at me. I broke out to the right and engaged in a dog-fight the two of them diving to 10 000 ft from 14 000 ft. After climbing again I saw 1 Me 109 about 150 yards in front of me and attacked him from beam with one long burst. The Me 109 turned left and dived with me

[12] Jeffrey Quill, *Spitfire: a Test Pilot's Story*, Arrow Books, London 1986.

following him and I gave him one long burst from dead astern. I saw him catch fire and crash near Wingham and explode."

It is believed that P/O Zenker shot down Hptm. Horst Tietzen, *Staffelkapitän* of 5./JG 51, and F/O Stefan Witorzeńć downed Lt. H. Lessing, also from 5./JG 51. Both German pilots were killed.

Similarly to 501 Squadron, 151 Squadron also moved its aircraft from the main base at North Weald to Rochford, to meet coming formations in better time. About 5 pm all aircraft went back to North Weald, and a few minutes later the Hurricanes were scrambled. The formation consisted of:

S/Ldr Gordon	P3940
Sgt Clarke	P3312
P/O Smith	V7411
P/O Ramsey	R4181
P/O Ellacombe	L2005/DZ-D
F/Lt Smith	L1750
F/O Milne	R4182
P/O Kawalecki (Polish)	P3306
P/O Debenham	R4183
P/O Czajkowski (Polish)	P3320

P/O Tadeusz Kawalecki and P/O Franciszek Czajkowski had been engaged in the air fighting over Poland during the 1939 campaign; P/O Kawalecki had managed to damage a German aeroplane at that time. The Hurricane pilots intercepted the enemy coming out of clouds a few miles south of Chelmsford. They spotted Junkers 88s and Heinkel 111s, escorted by Messerschmitt 110s and 109s. At least two pilots claimed the destruction of a Messerschmitt 110, one of them being P/O Czajkowski:

"The squadron was ordered off to intercept enemy raid approaching aerodrome. We climbed to 10,000 ft and saw other squadrons of Hurricanes waiting. The bombers came through the gap in the clouds facing straight at aerodrome. Seeing the opposition they turned round and opened throttle heading for home. I was unable to keep up with Green 1 who engaged a bomber. Me 110's came down on me and I successfully evaded one on my tail. Many Me 110's were being chased out to sea and I followed with Hurricanes of another squadron. I attacked a 110 and broke away after a short burst. Another Hurricane also fired at this 110 which went down with smoke coming from both engines. I did not see it crash as I was following up the attack of another Hurricane on a 110 and when he broke away I closed with this Me 110 and after a short burst he turned on his back and went down in a spiral and crashed in the sea. I now returned to base."

Czajkowski probably joined 85 Squadron Hurricanes that were chasing a Messerschmitt 110 of 4./ZG 26. This latter unit lost four aircraft in this encounter and only one ditched in the sea. Credit for the destruction of Bf 110C crewed by Uffz. Baar and Fw. Gierga goes in fact to 85 Squadron pilots; Czajkowski was however, the last to fire at this 4./ZG 26 aircraft, coded 3U+CM.

Chapter Two

POLISH SQUADRONS ENTER THE BATTLE

19 August – 4 September 1940

"I must confess that I had been a little doubtful of the effect which their experience in their own countries and in France might have had upon the Polish and Czech pilots, but my doubts were soon laid to rest, because all three Squadrons swung in the fight with a dash and enthusiasm which is beyond praise. They were inspired by a burning hatred for the Germans which made them very deadly opponents."

ACM Sir Hugh C. T. Dowding

19 August 1940

Instruction sent to Group Controllers and Sector Commanders, for Sector Controllers on 19 August 1940 by AVM Keith R. Park, No 11 Group CO stated:

"The German Air Force has begun a new phase in air attacks, which have been switched from coastal shipping and ports on to inland objectives. The bombing attacks have for several days been concentrated against aerodromes, and especially fighter aerodromes, on the coast and inland. The following instructions are issued to meet the changed conditions:

"... g) No 303 (Polish) Squadron can provide two sections for patrol of inland aerodromes especially while the other squadrons are on the ground refuelling, when enemy formations are flying over land; ..."

302 (Polish) Squadron had also began making operational sorties on 19 August. The first such were undertaken by the section:

F/Lt Riley	R4095/WX-M
F/Lt Jastrzębski	P3923/WX-U
P/O Chałupa	P3934/WX-T

20 August 1940

Two sections from "B" Flight, 302 Squadron, were ordered to patrol the Leconfield area. About 6.50 pm there were six aircraft in the air. Squadron Leader William Arthur John Satchell described his action.

31

"I took off at 18.53 and was slightly late starting, and caught up the Flight over the coast. As I joined it I received the order to patrol Hull at 5,000 ft. On approaching Hull I observed a twin engined aircraft flying in an Easterly direction below my starboard bow. I dived at once to a position above and slightly behind and saw the German black crosses and at the same time identified the aircraft as a Ju 88. The e/a immediately shot into the clouds endeavouring to avoid me. I followed and got in a short burst using full deflection and both aircraft turned before the e/a went into another cloud. I climbed above this cloud and as the enemy aircraft emerged on the far side I got in another burst and when he emerged a second time I dived and got in a long burst, opening at 300 yrds and ceasing fire at about 50 yrds when I had to pull out quickly to avoid a collision. Soon after opening my second burst the rear gunner ceased fire, as I saw no more tracer. I observed my tracer penetrating the e/a all around the centre of the fuselage, all my attacks being delivered from above and slightly behind, I received a bullet in my propeller. During the attack I observed smoke coming from the e/a's engines due apparently to overboosting. The main tactics of the enemy were steep left hand turns. After I had broken away I observed Green 2 on e/a's tail for a very short period before the e/a went into clouds. It was not seen and was presumed to have crashed. This was confirmed later by telephone. At an interview between Flying Officer Robinson, Interrogation Officer, and the four prisoners it was stated that my third attack from above set the cockpit on fire."

The enemy aircraft was spotted about 7.10 pm, flying at an altitude of 3,000 ft somewhere between Hull and Spurn Point. The German bomber was on its way back home, having bombed Thornaby airfield. After the successful attacks of S/Ldr Satchell with some attempted assistance by P/O Chałupa, the Junkers 88A-1 (coded 4D+IS, of 8./KG 30) crashed at Patrington, about six miles south west of Withernsea. The crew of the bomber were taken prisoners, with the exception of the pilot, Uffz. W. Rautenberg, who was lost. The credit for the first success of a Polish-manned unit in Britain thus went to its British OC, Squadron Leader Satchell. Other pilots who took part in this mission were as follows:

F/Lt Riley	R4095/WX-M
Sgt Paterek	P3930/WX-X
F/Lt Jastrzębski	P3923/WX-U
P/O Chałupa	P3934/WX-T
P/O Wapniarek	P3924/WX-Y
S/Ldr Satchell	P3812/WX-L

21 August 1940

Lack of order in the surviving official papers of 302 Squadron may lead to confusing conclusions as to the next aerial victory of this Polish unit. Many publications quote it as achieved on 21 August 1940[13]. However, the fundamental source document, the Operations Record Book (preserved at the Public Records Office, Kew) states that

---

[13] This version of events is supported by John Foreman in *Fighter Command War Diaries* (Air Research Publications 1997), for example, who states that 302 Squadron claimed one enemy aircraft shot down and two probables that day.

this next encounter did not take place until 22 August! The same document comments that two Ju 88s were downed on the 22nd (one into the sea and another four miles off the coast). Neither claim was confirmed by the RAF Intelligence. However, no personal combat reports dated 22 August appear to exist.

The same document, under the date of 24 August, describes a patrol when P/O Stanisław Chałupa of Blue Section attacked a Ju 88 and shot it down. On the way back the engine of his Hurricane seized and P/O Chałupa was forced to land immediately. His Hurricane I P3934/WX-T crashed on the edge of the airfield with undercarriage retracted.

It seems that in fact all the events described above (under different dates) took place on the same day, 21 August, about 3.50 pm. The personal Combat Report of P/O Chałupa (Blue 2), dated 21 August 1940 describes the sortie in detail:

> "While I was patrolling over the sea at 12,000 ft I noticed a Ju 88 flying on our port side in a dive. After turning the leader attacked from above and behind. Being about 200 meters away from him I opened fire and noticed that little bits of something flew off the e/a. After three bursts the e/a flew into a cloud with the whole section behind him. After emerging from the clouds I saw the e/a below me and behind him Blue 1. Having got in another burst the Ju 88 disappeared into a second cloud. After this burst I did not see the e/a again but only the aircraft of the section leader who I was following.
>
> "Second engagement.
>
> "Whilst patrolling later on with Blue 1 I saw an aircraft about half mile away. I approached Blue 1, waggled my wings and turned off in the direction of e/a. I could not recognise it at once because I was approaching into the sun which was on my starboard bow. Having approached to within 200 yards I recognised the aircraft as a Ju 88. Having attacked and got in about 3 bursts from about 150 yards I saw certain objects flying off from the aircraft and a lot of black smoke poured from his port engine. In this state the e/a started to dive and flew into the cloud. Owing to the fact that my engine began to function badly and gave forth white smoke from beneath its cowling I throttled back and tried to glide towards the aerodrome. Being at about 2000 ft the engine began to vibrate. Being unable to reach the aerodrome I landed on the edge of it without dropping my undercarriage."

The date of the crash of Hurricane I P3934/WX-T with P/O Chałupa as a pilot is still repeated as 24 August by some publications[14].

Apart from the Junkers 88 probably destroyed by P/O Chałupa, discussed above, one probable also was claimed by F/Lt William Riley who led the Blue Section.

> "Blue Section took off at 15.23 and was ordered to patrol Bridlington at 12,000 ft. Circled there for about 15 minutes and sighted Ju 88 heading due West at about 500 ft above cloud top. Enemy aircraft dived as soon as Blue Section was sighted. Blue 1 led attack from above enemy aircraft on its starboard side opening fire at about 400 yards with burst of 5 seconds. Enemy aircraft jettisoned bombs before

---

[14] Authors usually refer this information to Francis K. Mason's *Battle over Britain*, McWhirter Twins Ltd.

attack was delivered and during bursts pieces were seen to disintegrate from the fuselage. Enemy aircraft entered cloud and on emerging after about 10 secs. Blue 1 again attacked from above and to starboard. Blue 2 and 3 attacked almost at the same time from beams. Enemy aircraft again entered cloud with starboard engine smoking, at about 8,000 ft and was not again seen as broken cumulus reached down to about 4,000 ft. During attacks ice coated windscreen of Blue 1 aircraft and he could not see details of enemy aircraft."

22 August 1940

In the morning, between 8.00 and 9.00, convoy "TOTEM", passing through the Straits of Dover, became a very visible target for the heavy gun battery on Cap Gris Nez. The outbreak of shelling caused 32 Squadron to scramble, to protect the convoy from presumed air attack. The Hurricane patrol was fruitless, but on the way back P/O Jan Pfeiffer crash landed at Hawkinge, damaging his Hurricane P3205.

A more successful patrol for 32 Squadron began in the evening, when Messerschmitt 110s of ErpGr 210 were targeted to bomb Manston airfield. P/O Karol Pniak claimed damage to a 'Dornier 17', as he mistook a Bf 110 for a Dornier. None of the 110s taking part in the Manston raid were lost and no damage to any aircraft was reported. A similarly unresolved claim was made by another Polish pilot taking part in the same interception. 65 Squadron was detailed to intercept the raiders, but the Spitfires were engaged by Messerschmitt 109s. This action was described by P/O Władysław Szulkowski, who flew Spitfire R6712:

> "I was flying in the position of Blue 3 when we engaged many Me 109's over Dover at 20,000 ft.
> "I became separated from my section and attacked one of the stragglers. Before he could attempt evasion I fired several bursts from 350 yards closing to 100 yards and the e/a burst into flames and crashed down into the sea; where I saw it before turning back to base."

P/O Szulkowski had been posted to this unit from 5 OTU on 5 August 1940, and it was not his first combat. Despite his description of a Messerschmitt 109 crashing in mid channel off Dover at about 5.00 pm, apparently no Messerschmitt 109 was reported missing due to combat on that date.

23 August 1940

P/O Jan Pfeiffer of 32 Squadron suffered continued bad luck, when he crashed his Hurricane I P2795 as he had the day before. The Polish pilot tried to land on one wheel when coming back from patrol at 7.15 am; he escaped without injuries.

24 August 1940

This was the busiest day for 501 Squadron during the whole Battle of Britain period. It was also a day of great successes for British and Polish pilots in this unit. The ORB states:

> "Weather fine and clear. The squadron left [Gravesend] for Hawkinge at 9.35am and patrolled without landing at forward base. They intercepted an enemy formation of 30 Dorniers escorted by Me 109's. Red 1 entered into a beam attack

on the bombers and the formation was broken up. Enemy jettisoned bombs before turning East. P/O Zenker was reported missing – believed killed – after this engagement. Enemy casualties were 1 Me 109 destroyed and 1 Do 215 damaged."

The attack by Messerschmitt 109s on "B" Flight and the death of P/O Paweł Zenker, flying the Hurricane I P3141/SD-W, were clearly seen by Green Section. Sgt Antoni Głowacki, flying as Green 2, made the only claim for a Messerschmitt shot down in this encounter.

"We circled round and A Flight attacked the rear formation of the bombers and I saw, from the rear, German fighters (Me 109) attacking B Flight. I had a dog-fight with an Me 109, which I shot down. The e/a which I followed down hit the ground and exploded. As the bombers were attacked I saw them jettison their bombs about 10 miles South East of Canterbury."

It is probable that Sgt Antoni Głowacki (flying his lucky Hurricane I V7234/SD-A for Antek) probably destroyed a JG 51 Messerschmitt. Antek was his Polish nickname, but he was better known as Toni among his British colleagues. The team during the early morning encounter was as follows:

Sgt Głowacki (Polish)	V7234/SD-A
F/Lt Putt	R4105/SD-U
P/O Dafforn	R4223/SD-L
Sgt Green	V6545/SD-T
P/O Zenker (Polish)	P3141/SD-W
F/Sgt Morfill	P3397/SD-M
P/O Gibson	P3102
F/O Witorzeńć (Polish)	P3803/SD-Z
Sgt Farnes	N2329/SD-K
Sgt Lacey	P8816/SD-F
P/O Hairs	V7357/SD-G
P/O Aldridge	L1868/SD-D

Further encounters with Messerschmitt 109s, mentioned in Głowacki's combat statistics sheet[15], brought no result, until one which took place about 12.45 pm.

501 Squadron was sent to help other squadrons protecting Manston airfield. Meanwhile, during defensive combats over North Weald, 151 Squadron had a fierce clash with Bf 109s. P/O Franciszek Czajkowski of 151 Squadron, flying Hurricane I V6537, shot at one of the raiders, claiming it as probably destroyed.

501 Squadron intercepted a force of 30 bombers which had just bombed Manston, escorted by Messerschmitt fighters:

---

[15] Evidence of combat activity of Polish airmen in Britain was prepared by the Polish Air Force Inspectorate during the war and later was used for statistics, awards decoration and setting up of the List of Victories of Polish Fighter Pilots etc. Some sheets preserved at the Polish Institute and Sikorski Museum list operational and combat sorties of Polish fighter pilots.

"The enemy fighter escort were late in attacking our aircraft and the Squadron accounted for 2 Ju 88's destroyed and 2 damaged and 1 Me 109 destroyed."

said the Squadron Operations Record Book. F/O Stefan Witorzeńć, flying Hurricane I P3803/SD-Z, managed to shoot at one of the bombers and claimed it damaged.

"I was No 2 in Yellow section when the squadron left Hawkinge on patrol. While in the vicinity of Dover we were told that e/a had crossed the coast and had turned North towards Manston. We turned North to follow them and sighted about 20+ Ju 88 beginning to dive slowly down towards Manston aerodrome. They were seen to bomb the aerodrome from about 4,000 ft after which they turned right and out to sea. I saw a Ju 88 not in formation and attacked him as he crossed the coast. After firing all my ammunition from astern I saw white smoke come out of him. He turned slowly to the right gradually losing height. I was not attacked by enemy fighters."

The most successful pilot of this combat was again Sgt Antoni Głowacki, who claimed a Ju 88 and a Bf 109 destroyed.

". . . We turned across and intercepted them as they turned out to sea. The whole squadron attacked the bombers first as the fighters were too late in attacking us. I shot down a Ju 88 in flames into the sea and saw how a Messerschmitt shot down either a Hurricane or a Defiant. I attacked the Me 109 and was able to shoot him down in flames."

Sgt Głowacki had witnessed the downing of one of three Defiants lost by 264 Squadron in this surprise attack on Manston airfield. Defiants taking off under falling bombs had little chance to enter the battle, a situation which happened on two occasions for these unfortunate two-seaters.

Sgt Głowacki achieved further success when 501 Squadron was scrambled two hours later. Eleven Hurricanes of this unit took off at 3.30 pm to patrol Dover. Flying at 20,000 ft, the Squadron attacked a section of German bombers near Graystone. A dog-fight with enemy fighters followed. Sgt Głowacki described his experience in claiming his fourth and fifth victories of the day.

"The enemy formation of bombers and fighters were sighted at 13,000 ft coming from the direction of Lympne and executing a turning movement like the letter 'S' towards London. We turned West and attacked them South-West of Maidstone. The escort of Me 109's circled round and attacked from the up-sun side. I had a dog-fight with an Me 109 and shot him down in flames. I climbed again and attacked the last aircraft of a formation of bombers from astern and finished my ammunition on it. I saw white smoke come out of him and observers on the aerodrome saw him spinning towards the ground."

The successes of 501 Squadron during the whole day had cost two aircraft and one pilot lost. During the afternoon combat P/O Aldridge had to bale out, while P/O Zenker had lost his life early in the morning, as already described. The next patrol over Dungeness at about 7.00 pm brought a minor engagement, but without casualties on either side.

Almost at the same time that Sgt Głowacki was close to finishing off his fourth and fifth victims, a Polish pilot of 32 Squadron, flying Hurricane V6572 over Folkestone, tried to shoot down a Bf 109 of JG 3. However, in a split-second his very life became menaced. P/O Karol Pniak said in his combat report:

"I was flying No 3 of Blue Section when we met 12 Me 109's at about 20 000 ft. They were above us and attacked us, I was attacked by a Me 109 from head on and above. I circled round on his tail, and closing to 150 yards gave him 2 two-seconds bursts, he started to smoke from the engine, I followed him and gave him two more bursts, much black smoke came from the a/c, and he was diving just after this. I felt my machine vibrating and saw smoke coming from the engine and the right wing, and flames also appeared from the right wing. I switched off everything and put my a/c into a dive to land, but when I reached 5000 ft the flames were so big, that I turned my plane on one side and jumped. I landed very fast because my parachute was not properly open and full of holes, I landed 3 miles NW of Hawkinge, my ankle and knee were injured, and I was taken to hospital."

P/O Karol Pniak's aircraft crashed at Rhodes Minnis near Lympne, but the aircraft he had been attacking, from 7./JG 3 is presumed to have landed safely on the other side of the Channel.

Activity by German aircraft decreased gradually. Late in the afternoon the last Luftwaffe raid was plotted, heading towards Portsmouth. A dozen aircraft of 234 Squadron were scrambled to intercept this raid, including four flown by Polish pilots:

S/Ldr O'Brien	P9466	Red 1
Sgt Szlagowski (Polish)	X4035	Red 2
Sgt Wotton	X4251	Red 3
P/O Mortimer-Rose	X4010	Yellow 1
Sgt Klein (Polish)	X4023	Yellow 2
P/O Gordon	R6957	Yellow 3
F/Lt Hughes	X4009	Blue 1
P/O Oleński (Polish)	N3279	Blue 2
Sgt Boddington	P9494	Blue 3
P/O Lawrence	X4009	Green 1
P/O Żurakowski (Polish)	N3239	Green
Sgt Bayley	X4182	Green

S/Ldr O'Brien and P/O Gordon claimed the destruction of one Bf 109 each, P/O Lawrence claimed one Bf 110 damaged while P/O Oleński was the only Pole to achieve any success. In his personal combat report he claimed a Bf 109 probably destroyed:

"I was Blue 2. Over interception point I saw 7 Me 109 and was about to attack them when two Me 109's attacked from behind and I saw pairs of Me 109's stepped up 500 feet above each other. I swerved to the right and attacked the last pair from astern, gave a short burst and it dived wildly with smoke coming from fuselage."

However P/O Janusz Żurakowski was shot down by the team of Oblt Hans-Karl

Mayer and Lt. Zeiss of I./JG53; he baled out over the Isle of Wight. This event has often been mistakenly described as a case of a crash-landing, but Żurakowski's account tells how it really was:

"[...]during a sortie on August 24, 1940. I was attacking a formation of Do 17 bombers that were on a bombing run of Southampton harbour. After my attack, I made the error of climbing to join the squadron. Some of the escorting Me 109s managed to put a few cannon shells into my Spitfire. I lost control of elevator and rudder. My Spitfire then went slowly into a turn, stalled, and ended up in a flat spin.

"Having no controls, I had to bail out. At about 18,000 feet I slid open the canopy, climbed out of the cabin, and jumped. I soon found I was descending faster than the Spitfire, which was spinning above my head. I was afraid to pull the rip cord to open the chute because that would have slowed me down, risking a collision with my spinning Spitfire.

"The ground was approaching fast, and when I could distinguish a man standing in a field with a gun, I decided to pull the rip cord. It was now or never! My parachute opened immediately. My Spitfire just missed me and hit the ground with a bang. A few seconds later, I landed on the field, next to the old man (from the Home Guard) who was armed with a double-barrelled shotgun. He was badly shaken by the crash.

"Suspecting that I might be German, he asked me if I spoke English. Since my English was poor, I decided to remain quiet. I tried to show him my RAF identity card, but his hands were shaking so violently that he could not take it.[...]

"A Spitfire's vertical speed in a flat spin was fairly low, so the damage to my Spitfire on impact with the ground was not severe. The main engine mounting failed and there was evidence of two gunshots (probably 20 mm calibre) in the rear-fuselage tail junction and one in the port wing.[...]

"Next morning I returned to my squadron. I was flying again, but learned from my friends in London that I had been officially killed. I had to send a report to the effect that I was very sorry, but that, since the day of the crash, I had carried out six operational sorties in August, so I was obviously alive. Shortly afterward, I received two letters addressed to me, marked 'Killed in Action' on the envelope."[16]

Also F/O Tadeusz Nowierski of 609 Squadron (sent over Portsmouth in parallel with 234) finished his combat over Ryde with a damaged Spitfire I (R6631/PR-Q). He landed successfully at Middle Wallop. This unfortunate combat was described in the 609 Squadron chronicle.

"Squadron was ordered to intercept raiders over Ryde, and found themselves 5,000 ft below a large formation of bombers and fighters, right in the middle of our own A/A fire, and down-sun. The squadron was attacked and fortunate to sustain no further casualties other then 2 aircraft damaged, of which one was a Write-off."

Officially 307 Squadron was formed at the Polish Depot at Blackpool on this date.

---

[16] Robert Bracken, *Spitfire: the Canadians*, Boston Mills Press, Ontario 1995.

25 August 1940

Two Spitfire Squadrons, nos. 609 and 234, full of Polish airmen again, were scrambled together with other units from Tangmere, Exeter, Warmwell and Middle Wallop late in the afternoon to intercept a raid that headed towards Weymouth Bay and then split to attack Warmwell and Portland. P/O Janusz Żurakowski (shot down the day before) did not take part in this engagement. For other Poles the combats ahead were full of events.

"Squadron had a big Tea-time party with a Hundred plus, mixed enemy force over Warmwell, and the Squadron Leader drew first blood, although none of the bombers (Ju 88's) were intercepted. 609 Squadron pilots caused 11 casualties among their escorting Me's, at the expense of 2 Spitfire Aircraft . . ."

– said 609 Squadron ORB. P/O Piotr Ostaszewski's aircraft was hit and he survived a real thrill. The history of 609 Squadron described this event:

"Fg Off Ostaszewski in R6986 [PR-S] had a narrow shave. A shell blew off his top rear armour plating which gave him a clout on the head. Another went through the top of his engine and out through the airscrew; a third severed the pipe lines to his brakes. His engine however kept going and he arrived back at base but ran through a hedge through lack of brakes. He escaped from this with a few scratches and a headache. Aircraft repairable."

609 Squadron hammered into the Messerschmitt 110s and then were surprised by 109s of JG 53. This attack caused damage to two Spitfires, but 609 Squadron's success was undeniable. They claimed the destruction of eight enemy aircraft with one probable and two damaged.

28 August 1940

P/O Stanisław Skalski, one of the most successful fighter pilots of the September 1939 campaign, had joined the Polish team in 501 Squadron on 26 August 1940. On 28 August the Poles had another opportunity to attack German bombers and claim more victories. Sgt Antoni Głowacki described his attempts to shoot down a Bf 109.

"We saw a formation of 17 bombers flying North-West of Canterbury at an altitude of 10,000 feet. While climbing we made a wide circle to attack them. Some twenty Messerschmitt 109s were turning above the bombers and while we were half a mile from the bombers, some Hurricane squadron attacked the bombers, and was itself attacked by the fighters. This moment we hurried with help to the Hurricane squadron and attacked the Messerschmitts from below at 13,000 feet. I saw a Me 109 on the tail of a Hurricane, and I shot at him from a long distance. When he entered the dive I hit him with two bursts from behind. The Me 109 started to burn, hit in the fuel tank, and the pilot baled out. The aircraft crashed and exploded in a field South-South-East of Canterbury."

Sgt Głowacki, in Hurricane I P5193/SD-O, together with other 501 Squadron pilots, had arrived to help 79 Squadron. The history of this latter unit still holds a mystery regarding another Polish airman. During the combat described by Sgt Głowacki, P/O

Zatoński of no 79, flying Hurricane I P2718, was hit and had to be sent to a hospital with burns.

The mysterious Zatoński joined the RAF via Canada, and was mentioned in the official Polish Air Force papers only once, in the section dealing with casualty statistics (after this particular combat). Some facts regarding his personal history were traced in the 79 Squadron Operations Record Book, which mentions his name several times. Hit and burnt on 28 August, he returned to his unit on 4 December 1940. His health must have been in bad shape still, because very soon, on 20 December, he was sent back to St Athan Hospital. Later P/O Zatoński was posted to 238 Squadron, with which unit he was killed in North Africa, on 6 December 1941. Following this a local Canadian newspaper issued at Brandford, where Zatoński's parents lived, gave more details of his short life:

"A Polish boy, P/O Zatoński started for Poland shortly before hostilities began in September 1939, but found it impossible to reach that country. He returned to England and has been with the RAF ever since.

"After some months training he was attached to a fighter squadron near London, flying Hurricanes.

"Once he was shot down in an air battle, baled out from a height of 24 000 ft (almost four and a half miles) and landed in the English Channel. He suffered a bullet wound in one leg and was painfully burned, but, as he wrote his friends here, 'got away quite lucky'.

"The drop 'took me about half an hour to get down' to the Channel."

In the engagements recorded by 79 and 501 Squadrons, the German fighter cover of JG 26 Bf 109s lost two aircraft that crashed in the Canterbury area, and two pilots: Hptm. Beyer, the *Geschwaderadjutant*, and Fw. Straub were taken prisoner. 501 Squadron returned without loss.

Although one of the downed JG 26 Messerschmitts could be the victim of Sgt Głowacki, neither was reported to have crashed in the area described in the latter's report. Quite a different description of the claim was given in Głowacki's memoirs.

"Immediately after sunrise we landed as a whole squadron at Hawkinge, near the Channel. During the flight I noticed that the oxygen system in my aircraft stopped indicating the oxygen pressure in the cylinder. Upon landing I called a fitter. He found a fault that could not be repaired at the airfield. I reported that to my OC. He frowned and told me to fly back to Gravesend and replace the aircraft. Angry that I could miss an operational mission and a combat with the Jerries, I nevertheless jumped into my Hurricane and took off.

"The day was getting beautiful, sunny. I set course for the base, and staying at 100 m, like I had been told, flew to Gravesend. After I got a few miles from the airfield, I decided to try my machine for speed. I was curious how much it would show on the speed meter. I got down to the ground and gave full throttle. The speed hand started to move, from 240 to 280 – 300 – 320 . . . and slowly reached 351 miles. 580 kilometres per hour. Excellent! . . .

". . . Far to my right quite a big city appeared – I recognised Canterbury with its wonderful old gothic cathedral. I went around it, so as not to raise panic and shooting. Looking towards the city for a moment I noticed a small, slim aeroplane flying in the opposite direction, South. It flew immediately above the ground, like myself, and only when it hopped trees or houses did it show for short moments against the clear sky. Suddenly I noticed artillery bursts near the aircraft. What could this be! Why does the artillery fire at it? Intrigued, I made a sharp turn to get closer to Canterbury and this aircraft.

"By God! It was a Messerschmitt 109 – lonely, escaping to France after a reconnaissance. Pulling the stick with all my power I turned through 180 degrees, until I blacked-out – and chased the Messerschmitt. I descended to the very ground, so the Jerry would not spot me. Faster, faster! What luck that I had flown at full throttle and had my machine at high speed. Faster! My fingers shaking with emotion, I switched the electric sight on and armed the 8 machine guns. Still some 1,000 metres between us. I speed at full throttle and full revs, looking out of the corner of my eye at the temperature and pressure clocks . . . everything all right.

"Meanwhile the Messerschmitt has passed Canterbury and the artillery has stopped firing. The distance between us starts to shrink slowly. Very well! Obviously the Jerry does not know I am on his tail. You are mine!

"Only 500 metres, 400, 300, 250. The Messerschmitt silhouette starts to fill the entire sight. 200 metres – I can fire. I set the cross of the sight at the cockpit, and push the trigger of the machine guns. I fire a long burst at once . . . He's had it! He's had it! Smoke from the engine, pieces of metal flying away. I get in at 100 metres. I shoot again. The Jerry pulls up, I can see the propeller slow down its revs, the engine must be spluttering, but the aircraft gains height with its inertia. I close the throttle a bit, and follow him. Suddenly something large falls apart from the Messerschmitt! That is the cockpit canopy. I push the stick and the canopy flies some 2-3 metres over my head. I almost hit it. I feel hot suddenly. I jump sideways and now fly some 20 metres away from the Messerschmitt. I can see flames coming out of the engine, I can see the pilot trying to get out from the burning machine. He struggles, fights and . . . suddenly he is flying, free, cartwheeling. A moment later the parachute opens and the pilot is hanging under the white umbrella. I leave him and follow the machine which emits in turns white and black smoke. It must have been hit in its radiator and oil tanks. The aircraft glides towards the earth, and its shadow moves along on the ground. The aircraft and the shadow get closer and closer to each other, to meet at the spot where the empty aircraft hits the ground in some orchard. Flash, explosion, smoke – pieces of the machine fly away, the burning engine becomes detached from the fuselage and cartwheeling bounces several times on the ground, eventually coming to a halt among the trees. I circle the spot and go back to the pilot, slowly floating down under his white umbrella. I make a circle around the pilot, to get a good look at him. For him the war is over.

"What the hell! the arrogant pilot stretches his hand as if in the nazi greeting. Just you wait, bastard – I will give you 'Hi Hitla'. I fly away a short distance, turn back and dive onto the Jerry. I set my sight just below the feet of the nazi, and push the trigger. A short burst . . . I can see tracer rounds almost shave him. The Jerry draws his legs up and starts waving his hands. I make another attack and again I shoot just below his feet. This time the Jerry has had enough. He stretches his both hands upwards and keeps them straight up. Great hero, who has just shown me his 'Hi Hitla'. Just in case I attack once again and give another burst below his feet. The Jerry has had more than enough, he hangs powerless below the parachute, and heavily lands like this a moment later in a ploughed field. I circle above him. The Jerry has been scared like hell and is now lying motionless. I pull some 300 metres up, and the Jerry sits up immediately, so he's alive, he's all right. He was just pretending, so that I don't shoot at him again.

"I can see people running from various directions towards 'my' German . . .

". . . From a nearby town comes a military motorcycle with a sidecar. It jumps across holes and ditches. It has stopped in a cloud of dust next to the Jerry. Well, I can leave now in peace, the soldiers will take good care of him.

"So I go back to Gravesend. At the airfield they have already got another Hurricane waiting for me with the engine running. I only managed to shout at the fitter 'Check oxygen!' and jumped into the new machine. Take-off straight from under the hangar, and at tree-top to Hawkinge . . . quiet at the airfield, all machines on the ground. My fitters immediately topped up the fuel, and three minutes later my machine was ready to fly. I went to the pilots' tent. Some played cards, some were taking a nap. I approached the OC, and in my then poorish English reported shooting down a Messerschmitt along the way. At first the OC could not understand what I was talking about. What Messerschmitt? There were no Messerschmitts over England. Eventually he grabbed the phone and called the Sector HQ. I can see his face clear up, he is smiling at me. He hung up the phone and reached out his hand to me – 'Well done, Tony, Congratulations.' Others herd around us, everybody asking about the Messerschmitt, the dog-fight . . . I tell them there was no dog-fight. I simply got onto his tail and shot him down. But they wouldn't listen. From their congratulations my whole back was aching . . .

"A week later I read in the 'Flight' magazine about a German shot down over Canterbury, who baled out and was taken prisoner."

This colourful story could possibly qualify as a "tall tale", but some elements fit quite well. On 28 August Messerschmitt Bf 109E-4 Werk Nr. 5395 crashed exactly south/south east of Canterbury[17] at South Barham Farm, Denton, in accordance with the details in Głowacki's report. Its pilot, Oblt. Kircheis – *Geschwaderadjutant* of Stab./JG 51 – baled out and was taken prisoner. The German airman broke his leg during landing, Głowacki's action may have been the cause of this injury. The most important fact is that Kircheis was flying alone and was downed about 9.10 am, before the whole 501 Squadron was scrambled, which again fits the account of the Polish airman.

During that day also, 306 Squadron was officially formed at the Polish Depot at Blackpool.

The next few days brought no successes for Polish airmen – not until 30 August, the day when the legend of 303 (Polish) Squadron began . . .

30 August 1940

On this day waves of German aircraft began their onslaught at 10.00 am. 501 Squadron Hurricanes were airborne at 10.25 am. Soon they engaged a force of about 50 He 111s and Do 17s with a large fighter escort. Engagement took place east of Dungeness, Hurricane pilots claiming two He 111 destroyed and two Bf 110s

---

[17] Direction and site exactly described in Głowacki's report. Pilots of JG 26 were downed south east of Canterbury – but to the west of the city.

damaged. One of the damaged Messerschmitts was credited to Sgt Antoni Głowacki, who described his attack:

"Blue 1 led the attack on bombers but the enemy Me 110s attacked us from astern, diving down. 'A' Flight continued to attack the bombers, while 'B' Flight was involved in a dog-fight with the Me 110s. I attacked a Me 110 who was diving upon one of our own aircraft, and he broke away from the formation and turned towards the coast. Then I attacked an Me 110 from a defensive circle, and put the rest of my ammunition into him. He dived down emitting white smoke. I returned home as I was attacked by another plane in the circle."

The pilots of the County of Gloucester Squadron taking part in the morning battle were as follows:

F/Lt Putt	R4105/SD-W
F/Sgt Morfill	P3397/SD-S
Sgt Głowacki (Polish)	V7234/SD-A
P/O Duckenfield	V6540/SD-P
Sgt Pickering	P5193/SD-O
P/O Dafforn	V6545/SD-T
Sgt Lacey	P8816/SD-F
Sgt Farnes	P2760/SD-B
P/O Hairs	P5194/SD-J
P/O Skalski (Polish)	P3803/SD-Z
Sgt Green	V7357/SD-G

Fourteen Hurricanes of 253 Squadron, newly arrived at Kenley, were airborne at 10.59. At the beginning of the patrol they were sent to the Maidstone area, with orders to wait for enemy aircraft coming back from Croydon. The Flights split and then received an order to return over their base. After 35 minutes of fruitless patrolling, an additional five Hurricanes joined the formation and all headed south. At 18,000 feet near Redhill they spotted three formations of three bombers each, covered by more than 30 fighters: Bf 109s and 110s. "B" Flight headed into the bomber formation but without apparent result. Only P/O Tadeusz Nowak, flying Hurricane R2883, claimed damage to a "Do 215":

"I was Green 3 flying in Flight vic formation when I sighted formation of bombers and fighters 5-10 miles East of Gatwick. I was at 15 000 ft when I attacked number 3 of the leading section of bombers giving him 3 bursts from astern and beam. I observed incendiary entering the cockpit on my last attack entering tanks and wing."

"A" Flight, flying behind, then joined the attack. Yellow 3 – P/O Greenwood – got an He 111 with all his ammunition, and the bomber had to force land and four of the crew baled out. After shooting down this He 111H-2, Werk Nr. 3305, coded V4+HV, individual dog-fights began and another Pole – P/O W. Michał C. Samoliński described his action:

"I was No. 2 in Blue Section flying in vic formation at 12 000 ft when we attacked formation of bombers and fighters. My leader attacked the bombers which were Do 215, He 111 and I engaged 3 Me 110. I attacked first one from astern, and slightly above, giving a 6 sec burst silencing the rear gunner and saw my bullets entering wings and fuselage. Enemy aircraft dived in spiral towards the ground. I then engaged a second enemy aircraft Me 110 in a similar attack silencing the rear gunner. I was then attacked by the third Me 110 which dived onto me and I fired the rest of my ammunition at him in a head on position but was unable to observe damage. It was South East of Uckfield."

A third group of Hurricanes led by S/Ldr Gleave attacked some Bf 109s which were preparing to dive on the tails of the other Hurricanes, saving the "A" and "B" Flights from suffering heavy casualties. In total the 19 Hurricanes of 253 Squadron claimed one He 111 and three Bf 110s shot down, two Bf 109s and one Do 215 probably destroyed and one damaged Bf 109. This success cost the RAF unit three Hurricanes and their pilots lost. The rest of the squadron returned to Kenley, some in shot-up Hurricanes, like P/O Samoliński with his P3717.

151 Squadron had left North Weald and moved to Stapleford on 29 August, then patrolling the airfield area. Numbers of enemy planes appearing in the sky grew hour by hour. About 4.00 pm 151 Squadron took off for the third time that day. During the second encounter the squadron had lost its Officer Commanding. This time pilots of the unit took revenge by downing three bombers. One of the victors was P/O Franciszek Surma, who claimed an He 111 as probable:

> "We took off from Stapleford to engage bombers and intercept them over Thames Estuary. There were 8 Hurricanes of 151 Squadron, two sections of three in front and two aircraft just above us. The enemy aircraft were approaching us from the sea and we dived at the first bombers from the beam and continued down beneath them; after this attack I saw one He 111 turn away to the right and make for the sea. I was below and chased after him and fired a short burst under him. There was no return fire and I closed in and gave a longer burst from direct astern at about 80 yards. I used all my ammunition and the enemy was then down to about 6,000 ft and continuing in a series of slow turns towards the sea. I consider the crew were injured or dead."

Sadly, during this combat another Polish pilot was posted missing. Sgt Feliks Gmur, flying Hurricane I R4213 as rear cover, attacked the bombers and afterwards was attacked himself by enemy fighters. Shot down, the aircraft crashed at Jacks Hatch, Epping Green with the pilot still in the cockpit.

501 Squadron also took part in this encounter, whilst undertaking its fourth patrol of the day. Taking off from Hawkinge about 4.30 pm, Hurricanes of this Auxiliary Air Force Squadron attacked bombers over Southend. In this action two Poles claimed He 111s damaged: Sgt Antoni Głowacki and P/O Stanisław Skalski. The latter added the destruction of another He 111 to his score. Sgt Głowacki describes the action:

> "I was No. 2 in Green Section, when the Squadron intercepted a large formation of He 111 and fighter escort, flying along the Estuary, towards London and circling North over Southend. We attacked the second 'vic' of the bomber

formation head-on. This broke up, and I fired at the same aircraft which had turned, and dived down towards the river, jettisoning its bombs. The port engine was emitting white smoke and the enemy aircraft was travelling very slowly. I broke away near Fareham."

While Polish pilots of Squadrons based at Kenley (253), Hawkinge (501), Debden (601), Biggin Hill (32) and Stapleford (151) engaged the bomber formations over the coast and the Thames Estuary, the all-Polish 303 Squadron was practising formation flying. For the last two days they had been undertaking gunnery training at the firing range at Sutton Bridge. On 30 August the Squadron took off in a formation of two Flights for interception practice. They were ordered to intercept six Blenheim bombers. "B" Flight was flying in a six aircraft formation:

S/Ldr Kellett	V7284/RF-A
F/O Łapkowski	R4179/RF-Q
P/O Daszewski	V7243/RF-P
F/O Paszkiewicz	R4217/RF-V
P/O Łokuciewski	R4175/RF-R
Sgt Wojciechowski	P3975/RF-U

One of the pilots of "B" Flight, F/O Ludwik Paszkiewicz became the hero of this sortie, which he described in his memoirs:

"After climbing to 10,000 ft we flew northward. After a while I noticed ahead a number of aircraft carrying out various turns. The centre of the commotion seemed to be about 1000 feet below us to starboard. I reported it to the Officer Commanding, S/Ldr Kellett, by R/T and, as he did not seem to reply, I opened up the throttle and went in the direction of the enemy. I saw the rest of the Flight some 300 yards behind me; below me were the burning suburbs of a town and a Hurricane diving with smoke trailing behind it. Then I noticed, at my own altitude, a bomber with twin rudders – probably a Dornier – turning in my direction. When he noticed me he dived sharply down. I turned over and dived after him. When turning over I noticed the black crosses on the wings. Then I aimed at the fuselage and opened fire from about 200 yards, later transferring it to the port engine, which I set on fire. When I drew very close I pressed down under for a new attack and then saw another Hurricane attacking and a German baling out by parachute. The Dornier went into a steep turn, and I gave him another burst. He dived and then hit the ground without pulling out of the dive and burst into flames. I then approached the other Hurricane and saw his markings: VCI, and then I went upwards, but found nobody over the burning town, so I returned to the aerodrome, where I circled, waiting what would happen. After receiving an order I landed, having made a victory roll, with my joy spoilt by the thought of the Flight fighting somewhere while I had chased a single machine. Unfortunately, after the Flight returned it turned out that the English hero carried on with attacking the Blenheims.

"I have been firing at an enemy aircraft for the first time in my life."

During this flight F/O Paszkiewicz also spotted a He 111 bomber formation of KG

53 escorted by fighters. It was the third wave of bombers which appeared over Kent and the Thames Estuary that day. The targets of this formation were airfields at Luton, Oxford, Slough, North Weald, Kenley and Biggin Hill. He also noticed a Hurricane falling, which belonged to 56 Squadron, as had the other aircraft which joined Paszkiewicz to attack the enemy. Paszkiewicz identified the code letters of this aeroplane as "UC-J" rather than US-J. 56 Squadron lost two Hurricanes, N2668 and R2689, in action about 4.45 pm.

Paszkiewicz claimed the destruction of a twin tailed aircraft which was incorrectly identified by the Intelligence Officer as a Dornier 215. F/O Paszkiewicz was not sure himself if it was a Dornier or another type. Many years after the war Jerzy B. Cynk, the Polish aviation historian from London, identified Paszkiewicz's victim as being in fact one of the long range fighters of 4./ZG 76. About 4.45 pm on 30 August two Messerschmitt 110s of this unit were lost in the area where 303 Squadron carried out its exercises. No Dornier bombers were lost at that time. Most probably Paszkiewicz shot down Bf 110C Werk Nr. 3615, coded M8+MM, which crashed at Barley Beans Farm, Kimpton.

Disobedience by Polish pilots (shown later in the *Battle of Britain* film) became a legend, but it was not pleasing at all for the British officers of 303 Squadron. The atmosphere concerning such incidents at the international airfield, which Northolt had become at that time, was not favourable. A few days before this Polish incident, 1 RCAF Squadron went into action, shooting down in error two Blenheims of 235 Squadron, and everybody had become very sensitive about any unauthorised actions in the air. Confirmed destruction of the Messerschmitt brought 303 (Polish) Squadron into the line of operational squadrons, so needed by 11 Group in defence of the south east of England.

The moment when 303 Squadron became operational changed completely the situation for those Polish personnel who had been waiting for about a year to fight the Germans again. Further, the British officers of this unit soon changed their minds about the Poles. At the first stage of establishing the Polish unit, they may have felt that they had been banished to a colony of strangers lacking any knowledge of the English language or of RAF tactics. The ensuing days proved, however, that the Poles were valuable fighters.

"Intelligence Patrol Report   30.8.40

"No. 303 (Polish) Squadron, "B" Flight

"Hurricane up: Northolt 16:15
"Hurricane down: Northolt 17:35
"Contact at 16:35 near St. Albans

"1. Flight took off for interception exercise with Blenheims, arrived St. Albans 16:35 and met Blenheims at 9000 ft. Five aircraft remained with Blenheims and escorted them back to Northolt.
"2. At about 14,000 ft. Some sixty D.O. 17 or 215 were flying Eastwards, escorted by some sixty Me. 110. DO's in pairs wide apart, Me.110 in vics of 5-9 aircraft weaving between the bombers, above and a little behind. Unknown number of our fighters were attacking. Smoke was on the

ground and A.A. shells were bursting under enemy formations.

"3. Green 1. (F/O Paszkiewicz) tried to communicate with Apany[18] leader by radio, then went in front of formation and waggled his wings, turning towards enemy who were above and flying eastwards. He then saw a Do.17 or 215 , which was below this formation, banking towards him. When Enemy aircraft was almost head on, he saw the Hurricane and dived steeply followed by Green 1. When Enemy aircraft straightened out, Green 1 closed and fired a burst at 250 yards at the fuselage from dead astern – no effect apparent. Green 1 closed to 100 yards, and getting under Enemy aircraft fired a long burst at the starboard engine, closing to point blank range. Engine stopped and caught fire. Green 1 broke away. Hurricane UC.J. came in to attack just as a parachute left Enemy aircraft, which then dived, Green 1 attacked again with a short burst, though he realised at once that it was unnecessary. Enemy aircraft crashed and exploded.

"4. Green 1, regained height, failed to locate his flight and returned independently to Northolt, landing a few minutes before they returned.

"Enemy Casualties.   One Do. 17 or 215.   Destroyed
"Our Casualties   – Nil.
"All our aircraft serviceable.

"Intelligence Officer
"No.303 (Polish) Squadron,
"R.A.F. Station, Northolt."

31 August 1940

The last day of August was very significant for the Poles assigned to 601 Squadron, based at Tangmere. That day F/O Jerzy Jankiewicz, flying Hurricane I R4214, managed to shoot up a Bf 109. He and F/O Juliusz Topolnicki were the two most recent Polish pilots to join this unit and they had become more active after 20 August. On 31 August a 601 Squadron formation including F/O Jankiewicz were directed to catch a formation of bombers, which had reached Debden airfield and were bombing it, causing damage to the facilities and a few Hurricanes on the ground.

"I was Red 2. We took off at 08.27 hrs with orders to patrol base at 15 000 ft. When at 12 000 ft and still climbing, a formation of enemy bombers were sighted about 10 000 ft above, over base going NNW, and at the same time I saw bursts of AA fire and also bombs exploding on Debden aerodrome. We continued to climb and on turning around I saw a defence circle of about 6 Me 109's about 5000 ft above and behind. I broke away from our formation to observe these e/a and simultaneously one dived down and opened fire head on. He banked steeply to the left and I delivered a beam attack with full deflection. A few seconds after I saw black smoke coming from starboard side of e/a. E/a dived and I followed firing short bursts continually. The Me 109 drew away from me going SE."

---

[18] "Apany" – 303 Squadron radio call sign.

Jankiewicz claimed to have damaged the Bf 109 along the line from Stradishall to Colchester. Probably his opponent from JG 77 reached the other side of the Channel without much damage.

One of the next raids was encountered by Hurricanes of 151 Squadron. They flew in a formation of eight aircraft that day:

F/Lt Blair	P3183
P/O Smith	V7384
P/O Ellacombe	P2826
P/O Surma (Polish)	P3739
P/O Patullo	V6537
Sgt McIntosh	R4185
P/O Czajkowski (Polish)	P3301
F/Lt Smith	V7630

The success of 151 Squadron in this combat was paid for by the loss of two Hurricanes and two pilots sent to hospital with wounds. One of them was P/O Franciszek Czajkowski, who described his combat with a Bf 109 in this laconic report written in St Luke's hospital at Bradford:

"Took off from Stapleford about 10.00. First attack in formation, no serious damage observed. Intercepted by escort 109's, dog fight ensued with one. Fired 4 sec. burst at 300 yds, closed to 150 yds, fired 6 sec. burst, large volumes of black smoke poured engine, 109 dived and I followed, firing a 2 sec. burst at 150 yds, more smoke and 109 went into a spin. I turned left to avoid a 109 on my tail, but was attacked from the front. I fired at him but had only 1 sec ammunition left. At this moment I was hit by cannon shot in the right wing, engine and cockpit, and was wounded. I turned towards the land five miles away. The engine was only running irregularly and petrol and oil fumes poured into the cockpit. I force landed about five miles North of Shoeburyness with a dead engine and wheels up. The hydraulics had failed. I was lifted from my machine by a civilian, and a soldier was left guarding the machine."

After his crash landing at Foulness, his Hurricane P3301 was written-off. The Polish pilot, with a Bf 109 claimed as probable, was sent to a hospital at Shoeburyness. Doctors treated bullet wounds in his right shoulder and arm, bullets in both feet, shrapnel in feet and legs, and cuts to his nose and eyebrows. For P/O Czajkowski the Battle of Britain had ended. Unfortunately, his medical treatment and convalescence lasted a long time, and tragically, he was later killed in a hospital at Torquay when it was hit by German bombs on 25 October 1941.

Raids on airfields during 31 August continued, and about noon seven Hurricanes of 253 Squadron took off from Kenley.

F/Lt Wedgewood	P3032
S/Ldr Gleave	P3115
P/O Nowak (Polish)	P2883
P/O Samoliński (Polish)	P3804
Sgt Kee	V6640

| P/O Murch | P3337 |
| P/O Clifton | P3351 |

All seven aircraft were sent to intercept Raid 20 closing from the north on Kenley airfield. The bombers were on their way back after successful action over Biggin Hill which had again disabled this airfield by cutting all telephone lines. Blue Section attacked the bombers without apparent effect, then Red Section had its chance. Only P/O Nowak managed to shoot down a German aircraft in this encounter.

"I was Red 2 in formation Vic when I saw the enemy aircraft $2^1/_2$ – 3 miles away on port side. We attacked bombers in section Vic starting 300 yards away in a beam attack finishing at 200 yards in a quarter attack. I gave a burst of 1 seconds on He 111 flying at 12 000 ft. The enemy aircraft broke away and circled down toward the ground. After my attack two Me 109's were on my tail so I also broke away. I followed the He 111 to the ground where I saw it force land with its undercarriage up in a field."

P/O Clifton claimed damage to another He 111 in which he silenced the rear gunner, white smoke appearing after his attack. During this engagement 253 Squadron lost its second Squadron Leader that day, when S/Ldr Gleave had to bale out and was sent to hospital. S/Ldr Starr had been lost during the morning patrol at about 7.35 am, in which P/O Nowak and P/O Samoliński had also taken part.

501 Squadron pilots also engaged enemy aircraft during a patrol at about 1 pm.

"The enemy casualties were two Me 109's and 1 aircraft (type not known) destroyed."

– said 501 Squadron ORB. The unidentified aircraft claim was credited to Sgt Antoni Głowacki who was also shot down during this encounter. Later he wrote:

"I was acting as rear-guard when the squadron, consisting of Hurricanes, was ordered to patrol Gravesend at a height of 15,000 ft. I sighted two waves of bombers with escort of 109's immediately behind at 15,000 ft, and above them a cloud of Me 110's scattered all around them. I attacked the bomber formation, which was broken up by very accurate A.A. fire. I saw the last enemy aircraft catch fire and dive, I had attacked it. It was diving down towards Margate. As he dived the next bomber fired at me and the bullet entered my petrol tank and radiator. On landing my aircraft burst into flames, but I jumped clear, and was only slightly injured."

Sgt A. Głowacki probably shot down a Do 17 of KG 3. His Hurricane V6540/SD-P crashed and burnt out. It is worth noting that on this occasion Toni was not flying his favourite Hurricane, V7234/SD-A. Another claim for a Messerschmitt 109 was made during the day by P/O Stanisław Skalski, flying Hurricane P5194/SD-J.

The diary of 303 Polish Squadron, described 31 August in these words.

"On the 31st day of August 1940, the eve of the day our war against Germany started, we were scrambled as usual."

"Scrambled as usual" sounds like a joke for a squadron that had never been scrambled before, but P/O Mirosław Ferić, who wrote these words (as well as a number of his colleagues), had been scrambled innumerable times during the September 1939 campaign as a fighter pilot of the PAF Pursuit Brigade, and in the spring of 1940 in France as a pilot in GC I/55.

On 31 August 303 Squadron made its first operational flight at full strength.

"A" Flight:

S/Ldr Kellett	R4178/RF-G	(Red 1)
Sgt Karubin	R2688/RF-F	(Red 2)
Sgt Szaposznikow	V7242/RF-B	(Red 3)
F/O Henneberg	V7290/RF-H	(Yellow 1)
Sgt Wünsche	V7244/RF-C	(Yellow 3)
P/O Ferić	P3974/RF-J	(Yellow 2)

"B" Flight:

F/Lt Forbes	R4217/RF-V
F/O Łapkowski	P2985/RF-Z
P/O Łokuciewski	R4179/RF-Q
P/O Daszewski	V7243/RF-P
Sgt Rogowski	R4173/RF-T
Sgt František	R4175/RF-R
F/O Paszkiewicz	P3975/RF-U

P/O Mirosław Ferić continued to recall this operational sortie:

"We sprang into the air at 17:50. Bearing 90 degrees. After over a dozen minutes flying, and passing a flight of Spitfires, Sgt Karubin brought to the attention of the 'red section' commander that he can see the enemy. Indeed, some 60 to 70 machines North East of us are flying exactly at our course. We open up our throttles and push towards them. We are closing in. But further from the enemy formation and closer to us we notice three ME 109s that probably have not seen us yet, as we are coming from the sun. In order to approach the whole enemy formation and have safe rears, we had to get rid of the 109s first. The surprise is complete. S/L Kellett's section bursts in pursuit of the dispersing three. Everybody after his one. And what about us? Don't have to wait for long. Another trio of Me 109s, that must have been going well above the first one, went to the rescue of their lot, passing myself and Sgt Wünsche, with whom we have been some 200-300 metres behind the first section, as the cover. And just as well, since one of them has already started to strike his bursts to Sgt Karubin, who was busy with his Messerschmitt. Wünsche gets onto the tail of this one. Pulling 12 lbs boost I get on the tail of the other one that tried to get to the first section. I close in on him easily, he grows in my sights, his fuselage now fills the entire diameter of the luminous ring. That was the right time to open fire. I strike at him completely calm, somehow without excitement – I feel surprised and puzzled that it is so easy, quite different than in Poland, where one was really tired, sweating, nervous, and eventually got nothing, and was blown away oneself.[19]

[19] Ferić, flying a P.11c fighter "4" was shot down by a Bf 110 on 3 September 1939.

"A short burst of 20 rounds from all guns. Result immediate and wonderful. The Jerry, hit lethally, burns like a candle. Flame the length of the fuselage, he executes a bunt, flashes his white belly and the crosses – and goes down. I follow him. The pilot bales out – parachute opens. I feel like blowing him away, but too many witnesses. There may even be the English – and we have our accounts to settle from Poland. I leave him alone. Anyway he's going down on land. They'll get him. The hell with you. We land at 18:55 individually. It turns out that everyone has a Jerry of his own."

Mirosław Ferić started his diary on the very first day of the war. The third part of it became the 303 Squadron chronicle, and included battle descriptions in full detail. He also forced (literally) his companions to immortalise their impressions on paper. This time Ox, as Ferić was known to his colleagues, had described how Yellow Section fought with Bf 109s of 3./LG 2. His victim – Olt. von Perthes' Bf 109E-7, Werk Nr. 5600 – crashed at Chathill Park Farm, Crowhurst. Both Sergeants mentioned in Ferić's story also added a few words.

"I can see the enemy, I push ahead, pointing the direction of the enemy to the Flight commander. We have opened up our throttles – pursuit. We are closing in. The moment of revenge grows with every second. Three Jerries in my sights burst away. Dive after dive, attack and a short burst. The Jerry pulls up. That's what I like, another burst. The white belly of the Me 109 vomits smoke and fire, like a smoky torch going towards earth. Nevertheless I fired another short burst. Great joy came after the victory. After the victory I circled the spot where we fought for a while and with great joy swooped down, landing at the airfield.

Sgt Stanisław Karubin"

"Flying as Yellow 2, I was protecting the Flight from behind, together with F/O Ferić. Seeing the Jerries attacking our Red section, I went for one of them who attacked Sgt Karubin. Of course the manoeuvre was only intended to scare the enemy off, or divert his attention. However, he then executed a rapid bunt, showing his crosses which gave me even more hatred. Suddenly one of the Messerschmitt 109s came up in front of me, below to the left. Without thinking I pushed the trigger button, and I spotted smoke. Not being quite sure I fired another burst just in case, after which the burning Me dived to the ground. I made a few circles at the site of the encounter, looking for the others. But in vain, as they could not be dragged away from the parachutist, a German. They were 'protecting' him, so that nothing bad happened to him in the air.

"Upon landing it was difficult to realise, how it all happened. And it was just a few seconds.

Sgt Kazimierz Wünsche"

At the end of the day the pilots of 303 Squadron received a telegram message from the Chief of the Air Staff, which gave them a lot of satisfaction.

"Magnificent fighting 303 Squadron. I am delighted. The enemy is shown that Polish pilots definitely on top."

1 September 1940

The first successes of 303 Squadron made Polish airmen very attractive to Polish and British war correspondents. Northolt was not too far from London to pay a visit and almost every day its activities made headline news. Peter Matthews described his meeting with foreign pilots:

> "I watched an English sergeant-pilot giving instructions to some Polish aircraftmen in a mixture of English, French, Polish – and dumberambo. It was an efficacious mixture. Most of the men now have a rudimentary knowledge of English and some speak it fluently, but I rather think their military duties leave little time for the study of languages.
>
> "As I watched a flight of Hurricanes taking off within three minutes of receiving the order at their dispersal point I realised that the language problem made not the slightest difference to the clock-work efficiency of their performance. The British squadron leader told me that it took a maximum of 5 minutes to have the whole squadron in the air.
>
> "The squadron was due to conclude its advanced training on August 31 and to start operational work the following day. Actually it achieved its first in the course of its final training flight.
>
> "It was carrying out a practice flight as an escort for Blenheim bombers when a large formation of Messerschmitts was sighted: The British squadron leader confessed to me that when he first sighted the enemy planes he had a moment of anxiety for his charges. But in fact Poles not content with warning off the enemy from the British bombers destroyed one of the Messerschmitts, which was brought down by a Polish flight commander."

This press account of first combats by the Polish squadron, differs slightly from the original personal reports.

A different view regarding the presence of Polish airmen in RAF units was to be found in some documents from that period, including the 238 Squadron Operations Record Book, which stated:

> "2 sorties comprising 2 a/c of yellow section patrolled Falmouth at 20 000 ft. 1 Ju 88 sighted by Sgt Batt 10 miles NW of Lizard at 18 000 ft. No interception as e/a was too fast and Sgt Batt's a/c and engine performance was not at best. Also slight difficulty in air to air communication as Yellow 2 is a Polish pilot . . ."

Although radio communication in English was difficult to learn for the Poles, their shooting could be close to perfection. During the afternoon of 1 September, a dozen 501 Squadron Hurricanes were directed against about 30 Messerschmitt 110s. During this encounter in the Tunbridge Wells area only P/O Stanisław Skalski managed to engage, and he claimed a Bf 110 damaged. The same pilot would show his mastery the next day.

2 September 1940

About 7.30 am all 12 aircraft of 501 Squadron were scrambled. P/O Duckenfield had some troubles during take-off and joined the squadron a few minutes later in a replacement aircraft. The Squadron was ordered to patrol Gravesend, but they were too late to prevent the airfield being bombed. Twenty minutes after their take-off the first bombs fell on the lower part of the aerodrome, causing wounds to two airmen. The Hurricanes then engaged about 30 Do 17s under the cover of Bf 109s. After returning from this patrol F/O Witorzeńć reported:

> "I was No 3 in Red Section when No 501 Sqn was ordered to patrol base at 20,000 ft. The enemy was sighted coming from Folkestone towards Maidstone at about 18,000 ft. There was one wave of Dorniers, with about 20 Me 109's behind them, some above, and some below. I attacked two Me 109's over Charing when the squadron attacked the formation above the formation of bombers. The Me 109's climbed and formed into a defensive circle. Then I saw a Dornier flying SW over Ashford, and I attacked from astern, and finished my ammunition on him at close range. The Dornier emitted black smoke and dived steeply."

A general report, signed by Skalski, also gave some additional details. He mentioned that Sgt W. B. Henn was missing, believed killed. A flight of 501 Squadron Hurricanes had met Bf 109s from JG 53. Skalski claimed two Bf 109s destroyed in a dog-fight which took part over Ashford. The two Messerschmitts were from 3./JG 53, and it is believed that his victims were Lt. Herbert Riegel and Obfw. Kuhlmann, both missing in action. Fortunately, this surprising action cost the RAF squadron only two Hurricanes, one of which Skalski force landed . . .

> "I was in yellow section, when the squadron left Gravesend, to patrol base at 20,000 ft. The squadron flew south over Ashford and sighted a large force of Do's with an Me 109 escort spread out in wide formation behind them. I attacked an Me 109 over Ashford from astern, and he crashed near a Do which was shot down by F/O Witorzinc [sic] and had landed in a road near Newchurch. Then I flew west to Lympne and I shot down a Me 109 which was attacking men working in the field. The Me 109 flew out low over the sea, and came down 3 or 4 miles south east of Hythe. I forced landed near Sellindge with a pierced aux. pipe, and my engine had stopped."

The dozen pilots and 13 aircraft of the County of Gloucester Squadron involved in the morning engagement were as follows:

F/O Witorzeńć (Polish)	L1868/SD-D
Sgt Gent	P5194/SD-J
Sgt Henn	P3803/SD-Z
Sgt Lacey	V7357/SD-G
Sgt Farnes	P2760/SD-B
P/O Skalski (Polish)	V7230[20]/SD-H
Sgt Adams	V7234/SD-A
F/Lt Gibson	R4105/SD-W
F/Sgt Morfill	P3397/SD-S
Sgt Whitehouse	V7402/SD-L

---

[20] The Flying Accident Card (Form 1180) gives the Hurricane number V7226.

| P/O Duckenfield | P5193/SD-O, later V7403/SD-N |
| Sgt Pickering | V6545/SD-T |

About 5.30 pm a dozen Hurricanes of 303 Squadron took off from Northolt to intercept Raid No. 6, and later Raid No.17, as displayed on the maps in the Operation Rooms of 11 Group. After a few changes of course they were ordered to patrol the Ashford area. This time the two flights of 303 Squadron were led by a Canadian, F/Lt Johnny A. Kent:

"A" Flight:
F/Lt Kent	P3974/RF-J
Sgt Szaposznikow	V7242/RF-B
F/O Henneberg	V7246/RF-D
P/O Zumbach	P3700/RF-E
Sgt Wojtowicz	R2688/RF-F
P/O Ferić	R4178/RF-G

"B" Flight:
Sgt František	P3975/RF-U
F/O Paszkiewicz	V7235/RF-M
Sgt Wojciechowski	R4173/RF-T
P/O Łokuciewski	R4179/RF-Q
Sgt Rogowski	R4217/RF-V
F/O Łapkowski	P2985/RF-Z

Near Dover about ten Bf 109s of JG 3 and JG 77 attacked the squadron at 19,000 ft out of the sun. The weavers protected the Hurricane formation well from a sudden attack and warned the others, whilst themselves heading towards the Messerschmitts. Sgt Rogowski attacked a Bf 109, which finally ended its sortie in the sea ten miles off the French coast. Sgt František also chased a Messerschmitt and would not give up until he was warned off by anti-aircraft artillery fire over the French coast. The enemy aircraft he had pursued appears to have been Bf 109E-1 W.Nr.2695 of 3./JG77 which crash landed at Wissant with severe damage. Two other Polish pilots pursuing the Messerschmitts followed their quarry further over France. F/O Henneberg described this as follows:

"After a few moments of suspicious 'sniffing' of each other, the Messerschmitts and Hurricanes start to dog-fight. The whole 'gang' roll over towards France. In the forefront, like scared deer, the Messerschmitts. My machine somehow runs quite well. I select a less speedy Me and am glad to find that the distance between us is shrinking. I start at 200 metres. The Jerry pulls up from his dive and gets a long burst from 100 metres. He starts to smoke and executes a bunt. I repeat his manoeuvres, but the distance between us is increased for a moment. I close in on him easily, though, and the situation is repeated. We are over France already. I keep on chasing him, quite surprised that the Jerry, after four good bursts, somehow doesn't want to go down, even though he vomits thick dark grey smoke, and flames are jumping over his engine. Some suspect noise comes to my ears. After a while I realise it's machine guns. I turn around and see: on my right goes a smoking

Me. He is too far to shoot, though, as proved by the lack of tracers around my machine. It turns out that they are shooting at me from the ground. I fire another burst at my game and peek at the Jerry after me. I can see flashes from his barrels. I break port – the burst goes past me. No way I can continue chasing that Jerry. Very grey puffs of smoke with flashing grenade bursts surround my machine. Making shallow turns to port and starboard I leave unfriendly France, chased by the artillery fire far into the sea. The Jerry has run away, but still he's got what he's got, and he must have been scared like hell.

"The other Jerry, that chased me, had been, as it turned out, shot up by Sgt František."

Eleven Hurricanes were back at Northolt between 6.35 and 6.50 pm. Only F/O Ferić force landed near Dover after a long chase across the Channel and back, full of unexpected events. His Hurricane R4178/RF-G suffered damage assessed as Cat. 3 and never returned to the Polish unit.

"Me 109s somehow scattered in escape. And I, having selected one, decided to blow him away. I switched on the 'emergency boost' and somehow started to close in on him, perhaps because the Jerry was twisting and turning his machine nervously. He turned his machine on its back and, to my surprise, performed a full roll. All this happening in dive. At 250 metres I open fire, letting the Jerry know three times that his end is imminent. I repeat all manoeuvres after the Jerry, and since I am better at it, I get closer by 50 metres. From 200 metres I pour another burst over him. In a moment he should start to burn, but somehow he seems very hard – must be well armoured. I am shooting without deflection. We are both over the French coast. We have dived from 20,000 feet to 10,000. Here the Jerry has put his Me. on its head, me after him and I fire a burst. I am quite surprised by the darkness, or rather the eclipse of my windscreen. Needless to say, oil piping has given in and hence the tragedy. I break the chase, make a turn and go back to England.

"I have my heart in my mouth, now, hoping nobody catches me. I open the cockpit, wipe the bullet-proof glass with a handkerchief. This very moment the exhaust pipes start vomiting a lot of very thick smoke, which scares me and forces me to undo my harness just in case. Should the 'boneshaker' start to burn, I will have to bale out. And the Channel does not look very inviting. The engine starts to shake violently. I switch off contacts and the petrol. I glide.

"How lucky I still had 10,000 feet of altitude over the French coast. England is approaching quite fast. Two Hurricanes, F/O Paszkiewicz and P/O Łokuciewski are covering my return. Over the English coast at Dover I am covered by Sgt Rogowski. I decided to crash-land. I re-do my harness. Having selected the best and most convenient field, I landed with my wheels and flaps down without major snags. At the end of the run the machine came to a stop against bushes. The landing took place after 50 minutes of flight, at Elvington Eytone near Dover, Kent. Local people hosted me very kindly. I was taken by car to an artillery post, where I was given a dinner. Having taken the ammunition from my machine, at nine in the evening I left by a specially ordered car, and at twelve I was in my bed at Northolt."

News of the actions of the Polish fighter pilots in following the German fighters to the far side of the Channel reached 11 Fighter Group HQ. Like the day before, the Poles received an official message. This time less pleasant.

"The Group Commander appreciates the offensive spirit that carried two Polish pilots . . . (Henneberg and Ferić) over French coast in pursuit of the enemy today. This practice is not economical or so sound now that there is such good shooting within sight of London."

3 September 1940

"Altogether it was quite a day. Henneberg had tangled with four Messerschmitts and his aeroplane was pretty badly shot up although he himself was all right. Poor František, however, had begun to wonder whose side he was on: during an early patrol he was attacked by a Spitfire and later in the day by a Hurricane! Even so he did manage to destroy one enemy machine which he was pretty certain was a Heinkel He 113."[21]

So wrote John Alexander Kent, then Flight Commander of 303 Squadron. He was leading "A" Flight which took off at 10.20 am. His six Hurricanes were sent to intercept a big raid of bombers, but finally they were attacked by Bf 109s over Dungeness. This surprising attack was possible due to the haze. Kent followed a Bf 109 and he himself was chased by more 109s with Hurricanes on their tails. P/O Zumbach, seeing his Flight Commander in trouble, joined in the chase and attacked Kent's follower. The Hurricane of F/O Zdzisław Henneberg was hit in the fuselage and tail, but he landed his V7246/RF-D without trouble.

Sgt Wojtowicz who shot at a Bf 109 from close range, was hit himself and the propeller and engine cowling of his Hurricane were shot off. He had to force land near Ashford but was unhurt. The smoking Hurricane, R2688/RF-F, flown by Wojtowicz, was seen by F/O Wojciech Januszewicz as it finally reached British soil. Wojtowicz described his efforts:

"After climbing to 2500 feet we found ourselves over Dover. We flew along the coast. On my right I noticed two machines that were definitely higher than us, flying towards the English Channel.

"As the closest, I pulled up my machine to the altitude of the aircraft flying above us and started to cut across their path. At closer distance I recognised the Me 109s. I performed final pre-firing checks, but my opponents must have noticed me, too, as the first one executed a bunt, and the other one went upwards. I saw F/O Henneberg close to the second one, so without much thought I went back after the first one. I started to fire at a very close distance. My first and second bursts were well aimed. My opponent started to smoke and went starboard into a climbing turn. I put my machine slightly to the starboard and pushed my trigger for the third and last burst of fire in this fatal attack. The guns fired, but at the same time my machine showered oil and a quite strong wind pushed my 'boneshaker' away from its flightpath. I regained my nerve and thought of the invisible enemy behind. But I could not run, as my machine refused to obey. I saw malicious flames on the port side of the engine. My first thought – like

---

[21] Kent, *One of the Few.*

anybody else's in my place – was to bale out. I undo my harness and try to jump out. But too high a speed pushes me back. There is only one way left – to pull the machine up. This was not easy, but after a long struggle it gave in. I can bale out now, but the water in the English Channel somehow has no appeal. So I fly on, or rather glide towards land. The flames on the engine are out now, just the acrid smoke in the cockpit that forces tears out of my eyes. I decided to land. I still had much height, so I glided to the land and landed near Tenterden in one of the bigger fruit orchards. From there I was taken to an infantry unit at Woodchurch, where I was kindly welcomed by English officers and NCOs of both sexes. From Woodchurch I returned to my base by car. This was my second encounter with the enemy over England and in an English machine."

Late in the afternoon three sections of 303 Squadron were in the air again. They patrolled the Maidstone and Dover area at 22,000 ft. In this area they intercepted 253 Squadron Hurricanes, which they nearly attacked, mistaking them for Messerschmitts. The haze and their experiences that morning caused them to take a more cautious approach. Only Sgt Josef František, in his usual way, got separated from the Squadron and went to attack an unidentified formation of fighters flying 14,000 feet below. Soon he recognised them as Spitfires, and switched his aim to a single aircraft flying under cover of clouds just above the surface of sea level.

"I went below clouds and saw a He 113. I dived on it and fired for 2 seconds from above at 100 yards into the cockpit. I must have killed the pilot as the enemy aircraft dived slowly right into the sea and disappeared."

Most probably the victim of Sgt František, recognised by him as an 'He 113' was the Bf 109E-1 (Werk Nr. 6290) of 9./JG 51 which was lost over the Channel, although its wounded pilot was subsequently rescued.

4 September 1940

At the beginning of September 1940 more RAF units were joined by Polish airmen. F/O Janusz Maciński and P/O Zbigniew Kustrzyński joined 111 Squadron, which on 3 September moved to Croydon to release 85 Squadron for a rest. Kustrzyński made only three operational flights in this unit and a week later moved to 607 Squadron. P/O Maciński was less fortunate, being killed in his first combat with 111 Squadron on 4 September.

Treble One Squadron had been the first unit in the RAF to be equipped with Hurricanes before the war. During the Battle of Britain this unit received the first Hurricanes of the new Mark IIA Series 1 version. Although the replacement aircraft had begun arriving from 2 September, at dawn on 4th the squadron had only eight available aircraft. About 8.30 am these scrambled from the forward airfield at Hawkinge. One of the aircraft failed to take off, and only seven pilots took part in the encounter, the Pole among them.

F/Lt Giddings	Mk II Z2315/JU-E
F/O Bowring	Mk II Z2308
F/Lt D. C. Bruce	Mk I R4172
P/O Simpson	Mk II Z2312

P/O Atkinson	Mk II Z2310
P/O J. Maciński (Polish)	Mk II Z2309
Sgt Wallace	Mk I R4226

Five brand new Hurricane IIs and two old Mk Is were directed to intercept a formation of bombers flying five miles west of Folkestone. Before they managed to attack the bombers, they were themselves bounced by fighters of JG 2 and JG 54. In this attack P/O Janusz Maciński was shot down and had to bale out. Descending by parachute, he was attacked by several Messerschmitts firing as he fell. Sgt Wallace tried to protect the helpless Pole, but himself was attacked by a Messerschmitt and joined the dog-fight. In the melee the leader of the Hurricane formation – F/Lt Giddings – managed to claim two Bf 109s shot down, but then was forced to land at Staplecross. Other pilots added to their score claims for three more Messerschmitts destroyed and four damaged. In this action 111 Squadron lost two pilots and two aircraft. Two other Hurricanes were severely damaged.

Further Luftwaffe attacks on 4 September were mostly aimed at the aircraft industry. Apart from the prelude of early morning attacks, the main force of Bf 110 *Zerstörern* was prepared to strike in the early afternoon. A large force, flying west along the coast, was severely mauled by RAF squadrons. The main defensive screen of fighters was waiting north west of Worthing. Near Haslemere a dozen aircraft of 234 Squadron engaged about 65 Bf 110s and followed south east in a deadly race. The Operations Record Book of this unit mentioned that:

> "14 Me 110's and 1 Do 17 were destroyed and 7 Me 110's were damaged, making a record bag for the Squadron."

No casualties were suffered. There were three Polish pilots in the defending forces.

"A" Flight
F/Lt Page	P9508
Sgt Szlagowski (Polish)	X4251
P/O Doe	X4036
P/O Horton	X4010
Sgt Klein (Polish)	R6896
Sgt Harker	R6957

"B" Flight
F/Lt Hughes	X4009
Sgt Boddington	N3057
Sgt Bailey	X4279
P/O Oleński (Polish)	X4182
Sgt Hornby	X4183
P/O Lawrence	R6959

Sgt Józef Szlagowski made two claims – one Bf 110, one Do 17.

> "I was Red 3. After my shots enemy aircraft dived steeply into water and I could see big splash. I then attacked Do 17 with another Spitfire. I gave it 3 sec. burst with deflection. Do 17 was on fire and went into sea off Hove."

The other Spitfire which joined Sgt Szlagowski in his second attack (although presumably at a Bf 110 of ZG 76, not a Do 17) was flown by another pilot of the squadron. Sgt Zygmunt Klein also shared his victory with another Spitfire pilot. He reported:

"I was Yellow 3 and attacked an Me 110 which broke from a circle. I did a head-on attack and one engine caught fire. I broke away as another Spitfire attacked from astern. After he broke away I flew astern of him firing short bursts of 1 sec. and he crashed on land."

Their victims seem to have been ZG 76 Messerschmitts, three of which crashed north-west of Worthing, while two other aircraft crashed in the sea. P/O Zbigniew Oleński in his report described another Bf 110 downed in the same area – "east of Tangmere" about 2.00 pm. Unfortunately Oleński's Spitfire was damaged by return fire, but he landed successfully at the main base.

"I was Green 2. After my burst e/a dived steeply quite low. I could hardly see anything because of oil on my windscreen (engine hit). I pulled out because of low height and could not see enemy but saw smoke and fire in the corner of small wood. I circled over him but could not distinguish whether this was aircraft or bomb fire, but some people there saw it and could say."

Meanwhile 601 Squadron joined the same battle, P/O Jerzy Jankiewicz amongst their pilots and like Oleński, he enjoyed mixed fortunes on this occasion. His combat report stated:

"After taking off from Tangmere at 13.12, we orbited base for about 10-15 minutes, and were then vectored towards Brighton. When west of Worthing we saw a battle taking place over Worthing at 10 000 ft. We climbed to 12 000 ft and attacked the e/a which were identified as Me 110. They were being attacked by friendly a/c. I broke away and attacked a Me 110, which climbed and turned. I gave him many bursts at very close range, and saw something fly out of the cockpit. He then turned on his back and dived steeply, upside down, for the sea. At the same time I received a burst of fire from the starboard side. Glycol and oil filled the cockpit and the gravity tank caught fire. I was then SW of Worthing. After a short time (a few seconds) the fire stopped, and I glided towards land. I forced landed in a small field near Goring by Sea, after avoiding a high tension transmission line and telephone line."

F/O Jankiewicz and his colleagues claimed five enemy aircraft destroyed and two probably destroyed. Among them was the Bf 110D-0 W. Nr. 3390, coded S9+AB, flown by Hptm. von Boltenstern, the Gruppenkommandeur of ErpGr 210. His aircraft crashed near Littlehampton, killing the crew.

At the same time as the Spitfires of 234 Squadron prepared to attack, nine Hurricanes of 253 Squadron were scrambled to patrol the Kenley and Croydon area. They left Kenley and sighted what they described as Messerschmitt Jaguars[22] about to

---

[22] At that time it was believed that a bomber version of the Bf 110, featuring a glazed nose containing a bomb aimer, had entered Luftwaffe service under the name 'Jaguar'. In fact this version had never progressed beyond the prototype stage. The aircraft attacked were undoubtedly standard Bf 110s.

attack Brooklands Aerodrome (as stated in the 253 Squadron ORB). The Hurricanes in a wide curve went into a good position to attack out of the sun; the haze favoured a surprise attack. The Hurricanes, led by F/Lt Cambridge, dived from 12,000 ft onto Bf 110s flying 6,000 ft below. Cambridge attacked one of these, expending all his ammunition, and the Bf 110 started to burn, then crashed in a field. P/O Michał Samoliński followed his leader:

> "I was No. 2 in Blue section and in attack followed the leader. I sighted Me 110 Jaguar from 300-100 yards. I gave two bursts, each about 3 sec. I saw after bursts fire in cockpit and plane turned left into dive. What happened later I do not know because I went up to find our planes."

Similar reports were submitted by Sgt Innes (Blue 3), F/Lt Wedgwood (Red 1), P/O Corkett (Red 2), Sgt Kee (Red 3), F/O Watts (Green 1), Sgt Dredge (Green 2), and by another Pole – P/O Tadeusz Nowak (Green 3). The latter wrote:

> "I was No. 3 in green section in echelon left in B flight. I sighted an Me 110 from 200-150 yards. One burst of 3 seconds and later I observed smoke from fuselage. Me 110 Jaguar dived down and crashed."

In this encounter the pilots of 253 Squadron claimed the destruction of six Bf 110s plus one damaged (by P/O Samoliński). In fact four Bf 110s of the LG 1 which were attacked by 253 Squadron crashed on British soil. The scattered formation of Messerschmitts was on its way back from the Brooklands area, where it had bombed the Vickers factory.

During the day another Polish unit, 306 Squadron, was officially established at Church Fenton.

Chapter Three

HARD DAYS IN SEPTEMBER

5-14 September 1940

"First encounter with the enemy after a year. Nothing much has changed. Perhaps only the feeling that we are in the battle and can take active part again. We have to fight today, not only for a free homeland. We have to struggle in every field, in every area, to bring our nation into this historic arena.[...]

Today, when our brothers have covered Poland's name with glory on the ground, at sea, and in the air. Today, when so many of our brothers have laid their lives in the fields of Norway, Denmark, Holland, France, and England. Today I believe that their blood was not shed in vain."

From the personal diary of P/O Władysław Różycki,
238 Sqn RAF, 11 September 1940

5 September 1940

501 Squadron took off to patrol over Canterbury at 9.15 am. At 22,000 ft the squadron engaged a formation of Bf 109s and bombers. Dog fights ensued, and the squadron claimed one Bf 109 destroyed, 1 probably destroyed and 1 damaged. Two Polish pilots, F/O Stefan Witorzeńć and P/O Stanisław Skalski, took part in this action. The latter, flying V6644/SD-B, was shot down and admitted to Herne Bay Hospital.

According to Skalski's verbal recollections, he shot down a He 111 and two Bf 109s during this sortie. As he was shot down himself and suffered wounds, he was not able to write the combat report. Apparently in the hospital he met Sgt J. H. Lacey who was soon going back to the squadron, and asked him to report his account, but there is no known documentary evidence of this.

About 2.40 pm 303 Squadron was airborne:

S/Ldr Kellet	V7284/RF-A	Red 1
Sgt Karubin	P3975/RF-U	Red 2
Sgt Wünsche	V7289/RF-S	Red 3
S/Ldr Krasnodębski	P3974/RF-J	Yellow 1
P/O Ferić	V7243/RF-P	Yellow
F/O Urbanowicz	V7242/RF-B	Yellow
F/Lt Forbes	R4217/RF-V	Blue 1

| F/O Łapkowski | P2985/RF-Z | Blue 2 |
| Sgt František | R4175/RF-R | Blue 3 |

S/Ldr Kellet led the formation to 22,000 ft over Gillingham. There he saw intensive anti-aircraft fire on the other side of the Thames and the unit attacked. Red Section engaged Bf 109s of JG 3 and II./JG 53 that were circling over about 35 Ju 88s.

> "We await the order of the combat course. I heard on the radio: '100 bandit'. This moment I spotted a bomber formation with Messerschmitt escort. I jumped forward, giving a sign to the commander. We engaged in a combat. I attacked a Me 109 with two short bursts. It went down, burning. I escaped upwards as I was attacked by a Me 109. It was run over by Hurricanes and went down smoking badly – me behind him. We descended to tree top height. Chase. I hit the 'boost'. I closed onto him firing several bursts. The Me was still running. This made me nervous and I fired a burst of my last rounds. The Jerry is running. This made me even more angry and I decided to finish him off. I gave 'boost' again, got very close to him and ran a 'razor' over him. The Jerry's scared mug flashed before my eyes. This very moment he hit the ground, squirting smoke with lumps of soil. I pulled up, circled him and took a look at the remnants of the burning machine. I opened the throttle, going at altitude towards the aerodrome."

The story above was told by one of the Red Section pilots, Sgt Stanisław Karubin, whose combat report from this action is not available. Kellet's other wingman, Sgt Kazimierz Wünsche, described his attack in 303 Squadron's chronicle:

> "One Me 109 immediately got onto the commander's tail. Without much thinking I came to the rescue at once. The distance between the commander and me was some 200 metres. Suddenly a Me 109 flew between us. I opened fire. The rounds kept going and going, but nothing in the end. I moved full ahead, to reduce the distance between us and made a curtain of rounds in front of the Messerschmitt. I could feel the relief when I saw him going through these rounds. That was a terrible picture."

His combat report added, claiming damage to the Bf 109 over the Thames Estuary:

> "I fired all my ammunition at it, as I was so afraid it would hit the other Hurricane. It turned onto its back, and the cockpit was a mass of flames. It fell slowly into the sea. As I had no more ammunition, I dived to the ground and came home."

Yellow Section (Krasnodębski, Urbanowicz, Ferić) did not follow Red Section, but attacked the next formation of bombers escorted by Messerschmitts. Then the Poles were joined by 56 Squadron aircraft, and together they attacked the bombers from below, but without apparent effect. Blue Section (Forbes, František, Łapkowski) followed Red Section and attacked bombers in the centre of the formation. Łapkowski tried to shoot at his Ju 88 but was discouraged by escort fighters. As he described:

> "I at once made a second attack, firing at 150 yards and closing from above. Both engines were set on fire, and e/a began to dive. At this time I saw the aircraft at

which F/Lt Forbes had fired falling in such a great cloud of smoke that the aircraft became invisible. I am quite certain that this aircraft was destroyed. Then I was shot by a cannon from behind. My engine caught fire. I turned over on to my back, opened the cockpit cover and on getting out I broke my left arm near the shoulder. I was also burnt in the face and left leg. I came down near Rochford, Southend and was taken to Rochford Hospital."

Łapkowski's aircraft crashed at Bonvills Farm, North Benfleet. In September 1978 the Essex Aviation Group dug out remnants of the Hurricane, and some parts were presented to the Polish Museum and Sikorski Institute in London.

F/Lt Forbes, leading Blue Section, added more details of the melee around the bombers:

"I lost Red Leader when he became involved with Me 109's and just beyond AA fire I saw five Vics of 3 Ju 88's formed in a Vic. I led into attack. Blue 2 F/O Łapkowski broke from the section to settle some Me 109's. Blue 3 Sg František saw a Me 109 attacking a pilot who had just baled out of a Spitfire, and shot it down. He then caught up and followed me to attack the bombers. I took No. 3 and he took No. 2 of the rear most section. After an attack from dead astern, I attacked head on to the starboard quarter. A shower of oil came from the starboard engine, covering my machine. I attacked the starboard engine and this time from astern, and it burst into flames. I had expended all my ammunition. I pulled up to watch, but an Me 109 got on to my tail and I saw tracer on my port side. I broke away to starboard and dived to the ground to go home."

Finally the claims for 303 Squadron were as follows: S/Ldr Kellet – one Bf 109 destroyed, one Bf 109 probably destroyed; F/L Forbes – one Ju 88 destroyed; Sgt Karubin – two Bf 109 destroyed; F/O Łapkowski – one Ju 88 destroyed, Sgt Wünsche – one Bf 109 destroyed; Sgt František – one Ju 88 destroyed and one Bf 109 probably destroyed.

The Luftwaffe did not lose any Ju 88s over Britain that day, so possibly the bombers attacked by the Polish Squadron were He 111s. Their escort consisted of Messerschmitts from JG 3 and JG 53. II./JG 53 lost two aircraft which crashed on their airfield, having previously been damaged by fighters over England.

Sgt Josef František was the only one to return to Northolt in a severely damaged aircraft, but Hurricane R4175/RF-R was later repaired by 303 Squadron "M" Flight.

During 5 September 234 Squadron made one interception flight by a dozen Spitfires:

"A" Flight

Sgt Harker	N3061	
S/Ldr O'Brien	P9466	
P/O Doe	X4036	Red 3
F/Lt Page	P9508	
Sgt Szlagowski (Polish)	X4251	
P/O Gordon	X4035	

"B" Flight

F/Lt Hughes	X4009	Blue 1

P/O Żurakowski (Polish)	N3279	Blue 2
Sgt Boddington	N3057	Blue 3
P/O Oleński (Polish)	N3191	
Sgt Hornby	X4183	
P/O Lawrence	R6959	

The squadron engaged a large formation of enemy aircraft over Kent about 3.45 pm. Five Bf 109s were claimed destroyed. (F/Lt Hughes got two, Sgt Boddington one, and P/Os Żurakowski and Doe destroyed one each). The Polish pilot reported after the combat:

> "I was Blue 2. We were flying at 22,000 feet. I went down to investigate 2 machines and then saw a Me 109 flying South at 14,000 ft. I approached from astern and as he turned I gave a short burst from 100 yards. He half rolled and dived and flew very low due South. I stayed on his tail firing one 3 second burst at 120 yards, and then the rest of my ammunition from very close. He crossed the coast near Hastings. After my first attack he was smoking slightly and later heavily. Enemy pilot pulled open his hood as the machine landed on the sea. Pilot got out and 2 minutes later a/c sank.
>
> "I used all my ammunition. The Me 109 outdived me but I overtook him easily when flying straight and level."

Probably Żurakowski's victim was Bf 109E-1 W.Nr.6252 of 9./JG 53 flown by Fw. Ochsenkühn, reported missing in action over the Channel.

In the meantime P/O W. Michał C. Samoliński of 253 Squadron crash landed his Hurricane P5181 at Charing.

Another Polish unit, 307 Squadron, was established at Kirton-in-Lindsey during the day.

6 September 1940

Early in the morning three sections of 303 Squadron took off with orders to patrol West Kent. The nine aircraft and pilots that took off at 8:40 am were:

S/Ldr Kellet	V7284/RF-A	Red 1
Sgt Karubin	V7290/RF-H	Red 2
Sgt Wűnsche	V7289/RF-S	Red 3
S/Ldr Krasnodębski	P3974/RF-J	Yellow 1
F/O Urbanowicz	V7242/RF-B	Yellow 2
P/O Ferić	P3700/RF-E	Yellow 3
F/Lt Forbes	R4179/RF-Q	Blue 1
Sgt František	R4175/RF-R	Blue
Sgt Rogowski	V7243/RF-P	Blue

After receiving various orders, the squadron saw very large formations of enemy aircraft over the coast to the east of them, and above. Their lack of altitude forced them to attack while still climbing, and at only 140 m.p.h., which contributed very largely to heavy casualties.

S/Ldr Ronald G. Kellet, leading the Hurricanes, wrote in his report:

"This was the biggest formation I have seen. It covered an area 20 miles x 5. There were many big planes, Dorniers, He 111 and some 4 engined. There were the usual Me 110's among them, and formations of Me 109's up to 25,000 ft fully 300 to 400 enemy aircraft."

He attacked one Dornier, but after the second attack his Hurricane was hit. He realised it was difficult to control the aircraft because it had a big hole in the starboard wing and no elevators or rudder.

"Ronald Kellet was badly hit, having practically all the fabric shot off the rear of his aircraft and he himself received a minor wound in the leg. His aeroplane was barely controllable and he had to make a very fast landing at Biggin Hill where he was somewhat unceremoniously dragged out of the cockpit and into a shelter as they were still receiving some attention from the Germans."[23]

John Kent later described it thus.

Sgt Stanisław Karubin, flying in S/Ldr Kellet's section, claimed one He 111 shot down and, using the same tactics as his leader, suffered the same fate. Hit by return fire, he crash-landed his aircraft, V7290/RF-H, at Fletchers Farm, Pembury. The Polish pilot, slightly wounded, was taken to Pembury Hospital.

This combat made Karubin an "ace". He had claimed his fifth victory of the war (of a total of seven). During the Campaign of 1939 he was in the *Brygada Pościgowa* and claimed his first victory on 3 September 1939, shared with Wojciech Januszewicz of the 111 *Eskadra Myśliwska*. A few months later in France he joined the Polish flight of GC I/55, led by mjr. Zdzisław Krasnodębski. During a patrol he damaged an enemy aircraft, but this was never confirmed officially. In England, again under command of S/Ldr Krasnodębski, he found himself in 303 Squadron. He was one of the lucky five to open 303 Squadron's scoreboard on 31 August 1940. He claimed two Bf 109s on 5 September, and a Heinkel 111 on the 6th. Slightly wounded in the leg during the latter combat, he would be away for the next few days.

His team-mate, Sgt Kazimierz Wünsche of the same section, was more lucky on 6 September. He did not attack the bombers without first looking carefully around:

"Two Messerschmitts were attacking a Hurricane out of the sun. One broke away and one I banked round and gave four bursts at the Me which was firing at the Hurricane. The Hurricane went down out of control, and the Messerschmitt went down after it in flames. I turned right, thinking the other Messerschmitt was on my tail but I could not see it. A Messerschmitt then attacked me head on and we turned round each other. After 1½ turns I was on its tail and gave him two long bursts and ran out of ammunition. I hit the engine, and the Messerschmitt broke off with thick black smoke pouring from the engine. I circled round a British pilot who had baled out, and saw him land safely. Then I went home."

Sgt Wünsche claimed one Bf 109E destroyed and one probable. He had then given cover to P/O G. E. Goodman of 1 Squadron RAF, who had been shot down by a Bf 109 south of Penshurst and baled out. The Yellow Section leader of 303 Squadron –

---

[23] Kent, *One of the Few.*

S/Ldr Krasnodębski – soon had to bale out too:

"... we are flying towards the Channel. On our way we come across other squadrons. They are flying into the same zone. German bombers going to London show on the horizon. Our position is coming out of the sun, convenient to attack. I turn if there are no 109s behind. Looking up the sun is difficult, but I can see no enemy machines, so full throttle and on to the Jerries. My whole attention has moved forward now, to go as quickly as possible and aim as accurate as possible. The will of victory is so great that you forget everything that happens around you – you can only see the enemy.

"Suddenly the glass of the clocks shatters, the tank riddled with bullets – burning petrol pouring out. The whole cockpit is filled with fire. I want to bale out as quickly as possible, but cannot unfasten my harness. A short moment of surrender. But the will to live wins. Finally I unfasten the belts, open the cockpit, the door and bale out. Remembering the sad experience from Poland, I do not open my parachute to leave the combat area as fast as possible and not to be a target. After a while I decide to open the parachute, but here is another problem: when abandoning the machine my parachute has shifted and I cannot find the ripcord, and the ground is coming fast. At last I find the ripcord and pull. Strong jolt – sudden peace and quiet, only the sounds of battle coming from above. After a moment I heard a machine approaching, and thought of history repeating itself[24]. Fortunately it was a Hurricane which protected me down to the ground. I later learned that it was Witek Urbanowicz, who at first took me for a German and intended to reverse the direction of my journey.

"Coming to the ground I thought that would be the end of my adventures, but it was not, as silhouettes of Homeguardians, with their guns ready to fire, started to emerge out of houses and bushes, looking to have some sport with a German paratrooper, but the calm Englishmen kept their nerves and did not fire."

Zdzisław Krasnodębski, who thus described his experience in the Squadron diary, was taken to Farnborough Hospital and later underwent long treatment because of his burns. In the Queen Victoria Hospital at East Grinstead, the famous surgeon Archie McIndoe performed plastic surgery on him, as a result of which he becaome a member of the Guinea Pig Club. He returned to operations almost a year later. The wingman mentioned in his account, F/O Urbanowicz, joined the melee with the Messerschmitts and later reported.

"Red section went into attack. I saw Me 109's and Hurricanes flying across from left to right on each other tails. One Me 109 then attacked me from starboard. We had a short dog fight. I fired 3 or 4 seconds at 200 yards. The engine caught fire and enemy aircraft fell vertically to earth. I lost my section and orbited. I saw bombs dropping in one place and Me 109's circling round that place and much AA fire. I circled there and attacked a bomber. One Me 109 was in the way and two more attacked me. I had to dog fight with three Me's. I had no chance to fire. I escaped over some balloons by the sea and the Me's climbed up. I heard 'All Apany pancake' and I came home."

---

[24] In September 1939 Zdzisław Krasnodębski baled out and was then shot at by a German fighter.

P/O Mirosław Ferić, the other wingman of S/Ldr Krasnodębski, also managed to claim one Bf 109. In his combat report he described how he was engaged in a dogfight in which Spitfires also took part. He fired at a Messerschmitt which suddenly appeared in front of him. His victim, "painted white from his nose to the end of the cockpit", burst into flames and fell to the ground; the pilot of the Bf 109 did not bale out. Back at Northolt, P/O Ferić stated:

"No Forbes and Rogowski, of which we know that one has bailed out, and the other force-landed. Also Krasnodębski, Kellet and Karubin are missing, and there is not trace of them, while František has a shot up machine."

The situation of Blue Section, led by F/Lt Forbes, became hopeless at the very beginning. Forbes later complained that he heard very little on the R/T and could not get in touch with S/Ldr Kellet because of very heavy interference.

"At the beginning I experienced difficulty in hearing and later on I heard nothing at all"

wrote Forbes, but soon after Red Section attacked the air was full of excited voices. F/Lt Forbes and his wingmen were engaged by the escorting Messerschmitts.

"I chased one, coming up from behind underneath and to port. After a short burst at 200 yards, I saw black smoke and flames appear under the engine, and port wing of the enemy aircraft. I was just sighting to get another burst when I realised there was something on my tail. I broke away left and flew round for several minutes trying to get another one. The Me 109's outclimbed me every time. Eventually I got on to the tail of a Me 109 as it broke away from attacking another Hurricane. I gave it a very short burst and something fell off on the starboard side of the cockpit. Enemy aircraft flicked over and fell out of control. Before I could do any more some bullets came through the Perspex and hit the safety glass windshield and tank in front of me, which poured forth petrol. The suction in the cabin made the petrol hit me in the face, and blinded me. I broke away and dived. Near ground I was feeling faint with fumes. I turned the oxygen full on and finally chose quite a good field. Every time I opened the cockpit to land petrol came out even more violently, so I eventually landed with the cockpit closed, overshot and hit a bank."

After this morning combat F/Lt Johnny Kent became 303 Squadron's Acting Officer Commanding for almost half a day, but with rapidly decreasing numbers of aircraft and flying personnel available. Kent wrote in his memoirs with sarcasm.

"Atholl Forbes was wounded in the neck and got a crease across the bridge of the nose, but was not seriously injured. Squadron Leader Krasnodębski, Sergeant Karubin and Sergeant Rogowski were not so fortunate all three being shot down and badly burned. By the evening the squadron was reduced to three serviceable aeroplanes and – this was just when No. 12 Group was trying to force its wing philosophy onto No. 11 Group – the Northolt 'Wing' was scrambled with myself leading all three squadrons with a grand total of nine aeroplanes, all that were left on the airfield!"

F/Lt Forbes's aircraft (R4179/RF-Q), hit by a Messerschmitt cannon shell and damaged during his forced landing, as well as Rogowski's V7243/RF-P, were written off. The latter pilot was sent to a hospital, wounded in one leg. The luckiest Blue Section pilot was Sgt Josef František. He was back at Northolt, like three other 303 Squadron pilots, about 9.25 am, flying a slightly shot up Hurricane. He had shot at a Messerschmitt from about 150 yards and fired across the cockpit when the enemy entered a dive. Then the Bf 109 turned onto its back and dived towards the ground, flames issuing from the right side of its engine. At the end of this action he was himself shot up by Messerschmitts, as on the previous day. This time he claimed the destruction of a Bf 109 in the Sevenoaks area. P/O Mirosław Ferić, the diarist of 303 Squadron, summarised the action of his unit on 6 September in these words:

"The raid was enormous, and we were few, as apart from us I saw a Squadron of Spitfires, so in this whole upheaval we had to avoid the enemy, numbering some 100 aeroplanes, and think more of own safety than fight according to rules. I am certain that the Englishmen are too moderate in sending more Squadrons to completely annihilate the enemy, and even more so to create chaos in his lines.

"I noticed new tactics by the Jerries: From the Channel into England, along the path of the bombers, the fighters form a sort of path, or rather bridge, or lucky chain, up to the spot of bombing and under this cover of circling squadrons, bombers fly in peace and quiet and it is really difficult to get at them."

Almost at the same time, a little further south east, eleven Hurricanes from 601 Squadron, vectored to patrol Mayfield area at 15,000 ft, joined the battle with the Messerschmitts. F/O Herbert Ashley, the Intelligence Officer of this unit, wrote:

"about 50 Me 109's were seen at 20 000 ft in sections of 4 or 5 milling around, apparently having been engaged by other fighters. No e/a bombers were seen in the neighbourhood. Our fighters climbed to attack and a series of dog fights followed. P/O Topolnicki, who baled out slightly wounded, claims two Me 109. His combat report, with that of F/O Humphrey Gilbert, who also baled out and was slightly wounded has not been obtained."

The only Polish pilot who took part in this party, F/O Juliusz Topolnicki, mentioned in Ashley's report, shot down the Bf 109E-4 (Werk Nr. 5044) flown by Lt. Schimmelheler of Stab./JG 2, which crashed at Headcorn. This claim is shared with another pilot of 601 Squadron. Topolnicki managed to write his report in hospital, and added some details to the combat which ended with total claims for five Me 109 destroyed and one Do 17 damaged. 601 Squadron lost F/Lt Rhodes Moorhouse and F/O Davis, both missing. Two others, P/O Topolnicki and F/O Humphrey Gilbert, were slightly wounded. Topolnicki claimed to have shot down by a Messerschmitt, and described his effort.

"I was Red 3. We took off from Tangmere at 08.52 and flew to the vicinity of Crowborough, then turned NE. When over Staplehurst at 20 000 ft I sighted 2 Me 109's behind me, flying at 20 000 ft in a westerly direction, in close formation. I informed Red 1 and broke away to attack them from behind. I carried out astern and quarter attacks. Black smoke came from the e/a's engine and he dived steeply with smoke increasing. In the meantime I had been wounded by what appeared to be splinters and therefore did not observe the e/a crash. After making sure that my Hurricane was quite under control, I observed the other Me 109 below and in front. I delivered a beam attack at point blank range after diving down on him, following up with astern attack and fired many short bursts. I then saw another plane coming up from behind me who also attacked the Me 109. My engine then started to miss and I could not keep up, but almost immediately I saw the e/a climbing and the pilot baled out. I then turned to fly back to base, but when near Sutton Valence I received what appeared to be a burst of machine gun fire in the engine and past the cockpit and on looking up saw a/c milling around high over head. My Hurricane then went out of control and I was obliged to bale out. I landed on top of a tree near Sutton Valence but was unhurt apart from my wounds. I was taken to a hospital at Leeds Castle."

An hour later the next wave of bombers heading towards the British coast was intercepted by Middle Wallop-based Spitfires. About 9.40 am 234 Squadron engaged a large formation of enemy aircraft north of Beachy Head. In the resulting engagement eight Bf 109s were claimed destroyed, two probably destroyed and three Do 17s damaged. Among the pilots only one Pole, P/O Janusz Żurakowski, claimed a victory over an enemy aircraft. It is believed that he shot down the Bf 109E-1 Werk. Nr. 3578, flown by Gefr. Biecker of 7./JG 26. This Messerschmitt, coded '5 and vertical bar', crashed at Swamp Farm, Old Romney.

"I was Blue 2. Saw Blue 1 attack and reformed with Blue 1. Saw formation of Do 17 with Me 109's. Attacked a Me 109 in front of the bombers from the front and from a beam. He holed my wing. He went over on his back, dived and I followed him. He climbed and went on his back again: fired second burst, and third burst and he crashed. Three Me 109 attacked me at 3,000 ft. Saw close formation of Me 109's in Southerly direction, far away. Returned to base and my machine overturned on landing."

Because of the damage to his Spitfire, N3279, P/O Janusz Żurakowski did not take part in a further action by his unit, which ended with the downing of a Ju 88 off Portland.

After 1.10 pm the "A" Flight of 303 Squadron was airborne again. This time 303 flew in company of 1 RCAF Squadron. The patrol was fruitless, but for F/Lt John A. Kent it proved quite eventful, as his Hurricane, P5180/YO-R[25], suddenly caught fire:

"We climbed to about 11 000 feet and then, without any warning, there was a loud bang as my engine blew up and caught fire. Flames were licking around the canopy and sparks darted around inside the cockpit. I switched off the ignition, turned out the fuel, turned up my oxygen supply and started side-slipping in an effort to keep the flames from reaching the reserve petrol tank situated just behind the

---

[25] Due to shortage of aircraft F/Lt Kent was flying a Hurricane borrowed from 1 RCAF Squadron. Various sources gives different data i.e. 303 Squadron ORB – R2685/RF-G, but P5180/YO-R appears in Kent's Log-Book as well as in Flying Accident Card (Form 1180). Certainly the latest Hurricane never belonged to 303 Squadron, although its photograph was put into its chronicle.

firewall bulkhead. My aircraft rapidly lost speed and the other aircraft shot past me, or all except one which came into tight formation – it was Hilly Brown who called me on R/T saying: 'Haw, bloody haw! You gettin' hot in there, Bud?' This was a reprisal for a lot of ribbing I had been giving him for having been shot down and burnt a few days before, but I thought he could at least have waited until I got down!

"I was, in fact, in a bit of a predicament as I was right over the centre of London and, if I baled out, the machine would crash into a densely populated area – though why I should think that would be worse than the bombs already falling there, I don't quite know! Anyway, I decided to stay with the aircraft and hoped that the fire would be blown out and that I might reach open country or possibly even my own airfield.

"I called the Controller and told him what had happened and what I was trying to do. Nothing much was said for some minutes and then the Station Commander, Stanley Vincent, came on to the radio and asked if I was going to bale out. By this time it was too late and I was already starting the final approach and had pumped down both wheels and flaps. Although the smoke had died away quite a bit I was far from happy, but it was good to see two beautifully sited fire engines converging on me as I touched down. They started to throw foam at me as I was completing my landing roll but the operators had never been given instructions in deflection shooting – while they were aiming at the engine, they managed to hit me, so after stopping ten yards from the spot where I had started my take-off, I got out looking rather like a snowman."[26]

That was not the last event for 303 Squadron that day. About 5.25 pm four aircraft of "B" Flight were on patrol with 1 Squadron, RAF, but this patrol proved fruitless. In the meantime, about 5.45 pm, F/O Januszewicz went off with 1 RCAF Squadron in a machine (P3089/RE-F) he had borrowed from 1 Squadron, RAF. They got into combat with Bf 109s and 110s over Lenham, where Januszewicz apparently got one probable[27], but was himself shot down, fortunately without being wounded. He force landed and soon was hosted by Mr and Mrs W. K. Vinson at Boughton Place, Boughton Malherbe. He was back with the Squadron next morning. A summary of this day was provided by Johnny Kent in his memoirs.

"Altogether it had been an expensive day and 303 Squadron ended the day with only two of the eighteen aircraft with which it had started. Strangely enough no one was killed although several had been wounded and burned. It reflects great credit upon those who were responsible for the supply of replacements and upon the Air Transport Auxillary who delivered them, that, by ten o'clock the following morning, the Squadron was again up to strength and fully operational."

7 September 1940

The absence of S/Ldr Krasnodębski, the Polish Officer Commanding 303 Squadron, caused a temporary replacement to be made. The senior Polish officer, F/O Witold Urbanowicz, became the new OC, but this promotion was not approved by the Polish authorities. He later recalled that a new commander was appointed by the Polish Air

---

[26] Kent, *One of the Few*.
[27] This is not recorded in any existing documents of 303 or 1 RCAF Squadrons, but was mentioned in Kent's *One of the Few* p. 107.

Force HQ, but had no knowledge of this unit at all, and was soon re-posted; this story was supported by other Polish pilots. It is a fact that S/Ldr Jerzy Orzechowski was posted to 303 Squadron on 16 September, and this posting was cancelled five days later, although no official document confirms that he was intended to replace Krasnodębski as the unit OC.

Meanwhile, six replacement aircraft arrived early on 7th. Also, most of the shot up and unserviceable aircraft were repaired during the night, and were back ready to fly, thanks to the unit's groundcrews. When the day dawned, the Squadron Intelligence Officer, F/O Żyborski wrote:

> "From early morning the English radio roars with congratulations for no. 303 (Polish) Squadron. The Secretary of State for Air Sinclair sends appraisal for the Polish Air Force to Gen. Sikorski.
> "Something strange is happening today. Beautiful weather and such calm. In the afternoon we found that this was the calm before the storm. Adolf has prepared for a major raid, which took off from France at 16:00 numbering some 500 machines."

About this hour a 1,000 aircraft formation was airborne and heading towards the English coast, watched by *Reichsmarschall* Herman Göring from the cliffs at Calais. The main target was London – the capital city of the British Empire. This one big target, easy to predict, allowed a more effective defence to be mounted, and made it easier to command the weakening defending forces.

About 4.20 pm 11 Hurricanes of 303 Squadron were airborne from Northolt, which still had less than a dozen serviceable machines. The Poles had to borrow an aircraft from 1 RCAF Squadron, which was also based at Northolt.

Aircraft of 303 Squadron joined 1 Squadron, RAF, airborne earlier, and the combined formation headed east at 15,000 ft. Receiving information regarding the huge raid coming in from France, they climbed to 24,000 ft and prepared to attack out of the sun, making a big circle. The moment that 1 Squadron attacked the bombers, the rear group of enemy aircraft split and went directly east. Through the gap the German bombers were attacked by the Polish squadron:

F/Lt Forbes	R4217/RF-V	Blue 1
P/O Daszewski	P3890/RF-N	
F/O Paszkiewicz	V7235/RF-M	
F/O Pisarek	R4173/RF-T	
P/O Łokuciewski	P3975/RF-U	Green 2
F/O Henneberg	V6605/YO-N[28]	
Sgt Wojtowicz	P3939/RF-H[29]	Yellow
P/O Zumbach	V7242/RF-B	Yellow 2
Sgt Szaposznikow	V7244/RF-C	Red
F/O Urbanowicz	R2685/RF-G	Yellow 5
F/O Żak	V7289/RF-S	

[28] Aircraft borrowed from 1 Squadron RCAF.
[29] The ORB gives under this date the number V7290 – of an aircraft definitely destroyed on 6 September 1940. As the personnel usually referred to individual machines by their code letters, it was not unusual to quote in documents serial nos. of destroyed aircraft for a few days after they had been written-off. In this case, P3939 took over from the unfortunate V7290 as the new RF-H.

Forbes stated in his report:

> "I led the squadron up to 24,000 ft, determined after our experience yesterday not to be caught napping at too low an altitude. It is easy to get down to the enemy, and impossible to attack climbing when the slow speed makes one an easy prey to the Me 109's. I sighted a formation of about 40 enemy bombers flying Northwards. Their rearguard of Me 109's were engaged with Spitfires at 25,000-30,000 ft. No 1 Squadron went in to attack the enemy's tail and drew off most of the remaining fighter escort. It was a perfect combination of circumstances. We were flying in Vics line astern. The enemy was flying also in Vics line astern with 3 and 5 aircraft in each Vic. The AA fire had loosened their formation. As soon as No. 1 Squadron attacked, the enemy wheeled Eastwards, and we caught them on the turn. We reformed towards the enemy and launched the attack in Vics abreast, striking the formation a little to the rear of centre. They were easy meat. We came at them from partially up sun at great speed as they turned away from us. I led in and attacked a Do 215 hitting the starboard wing. Great chunks fell off the wing and engine, which stopped. I gave another good burst into the cockpit, and more stuff fell off. Enemy aircraft fell away sideways in a long glide and hit the sea. I broke away and whilst in a steep turn, a shell hit my starboard wing root and exploded. I felt my leg was wounded and there were 3 or 4 glycol and hydraulics system leaks in the cockpit. I decided to try to return to an aerodrome and get the machine down whole. I succeeded in regaining Northolt and landing without mishap."

F/Lt Johnny Kent helped to get the wounded Forbes out of his cockpit and took over his duties until the end of the day.

P/O Witold Łokuciewski, known as Tolo to his friends, described the combat he had fought, accompanied by F/O Paszkiewicz and F/O Pisarek.

> "I took off with Paszka [Paszkiewicz] and Marian [Pisarek] at 16:20. After a few rounds at 30,000 ft we spotted flocks of enemies. We attacked the bombers, as the Messerschmitts were being attacked by other squadrons. Before I had the time to attack mine, Paszka's Dornier was already on fire. Mine started to burn, too, and finally burst like a bubble of soap water. After this success I took to another one. I fired a few bursts. He started to smoke, but an Me 109 prevented me from further attacks, so I broke to one side and spotted two Me 109s on my starboard, creeping up to me. I made such a dive that I finished at the aerodrome. Anyway, I landed because that was what I was told on the radio. On the ground it turned out that the propeller was damaged, then the wings and tailplane – some rounds went near the cockpit[30]. That was my first success on Hurricanes[31]."

Paszkiewicz claimed the destruction of two Do 17 and, after firing all his ammunition, was back at Northolt without trouble. The third pilot of Yellow Section, F/O Marian Pisarek, was not as lucky as his comrades, being shot down during this engagement. Fortunately, he escaped without wounds and was able to describe his efforts.

---

[30] Despite this damage the aircraft was back in service next day.
[31] In September 1939 Witold Łokuciewski, flying a PZL P.11c, shot down a Ju 87. In France he claimed the destruction of a He 111, flying a Morane Saulnier MS.406C-1.

"I took off for my first combat sortie over England together with Paszka [Paszkiewicz] and Tolo [Łokuciewski]. I was starting to think the mission would be a waste, when suddenly I spotted AA artillery puffs to let us know that the enemy was near. Paszka also spotted the puffs and started to wag his wings violently, as a sign to prepare ourselves to attack. He made a turn to the starboard towards the enemy and attacked the last two Dorniers. After a moment one started to burn. That left two of us in the section for one Dornier. There was nothing for me to do. Below to our port a battle was going on, too. I decided to go there. And suddenly, an aeroplane with a swastika on its tail appeared in front of me. I had advantage of height, so I attacked it with no difficulty from behind and above. I noticed flames bursting from it. This was a Me 109. But after a moment I got a series of strikes from behind myself, and my Hurricane started to smoke heavily and to go into a dive. I unfastened the belts and took off my headgear. At this moment I was thrown out of the cockpit, as the aeroplane was nearly on its back. How things change . . . To add insult to injury I landed by parachute without one of my shoes, as during the bale-out it had stuck against something in the cockpit."

Pisarek's life was saved, but his Hurricane, R4173/RF-T, abandoned by him over Loughton, caused the death of three civilians, when it fell on an urban area and hit the air raid shelter in a corner of the garden at 40 Roding Road.[32]

Five aircraft of "A" Flight, led by F/O Zdzisław Henneberg, followed "B" Flight in the attack on the bombers. Henneberg attacked a formation of Dorniers, firing three bursts at the port side of one of these. He recalled:

"My engine began to falter and I fell back a little where I was engaged by three Me 109's, my engine now working normally. After a few seconds one began to smoke, but I had to break away as I was being attacked from the rear. I climbed and met another formation of Me 109's. I attacked from the rear and after firing two bursts saw enemy aircraft burst into flames and fall to earth."

P/O Jan Zumbach, who claimed destruction of two Dorniers, told his story:

"Above us were two squadrons of Spitfires and one of Hurricanes. We approached from the port side, and from a turn to starboard we moved onto the bombardiers. At the last moment I noticed how two upper Squadrons engaged the Messerschmitt 109 escort. Under me I saw a Do 17, or a Do 215, that had left the formation. I got onto its tail. At this moment the Adolffie squirted a short burst at me. It was short, as apparently with my first rounds his soul was hitting the Land of Eternal Ghosts, into the arms of the good Manitou.

"The second burst did not give any result. It took the third, very long one, to put his starboard engine on fire and the Dornier fell down. I escaped from underneath it and started to close in onto the formation by a left turn. Now I noticed another one slightly above me. He must have left his formation, which had already been broken by ours. I saw Szaposzka's one burn, as did two more enemy aeroplanes, seemingly those of Paszka and Tolo.

---

[32] In 1976 a team from the London Air Museum undertook excavation works and found many parts of this aircraft and, amazingly, Marian Pisarek's left shoe.

"I also saw three Me 109s that hurried towards Dzidek [Henneberg]. I yelled over the radio, but it seems he saw them himself, and broke away. Until my last round I was pounding from 20 metres, with a 3 sec. burst after which his left engine started to burn. I was so close I dropped the aircraft's nose violently. After recovery I 'blackouted' so much that I did not wake up until 10,000 ft below. Meanwhile Adolffies were making their way across the River Styx to the Land of Eternal Ghosts. After hearing the course I returned to the aerodrome."

Two young sergeant pilots also claimed the destruction of enemy bombers. Sgt Szaposznikow, after firing two bursts which caused a Dornier fall, wrote:

"I dived and having satisfied myself that the enemy aircraft was finished I pulled out of the dive and in climbing attacked a Me 109 from a forward position. He also burst into flames and fell to earth."

Sgt Wojtowicz added to his colleagues' accounts:

"We were flying over London. On my starboard I saw AA bursts. I gave a sign to the commander and we changed course two more times, and then on my right I saw Dorniers flying in close formation. There was a lot of them. Our squadron, also in close formation, got at them from behind. The first of our sections were already attacking, and I could see some smoking Dorniers. I got closer to them. They were in the process of getting back into formation, as the formation must have broken under our first attack. I attacked the first on my right. After the third burst the Dornier burst into flames and went down. I did not have to look for another, as it flew into my gunsights. After a small deflection I pushed the trigger, but the Jerry was harder, his starboard engine started to burn only after six bursts, and then his whole starboard fuselage was on fire. I looked now where my first victim was falling, but instead of a Dornier, I saw a burning Hurricane slightly behind, that was flying towards London. I now went at full throttle after the Jerries and could see four more Dorniers smoke, but I could not catch them – they were too far away. I could see some columns of smoke on the Channel. Those were Jerry aircraft ending their existence. I was returning from this combat not satisfied at all, in spite of two kills. The whole eastern suburb of London was burning. Very upsetting view. I recalled a year ago in Poland, over Lublin – a very similar one."

F/O Witold Urbanowicz landed at Debden after the combat, and having refuelled there was back at Northolt about 7:50 pm. He reported to the intelligence officer that after three bursts his bomber exploded in flames and he saw it crash. Then he attacked a Bf 109 and, after several bursts from close range, its engine began to smoke furiously. Unfortunately, Urbanowicz had to evade another Messerschmitt attack and did not notice what happened to this smoking opponent, so he claimed one "Do 215" destroyed and one Bf 109 damaged.

Only P/O J. Daszewski was seriously wounded; F/O Hadwin, Intelligence Officer of 303 Squadron, learned from telephone conversations with the Matron of Waldershire Hospital, Kearnsay, near Dover, that the Polish pilot had dictated a report stating that he brought down one "Do 215" destroyed, and probably another, one engine of which was in flames. His Hurricane was hit by shells and when it caught fire he baled out, seriously wounded. The aircraft crashed in flames near Canterbury Gate, Selsted, and the pilot landed nearby.

During operational sorties on 7 September the Spitfire-equipped 54 Squadron lost two pilots. P/O Saunders was killed when his aircraft dived into the ground from low altitude. The same day one of the Poles, P/O Walenty Krepski, was reported missing during an operational flight in the Whitby area. When his section was vectored home no R/T response could be obtained from him. Probably his Spitfire I, R6901, hit the water while flying low near Flamborough. 54 Squadron ORB stated that

> "his very limited English vocabulary was certainly a contributory factor in this unlucky and regretted mishap."

Only a few days before, on 3 September, 54 Squadron had moved from Hornchurch to RAF Catterick. By this time only seven pilots remained of the original team from the early stage of the Battle of Britain. Among replacement pilots were two Polish airmen: P/O Krepski and P/O Ludwik Martel. Krepski was the second Polish pilot lost by this squadron after Kloziński was shot down and wounded on 15 August. P/O Ludwik Martel, on the other hand, would fly Spitfires throughout the rest of the Battle of Britain, although at the end of this month he would move to 603 Squadron.

Before 303 Squadron's big engagement in the vicinity of London had commenced, Spitfires of 234 Squadron (based at Middle Wallop) had intercepted large formations of enemy bombers between London and Brighton. The unit lost its Squadron Leader and one of the flight commanders during this engagement, but its attack prevented two bombers and three covering Messerschmitts from reaching their target. One Do 17 and one Messerschmitt 109 were also presumed damaged, and another aircraft probably destroyed. As usual, there was a Polish pilot among the victors, and he claimed a Do 17 probably destroyed, which by error would be listed as a Messerschmitt in 234 Squadron's Operations Record Book. Sgt Zygmunt Klein, flying the Spitfire I R6896, wrote in his report:

> "I was Yellow 2. I attacked the e/a from astern and put all ammunition in fuselage and engines. The port engine started smoking and rear gunner stopped firing. Then starboard engine began to smoke and the aircraft began to lose height over the Channel and at 4,000 ft. I had to break away owing to lack of fuel. The aircraft was still losing height and smoking from both engines."

Early in the evening 609 Squadron, also based at Middle Wallop, was called to reinforce No. 11 Group in the defence of London. P/O Ogilvie reported later:

> "The Squadron was ordered to patrol Brooklands. Many bandits were sighted over London above us. We climbed to 20,000 ft and attacked from the sun."

Led by F/Lt McArthur, eight pilots claimed six destroyed, four probably destroyed and two damaged, later upgraded to six probables and four damaged.

The only Pole to take part in this victorious engagement was F/O Tadeusz Nowierski, flying Spitfire I R6922/PR-T who later reported:

> "I was blue 2. I followed leader and attacked a big formation of Do 17 (or Me

110), type of enemy aircraft is not definitely known. Beam attack developing with astern 2 bursts of 2 seconds no results observed. I dived away and then climbed up to 15,000 ft and saw a Me 109. A dogfight developed but I lost sight of the enemy aircraft. I then saw a Do 17 and attacked from astern at 150 yards range, three bursts of 2 secs., the last burst caused the enemy aircraft to catch fire between the starboard engine and fuselage. A Me 109 then attacked me but I broke away downwards and evaded him."

9 September 1940

"The 9th of September was quiet and nothing happened until about five o'clock when we were ordered off in company with No. 1 Canadian. At first we saw nothing but Spitfires and 109's high above us and I thought that it was to be another abortive sortie . . ."[33]

In these words F/Lt Johnny Kent began his recollections of the day. About 5.35 pm he led a dozen Hurricanes of 303 Squadron against large formations of German bombers and fighters heading towards London:

"A" Flight

F/Lt Kent	V6665/RF-J	Red 1
P/O Zumbach	R2685/RF-G	
P/O Henneberg	V6667/RF-K	Red 3
F/O Urbanowicz	P3939[34]/RF-H	
Sgt Wünsche	P3700/RF-E	
Sgt Szaposznikow	V7242/RF-B	

"B" Flight

Sgt Wojciechowski	"R4173"[35]
P/O Łokuciewski	V7235/RF-M
F/O Pisarek	V7465/RF-V
Sgt František	P3975/RF-U
Sgt Kowalski	V7289/RF-S
F/O Żak	P3089/RF-P

They met about 40 Ju 88 and He 111 bombers, escorted by Bf 109s and Bf 110s in large numbers, over Beachy Head about 6 pm. The enemy was escaping southwards at great speed, losing height. When first seen the hostile aircraft were 1,000 ft above the squadron; they were engaged by the leading aircraft at about 13,500 ft. However, only F/Lt Kent, F/O Zumbach and Sgt František managed to engage and to have the opportunity to make claims. Kent later described this fact in his memoirs:

"They were in a shallow dive and moving fast, so I picked on a Ju 88 and gave chase. It took a little time to accelerate so I pulled the boost over-ride plug and

---

[33] Kent, *One of the Few*.

[34] Another occurrence of the erroneous serial no. V7290 in the ORB. Compare the footnote under 7 September.

[35] Yet another erroneous serial no. R4173/RF-T appears in 303 Squadron Operations Record Book and is repeated in many publications, but it had been shot down on 7 September. Probably Wojciechowski was flying R4175/RF-R that day.

opened the throttle wide. Very slowly I began to gain on the German but, at the same time, I could see one of the 109 escort fighters diving down after me. I kept on in the hope of catching the Junkers before the 109 caught me, but it looked very much as though I was going to lose the race; I was on the point of breaking away as the 109 was getting uncomfortably close when a Hurricane flashed across in front of the 109 and forced its pilot to pull up. As the Hurricane climbed above me to reposition itself I recognised Henneberg's machine and so, with him as my protector, I carried on after the Junkers and opened fire from 400 yards while Henneberg repeatedly chased the Messerschmitt off my tail. After two bursts the starboard engine of the 88 burst into flame and the aircraft rolled over and dived into cloud. I followed the trail of black smoke hoping it would guide me to the 88 under the clouds where I could finish it off but, on breaking cloud, I found myself over the Channel and not a sign of a German machine.

"The light was poor so I set off towards the French coast hoping that I might find the damaged bomber when, quite unexpectedly, I saw a twin engined aircraft that, at first looked like a Hampden. I could not think what a Hampden would be doing over the Channel so I approached it rather cautiously to make a positive identification. As I got closer it began to look less familiar and then its rear gunner opened fire so, even though it was not the Ju 88 I was looking for, I immediately attacked. It was quite fascinating and made a pretty sight in the gloom watching my tracer sail gracefully towards the German while at the same time his came streaming back at me like a string of gleaming red beads. After my third burst the enemy made a sharp turn to port and the silhouette it presented was that of a 110. I can remember the picture it made so terribly clearly, it was like a picture out of a book on air firing – 'At this angle place your sights there and FIRE!' which is precisely what I did and his starboard engine blew to bits. He was obviously badly hit and turned back towards England whilst I flew alongside but out of range of the rear gunner just in case he was still alive and active.

"As I followed the stricken machine smoky fingers streamed past on my port side, I did a fast turn and found a 109 intent on evening the score. Fortunately I could outturn him easily at this low altitude and got two bursts into him after which he quickly disengaged and flew off towards France. Although I think I hit him I could not be sure as the light was so bad.

"By this time the 110 was getting very low and the smoke from its starboard motor was getting thicker and thicker. Finally, about ten miles from Dungeness, it hit the water and exploded. I came down low and could see the twin tail sticking out of the water and what appeared to be an empty dinghy nearby, but of the crew I could see nothing at all."[36]

F/O Zumbach was attacked by Bf 109s and during the combat he found himself over France. Luckily, he recognised the unfriendly coast and headed back to England. He described his combat as follows:

"When we saw the bombers and the Me's which were fighting with the Hurricanes and Spitfires, I saw a bomber being attacked by a Hurricane (Sgt. František). This Hurricane was being attacked by two Me's, and escaped into cloud. I looked and

[36] Kent, *One of the Few.*

saw one fighter in front of me. Thinking it was F/Lt Kent I went up to it and at 50 yards I saw it was a Messerschmitt with yellow strips on wings and nose to make it look like a Hurricane. I only recognised it by the struts on its tail. I gave it a two second burst, and from the starboard wing root many pieces fell off and the e/s burst into flames. At this moment I was attacked by an Me 109 on my port side 800 yards away which missed me from 800/600 yards. I began dog fighting with him. After a few minutes four more Me 109's appeared, three from below and one from above, and attacked me. Two gained height as I made tight circles and dived on me giving long bursts. I should not like to have that happen to me again. I continued doing tight circles. One of the Me's came up towards me, and I gave him about 60 rounds from 150 yards. He turned over on its back, smoking and fell into cloud.

"I was now very tired and also got into cloud and came out on the French side of the Channel. At first I thought it was England, but the AA fire woke me up. I made for England and on my way I met an Me 109 but I was too tired to attack it. I decided to go down at the first aerodrome I saw and landed at White Waltham. Men ran to me and I got out and rested for ten minutes, and came home."

Sgt František claimed to have destroyed one Me 109 and one He 111, then force landed in a cabbage field beside Downs Hotel, 1½ miles north east of Woodingdrine, Brighton, making an excellent landing. The pilot was uninjured, but the Hurricane had been shot-up. František described his adventure in a lengthy combat report, which was attached to the composite report submitted by the Intelligence Officer at the end of the day:

"When we arrived in sight of the Germans, swarms of Me 109's dived from a great height to attack us. I saw one Me.109 going in to attack a Hurricane in front of me, I attacked it, starboard beam, firing at 150/100 yards at the engine, which began to burn. He tried to escape by climbing, and I saw him open the cockpit preparatory to jumping. I shot at the cockpit and the pilot collapsed. The e/a fell in flames to the ground (Horsham area). I then saw a Hurricane in flames and the pilot jumped. A Spitfire came down to circle round the pilot. I went for a He 111, and two Me 109's attacked me. I hid in a cloud at about 17,000 ft for seven minutes – I played hide and seek with them in the cloud. During a right turn I came out of the cloud, and saw in front of me, 10 yards away, also coming out of the cloud, a He 111. I very nearly collided with it, and fired at the front of the fuselage at an angle of 45 degrees from above and behind. The front of the e/a fell to pieces with the cockpit and both engines in flames. I do not know if this e/a fell on the ground or in sea, owing to the clouds. As I broke away one Me 109 attacked me from above, and another from below. I hid again in the clouds and flew towards France to keep under cover. Over the Channel I climbed out of cloud and was hit by four Me shells one in the port wing, one through the left tank which did not catch fire, one through the radiator. It is only owing to the armour plating behind me that the fourth shell did not kill me. Two Spitfires came to my rescue, and shot down the Me 109 which was apparently the one which had hit me. I saw the damage which had been done, and was obliged to find a landing place as the engine temperature was mounting dangerously.

"On a little hill North East of Brighton, I found a field of cabbages and made an excellent landing. The police came immediately – not only did they not make any difficulty, but they were very kind to me. They anchored the Hurricane, shut off the petrol and oxygen and left the plane guarded by a policeman. They took me by car to Brighton, and I returned to Northolt by train. Sgt Wünsche's parachute was at the police station. I brought mine home.

"At the railway station the people were very kind to me, girls gave me some chocolate, and people photographed me. I am very grateful for the kindness which was shown me by everybody."

The rest of the Squadron failed to make contact with the enemy, and there was nothing to report. Sgt Wünsche, whose parachute was seen by Sgt František, had to bale out, and was admitted to Hove Hospital. He had been seriously wounded in the back and arm, but within months would be back in the unit.

308 Squadron, yet another new Polish fighter unit, was formed officially at the Polish Depot at Blackpool on this date.

10 September 1940
This rather calm day was marked with a lot of personnel movement. Three more Polish airmen arrived to join 111 Squadron: P/O Stefan Stegman, Sgt Michał Maciejowski and Sgt Bolesław Olewiński.

501 Squadron moved to Kenley from Gravesend, where it was rejoined by Sgt Antoni Głowacki, back from hospital. He appears to have lost a little of his self-confidence due to his recent experiences, and his return to action was marked by a more reserved approach.

11 September 1940
11 September began as a foggy day. Later the sky cleared and 303 Squadron was scrambled at about 3.15 pm. The squadron went on patrol to intercept enemy raiders coming from the south east towards London, leading 229 Squadron, another Northolt based unit. When they met the enemy, 229 Squadron, flying a little below and to the right, went straight in to attack the enemy bombers head on. A dozen Hurricanes of 303 Squadron wheeled round and attacked the centre and rear of the enemy formation, which appears to have been about 50 He 111s and 30 to 40 Do 17s strong.

"A" Flight

F/O Cebrzyński	V6667/RF-K[37]	Red 1
Sgt Wojtowicz	V7242/RF-B	Red 2
Sgt Brzezowski	V6665/RF-J	Red 3
F/O Henneberg	P3939[38]/RF-H	Yellow 1

[37] 303 Squadron Operations Record Book quotes incorrect serial nos. for F/O Cebrzyński's and Sgt Brzezowski's Hurricanes. According to the aircraft movement documents of their Flight (preserved at the Polish Institute and Sikorski Museum in London) F/O Cebrzyński was flying RF-K that day, and Brzezowski RF-J. The absence of V6667/RF-K in subsequent operations proves the correctness of the Flight documents and a mistake in the ORB. It is worth noting that the individual letter K was not used any more on Hurricanes of 303 Squadron.

This error is copied by many publications, and very often the aircraft V6665, V6667 and W6667 are confused. W6667/AK-P was the Hurricane flown by Sgt Aleksander Wójcicki of 213 Sqn RAF in which he was shot down by a Bf 110, also on 11 September 1940.

[38] Another occurrence of the erroneous serial no.V7290 in the ORB. Compare the footnote under 7 and 9 September.

| P/O Zumbach | R2685/RF-G | Yellow 2 |
| Sgt Szaposznikow | V7244/RF-C | Yellow 3 |

"B" Flight

F/Lt Forbes	V7465/RF-V	Blue 1
Sgt František	V7289/RF-S	Blue 2
F/O Paszkiewicz	V7235/RF-M	Green 1
P/O Łokuciewski	L2099/RF-O	Green 2
Sgt Wojciechowski	"R4173"[39]	
F/O Pisarek	L2026/RF-Q	

"Cebrzyński was on his first outing. We heard him shout: Look out! Look out! Four Messers to the left." P/O Jan Zumbach later wrote. Yellow Section then sought to attack the fighter escort, allowing the rest of 229 and 303 Squadrons to slaughter the bombers.

Yellow Section leader engaged four Messerschmitts 109s, but they escaped. F/O Henneberg later said:

"I was passed by one Me 109 which I attacked from the side and set on fire. I was then attacked by three Me 109's and in evading them I ran into a He 111 returning to France. After several bursts stopped both his engines he forced landed not far from the sea in a damaged condition."

His victim probably belonged to KG 1 or KG 26. The bomber chosen by P/O Zumbach of the same section escaped into cloud after his first burst, and he had to pick another victim. Finally he noticed a Bf 109, probably damaged, making its way home.

"I easily overtook him", said Zumbach "and after my firing about 100 rounds he burst into flames and crashed to earth. I then joined two Hurricanes and we attacked five Me 110's. Two Hurricanes broke off the engagement through lack of ammunition. I was left alone and having run out of ammunition and being short of petrol I succeeded in evading the e/a and landing at Biggin Hill to refuel."

The third pilot of Yellow Section enjoyed more success. Sgt Szaposznikow wrote in his memoirs:

"I took off as usual, on the port flank, and as usual in the section of F/O Henneberg. After a rather long, pointless search of the longed-for target we perform a flypast between two waves of German spectators. You are an interloper, so four Me 109s fall on our heads. So we fly away in all directions and everybody gets at their prey. I can see, though, that there is no point at all in losing height and chasing an evader. So I press on to the heart of the raid. They fly, as usual, in a herd. Two Me 110 are behind them. I get onto the tail of one and start firing. Since I was quite close, I was rather mightily battered around the sky and my burst moved rather unintentionally to the other machine. I take it for a

---

[39] R4173/RF-T was shot down on 7 September 1940 and probably Wojciechowski was flying R4175/RF-R. Compare the footnote under 9 September.

good omen and I start to shoot again and I let go of the machine gun button only after they have gone silent by themselves. Meanwhile the starboard one goes down with a burning engine. After a couple of seconds the same happens to the other one. Both Messies fall to ground like candles. And in general there was a lot of candles today, so much that I suspected some extensive flare dropping.

"Now I am considering the idea of not making any more kills, as the greatest tragedy lies in this outpouring onto innocent paper."

Thanks to this unpleasant duty of writing combat reports and memoirs, we now have a comprehensive view of the actions of 11 September, as well as other days.

The leader of the whole formation, F/Lt Atholl Forbes, reported:

"We were due North of the enemy when sighted, and turned South, attacking from the East up sun. We were actually being vectored across the enemy's bow, and it was the wonderful eyesight of the Polish that spotted them some 6/7 miles on our right.

"F/O Paszkiewicz spoke to me by R/T and wheeled round; noting that No. 229 were below and going in to attack the bombers, he led his section to engage the escort fighters above them."

F/O Paszkiewicz recalled:

"I told Blue leader over the radio and went to the front and led the formation towards the enemy. Whereas 229 Squadron was lower, I left them the bombers and attacked the fighters protecting them, in order to facilitate No. 229 Squadron. I was drawn into combat with a Me 110 which I set on fire, but as I was firing from quite a considerable distance away – about 300 yards – I used up all my ammunition and had to withdraw from the combat."

Paszkiewicz's wingman, P/O Łokuciewski, had more success with his efforts and described these in a more colourful manner:

"Since the Squadron leader failed to notice the enemy for a while, Paszka had to lead the attack. By a turn to starboard we closed in onto the enemy. And since we were the highest, it was our duty to engage the Me 109s and Me 110s, which we have achieved completely. Paszka was the first, me the second, and the whole gang behind us. We have been attacked head-on from above by a single Me 109. Of course a dog-fight ensued. I thought initially that it was a Hurricane flying straight at me, but I noticed machine gun trails, so I turned left, until my eyes blacked out, and here I am on the (enemy's) tail. Five short bursts – the one-o-nine is on fire and slides straight into the sea. I gave an additional burst, and some pieces flew away. The pilot did not bale out. In view of the above I gained height and just like Donald (Zumbach) I decided to lurk at the coast, waiting for the returning survivors, as I still had some ammo. And I was right! 8,000 ft – I spotted a Do 215, returning unusually calmly to France. I decided to attack head-on from above for the first time. With a slight advantage of height I attacked, but the result was poor, as he only emitted some smoke and jinked lightly to the left, so then I attacked again from above and behind. I fired bursts up to the last round. He first started to smoke, then to burn, and then in weird manoeuvres, unseen in aerobatics, went to the ground, or more precisely – to the sea. Definite result of my combat: 1 Me 109 and 1 Do 215."

Pilots' reports stated clearly that these attacks broke up the enemy bomber formations, and that large quantities of the bombs were jettisoned in wooded country some 25 miles south of London.

Sgt Brzezowski also claimed at least two Heinkel 111s:

"I engaged one and fired a burst from about 100 yards. Enemy aircraft immediately burst into flames and dived to earth. At that moment, I noticed bullets flying past my cockpit. I immediately dived and in pulling out noticed a He 111 which I attacked and fired four bursts at from a distance of about 150 yards. It burst into flames and one of the crew jumped. Enemy aircraft began to dive to earth. At the same time I noticed a Hurricane on fire. The pilot jumped and as there were a number of enemy aircraft in the vicinity I circled round the pilot in order to protect him. As my engine seemed to be covered with oil and smoking badly and also labouring, I prepared to jump, but seeing that there was no danger of the plane catching fire immediately I landed at Croydon. There is a small bullet hole in the port wing of my aircraft."

F/Lt Atholl Forbes, wounded, landed his shot-up Hurricane at Heston. He recalled this painful event:

"As I dived into the attack I saw the crew of one bomber in the middle of the formation bale out, and as far as I could see, they were not being attacked (this is not the first time that members of my Squadron have noticed a similar phenomenon, and we have also remarked that the German crews open their parachutes immediately, although they may be a great height up.) I took on the left-hand bomber of a section and dived right in on the port wing and engine, which came adrift. I had difficulty in avoiding the wing top and drew out in order to attack the right hand bomber of the next section. In fact, the slip stream of the bomber which I had just destroyed, threw me so far out that when I turned in again I found myself in the ideal position to attack the third machine up the line. This left the bomber immediately in front of the destroyed one on my tail. I nevertheless pressed home the attack, and got in a very good first burst from about 100 yds. on the port engine, wing root and cockpit. Large chunks fell away from all three, and the e/a immediately swang sharply to the left with its nose dropping. At this moment I received a severe blow in the back of the right arm, and right thigh. My arm was thrown forward, and I went into a steep dive. When I neared ground level I started to return to base, flying with my left hand. On nearing Heston I began to feel faint and effected a landing. After treatment I was driven back to Northolt. My machine is being brought back after small repairs ."

The Czech Sergeant Josef František proved the most successful pilot of 303 Squadron in this combat. He claimed the destruction of two Bf 109s and one He 111.

The final account of this encounter was summed up as 16 destroyed and one damaged enemy aircraft! This great victory by 303 Squadron was paid for by the loss of two of its members. Sadly, the unit lost F/O Arsen Cebrzyński and Sgt Stefan Wojtowicz who were shot down in circumstances which are not entirely clear. Cebrzyński's aircraft, V6667/RF-K, crashed at Pembury and the pilot fell nearby. He was taken to a hospital unconscious, but his wounds proved fatal and he died almost a week later. F/Lt Kent remembered a peculiar conversation with this Polish airman:

"It was strange really, as Cebrzyński knew he would be killed and he told me quite dispassionately only two days before that he would not survive long enough to see the end of the month. He was not morbid about it, he was just stating a fact which he accepted and merely wondered vaguely when it might be.

"Sgt Wojtowicz became separated from his flight and fought a long drawn out battle with six 109s single-handed and managed to shoot down two of his opponents before he himself was shot down near Westerham in Kent, not far from the Prime Minister's home."[40]

A few days later F/O Hadwin, who went to investigate Sgt Wojtowicz's crash site, reported:

"I went to Westerham and saw the body of Sgt. Wojtowicz – he had been shot in the forehead by a cannon shell and crashed in flames two miles East of Westerham Village. Several of the local Special Police stated that they had seen his Hurricane fighting with a number of Me 109's and Me 110's over the hills to the West of Westerham at about 16.30 hours on 11.09.40. During the few minutes of the combat two Me 109's crashed in the neighbourhood of Westerham and there is reason to believe that they were accounted for by Sgt. Wojtowicz, but no claim has been put in.

"I went to the Pembury Hospital to see Sgt Karubin who is doing well and to try to find out about the fate of F/O Cebrzyński. I was unable to obtain any information about his combat. He was shot in many places, and one leg was blown completely off. It appears most likely that his harness was severed, and that he fell out of the aeroplane when it turned upside down. It is obvious that he could have been in no position to try to open his parachute."

238 Squadron, with many Polish pilots on strength, also joined the action in defence of London. On 11 September this unit claimed three enemy aircraft destroyed, loosing three of its own Hurricanes and two pilots. One of these was Sgt Stanisław Duszyński, who was on his third combat sortie with the Squadron. Duszyński was shot down by Bf 109s while he was busy aiming at the tail of another Messerschmitt. His Hurricane, R2682, crashed at Little Scotney Farm, Lydd.

Another Polish pilot in this unit, P/O Władysław Różycki, flying Hurricane I P3618, shot down a He 111, but was himself forced to land at New Alresford. Later he flew back to Middle Wallop with his lucky mount on which he would claim two more victories. One of the He 111H-3s of 3./KG 26 attacked by 238 Squadron became P/O Różycki's victim (shared with others). This aircraft, coded 1H+ML (Werk Nr. 3157), crashed at Dormansland, near Lingfield.

At the same time further to the north 605 Squadron also met the stream of

---

[40] Kent, *One of the Few*.

bombers. One of this unit's Polish pilots, Sgt Jan Budziński noted:

"I left Croydon 15.43 hours with 605 Squadron B flight leading A flight in echelon left, we met the He 111's at 18 000 ft near Addington going north. They were in vic formation, a vic of 3 leading followed by vics of 5, with many Me 109's each side of them and 15 000 ft above with 20/30 Me 110's over and behind the bombers. I attacked a He 111 in the formation with a beam attack from 400 yards, with a 3 sec burst, with no visible attack. I broke underneath it and saw a Me 109 coming towards me. I made a head-on attack but with no effect. The Me 109 then dived and turned right handed, I turned into him and dived after it to 10 000 ft. I was then in a position to make an astern attack from above. I fired 5 sec burst from 250 yards, the enemy aircraft broke up and dived down to the ground SE of Gravesend. I then met another Hurricane and returned to Croydon aerodrome."

The Messerschmitt attacked by Budziński probably escaped, but he claimed its destruction. Another Polish pilot of this unit also had good hunting, P/O Witold Głowacki claiming the destruction of a Bf 110.

"We were in echelon port just before beginning our attack on the He 111's. We met the enemy formation coming from the East near Rochester. I attacked the port aircraft of the leading vic of 3 He 111's from port side with a diving quarters attack from 300 yards closing to 100 yards with 3 very short bursts with no visible effect. I then broke under it and circled left and climbed parallel to and above the leading bomber.

"I again attacked the same He 111 with a diving head-on attack without effect. At that moment I noticed a Me 110 behind me and diving on to me so I broke away down and to the right. The Me 110 was following me. I then did a climbing turn to the right and saw the Me 110 break away below me to the left, so I continued my turn and dived upon it from astern firing a five second burst from 350 to 150 yards when its port engine began to smoke and it turned sharp left and dived into the ground from about 8000 feet between Rochester and Gravesend. Then I was by myself so I climbed and searched for other enemy aircraft. I saw a He 111 going south east, being attacked by a Spitfire with a diving attack from astern, so I joined it also with a diving attack from astern, the Spitfire breaking left and I broke right climbing again to attack. When I made my second attack there were about 7 Hurricanes and Spitfires also attacking it. The He 111 dived from about 8 or 10 miles south east Maidstone, three of the crew baling out and two appeared to land safely but the parachute of the third did not open. I then returned to Croydon."

Another unit with a few Poles still serving with it also arrived over the Thames Estuary. 501 Squadron had taken off from Kenley in company of 253 Squadron to patrol the Maidstone area about 3.20 pm. When they approached the combat area, 501 Squadron was attacked by a part of the escorting Bf 109s. In the dog-fights only one Messerschmitt was shot down, as was one Hurricane piloted by Sgt Pickering. After this combat Sgt Antoni Głowacki brought home a big hole in the wing of Hurricane P5193/SD-O, a souvenir from a German 20 mm cannon. Pilots of 501 Squadron also claimed damage to four other German aeroplanes. F/O Stefan

Witorzeńć, flying Hurricane I P5194/SD-J, joined in the joint shooting at a single Do 17, but his claim is not certain.

Almost at the same time another Pole, F/O Henryk Szczęsny from 74 Squadron, flying Spitfire I X4167, claimed the destruction of a Bf 110. He described it in his combat report.

"I was Red 3 74 squadron which took off at 15.34 hrs to intercept hostile raid 44. At 20,000 ft over London I sighted two e/bombers, and delivered astern attack at 100 yards giving 3 x 1 sec burst but observed no apparent damage. I then saw two Me 109's attacking two Spitfires and closed to attack one e/a giving 4 x 1 sec burst at 200 yards range from astern. E/a dived steeply apparently out of control. I then sighted one lone Me 110 and closed to attack from astern giving 5 x 1 sec burst from 300 yards range. E/a dived and crashed on ground in flames. Owing to shortage of ammunition I returned towards base but was unable to obtain homing so returned to home base at 17.40 hrs."

Meanwhile, as the battle around London ended, another raid was heading towards Portsmouth and Southampton. Several squadrons of No. 10 Group were directed towards the bombers with their cover of Bf 109s and Bf 110s. 213 Squadron was the only Hurricane squadron to intercept this raid. Polish airmen marked their presence in this action, too. The 213 Squadron "team" was:

F/Lt Sing	AK-A
S/Ldr MacDonald	
Sgt Llewelyn	P3113/AK-F
F/O Kellow	P5202[41]
F/O Duryasz (Polish)	P3780[42]
Sgt Crosskell	AK-J
F/Lt Strickland	P3979/AK-V
P/O Sizer	AK-X
Sgt Snowden	AK-Y
Sgt Wójcicki (Polish)	W6667/AK-P
Sgt Dunscombe	AK-U
P/O Cottam	AK-W

They met their opponents over Selsey Bill and claimed the destruction of five enemy aircraft plus damage to two more, for the loss of one pilot and his Hurricane. F/O Marian Duryasz described his encounter with a Bf 110, which ended in his shooting this down into the sea:

"I was No 3 Yellow Section when we intercepted e/a over Selsey Bill. One broke away and I was below it and had a good target to give it five short bursts. Left engine started smoking and it started to dive down in a long left hand turn. I

---

[41] 213 Squadron ORB records individual letters and very occasionally serial numbers. Possibly the two Hurricanes flown that day by F/O Kellow and P/O Duryasz carried no code leters.
[42] Many sources give account that aircraft P3780 carrying letters AK-A was lost on 11 September 1940. F/Lt Sing abandoned his AK-A and baled out, but F/O Duryasz landed safely home. Thus the ORB entry seems to be very strange.

followed it down to within 1000 ft of the sea when it burst into flames and dived straight into water."

Unfortunately the other Polish pilot of this unit was lost in this encounter. Sgt Aleksander Wójcicki was shot down one mile off Selsey Bill by a Bf 110 and was reported missing.

Both F/O Marian Duryasz and Sgt Aleksander Wójcicki had began their operational flights in 213 Squadron in mid-August.

12 September 1940

"A" Flight of 302 Squadron moved to RAF Duxford on 11 September, followed by the rest of the squadron next day.

308 Squadron personnel, under the command of S/Ldr Stefan Łaszkiewicz, moved from Blackpool depot to Speke to start forming the unit.

13 September 1940

The weather on 13 September was not favourable for offensive operations, although single German aircraft penetrated over southern England. Two Hurricanes of 253 Squadron were airborne at 3 pm, taking off from Kenley. P/O Tadeusz Nowak (Polish) in N2455, led by F/Lt Watts in V7466, intercepted one such intruder. Nowak described in his report:

> "I was Green 2 flying in section of 2 aircraft on patrol to intercept single raiders. We were flying at 14 000 ft in the Hastings area when I lost Green 1, at the same time sighting a He 111 about 10 miles West of me flying NNE. I got into position and delivered an astern attack on e/a out of the sun and subsequently chased the He 111 in and out of cloud inland to Croydon, where I lost e/a in cloud. I delivered 5 separate attacks, all from astern. After 2nd attack I received no return fire from the rear gunner and after the 4th attack the port engine of e/a was smoking black very badly."

The only loss of a Heinkel 111 that day matches Nowak's report. Oblt. Eisenbrandt of 2./KG 1 nursed his shot-up He 111H-3, coded V4+OK, back to Montdidier aerodrome and then crashed on landing. Two of the crew were killed and two others were wounded.

During the day F/O Marian Duryasz of 213 Squadron was ordered to perform an unusual duty. He took off in his Hurricane V6866/AK-D at 4.10 pm with orders to shoot down a barrage balloon that had broken free of its moorings.

Duryasz, lonesome since the death of Sgt Aleksander Wójcicki the previous day, would soon be joined by P/O Własnowolski.

14 September 1940

307 Squadron at Kirton-in-Lindsey received its first nine Defiant night fighters, and soon began flying training with air gunners, leaving the Battles and Master, with which it had initially been supplied, for communication duties only.

Sgt Josef Kania, the second Czech pilot of 303 Squadron, apart from the famous Sgt Josef Frantisek, damaged newly arrived Hurricane L1696 (later coded RF-T) during taxying after landing at Northolt. "Caused by failure of the latch and possibly due to strain on previous occasions" – said the accident report.

Chapter Four

IMPACT OF THE POLES ON THE BATTLE OF BRITAIN

15 September – 14 October 1940

Gallants, who here patrol the sky
And strew the land with wreck of raiders,
There's a refinement you might try
In your reception of invaders.
The German, itching to oppress,
With well-thought-out humiliation,
Says yellow patches on the dress
Must now mark out the Polish nation.
Accept the badge, then: at this time
Let every Pole show like his fellow
And when to fierce pursuit you climb
Paint your avenging Spitfires yellow.
Gallants, a day will surely come
When you shall help to square the reckoning,
And though Fate's judgement-voice stay dumb,
I think we see a finger beckoning.
Is it no sign when we are told
How you press home in mid-air battle
And almost to the shock withhold
That deadly many-throated rattle?
Each of your triumphs earns a crown
Beyond what simple victory gives,
For, when a German crashes down,
Men know – that Poland lives
Stephen Gwynn –
To a Polish squadron which in a month destroyed 100 enemy machines.

15 September 1940

This quiet morning did not foretell the greatest air battle of the Battle of Britain, as the Luftwaffe prepared for its decisive encounter with RAF Fighter Command. About 11.20 am 501 Squadron together with 253 Squadron were airborne to patrol

Maidstone, and later intercepted a formation of Do 17s. They were in turn attacked by the fighter cover and a series of dog-fights ensued. 501 Squadron claimed three enemy aircraft destroyed, one probably destroyed and one damaged. The Polish participant of this combat, Sgt Antoni Głowacki, noted in his log-book:

"One Me 109 damaged unconfirmed. My own aircraft badly shot up".

Since his Hurricane, V7403/SD-N, was out of service, he did not take part in any further sorties that day.

Since early morning, sections of 302 Squadron were patrolling the Duxford area every half an hour. About 11 am the following section took off:

F/Lt Farmer	P3924/WX-Y
P/O Wapniarek	P3930/WX-X
Sgt Markiewicz	P3085/WX-A

A few minutes after take-off the section was left by its leader, who landed back at Duxford to join the rest of the squadron preparing for a bigger operation. The famous Big Wing, under command of S/Ldr Douglas Bader, was preparing to come to the aid of the 11 Group squadrons engaged near London. All Duxford's fighter squadrons were airborne at about 11.25. The Polish squadron was as follows[43]:

F/Lt Farmer	P3924/WX-Y	
F/Lt Jastrzębski	R2684/WX-B	Red 2
F/O Kowalski	P3935/WX-D	Blue 3
F/O Chłopik	P2954/WX-E	Red 1
Sgt Siudak	P3867/WX-F	
P/O Łapka	V6569/WX-K	
P/O Karwowski	R4095/WX-M	
S/Ldr Satchell	P3812/WX-L	Blue 1
F/O Czerwiński	V6571/WX-Q	Blue 2
Sgt Wędzik	P2752/WX-R	
P/O Chałupa	P3923/WX-U	Green 1
Sgt Palak	V7417/WX-T	Green
Sgt Paterek	P3086/WX-Z	Green

One of the participants in this operation, F/O Julian "Roch" Kowalski, years later recalled his first successful sortie in the Battle of Britain:

"We are at readiness, machines warmed-up, pilots ready to take off, air clear on the ground, but the sky completely covered up; ceiling about 10 thousand ft. Pilots sitting, lying on the grass, some walking, frequently taking a peek into the sky. Suddenly, from the loudspeakers: – Attention, attention. All Hurricane squadrons scramble! It boils up. Noise of machines starting-up and taking off in sequence: Canadians, Poles, Czechs. I am flying on the port side of the 302 OC, S/Ldr Satchell, Tadzio Czerwiński on his starboard. We break through the clouds. I

---

[43] Order as stated in 302 Squadron Operations Record Book.

squint upwards. In the blue sky hundreds of white trails scatter in great disorder, and along lines straight, semicircular, and full circles, cover the beautiful blue sky, some suddenly break and in a vertical, spiral, blue trail of smoke connect the sky with the ground. Every now and then white balloons open up there; it all looks like a great Christmas decoration, suspended under the dome of sky.

"'The combat is already on', I thought, 'Spitfires are welcoming the Me 109s.' Under us white, neat, puffy clouds, and formations of black German bombers against that background. Some are already scattered by squadrons of Hurricanes and several are heading back South in disorder, but still more and more appear on the horizon. Great noise in my headphones. I am not listening, why would I? I don't understand a thing anyway. Suddenly, how strange, a voice in Polish, shouting: 'Attack! Kill them, bastards!' 'That's Northolt', I thought. They were closer, we are flying almost on top of them. Terrible sight! I am glad I am not German. We carry on. Meanwhile, a huge formation of Dorniers approaches us, and after a moment I can hear the voice of Bader: 'Tally-ho!'

"The entire Wing almost simultaneously made a sharp turn, and fell at full throttle onto the tight Dornier formation. I did not go down to attack. I just caught onto the tail of one and fired a long burst straight into its fuselage from minimum distance, and the Dornier continued to fly as before. I gave it a thought and shouted aloud: 'Roch, get at the engine!' – After a rather short burst from my guns, the engine exploded, almost the entire wing fell off, and the German disappeared, spinning, under the clouds. I was positive its crew would miss their lunch today. I aimed at another. Suddenly, a Spitfire in vertical fall literally cut a Dornier in half with its wing. The attack of Bader's Wing must have been very effective, as after just one kill I could not find another. Avoiding some parachutes, and pieces of Messerschmitts coming down, I returned to the airfield."

Back at Duxford airfield, it turned out that Roch Kowalski was not the only one who had been successful. He described in his combat report:

". . . I noticed two more Dorniers, at which I did not shoot, as they were being attacked effectively by several of our Hurricanes. After a few seconds of combat both Dorniers went down in flames."

Excited pilots described their action to the 302 Squadron Intelligence Officer. In his composite combat report he filed claims for seven destroyed, two probables and one damaged enemy aircraft without any casualties in return. In the whole of Bader's Wing only one pilot was forced to land in a shot-up Hurricane.

This apparent success by Big Wing, including that of 302 Squadron, had in fact resulted in a significant proportion of overclaiming. Many of the victories credited were in fact shared among several pilots, as was clearly stated in some of their reports, for example that of F/Lt Czerwiński:

"At 12.10 we attacked in section formation with a beam attack the head of the enemy formation with height advantage and at a speed of about 300 mph. I got in two short bursts at 300 yards closing to 100 yards, results of my bursts I could not see as I broke left immediately after shooting. Climbing again I met a single Do 17 slightly above and in front of me. I attacked alone from behind and slightly above getting in three bursts whereas the enemy aircraft left engine caught fire and I broke off to the left and saw the enemy aircraft dive steeply. Then I saw three of our aircraft attacking this falling enemy aircraft. I went for one more enemy aircraft but it was already under attack by our aircraft and its crew had jumped out."

Similar remarks about a bomber chased by more than one fighter are included in the report of F/Lt Tadeusz Chłopik, who shared one bomber with F/Lt Jastrzębski:

"On seeing the enemy formation breaking up I attacked one Do 215 as it broke away to the left giving a short burst from the side, then a very long burst from behind until I saw port engine smoking heavily with black smoke and on fire and the starboard engine emitting blue smoke and the enemy aircraft diving on its back earthwards. A moment later three of the crew jumped out in parachutes. A moment later I attacked a Do 17 from behind and above. I got in a long burst and saw the port engine emitting smoke. This enemy aircraft was attacked immediately by a large number of Hurricanes and two Spitfires . . ."

The excited Polish voices heard by F/O Kowalski in his earphones had indeed come from 303 Squadron pilots, already engaged in the battle. The whole squadron took off about 11:15 am:

"A" Flight

F/Lt Kent	V6665/RF-J	Red 1
P/O Ferić	R2685/RF-G	Red 2
Sgt Andruszkow	P3939/RF-H	Red 3
F/O Henneberg	P3120/RF-A	Yellow 1
P/O Zumbach	P3577/RF-E	Yellow 2
F/O Grzeszczak	V7244/RF-C	Yellow 3

"B" Flight

F/O Paszkiewicz	V7235/RF-M	Blue 1
P/O Łokuciewski	P2903/RF-Z	Blue 2
Sgt Wojciechowski	V6673/RF-U	Blue 3
F/O Pisarek	V7465/RF-V	Green 1
Sgt František	P3089/RF-P	Green 2
Sgt Kowalski	V7289/RF-S	Green 3

F/Lt Johnny Kent, leading this formation, later described this flight:

"I led the first scramble of the day in company with 229 Sqn, which had replaced No. 1 a few days previously. We were vectored towards the south-east and when we arrived over the area to the south of Croydon No. 229, which was the leading Squadron, started a gentle turn to starboard. At the same time I saw a large formation of enemy aircraft approaching from the south which put us in a perfect position for a head-on attack. I waited for the Wing Leader to attack the bombers with 229 Sqn while I prepared to give him protection from the German fighter escort. It suddenly dawned on me that he had not seen the enemy as he continued his turn away from them and here we experienced one of those incidents which indicated just how impractical the wing theory was under the circumstances obtaining at this time. [...]

"We, No. 303 Squadron, were equipped with H/F radiocommunication equipment as was No. 229 Squadron but the two squadrons were on different frequencies and while we could both speak to the Controller in the Operations Room and receive messages from him we couldn't speak to one another! In this instance, when it became evident to me that John Banham, leading 229 Squadron, had not seen the German formation I tried to relay a message to him via the Controller but he could not understand me as we were just at about the extreme range of the radio which was only about forty miles![...]

"In this instance I had less than one minute in which to make up my mind as to what action I must take if this enemy formation was not to get away scot-free. I realised that it was hopeless endeavouring to get 229 into action at this stage so I sent down three sections of my squadron, nine aircraft, to attack the bombers while I and my section went for the fighters. By this time we were, unfortunately, in nowhere near as good a position and the bombers were already dropping their bombs."[44]

A very critical account of this part of the operation was given by F/O Ludwik Paszkiewicz:

"The whole is led by F/Lt Kent. I am flying as Blue 1 (third section in sequence). Kent was leading without any sense – manipulating his throttle and flying blind no-one knows where to. At one point he started to chase a distant formation of Me 109s and 110s. The Squadron broke up. I kept up with the trio of Kent. Tolo [Łokuciewski] has already downed an Me 109 that attacked us from one side. I peek upwards, what are the black 109s doing? Kent is firing all his guns like crazy, from a distance of some 1 kilometre."

F/O Paszkiewicz's section preparing to attack was attacked itself from the rear by four Bf 109s. Paszkiewicz was still following Kent, but his wingmen broke away. Suddenly a German fighter appeared in front of Paszkiewicz's Hurricane, so he fired short bursts at it and later claimed it as destroyed. His wingman – Tolo Łokuciewski mentioned above – did a sharp turn to set himself free from the Messerschmitts, and found on his course another German formation:

"To my great surprise, at some 600 metres I can see another bomber formation under strong Me 109 and 110 escort, flying towards London. I can also see a Hurricane Squadron feebly attacking this formation. I join in with that squadron, but a 109 flew in front of me, intending to attack me. Needless to say, a little turn to the left, several jinks, look to the rear and sides, and let's get on to the Jerry. I could sense a trap in it – and I was right. I fired my first burst – the Jerry is smoking, I fired my second – black smoke and fire appeared. I thought to myself: let's finish the bugger, but at this moment I heard a loud noise and my bursts were scattered. I broke violently and fell into the clouds."

In the cloud P/O Łokuciewski felt itching in both legs caused by shell splinters and

44 Kent, *One of the Few*.

the aircraft began to lose its speed. After he left the cloud a big hole in the wing caused by the explosion of a 20 mm shell could be seen. The glycol level also suddenly fell. Łokuciewski reached Northolt airfield, but landed without flaps, unable to operate them. Wounded in both legs he was taken to hospital, saying "But I got one Jerry!".

According to the account of Sgt Wojciechowski (the other wingman of F/O Paszkiewicz), who followed F/Lt Kent's section, he saw a Messerschmitt smoking slightly, and losing height. Wojciechowski followed it to the ground, where the Messerschmitt crash-landed; the German pilot stepped out of the plane, and was arrested. This was Uffz. Walburger, who crash landed near Ilfield and was taken prisoner. His Bf 109E-1, Werk Nr. 6147, of 2./JG 27 was one of those positively verified as falling prey to the Polish fighters.

Following this Sgt Wojciechowski claimed another victory:

> "I again climbed and another machine (from A Flight 'M') joining me, we attacked a Do and firing two bursts enemy aircraft crashed to earth and burst into flames."

The aircraft which joined Wojciechowski on the way back to Northolt was in fact the Hurricane coded H not M, and was flown by Sgt Tadeusz Andruszków who shared in the destruction of the bomber and also watched this fall in flames to the ground.

In the meantime, the Green Section leader, F/O Marian Pisarek, easily shot down a Bf 109 into the sea after a brief chase. His wingman, Sgt František attacked a Bf 110, the only pilot of 303 Squadron to do so, and claimed it destroyed.

F/Lt Kent, leading the whole formation, was very disappointed by his first attack and by the development of this action:

> "As there were about fifty enemy fighters, we three Hurricanes could not do very much except interfere with their attempts to go to the help of their charges, so our combat – while fast and furious – was still indecisive. Zumbach and I both got a lot of smoke out of a couple of 109s but the pace was too fast for us to see what happened to them."

P/O Jan Zumbach first went to the rescue of F/O Henneberg who was attacked by a Messerschmitt. He fired at the German fighter, and set it on fire while diving. Zumbach later recalled:

> "I cut across his path and pumped him a nice burst. He smoked immediately and went spinning down. I followed him and a polka started. Something got into his head, as he was performing fantastic aerobatics, hoping I would let him go. In order to stop him day-dream of escaping, or to give him more courage, I fired a little burst every now and then. Since I had spent a lot of ammunition this way, and he just continued to smoke, I decided to wait, until he got fed up with the fun, and started to fly straight. So he did. Being slightly to one side I turned and hit him from a direct distance. Pieces flew away from him and he started to burn at once. I struggled with him for some four minutes. Then I climbed and started to look for another . . ."

He then saw about a dozen Dornier 17s returning to France without protecting fighters. He signalled to another aircraft that joined him, and they attacked, but Zumbach was almost out of ammunition, so he gave up further action and went back to Northolt.

F/O Henneberg, attacked by three Messerschmitts and saved by Zumbach's action, was forced to break off the engagement with the bombers, but he left one Dornier with the right engine and petrol tank in flames. Later, flying south, he came across three Bf 109s making their way towards the Channel:

"I gave chase, and firing from a distance of about 300 yards saw one enemy aircraft dive in smoke, and spin down. I again fired a burst. Enemy aircraft then slackened speed, and approaching to a distance of about 150 yards, I fired a third burst from the rear left side. Enemy aircraft hit the water at an angle of about 30 degrees and disappeared 10 kilometres from the coast."

For F/Lt Kent also, the first part of the battle ended suddenly:

"The wild melee suddenly came to an end, the only enemy machines to be seen were away in the distance heading for France. Amazingly none of us three had received so much as one bullet in our aircraft, so we went off on a patrol of the south coast where we turned westward over the Rye area. As we completed the turn, I just caught a glimpse of two 109s diving down on our starboard quarter. Mike Ferić, my number three, also saw them and whirled to meet them, firing as he did so, but at the same moment his own aircraft was hit. I dived after the other which overshot its attack. As I followed, the German rolled on to his back just before I opened fire and then rolled back again and round until he was inverted again, then once more he rolled right side up and I saw a large piece of the aircraft come off and spin away over the top of my aircraft. We were both diving almost vertically by this time and he was outdistancing me, so I ceased fire and waited to catch him as he pulled out of the dive. To my surprise the aircraft dived straight into the sea just a few hundred yards off the tip of Dungeness; there was a vivid flash as it hit, a large cloud of black smoke billowed up and the petrol continued to blaze upon the surface of the water.

"I was told later by the Intelligence Officer that the large piece that had nearly hit my aircraft was the pilot who had baled out but whose parachute had failed to open. He was found lying dead on the beach at Dungeness."

This description of the noon combat was given by F/Lt Kent in his memoirs, but no document of 303 Squadron mentioned any claim by him on this date. His flying logbook, however, includes his own comment which differs slightly from the account above:

"[...] LATER ATTACKED 109 WHICH WENT INTO SEA. P/O FERIĆ HAD HIT IT FIRST."

The combat report of P/O Ferić states:

"After an hour flight looking for enemy aircraft I was attacked by two Me 109s over the coast at Dungeness. These were reinforced by three other Me's and in ensuing fight I shot one down, firing a long burst from a distance of 300 yards. Being myself engaged I could not follow subsequent flight of damaged enemy aircraft, but F/Lt Kent who was in the vicinity states that he saw enemy aircraft burst into flames and fall to earth."

This encounter of 303 Squadron ended with claims for seven Bf 109s, two "Do 215" and one Bf 110.

About 12.30 pm Red Section of 601 Squadron was sent on patrol. During this flight F/O Marian Duryasz, flying the Hurricane I, P3174/AK-G, followed his leader F/Lt Sing, in AK-A, shooting down a Do 17 near Edenbridge.

"I was Red 3 in A Flight when we engaged the bombers. We carried out a head on attack. One turned with it and I engaged it. He was attempting to dive down away from me into the cloud. I followed, firing all the time. He dropped all his bombs. I watched him blazing on the ground in a small wood."

The third member of this section, Sgt Bushell, flying the Hurricane AK-B, did not manage to join in the combat.

Douglas Bader's Big Wing was airborne again about 2.15 pm, 27 Hurricanes and 20 Spitfires being directed to the south again. This time 302 Squadron was represented by seven Hurricanes only:

S/Ldr Satchell	P2752/WX-R	Blue 1
P/O Pilch[45]	P3086/WX-Z	Blue 2
P/O Karwowski	R4095/WX-M	Blue 3
F/O Czerwiński	V6571/WX-Q	Blue 4
F/O Chłopik	P2954/WX-E	Red 1
P/O Łapka	V6569/WX-K	Red 2
F/O Kowalski	P3935/WX-D	Red 3

F/O Julian Kowalski recalled again:

"Soon after lunch we took off in sequence: Canadian 242, Czech 310 and Polish 302. This flight was arranged so that Tadzio Chłopik's section was the rearmost in the whole Wing. Stasio Łapka on the starboard side, and me on the port, the last pilot of the formation. This last pilot was generally an easy bit for the yellow nose Messerschmitts, but I was not worried, since when I was 12 a Gypsy fortune-teller told me that I would spend my life out of Poland, somewhere overseas, and would live long. Believing in this prophecy I was calm and sure.

"Meanwhile we entered clouds, thinner than in the morning. As the last, I flew the lowest and could see, far away on the horizon, a black line that, as I climbed, turned into a dark band, lightly waving against the white plumes of clouds, and flying straight at us. I could see first Dorniers immediately below us, so close below us that I instinctively pulled up to avoid collision.

"I could hear Chłopik calling Bader in English. I didn't understand what he was

---

[45] In place of P/O Pilch 302 Squadron ORB listed Sgt Paterek who in fact did not take part in this combat. The Composite Combat Report clearly stated that Blue 2 was P/O Pilch.

saying, but I am sure he reported the Dorniers below us. Having no answer, Tadzio shouted, this time in Polish: 'Attack', with a simultaneous turn backwards. Knowing Tadzio, I was ready for it and the whole trio turned back. Tadzio chose to attack the middle line of the Dorniers, and me and Stasio found ourselves among the formation lines. Since our speed after the turn was reduced to zero relative to the Germans, the Dornier that flew at the back crashed into Tadzio's aircraft. A great explosion followed, and debris from the Hurricane and Dornier sank in the clouds.

"I looked to the port. Exactly at my height, from no more than 20 metres, I saw the giant fuselage of a Dornier and its gunners aiming at me. Without thinking I shut the throttle in order to fall behind, a little of the left foot, and a long burst, first across the gunners, then into the starboard engine and the cockpit. The Dornier literally fell to pieces. Good reflex will save you . . .

"To the starboard and a bit in front I could see Stasio finish his German, already on fire, and at the same moment I could see a black trail of smoke behind Stasio's Hurricane. I put the transmitter on and shouted: 'Stasiu, jump! Stasiu, jump!' A moment later both the Dornier and Hurricane went behind clouds. I was left alone, but did not have the heart to withdraw. I still had ammunition left, and was dissnissive of my environment. I was flying in formation with the Dorniers. The Hurricane jumped around in the slipstream. I was so close behind the tail of a German, I could not miss. I aimed at the engines; another one on fire, the crew bales out. Dornier spins to hide in the clouds. The third one was lucky: a short burst and out of ammo. I shut the throttle a bit, and slowly sink down. I look above. The black band of Dorniers was broken in half. Four lay on the ground, several smoking wrecks were returning south – probably shot up. The whole group was turning back in disorder.

"My aeroplane was slowly going home, like an old cart horse, and I was thinking of my friends and those few minutes of my life. The aerodrome approaches. Flaps refuse to open, the undercarriage does not come out, I pump it – it's out! I come down. My machine goes violently left on touchdown. Fortunately it has stopped at the 302 dispersal. Fitters run to me with the question: 'What happened, where are the others?' I slowly climb out of the machine and look: the Hurricane is riddled with bullets! Somebody is counting the holes: '68!' he shouts. I stand still. Sergeants are touching me, as if looking for holes in my suit, too. I go into the hut to file my report and on my way I think about those two, whom I said good-bye to forever . . .

"I gave a short report from the sortie to the Intelligence Officer. There was not much to say. In the evening news came that the body of Tadzio Chłopik was found in the Thames Estuary. Stasio Łapka baled out safely, but on landing he broke his leg. His adventures were to be immortalised in the *Battle of Britain* film."

S/Ldr Satchell, leading Blue Section, turned to attack a small formation of about 15 enemy aircraft. Just before getting into position he noticed in his mirror a Bf 109 which was flying above him. Satchell waited until the Messerschmitt dived to attack, and then pulled sharply up, letting it pass below him. Then he got on its tail and gave several long bursts, whereupon the Bf 109 turned onto its back, with smoke issuing from its engine, and went into cloud in a spin. Meanwhile, P/O Pilch dived to attack the bomber formation and found that in the meantime Red Section Leader was doing the same. The enemy formation split up and entered clouds. Pilch waited below until enemy aircraft emerged, and then attacked a Do 17 head-on, silencing the rear gunner. Simultaneously a Spitfire attacked the same aircraft from behind. Pilch turned and attacked the bomber from behind, after which he saw black smoke issuing from the port engine. The enemy aircraft turned towards the Thames Estuary and dived away, burning. At this time a Do 17 emerged from the cloud and Pilch attacked it immediately, again silencing the rear gunner. After his next attack the port engine of the Dornier began to smoke. He then had to cease further action because of the increasing AA fire bursting all around. He waited for this to cease, and once more attacked the Dornier over the Channel, where he saw it fall into the sea near Margate. P/O Karwowski was not so fortunate. At the moment of attack his port machine gun panel became loose; it did not fly off completely, but caused very considerable drag, preventing proper control of the aircraft. He dived away and eventually found a field to land in, but the left undercarriage wheel caught in a rut and broke away. F/O Czerwiński, the last pilot of Blue Section, had to break off his attack due to an engine failure, and he returned to Duxford. So the afternoon engagement of 302 Squadron was not as successful as the previous one.

Like their comrades from the Duxford Wing, 303 Squadron's pilots were also airborne again about 2.25 pm. This time only nine aircraft were available to take off from Northolt:

"A" Flight

F/O Urbanowicz	V6684/RF-F	Red
Sgt Brzezowski	P3577/RF-E	
P/O Ferić	R2685/RF-G	Red
F/O Januszewicz	P3120/RF-A	
Sgt Andruszków	P3939/RF-H	

"B" Flight

S/Ldr Kellett	V7465/RF-V	
Sgt Kowalski	V7235/RF-M	
Sgt Wojciechowski	V6673/RF-U	Blue 3
F/O Żak	L2099/RF-O	

The Polish fighters, led by S/Ldr Kellett, were vectored onto a bomber formation protected by Bf 109s. Kellet later reported:

> "We reached 18,000 ft somewhere near Gravesend, we sighted about 400 enemy aircraft coming straight towards us from East South East. The bombers, the leaders of which were Do 215's, were in Vics of 3 sections in line astern stretching for several miles. There were Me 110's in Squadron formation between the bomber squadrons, and guarding the flanks. Above and stepped up to 25,000 ft were many formations of Me 109's of various sizes."

The initial attack by the squadron, developed into individual dog-fights and hide-and-seek games through the clouds. The only Bf 109 claimed on this occasion was credited to Sgt Mirosław Wojciechowski. He recorded:

"Being near a Messerschmitt I fired a burst after which he turned and made off towards the sea. I chased him for quite a long time, before I was able to shoot him down. The pilot jumped, and I saw him arrested as he landed."

Probably the Messerschmitt shot down by the Polish pilot was chased as far as Rainham, west of Chatham, the crash site of the Bf 109E-7, Werk Nr. 2061, flown by Uffz. Streibing. The pilot, from 1./LG 2, baled out and was taken prisoner exactly as described by Wojciechowski in his report. It was the second Bf 109 shot down by this pilot during the day.

At the beginning of the attack the squadron was a little slow in turning into position. S/Ldr Kellett found himself some way in front with Blue Section, and made a quarter head-on attack. The leading bombers then wheeled eastwards and the Red and Yellow Sections came in. At about the same time another British unit, (either 73 or 238 Squadron) about six miles away attacked the enemy from the west in the flank. The whole German formation, which had been very tight so far, loosened, and most of the bombers went east, some miles south of the river, while a few fled southwards. S/Ldr Kellett reported:

"I fired at a Do 215 from very close range – I saw pieces fly off both engines and front of the fuselage. I could not stay to see what happened as I was immediately attacked by four Yellow nosed Me 110's from all sides and had to dive to get out of it. I reached cloud and shook off the Me 110's by doing a series of turns. I climbed back where I could see streamers to the East. As I climbed I was again attacked, but by a single Me 110. I had no difficulty in evading him, and got on to his tail. I gave him two good bursts into his starboard engine from the quarter. The engine stopped and smoked, and flames burst from the wing. Enemy aircraft fell flaming into the cloud."

F/O Witold Urbanowicz of Red Section claimed to have downed two Dornier bombers quite easily.

"Enemy formation split into 3's. After a long chase I attacked and fired a burst from a distance of 200 yards. At that exact moment enemy aircraft hid in clouds. On emerging from the clouds I again attacked from a nearer distance, and in a short while the enemy bomber dived in flames and fell into the sea. I attacked another 3/4 from the rear, and after a long burst, one engine stopped working, aircraft lost speed, and began to lose height. Having satisfied myself that no enemy fighter was on my tail, I again attacked the bomber, and firing from a distance of 150 yards, saw him burst into flames and fall into the sea."

Another pilot of Red Section, P/O Ferić, was engaged by the fighter cover after his attack on the bombers.

"Since I had used up half my ammunition in attacking enemy bombers I approached to about 100 to 80 yards before firing a burst at a Me 110, which immediately burst into flames and fell into the clouds out of control. Having now used all my ammunition I took cover in the clouds and after a few minutes landed at Gravesend where I refuelled and returned to Northolt."

Sadly, Sgt Brzezowski failed to return (the only pilot lost by the squadron). Nobody was able to explain what had happened to him.

For S/Ldr Kellett, who led the victorious formation of fighters, this day proved to be happy one not only because of his claims, but also because he was now awarded a DFC.

17 Squadron RAF from Debden was one of eight units scrambled about 2 pm to intercept bombers approaching from Calais and Boulogne. For the second time that day 17 Squadron was sent into the Chelmsford area, at an altitude of 15,000 ft. Among the pilots of that unit was one Pole – P/O Paweł Niemiec. After returning to Debden, he claimed damage to a Do 17.

> "I was No 3 in Blue Section when we attacked a formation of 50 or more Dorniers with Me 110's behind and Me 109's above them. There were only two in my section as No 2 did not take off. I made a beam attack on a Do 17 and opened fire at 300 yards closing to 100 yards giving him a four second burst. Black smoke started to come from his starboard engine. I broke away under him, and saw another and bigger cloud of black smoke come from an engine which I thought was beginning to catch fire. I then joined up with two of our Hurricanes and coming down through cloud saw another Do 17. I broke away from the Hurricanes and after flying alongside the Do 17 I turned into him in a break in the cloud and gave him a short burst at 150 yards, but observed no result. The Do returned cannon fire, but my aircraft was not hit."

In all, 17 Squadron claimed the destruction of two Do 17s and damage to one more.

Polish pilots had been in this Squadron since 1 September, when P/O Tadeusz Leon Kumiega and P/O Niemiec arrived from 6 OTU at Sutton Bridge. This Polish team had grown to a trio on 10 September, when P/O Marian Chełmecki was posted in from 56 Squadron.

15 September was described in 238 Squadron's Operations Record Book as "a bright day", not only in terms of weather:

> "Twelve sorties comprising the whole squadron patrolled base, and subsequently went to Brooklands-Kenley line where strong formations of enemy were found. The squadron attacked in sections line astern out of the sun. The ensuing engagement was the most successful the squadron has yet had. Ten enemy were destroyed and only one of our pilots (Sgt. L. Pidd) was lost. Unfortunately he was killed. His aircraft P2836 and his body being found some days later in a wood near Tonbridge. F/Lt M. V. Blake's aircraft (P3920) was badly shot about and he landed at West Malling. The aircraft was struck off squadron strength, but the pilot was uninjured.
>
> "The toll of sky rats was as follows:
>
> "F/Lt M. V. Blake, P/O V. C. Simmonds, P/O J. R. Urwin-Mann, P/O C. T. Davis, one He 111 each = 4 He 111 destroyed. P/O A. R. Covington, Sgt J. Jeka (Pole), one Me 110 each = 2 Me 110 destroyed. Sgt J. Jeka (Pole) one unidentified aircraft = one unidentified aircraft destroyed, P/O W. Różycki (Pole) and Sgt R. Little damaged one He 111 each = 2 He 111 damaged. P/O J. R. Urwin-Mann probably destroyed He 111 = one He 111 probably destroyed. This makes a gross total of 10 enemy aircraft and our pilots, P/O J. R. Urwin-Mann and Sgt J. Jeka

(Pole) both made a double score.

"L2089 – P/O V. C. Simmonds, P3462 – P/O C. T. Davis, P3833 – P/O A. R. Covington were damaged beyond squadron repair."

During this encounter P/O Władysław Różycki flew Hurricane I, P3618, and Sgt Józef Jeka, P3219.

The day became notable for 607 Squadron also, which ended it with total claims of seven destroyed, one probably destroyed and four damaged enemy aircraft for the loss of one aircraft and a pilot wounded in action. A late afternoon interception of bombers heading towards Portsmouth and Southampton brought one victory to this unit's Polish pilot, P/O Bolesław Własnowolski describing his combat, which ended with shooting down a Do 17 near Poole:

"I was Red 3 flying in section and from this position I saw Do 17 at about 12,000 feet flying alone to my right over coast near Poole. I pursued e/a who tried to escape by taking zig-zag course above clouds so fired two bursts from behind and a little below. I saw engine catch fire and e/a dived below clouds. I followed him down and saw e/a dive into the sea in flames and sink. Enemy pilot sunk with plane. After this having became detached from section I rejoined base alone."

The following day cloud cover over England gave the RAF a break, following what had possibly been the busiest day of the summer.

17 September 1940

After taking part in the funeral ceremony for P/O Arsen Cebrzyński and Sgt Stefan Wojtowicz at Northwood cemetery, 303 Squadron together with 1 RCAF Squadron were airborne about 3 pm. They were ordered to patrol north of Biggin Hill. "A" and "B" Flight taking part in this patrol consisted of:

F/Lt Kent	V6665/RF-J
P/O Zumbach	V6681/RF-B
P/O Ferić	V7244/RF-C
F/O Henneberg	V7246/RF-D
F/O Januszewicz	P3120/RF-A
Sgt Andruszków	R2685/RF-G
F/O Paszkiewicz	V7235/RF-M
Sgt Kowalski	P3089/RF-P
Sgt Wojciechowski	P3975/RF-U
F/O Żak	L2099/RF-O

All ten aircraft had reached 20,000 ft when they spotted a formation of aircraft approaching from the east which proved to be a squadron of Hurricanes. RAF squadrons flying lower then Luftwaffe *Freie Jagd* Messerschmitts were ordered to avoid close encounters. Soon 303 Squadron was ordered back home. F/Lt Kent wisely refrained from trying to give battle to the Messerschmitts above the Hurricane's ceiling. In spite of this some Messerschmitts were attacked, and one of the Polish airmen of 303 Squadron became engaged.

"In the course of the patrol I saw several Messerschmitts attacking one Hurricane, and the Hurricane diving, I went in to attack and engaged the Me's at 17,000 ft. I fired one burst into one of them, which shook and dived towards the earth. The burst was accurate, but I could not follow the enemy aircraft down, as I was engaged with the others. I fired again at another Me. and after the second burst his right wing caught fire; I also saw flames inside the cockpit as he fell away from me, but I could not follow him down as I had another of them on my tail. I evaded this one in the cloud and afterwards could not find him. I then heard the order to return home."

Sgt Wojciechowski probably saved the life of F/O E. C. Briese of 1 RCAF Squadron who was chased by Messerschmitts; the oil system of his aircraft suffered damage which prevented him from being able to reach Northolt, and he had to force land at High Halstow. In return Sgt Wojciechowski certainly shot down one of three Bf 109s of 9./JG 53 lost over the Thames Estuary. His victim was probably either Olt. Herbert Seliger (Bf 109E-4 W.Nr.1228) or the *Staffelkapitän*, Olt. Jakob Stoll (Bf 109E-4 W.Nr.5141), both presumed missing over the sea.

Polish pilots remarked upon a similarity in the tactics used by the Germans on this occasion to those which they had employed in the air battles over Poland. The following notes were added to the composite report for the day by F/O E. H. L. Hadwin:

"In the early days the Germans sent over formations of bombers, escorted by fighters and suffered severe losses. They then adopted other tactics which they adhered to until the end of the Campaign. They sent over large numbers of Messerschmitts at varying altitudes in small formations of three and fives, and stepped up to a very great height. When the Polish fighters came to meet them, they harassed the Poles and split them up. When the Polish fighters had exhausted their ammunition and petrol the German bombers came in and bombed the aerodromes; they were accompanied by heavy escorts of fighters, and more waves of bombers continued to attack the aerodromes in order to catch the Poles when they landed. The radio signals from the first wave of fighters were intercepted. They kept their Control stations informed of the conditions of the Polish squadrons through the attack. In some cases they drew the Polish Squadrons away from the real objective of the attack and kept them occupied until their own bombers had finished their task and escaped."

The day proved to be happy one for Sgt Josef František, who was awarded the DFM. This was the first British award for a 303 Squadron pilot. In the recommendation, dated 7 September 1940, his Squadron Leader wrote:

"This pilot has proved himself exceptional not only as a pilot, but in fighting. He has taken part in practically every operational flight carried out by this Squadron and has accounted for the following enemy aircraft. 3 Me 109s, 1 Heinkel 113, 1 Junkers 88. These victims are the result of only one week's operations. This pilot not only has a fine spirit, but is an excellent NCO showing a great example to others in his Flight."

G/Cpt Vincent, Northolt Station Commander added that František:

> "at all times showed great gallantry in attacking vastly superior numbers of enemy aircraft."

18 September 1940

303 Squadron again took part in several patrols during the day, although that undertaken during the morning did not bring any encounters. After coming back to Northolt, the squadron was inspected by Gen. Władysław Sikorski, the Polish Commander-in-Chief. During this visit he awarded pilots of this unit with the highest Polish decorations: S/Ldr Krasnodębski, F/O Paszkiewicz, F/O Januszewicz, P/O Zumbach, P/O Ferić, F/O Urbanowicz, F/O Henneberg, F/O Pisarek, F/O Łapkowski, P/O Daszewski, P/O Łokuciewski, Sgt František, Sgt Szaposznikow, Sgt Karubin, Sgt Wünsche, and Sgt Wójtowicz were all awarded the Cross of Virtuti Militari (the highest Polish military decoration), while F/O Wodecki (medical officer), F/O Cebrzyński, Sgt Rogowski, and Sgt Brzezowski received the *Krzyż Walecznych* (Cross of Valour).

The visit was suddenly interrupted by a scramble at about 12:20 in which a dozen 303 Squadron Hurricanes joined 229 Squadron aircraft.

The Polish Hurricanes were as follows:

"A" Flight

S/Ldr Kellett	V6684/RF-F	Red 1
P/O Zumbach	V6681/RF-B	Red 2
P/O Ferić	V7244/RF-C	Red 3
F/O Urbanowicz	P3120/RF-A	
F/O Henneberg	V6665/RF-J	
Sgt Andruszków	P3901/RF-E	

"B" Flight

F/O Paszkiewicz	V7235/RF-M
F/O Żak	L2099/RF-O
Sgt Kowalski	P3089/RF-P
Sgt Wojciechowski	P3975/RF-U
Sgt František (Czech)	V7465/RF-V
Sgt Bełc	V7289/RF-S

After climbing to an altitude of 25,000 feet they appeared to be south of Biggin Hill. They saw and investigated many formations of friendly fighters. After nearly an hour flying they sighted an aircraft again identified as a Do 215 returning southwards at about 17,000 ft. The three leading sections went in to attack the Dornier from which three members of the crew baled out; the aircraft bomber fell in fields ten miles south of West Malling and broke up.

Sgt František who was "weaving" behind the squadron, seeing that it was unnecessary for him to follow the Hurricanes to attack the Dornier remained above:

> "I remained alone above them, and on a course looking towards the Channel I saw an Me 109 to the East of me proceeding southwards. It was going fast and the

engine was smoking a little. I dived towards it, and caught it up near the coast. I attacked it from starboard and a quarter behind. I gave it a burst into the engine without effect, then I gave it another burst into the engine and cockpit and it fell into the sea in flames. I think it is possible that this Me 109 had been fighting with our aeroplanes before I came upon it. When I returned to land I found F/O Ferić and we flew back to Northolt."

All were back at Northolt about 1.40 pm. Two Hurricanes were shot-up by friendly fighters but there is no record of how this happened – possibly due to a degree of over-enthusiastic firing at the lone Dornier. The victim this time appears actually to have been one of the rare Do 215s, one of the aircraft, Werk Nr.0038 coded G2+KH which crashed at Collier Street near Yalding. This bomber belonged to 4./*Aufklärungsgruppe Oberbefehlshaber der Luftwaffe*.

Almost at the same time as 303 Squadron left Northolt, 11 Hurricanes of 501 Squadron departed Kenley, sent together with 253 Squadron to the West Malling area. They sighted about 20 He 111s escorted by six waves of Bf 109s. S/Ldr Hogan who led the formation was shot down and had to bale out. The only success for his unit was credited to Blue 1 who was Polish. As in the previous missions there were two Poles amongst the County of Gloucester Squadron pilots: F/O Stefan Witorzeńć and Sgt Antoni Głowacki. The latter was the author of the claim for a Bf 109 probably destroyed.

"I was Blue 2 when the Squadron was ordered to patrol West Malling at 20,000 ft. We sighted 20 bombers approaching Maidstone at 18,000 ft and saw how they turned back towards France on being attacked by Spitfires which engaged the large fighter escort. A. A. fire was bursting among the bombers. A parachute below the bombers was attacked by two Me 109's at about 15,000 ft. I turned and attacked one of them from beam and quarter, and after my second burst he dived vertically from 15,000 ft down to a patch of cloud at 3000 ft. The last two bursts I fired as he dived dead astern. When he reached the cloud I went round it, having pulled out of the dive just in time. I waited on the side towards the French coast to intercept him but saw no trace of him. At the speed with which the Me 109 was travelling (i.e. 400 mph) it is not possible that he could have pulled out below 3000 ft. Had it done so, I must have seen him as I placed myself directly on his path home. It is most probable that it went straight in SW of Maidstone."

The parachutist, apparently under attack by Messerschmitts when spotted by Sgt Głowacki, was probably one of three pilots lost by 46 Squadron. One of them, Sgt G. W. Jefferys, was officially listed as killed due to parachute failure.

About 4.15 pm 302 Squadron was scrambled for the third time that day. The first two patrols provided no success, nor even contact with the enemy. This time luck was with them:

S/Ldr Satchell	P3812/WX-L	Red 1
S/Ldr Mümler	P3538/WX-J	Red 2
F/O Kowalski	P3935/WX-D	Red 3
F/Lt Farmer	V6734/WX-K	Yellow 1
F/Lt Łaguna	R2684/WX-B	Yellow 2

Sgt Wędzik	P2752/WX-R	Yellow 3
P/O Pilch	V7417/WX-T	Green 1
Sgt Paterek	P3086/WX-Z	Green 2
P/O Karwowski	P3085/WX-A	Green 3
F/Lt Riley	V6735/WX-M	Blue 1
F/Lt Jastrzębski	P3930/WX-X	Blue 2
P/O Wapniarek	P3924/WX-Y	Blue 3

The Duxford Wing again appeared as it had on 15th joining the battle south-east of London. Their opponents were spotted at an altitude of 16,000 ft. 302 was the last of three Hurricane Squadrons flying in line astern, with two squadrons of Spitfires on the flank above. About 5.20 pm some 30 enemy bombers were sighted, flying north-west in vics of five. As the wing approached, the enemy aircraft turned to starboard and the wing attacked in squadrons line astern. No fighter escort was seen, and 302 Squadron headed for the inside formation as it turned. The enemy formation was very loose by now, and S/Ldr Satchell attacked an aircraft to the right of the main body together with two Hurricanes of his Red Section. After two or three attacks from above by Satchell, his victim turned south, losing height. Satchell followed, and closing to about 80 yards got in a good burst from astern, after which the port engine caught fire. Then the bomber disappeared into a cloud and was not seen again. Before breaking away, the windscreen of Satchell's Hurricane was covered with oil from his burning and smoking target.

Satchell then noticed the crash sites of two enemy bombers shot down during this engagement. One crashed in flames into the sea off Sheerness and another on the peninsula between the Medway and the Thames; both were from 8./KG 77, which formed part of the formation attacked by Duxford Wing. Satchell and his wingman claimed one Dornier destroyed each. S/Ldr Mümler, who was flying as Satchell's wingman, attacked the enemy aircraft on the port side of the formation. He got in a long burst of about five seconds at 150 yards, then breaking away to make room for other Hurricanes. As he did so he definitely noticed flames coming from the rear gunner's turret. F/O Julian Kowalski, flying as Red 3, attacked a "Do 215" (as stated in his report) with a right hand turn from above, getting in two bursts, but he too had to break away sharply to make room for another section which was attacking from behind. Then Kowalski attacked a second Dornier, getting in three long bursts. At his last burst he noticed a full size parachute open from the rear gunner's turret, and become entangled in the tailplane. Bits of the enemy aircraft flew off the mainplane, causing him to break off the combat temporarily. After attacking another Dornier without apparent effect, Kowalski returned to base, and reported a "Do 215" probably destroyed.

The Yellow Section followed in line astern behind the leading section. The section leader, F/Lt Farmer, attacked a Do 17, firing in a burst about four seconds with no apparent results. Farmer then broke away to the west, and chased a Ju 88 which had left the formation. He fired the rest of ammunition and pieces of the aircraft flew off before it disappeared in the clouds; he claimed one Ju 88 damaged.

Yellow 2, who was F/Lt Piotr Łaguna, attacked with his section but could not focus his sights properly and was afraid of hitting another aircraft. The other wingman of Yellow Section, Sgt Marian Wędzik, broke away after his first attack on the bombers and then chased a Ju 88 together with another Hurricane. They followed their prey out to sea, forcing it down to 1,000 ft, attacking alternatively. Pieces fell off the enemy aircraft, but due to lack of ammunition Sgt Wędzik had to give up the chase.

Green Section attacked in turn from above and behind, causing the rest of the enemy formation to break up. Green Section leader got in two bursts at an aircraft in the middle of the formation, and noticed bits of metal flying off. Then P/O Pilch chased another Ju 88, like his comrades from the first two sections. The upper gunner of the Ju 88 under attack fired at Pilch constantly, as he attacked five times. After his first attack he noticed smoke coming from the port engine, and after the fourth the whole port engine was enveloped in flame. After his fifth attack another Hurricane attacked the enemy aircraft and one crew member baled out; Pilch reported one Ju 88 destroyed.

Sgt Paterek, flying as Green 2, chose a Ju 88 on the left of the formation and his first attack caused a port engine fire, which "burned well". After the next attack, Paterek saw three of the bomber crew bale out, and their parachutes opened at once. Another burst of fire caused pieces to fly off and hit his propeller, which made his aircraft flutter violently. An object from the enemy aircraft, possibly one of the crew, hit his radiator, and his reserve petrol tank broke, covering him with petrol. He switched off his engine and glided to earth, seeing the enemy bomber crash from 2,000 ft. He crash-landed at Sandon Lodge Farm, Danbury, and his aircraft sustained no further damage. Sgt Paterek reported one Ju 88 destroyed.

P/O Karwowski attacked the bomber formation twice without visible effect and eventually went for another aircraft flying immediately below him. He got in three bursts from a beam attack and saw some object fly away from the enemy aircraft which dived violently into the sea. At the same time one of the crew members baled out and opened his parachute. P/O Karwowski, who reported one Ju 88 destroyed, probably attacked the same aircraft as P/O Pilch.

Blue Section, led by F/Lt Riley, attacked from above and to starboard with the rest of the squadron. The Composite Combat Report said:

> "Blue 1 singled out a Ju 88 and fired 3 bursts of 3 seconds each from about 150 yards closing to less than 100. E/A fire ceased at once and both engines gave out much black smoke while very large pieces of fuselage dropped off causing the enemy aircraft to dive away apparently out of control. Blue 1 broke away to inspect fighters behind. Blue 1 then attacked another Ju 88 firing the rest of his ammunition and causing the E/A port engine to smoke fiercely while pieces flew off the fuselage and a stab of flame was seen to appear from the port side of the E/A fuselage. E/A dived sharply away. The second attacks were made from the port quarter of the E/A and astern. Blue 1 returned to base through lack of ammunition his a/c undamaged."

F/Lt Franciszek Jastrzębski, who later reported a Do 17 probably destroyed, attacked several times three different aircraft, expending all his ammunition. Only one bomber attacked by him dived sharply, probably evading his attacks. Later Jastrzębski saw seven bombers from the attacked formation returning in close formation across the Channel to France.

The last pilot of 302 Squadron to attack the bombers was P/O Stefan Wapniarek, who claimed a Ju 88 shot down. He attacked the aircraft on the right of that attacked by his section leader. His second pass on the same aircraft took place immediately after another Hurricane had attacked it, while Wapniarek was turning. As he approached, he saw black smoke issuing from the Junkers. After his subsequent bursts the rear gunner baled out near Southend on Sea. Later Wapniarek noticed another Ju 88 trying to escape into cloud and he attacked this. The rear gunner fired at him continuously, while he was closing to less than 100 yards. Due to shortage of ammunition (about 50 rounds for each gun) Wapniarek decided to make one, but well prepared attack. He fired all the ammunition from very close range, and the bomber glided down to crash into the sea, where it broke up completely. Wapniarek checked that it took him eight minutes flying over the sea before he reached the coast and landed at Rochford aerodrome.

The claims by 302 Squadron (seven bombers destroyed, three probable and one damaged) plus more then 15 claims by other pilots of Bader's wing, compare badly with the actual losses of Luftwaffe units taking part in this engagement – four bombers destroyed! Overclaiming caused by several pilots shooting at the same enemy aircraft was evident.

19 September 1940

Due to the strong defence of the British Isles by Fighter Command, Operation *Seelöwe* was postponed indefinitely by Adolf Hitler, but Luftwaffe aircraft were ordered to continue their attacks. German activity on 19 September was much reduced due to weather conditions however. Only lone raiders were sent, and some of these were intercepted by RAF fighters. One of such intruders was caught by 302 Squadron. "B" Flight took off from Duxford at about 10.25 and was directed over London. The group of fighters which attacked a Ju 88 was as follows:

F/Lt Jastrzębski	P3930/WX-X
P/O Pilch	V7417/WX-T
Sgt Markiewicz	P2752/WX-R
Sgt Wędzik	P3923/WX-U
F/Lt Riley	V6735/WX-M
F/O Kowalski	P3935/WX-D

The Operations Record Book stated:

> "Enemy aircraft caught fire after being attacked and dived steeply through clouds. After gliding for about two minutes it crashed to earth about four miles N.E. of Brandon."

The 1./KG77 Ju 88A-1 (Werk Nr. 2151, coded 3Z+GH) fell at Culford School, Bury St Edmunds with three of the crew on board. The only airman to survive was Uffz. E. Etzold, who baled out and was taken prisoner. The Junkers was credited to F/O Julian Kowalski.

20 September 1940

Two waves of Bf 109s flying *Freie Jagd* sorties were the main Luftwaffe action over England this day. Four Spitfire squadrons sent against them caused loss of three Messerschmitts. The only Hurricane unit engaged was 605 Squadron.

The 605 Squadron ORB stated:

"The squadron did one patrol today and encountered only Me 109's and He 113's. They were adopting different tactics from usual, flying alone, in two's, three's or four's over a wide area, which our pilots found very harassing, never knowing when they would swoop down upon them . . ."

This meeting with Luftwaffe *Jägers* ended with damage to two Hurricanes. One of the unfortunate pilots was P/O Witold Głowacki, who had been transferred from 145 Squadron to 605 on 31 August. The Bf 109s bounced the surprised pilots of 605 Squadron, and after a rather chaotic combat, P/O Głowacki returned to Croydon in V6722, hit by a 20 mm cannon shell. The effective shot probably came from a 6./JG 26 Messerschmitt flown by Obfw. Gottlob, who claimed two Hurricanes shot down in this encounter.

21 September 1940

F/O Juliusz Topolnicki, who had meanwhile returned to 601 Squadron, following his engagement on 6 September, burned to death in his Hurricane L1894 during take-off from Exeter at about 11.30 am. His aircraft had hit another machine of the same Flight and run into an anti-aircraft gun post. Topolnicki's friends included a short note about him in the 303 Squadron chronicle, and his efforts in the struggle in the skies over Britain were described there by F/O Z. Bieńkowski:

"F/O Topolnicki Juliusz posted in August 1940 to 601 Squadron at Tangmere shot down two Me 109s – was shot down himself and baled out, luckily landing in a tree. Before his numerous wounds healed completely he escaped from the hospital in a pair of borrowed trousers.

"He was killed while taking off for a combat sortie . . ."

23 September 1940

About 9.30 am a dozen Hurricanes of 303 Squadron took off from Northolt. They were as follows:

"A" Flight

F/Lt Kent	V6681/RF-B
P/O Ferić	P3901/RF-E
Sgt Szaposznikow	V7244/RF-C
F/O Henneberg	V7246/RF-D
F/O Januszewicz	P3544/RF-H
F/O Grzeszczak	V6684/RF-F

"B" Flight

F/O Żak	V7289/RF-S
Sgt František	V6673/RF-U
Sgt Bełc	V7465/RF-V
F/O Paszkiewicz	V7235/RF-M
Sgt Kowalski	P3089/RF-P
Sgt Wojciechowski	L2099/RF-O

The formation, led by F/Lt Kent, was joined by Hurricanes of 1 RCAF Squadron and 229 Squadron. The three squadrons were directed south of Biggin Hill, and then towards the Thames Estuary. Here they spotted about 20 Bf 109s above, circling at an altitude of 25,000 to 30,000 ft. While the whole wing was climbing to reach these intruders, another formation of 20 Bf 109s came from behind, trying to break up the Wing formation. In defence, the Hurricanes turned to the attack. Sgt Szaposznikow, one of two victorious pilots of 303 Squadron that day, wrote:

"I saw about eight Me 109s attack an isolated Hurricane of another Squadron. This Hurricane shot at the Me 109 which rolled away right. I attacked it from astern and underneath at 300 yards. The Messerschmitt dived down towards the sea. I used up all my ammunition on it, and it crashed into the sea in mid Channel."

F/Lt Kent performed a similar action, which also ended with shooting down a Bf 109 into the sea, but his efforts did not end with the one claim. He recalled:

"Without waiting for him to hit the water I turned for home. As I approached Dungeness I saw an aircraft low over the water and about five miles off shore. I flew towards it to investigate. It was with some surprise that I discovered it was a German machine – just what type I have never been absolutely sure, but from the recognition manuals it most closely resembled a Focke Wulf 158[46] – although I can't imagine what such a machine would have been doing there unless it was somehow connected with an air-sea rescue system. At any rate, it had large black crosses on it and that made it fair game. I immediately attacked, my first burst splattering around the rear cockpit, but I got no return fire so I had probably killed the rear gunner. On my second attack only a few bullets were left and my guns stopped almost immediately after I pressed the gun button. To my disgust I could do nothing but watch as the German headed towards France as fast as he could go."[47]

303 Squadron was reinforced by three NCO pilots who had been flying in 302 Squadron: Sgts Palak, Paterek and Siudak.

The windy morning with much broken cloud resulted in almost a repeat of the actions of 20th, when 605 Squadron was again engaged by *Freie Jagd* Messerschmitt 109s over Tunbridge Wells. The pilots involved were as follows:

S/Ldr Burront	P3677	Red 1
P/O English	N2557	Red 2
Sgt Jones	V6699	Red 3
P/O Muirhead	R4118	Yellow 1
P/O Głowacki (Polish)	P3583	Yellow 2
P/O Milne	P3832/UP-P	Yellow 3

This time however the RAF pilots were not surprised and managed to engage their attackers. P/O Witold Głowacki:

---

[46] As stated in Kent's memoirs. 303 Squadron ORB described this aircraft differently: "On returning F/Lt Kent saw probably a Potez flying low towards France . . ."
[47] Kent, *One of the Few*.

"While on patrol near Tunbridge Wells we were attacked by two Me 109s which dived on us out of the sun. The squadron was circling righthanded and losing height when a Me 109 broke into the formation firing at me. I was then rather higher than the rest of the squadron and the Me. after a short burst over-shot me and I was able to give him a long burst from 300 yards closing to 50 yards. I saw him shudder and try to climb away, but he could not do so and dropped away. This is confirmed by Yellow 1 but neither of us could watch him as another Me 109 was then in position to attack and we had to break away. The second enemy aircraft climbed back to join the rest of the formation alone."

During a midday patrol north of London, P/O Jan Pfeiffer of 257 Squadron had trouble with his Hurricane I, P3717/DT-R. While patrolling out of Castle Camps, he damaged his engine cowling when force-landing in a field.

24 September 1940

This day brought an end to the short history of P/O Witold Józef Głowacki's service in 605 Squadron. While on patrol over Beachy Head, P/O Głowacki together with P/O James Muirhead chased a Do 17Z. They followed an aircraft that belonged to 2./KG 76 (Werk Nr. 3317, coded F1+GK), repeating their attacks until it finally crashed five miles west of Cap Gris Nez. On the way back both were engaged by three Bf 109s. P/O Muirhead turned about and flew 21 miles inland over France, where finally he shook off the Messerschmitts and returned safely to base. Sadly, P/O Witold Głowacki was not so lucky. He was shot down immediately and crash-landed his Hurricane P3832/UP-P, which broke apart near Albermuse. Photographs taken by German propaganda just after the crash showed the Polish pilot in quite a good shape, with bandaged head. However, he was reported dead the same evening. The mysterious death of Głowacki in a Luftwaffe hospital gave birth to a story, later widespread among airmen, that the Germans killed Polish pilots. It seems more probable, however, that he died from an allergic stroke to an anti-tetanus injection.

25 September 1940

A precision attack of German bombers, escorted by Bf 110s, on the Bristol Aircraft factory at Filton surprised the Operations Room controllers of 10 Group, who had expected another raid against the Westland works at Yeovil. Not until they left their target, were the bombers caught by Hurricanes of 238 and 601 Squadrons, as well as by Spitfires of 152 and 609. Polish pilots excelled in three of those units.

P/O Władysław Różycki of 238 Squadron, flying Hurricane I P3618, claimed one He 111 destroyed during his one and a half hour mission, while other pilots of this unit claimed five destroyed and two damaged.

601 Squadron pilots taking part in the same engagement were:

F/O Mayers	R4218	Red
P/O Aldwinkle	P3675	Red
F/O Jankiewicz (Polish)	V6666/UF-J	Red
Sgt McCann	P2949	
P/O Grier	V6649	
Sgt Hetherington	V7236	

F/O Jerzy Jankiewicz, flying his favourite Hurricane I, coded with his initial letter, shot down one of the escorting Bf 109s.

"I was Red 2. We took off at 11.20 and were ordered to patrol Portland Bill, then Warmwell, then Yeovil at Angels 15. Sighted enemy formations a long way off 10-12 miles W of us flying NNW. Formations appeared to be bombers escorted by fighters flying 3000-4000 ft above bombers, and 2-3 miles astern. Turned North as we were ordered to patrol Weston-super-Mare. Orbited over Mendips and saw e/a returning South. Intercepted a few miles West of Frome. We delivered an attack in echelon right on some Me 110's which were wheeling around. Fired 2 short bursts at one e/a then broke away. I then saw an Me 110 which had been attacked by Red 1 with smoke coming from it, then saw some Me 110's below me and attacked a straggler from astern. The rear gunner returned my fire, and I saw black smoke coming from one engine. I broke away and renewed my attack. The rear gunner ceased firing and the other engine started to emit black smoke. By this time I was south of Shaftesbury and my ammunition ran out. I followed Me 110 South still with smoke coming from both engines and losing height and 7 miles NW of Bournemouth the e/a was at 6000-7000 ft. I was then about to be attacked by two other Me 110's and therefore broke away, dived low, and returned to base, landing at Exeter at 12.30. I carried no camera gun.

"Signed: F/O G[48]. Jankiewicz."

609 Squadron documents recorded that its Spitfires took part in a big battle just before noon. Over 200 Dorniers and Heinkels in three arrowheaded formations, escorted by at least 30 Messerschmitts, were caught just south of Bristol.

"The city's anti-aircraft fire, though well meant was more then disturbing for our pilots, none of which, however, were hurt. The Squadron obtained a very good bag, at the expense of only one machine (P/O Ogilvie) damaged by enemy fire."

Those responsible for enemy casualties were:

S/Ldr Darley	1 Do 17 and Me 110 damaged
F/O Dundas	1 Do 17 destroyed
Sgt Hughes-Rees	1 Do 215 destroyed
P/O Ogilvie	1 Do 17 probable
Sgt Feary	1 Do 215 damaged
P/O Staples	1 Me 110 probable
F/Lt McArthur	1 Me 110 destroyed
P/O Miller	
P/O Agazarian	} 1 He 111 destroyed
P/O Urwin-Mann (238 Sqn)	
P/O Curchin	1 He 111 destroyed
	1 He 111 destroyed (shared with P/O Wigglesworth, 238 Sqn)
F/O Nowierski	1 He 111 destroyed

---

[48] G – for George, English equivalent of his Polish name Jerzy. At that time Jankiewicz was one of the relatively few Polish airmen with quite fluent command of English.

"Several very good Cine-gun films emerged from this engagement."

Some of the footage of these cine-gun films exists to this date and is very interesting, indeed . . .

The Polish-manned 308 Squadron that had formed on 9 September, moved on 25 September 1940 from Speke to Baginton near Coventry. Its teething troubles were described in the squadron chronicle:

"We find the same difficulties here: lack of accommodation, the airfield is not equipped, still in construction, and only temporarily usable. Officers are accommodated in The Chace Hotel nearby with the ranks at the aerodrome. With a single Fairey Battle and a single Master, we commence our training."

In the history of 308 Squadron compiled after the war, F/Lt (P/O in 1940) Stanisław Wandzilak wrote:

"Immediately upon arrival at the new aerodrome, witnessed by the whole squadron, a Ju 88 bombs a factory in the centre of Coventry, flying across the entire balloon barrage. This speeds up the rate of our training."

26 September 1940

On 26 September 302 Squadron moved from Duxford to Leconfield.

Morning patrols by a few RAF fighter squadrons, sent against *Freie Jagd* Messerschmitts and some lone bombers, brought no spectacular success. 249 and 253 Squadrons were scrambled to intercept a single Dornier; 249's Red Section was able to chase and damage the Do 17, but believed that it would get back to France with a bit of luck. Less lucky was 253 Squadron, bounced by Messerschmitt Bf 109s of II./JG 77. They lost two Hurricanes and one pilot in action about 11.00 am. F/Lt G. R. Edge had to bale out and was rescued by a boat, but the Polish pilot P/O Włodzimierz Michał Czech Samoliński was shot down into the sea and killed.

The main Luftwaffe attack of the day became evident to the air controllers about 4 pm. Bombers of KG 55, escorted by fighters, headed towards the Spitfire factory at Woolston. Soon RAF fighter squadrons were airborne, but failed to prevent the bombers from reaching their target and causing much damage.

Exeter-based 213 Squadron was one of the first units to reach the raiders, but too late. F/O Marian Duryasz, flying Hurricane I V6541/AK-I, was the only pilot to engage in combat with a positive result. He claimed a Heinkel 111 probable. In his combat report he wrote:

"I was Red 3 and took over from Red 1 as his wireless was not working. We were given a vector of 260 degrees and then 280 degrees and after a few minutes I saw AA fire over Southampton. I became separated and saw enemy bombers approaching from SW. I climbed and waited about 1000 yds to the side of them until they turned back. AA fire had broken up enemy formation and I saw and attacked one of them. I carried out a stern attack and after two bursts he started gliding down. I followed firing all the time. I did not experience any return fire. I ceased attacking when I was out of ammunition. When last seen e/a was still going down and I left him 30 miles from coast 3000 ft up. Both Sgt Stevens who was watching the combat and myself are certain e/a must have landed in the sea."

Then other squadrons ran into the bomber formation. 238 Squadron from Middle Wallop arrived as the bombers were dropping their bombs; pilots of this unit claimed seven enemy aircraft destroyed and five damaged for the loss of one pilot – Sgt Vladimir Horsky (Czech). Two Hurricanes were lost and three others were severely damaged, including L1998 flown by Sgt Józef Jeka. Nonetheless, the Pole was then able to claim two Heinkel 111s, destroyed over the Isle of Wight.

607 Squadron from Tangmere claimed three destroyed and one damaged, but for the loss of one Hurricane only. Needless to say, this unit also included Polish pilots. One of them, P/O Franciszek Surma, described his attack which finished with a chase of a Bf 109 to mid-Channel.

"I was Blue 2 after the first attack on enemy bombers near Southampton. 607 Squadron broke up and individual attacks followed and while over the Solent I met a formation of about 20/30 enemy bombers, probably Ju 88's, turning away from Portsmouth towards the sea. I saw a bomber break away from enemy formation and tried to overtake him. At the same time I saw a Me 109 gliding down behind and above Ju 88. I followed e/a for considerable distance and when several miles south of St Catherines Point I made two or three long bursts from 100 to 150 yds on the tail of e/a who immediately went into a dive and crashed into the sea."

Early in the afternoon RAF Northolt was visited by His Majesty, King George VI. After visiting the Canadians, the King also inspected the "famous Polish squadron no. 303". All airmen on duty lined up and the King shook hands, and exchanged a few words with each of them. Then he was asked to sign the first volume of the illustrated squadron chronicle. As the Royal visit was coming to an end, the squadron was scrambled, two dozen Hurricanes from 303 and 229 Squadrons taking off as the King was leaving the station. About 4.10 pm both squadrons were vectored to the Guildford area to catch raiders attacking Portsmouth. The Polish part of the Northolt expedition consisted of:

"A" Flight

S/Ldr Kellett	V6681/RF-B	Red 1
F/O Januszewicz	P3544/RF-H	
Sgt Andruszków	V6665/RF-J	
F/O Urbanowicz	P3901/RF-E	Yellow 1
P/O Zumbach	V6684/RF-F	Yellow 2
F/O Grzeszczak	P3120/RF-A	

"B" Flight

F/Lt Forbes	V7465/RF-V	Blue 1
F/O Żak	V7289/RF-S	
Sgt František	R4175/RF-R	
F/O Paszkiewicz	V7235/RF-M	Green 1
Sgt Bełc	V6673/RF-U	Green 2
Sgt Kowalski	P3089/RF-P	Green 3

Flying at an altitude of 12,000 ft, as ordered by the controller, S/Ldr Kellett saw anti-aircraft fire about ten miles away in front of the fighters' formation, and then saw a raid approach from the south at 16-17,000 ft. He later wrote:

> "I climbed as hard as I could, continuing on the same vector. I saw about 50 He 111's with their escort a considerable way to their right and above them. Enemy aircraft were dropping bombs along the East side of Southampton Water. They turned sharply to the North of Hamble. I was approaching them up sun, so I wheeled round at full speed and attacked their rear from ¾ astern, and from partially up sun. The enemy aircraft were already in a shallow dive, making full speed for the French coast, and we intercepted their rear at about 14,000 ft over the Solent.
>
> "In view of lack of height and of lateness which necessitated high speed, it was impossible to operate efficiently as a wing. The other squadron was too low, and too far behind to catch the raid."

While Red Section, led by S/Ldr Kellett, went up to engage the fighter cover, other aircraft followed F/O Urbanowicz in an attack against the bombers. Immediately before the attack everybody heard 'Apany Leader Pancake', but this was too late, and 303 Squadron pilots were already shooting at the bombers. F/O Witold Urbanowicz in his third attack shot down an He 111 which

> "fell to earth entirely wrapped in thick black smoke".

His wingman, F/O Jan Zumbach, attacked the last bomber in the formation and it

> "appeared to explode in the region of the cockpit. Enemy aircraft fell out of control to earth."

Then he encountered a Messerschmitt Bf 109 and, after his two attacks,

> "the pilot must have been killed as enemy aircraft dived into the sea without any visible outward sign of damage. [...] Heinkel fell on the coast and Messerschmitt into the sea about 10 miles out."

Thus F/O Zumbach claimed one He 111 and one Bf 109 destroyed. Number three of the Yellow Section also claimed the destruction of one bomber; F/O Grzeszczak wrote:

> "Enemy aircraft began to smoke and dived steeply to sea. At that exact moment my machine was lifted badly owing to a shell bursting underneath me. I made a steep turn to the right breaking formation and joined up with aircraft FR.H which a few moments later let down its undercarriage and landed in a field."

After coming back home, Grzeszczak noticed several machine gun bullets holes in the tailplane of his Hurricane.

Hurricane RF-H (not FR-H, as stated in the report), which Grzeszczak spotted after the combat, was flown by F/O Januszewicz, who force-landed at Wyton Farm near Fareham. Januszewicz was flying in the section that went up with S/Ldr Kellett. It seems that Kellett's other wingman, Sgt Andruszków, did not go after the Messerschmitts, as in his first attack he shot at an He 111, and then at a "Do 215". Probably the aircraft claimed destroyed by Andruszków as a Do 215 was one of the escorting Messerschmitt 110s. His prey, attacked from a very short distance,

> "continued his dive and crashed into the sea."

In the meantime S/Ldr Kellett chased a Messerschmitt Bf 109:

> "I took the leading Me 109. He dived away and I dived after him. His engine caught fire and he crashed into the sea in flames. My throttle stuck open and I had proceeded a long way from the scene of the combat before I was able to control my machine. I then tried to rejoin my Squadron and was attacked unsuccessfully by two Hurricanes."

The Blue Section leader was also attacked by friendly fighters in the later stage of the combat. F/Lt Atholl Forbes attacked a He 111 which began to smoke from the port engine and which he claimed as destroyed because he saw

> "pieces come off and a dense trail of black smoke".

Later Forbes wrote:

> "As I broke away I looked in the mirror, and saw a trail of white smoke apparently coming from my machine. Thinking I might be on fire I prepared to bale out, but as no flames appeared I did a tight turn and found that the smoke had ceased. I found afterwards that an explosive bullet had opened up my port wing about a foot from the tip, leaving a jagged piece of metal sticking up and I assumed that the white smoke was due to condensation caused by the jagged metal in the dive. By the time I had finished investigating the white smoke, the enemy formation was breaking up and was at some distance. I was attacked by two Spitfires, and after evading them it was too late and I had to return to Northolt. Sgt František who was attacking another Heinkel behind me, was able to confirm that my Heinkel crashed soon afterwards into the sea in flames."

Sgt František claimed the destruction of two He 111s, chasing his second bomber over France, and later reporting:

> "I shot enemy aircraft down and he fell to earth in France. It was then that I noticed that I was over France and turned and flew back to Northolt."

Forbes' other wingman, F/O Żak, also claimed the destruction of two He 111s and damage to a third.

F/O Paszkiewicz, leading the rear section, managed to shoot down an He 111 which "burst into flames". Sgt Bełc and Sgt Kowalski both shifted their aim from bombers to Messerschmitts. Kowalski's victim, claimed as destroyed, "dived in smoke to earth" and he did not follow it, but Sgt Bełc, after downing one which fell in the neighbourhood of Portsmouth, chased another up to the French coast and then landed at Biggin Hill.

In spite of the glorious, propaganda-inflated, claims of that day, the *Oberkommando der Luftwaffe* reported that only a few aircraft failed to return from the Southampton area.

27 September 1940

"A great day in the air for the Squadron", reported 605 Squadron's Operations Record Book. "At 9.30 am they encountered 12 Me 110's at 18,000 ft above Kenley, F/Lt Currant, P/O Milne and Sgt Budziński each destroying one, Sgt Wright probably destroying another and F/O Passy damaging another . . ."

The Polish victor of the morning patrol on 27 September, Sgt Jan Budziński, described it as follows:

> "We orbited Croydon for some time, until ordered to attack some Me 110's which were already being engaged South of Kenley. Dog fighting between Me 110's and Spitfires was already going on. The Me 110's were circling, and we had to climb up to them. On my left I saw one Me 110 turning to the left, so I turned left and did a diving quarter astern attack from 250 yards, closing to 30 yards, with a fairly long burst, and I think I killed the rear gunner as he never fired at me. I broke away down and climbed up to the left, and the Me 110 went down a bit and turned to the right. I then did a diving head-on attack at 10,000 ft from 300 yards, closing to 100 yards, and I saw its port engine on fire. The Me 110 went down in flames, fairly gently until quite near the ground, when it dived straight down and exploded on hitting the ground East of Redhill, but North of the railway line. I then returned to Croydon."

His victim was probably the 15./LG 1 Bf 110C-2 Werk Nr. 3533, coded L1+LL, which crashed at Socketts Manor, Oxted – this site matched exactly Budziński's description. Oblt. Weckeisser and his gunner were taken prisoner.

The next two encounters by this unit during the day increased total claims to 6-2-5, but without any further Polish victories.

At the same time, about 9 am, 303 Squadron sent up 11 Hurricanes, accompanying the aircraft of 1 RCAF Squadron. The fighter formation was directed south at an altitude of 15,000 ft, to intercept about 30 He 111s escorted by "fifty plus" Bf 109s. Almost all aircraft in the German formation met over Horsham had a single white stripe on the tail, which from a distance looked very similar to British fin flash. 303 Squadron attacked in the following order:

"B" Flight

F/Lt Forbes	L2099/RF-O	Blue 1
F/O Żak	V7289/RF-S	
Sgt František	R4175/RF-R	
F/O Paszkiewicz	L1696/RF-T[49]	Green 1
Sgt Kowalski	P3089/RF-P	Green 2

---

[49] Usually F/O Paszkiewicz flew Hurricane V7235/RF-M, and many publications (and his comrades) mention that he died in an M-coded aircraft, but in fact he was shot down in the Hurricane L1696/RF-T. His "personal" V7235/RF-M continued to be used until the end of the Battle of Britain.

"A" Flight

F/O Henneberg	V7246/RF-D	Red 1
P/O Ferić	V6681/RF-B	Red 2
Sgt Andruszków	V6665/RF-J	Red 3
F/O Urbanowicz	P3901/RF-E	Yellow 1
P/O Zumbach	V6684/RF-F	Yellow 2
F/O Grzeszczak	V7244/RF-C	Yellow 3

F/Lt Forbes, who led the Polish Squadron, described his action:

"We were doing a broad side approach when for no reason that I could see, the Canadian Squadron started to wheel to the left on a course parallel with the enemy formation. I started to follow them wondering why they had done this, but was unable to see any other enemy formation, so I headed towards the enemy calling the Canadians by R/T to say that I was taking the lead. I was not hopeful of them hearing me, as I had received no message for some considerable time. I therefore led on towards the enemy crossing underneath the Canadians. After a short while the AA opened up single bursts unpleasantly close and all round me. I looked about to find out what effect it had on the rest of the Squadron, and discovered that I was alone, so I turned West to see what happened to the rest of the Squadron and the Canadians."

A completely different account was given by P/O Zumbach, who flew as a wingman in the rear section:

"After some time had passed I noticed smoke artillery bursts that pointed the direction of the approaching enemy. Almost against my better judgement, I raised my head and started to stare at the blinding sun, which I have never trusted. And indeed! – There they were! At the same time I heard the voice of Ox, who reported a bomber formation to our port. I turned my radio on and shouted in Polish: 'Attention! A hell of 109s above us!' The Squadron, already on its way towards the bomber formation, was hit as if by an electric current. The sections got looser, wingmen started to weave slightly with small esses as they followed their leaders, their attention focused on their backs. That was where the strike would come from any time now. The more dangerous, as it would fall upon us from a great height advantage.

. "Personally, I was in a silly position, as in patrolling I rose some 100 metres above, and now I had to come down, to reach my leader, who had for a while now been shelling the bombers that were approaching minute by minute. I looked ahead of me, in order to find my chief, when suddenly I saw a Hurricane in front of me, going down in a shallow dive with the starboard wing on fire, followed by an Me 109. I pulled up violently and started to shoot, aiming at the tail. The Messerschmitt went across the burst, broke up, and went down. The same moment I received a burst of fire. Fortunately, it went high. I threw my machine in a starboard turn. Two Me 109s went past me. I started to run towards the Sqdn, the first section of which was already pounding the Heinkels."

The burning Hurricane which crossed Jan Zumbach's course belonged to Sgt Tadeusz

Andruszków, who was killed, his aircraft falling at Holywych Farm, Cowden. Two other pilots of "B" Flight ran out of luck. The first two sections, left by F/Lt Atholl Forbes, attacked the bombers; F/O Ludwik Paszkiewicz was shot down immediately after his first attack, as was F/O Walerian Żak. The former crashed at Borough Green. F/O Urbanowicz visited F/O Żak, who had suffered burns, in hospital:

> "It turns out that F/O Żak shot down an He 111 and that very moment he received a lethal burst from behind. His middle tank blew up. He was covered with petrol, and started to burn, he flew on until the fire was out, before opening his parachute. His face is terribly burnt . . ."

Only Sgt Josef František was able to claim a Ju 88 and later a Bf 110 shot down. Sgt Kowalski claimed an He 111 damaged, but his report ends with the words:

> "Enemy aircraft began to fly South losing height. I returned to Northolt through lack of ammunition."

"A" Flight, led by F/O Henneberg, was in big trouble. After shooting down one Messerschmitt 109 which "burst into flames and fell to earth", his aircraft was hit by three cannon shells. When smoke began to fill the cockpit, Henneberg immediately headed back to Northolt, where he landed safely with a punctured radiator. Sgt Andruszków from the same section was shot down, the other wingman, P/O Ferić, being left on his own. Later he described the action:

> "I attacked an Me 109, and after a short burst enemy aircraft exploded into flames and crashed to earth. I then approached the bombers who were already being attacked by some of our aircraft. I attacked a Heinkel and fired three short bursts. The pilot was evidently killed as the machine dived without smoke or flames, and crashed between Croydon and Gatwick. As my aircraft had been hit by machine gun bullets I returned to Northolt."

The aircraft attacked by many Hurricanes which crashed close to the area described by P/O Ferić would be the Ju 88A-1 Werk Nr. 8095, coded 3Z+HK, of 2./KG 77 which went down in flames and crashed on Folly Farm at South Holmwood.

Like P/O Zumbach, F/O Grzeszczak also noticed Sgt Andruszków's Hurricane chased by several Messerschmitts, one of which he claimed to have shot down. Messerschmitts then attacked his Hurricane, but after evasive action he returned to Northolt. His leader, F/O Urbanowicz, after engaging Bf 109s, noticed about 40 Bf 110s which were making for London in single line astern. He recalls:

> "Several Hurricanes[50] cut them off and enemy aircraft immediately formed a ring. Seeing one enemy aircraft break away from the ring and make as if to return to France I attacked him. I chased him for about seven minutes. During this time I fired several bursts but owing to his continually zig zagging I was unable to score a hit. Approaching however to about 50 yards I fired the last burst. Enemy aircraft began to smoke and falling on its left side dived, and crashed to earth about 35

---

[50] Probably the Canadians.

miles South of London by the side of some railway lines. One of the crew jumped by parachute."

After this attack Urbanowicz tried to attack another 110, but was attacked himself by a pair of Bf 109s. Engaging them, he shot down one which fell in flames. Due to lack of ammunition he then returned to Northolt.

Finally, F/Lt Forbes was back with the squadron, but too late. He saw the attacking Messerschmitts from a distance.

> "I flew towards the diving fighters, but was unable to reach them before they engaged the rest of the squadron. Then I saw a He 111 leave the combat and start diving towards the coast. As no one followed him I dived on to him, and caught him up at about 10,000 ft. I closed and after two short bursts, three or four of the crew baled out. As the enemy aircraft continued in an even dive I thought that the pilot might still be in his place. I therefore decided to destroy the e/a and set fire to the port engine. It crashed in flames either on the shore or just in the sea on the east coast of Kent."

His victim probably ditched in the sea off Lydd. Two crew members of the 2./KG 77 Ju 88 were captured unhurt and two others killed.

P/O Zumbach who re-joined the combat after his attack on a 109, continued in his dramatic manner:

> "I attacked a Heinkel 111 that popped out of the formation. With some others I started to pound him in turns. After a moment the gunner baled out. We were joined by three more machines which, hell knows why, decided it was their duty to shoot at this particular machine, while they had a whole lot of others above us. I got to it once more. After the burst it wheeled and rammed into a small town, knocking one house down and setting another one on fire."

Only seven of 303 Squadron Hurricanes returned to Northolt, some of them badly shot up.

In the meantime, the Luftwaffe attempted to bomb Filton. Just after 11.00 am German raiders were caught by Spitfire and Hurricane squadrons. Sgt Józef Jeka of 238 Squadron, flying the Hurricane P3836, shared in the destruction of one Bf 110 south of Bristol, while his squadron comrades damaged two others. The other unit with Polish personnel that engaged over Swanage was 609 Squadron, flying Spitfires. F/O Tadeusz Nowierski in N3223/PR-M damaged a Bf 110 over Portland.

The next great strike against the London area came about 3 pm. Six Hurricane and seven Spitfire squadrons were ordered to take off in response. About 3.10 pm only six aircraft of 303 Squadron were able to intercept the coming bombers:

"A" Flight

Sgt Szaposznikow	V7244/RF-C	Red 3
F/O Urbanowicz	P3901/RF-E	Red 2
F/Lt Kent	V6684/RF-F	Red 1

"B" Flight
F/O Pisarek	R4175/RF-R
Sgt Palak	L2026/RF-O
Sgt Paterek	P3089/RF-P

They were ordered to take off and rendezvous with 1 RCAF Squadron over base. As soon as all 303 Squadron Hurricanes were airborne, F/Lt Kent, leading the six aircraft, saw enemy bombers coming from the south east towards London. They climbed as rapidly as they could, leaving behind 1 RCAF Squadron which had not finished forming up. "B" Flight section failed to follow the three aircraft of "A" Flight. F/Lt Kent wrote in his combat report:

> "Six bombers turned back long before we could reach them and started a shallow dive for the coast. When we had reached 8000 ft, I saw some bombers on our left at about 15,000 ft. We were ordered to look out for enemy bombers on our right at 15,000 ft – there was nothing in that direction at all. The enemy bombers turned South East. I pulled the plug and flew along level as the bombers were losing height, meaning to intercept them at the coast. There were about seven bombers escaping in very close formation."

After watching Spitfires shoot down one of the bombers, Kent eventually got behind one of the latter. He described further events in a brief but comprehensive note in his logbook:

> "I CAUGHT ONE ABOUT 10 MILES FROM COAST. REAR GUNNER FIRE FAIRLY ACCURATE. NICKED MY AIRSCREW AND WIRELESS MAST. SHOT GUNNER THEN STBD. ENGINE, COCKPIT THEN PORT ENGINE. SMOKING BADLY. JUNKERS JUST CLEARED HOTEL AT HASTINGS AND HIT THE SEA. I SAW ONE MAN SWIMMING."

F/O Urbanowicz, wingman of the leader, attacked one bomber which then smoked for quite a time but did not slacken its speed. After his second burst the right wing of the bomber burst into flames and the aircraft crashed into the sea about 300 yards from the shore at Brighton. Afterwards, Urbanowicz attacked another bomber and after firing for six seconds, this also fell into the sea. Later he recalled:

> "Enemy formation was maintained in flight from London to the coast. Smoking aircraft held their formation until forced to drop behind."

Kent's other wingman, Sgt Szaposznikow, also failed to catch the bombers, later reporting:

> "I was left behind alone as I could not keep up the speed of the others, and was attacked by a Me 109 who dived onto me and then rolled. I got onto his tail and fired two bursts. Enemy aircraft continued its dive and fell into the sea off Brighton."

Top left: A few years before the war Deblin-based Polish Air Force College cadets could hardly have imagined their long journey to Britain. Front row, left to right: Jerzy Czerniak (302 Squadron pilot in the Battle of Britain, KIA in 315 Sqn in 1941); Stanisław Zatorski (shot down by Soviet fighters in 1939). Back row, left to right: Kazimierz Rutkowski (an ace, flew in 306 and 317 Sqns, becoming a Wing Commander later in the war), Leszek Grzybowski (306 Sqn), Marian Szalewicz (316 Sqn), Tadeusz Nowak (253 Sqn pilot in the Battle, later in 315 Sqn, KIA in 1941), Stanislaw Łapka (in 302 Sqn in the Battle of Britain, later OC 306 Sqn), Stanisław Skalski (the Polish WW2 top scorer), Janusz Łabicki (wartime fate unknown). *(CBW)*

Top right: The father of the modern fighter operations in the Polish Air Force – plk Stefan Pawlikowski.
(W. Matusiak)

Middle: PZL P.11's and P.7's of the Advanced Flying Course at Grudziądz in 1938. A year later these obsolete machines took part in combat against top Luftwaffe aircraft. *(T. Kopański)*

Above left: Groups of airmen, often referred to as "Sikorski's tourists", sneaked out from internment camps in Roumania. This particular one was led by por. Witold Urbanowicz (in the middle), the future Battle of Britain ace. October 1939. *(W. Urbanowicz)*

Above right: The main gate of the training camp at Lyon-Bron in France invited them with big sign saying "Polish Army". October 1939. *(Author's collection)*

Bottom: The experienced Polish Air Force personnel did not have much opportunity to prove their value in combat during the Battle of France. Here is one of the sections attached to French GC III/1, consisting of por. Kazimierz Bursztyn, ppor. Władysław Gnyś and ppor. Władysław Chciuk. May 1940. *(Author's collection)*

Above left: A circle of soldiers on a Blackpool beach, watched by a few Britons walking along the promenade. Lack of lecture rooms in the camp caused this unusual sight – this was in fact one of the lectures held in the open air. *(J. Solak)*

Above right: A group of Polish airmen at RAF Eastchurch just after arrival from France. Management of people without any command of spoken English language was difficult. Here, they wear two-coloured bands with numbers, awaiting their postings. In the centre (light jacket) is Piotr Łaguna, soon the OC of the first Polish fighter squadron. *(J. Zieliński)*

Top left: Farewell to France on board s/s "Arandora Star" heading for Liverpool. June 1940. *(G/Cpt S. Wandzilak)*

Top right: The Poles arrive at Blackpool – the PAF main depot in Britain from 1940 throughout the war. 29 May 1940. *(Author's collection)*

Middle: As they marched along Blackpool promenade, groups of Polish airmen were a tourist attraction in 1940. *(J. Solak)*

Bottom left: Poles at the field camp at Gloucester which accommodated over 1,200 airmen (including nearly 250 officers) immediately after the fall of France. June 1940. *(MLP)*

Top: Bird's eye view of RAF Sutton Bridge. No. 6 OTU trained almost all the Poles that joined RAF Squadrons during the Battle of Britain.

(Author's collection)

Middle left: A trio of 145 Squadron pilots. First from the left is F/Lt Roy G. Dutton – 23 years-old veteran of the Battle of France, who led a section which on 19 July 1940 claimed a He 111. In the middle is OC 145 Squadron, S/Ldr John R. A. Peel. At far right is 29 years-old P/O Antoni Ostowicz – the pilot who on 19 July 1940 opened the scoreboard of Polish fighters in Britain, sharing in the destruction of the He 111 with F/Lt Dutton. He was also the first PAF fighter pilot killed in combat in Britain.

(RAF Museum)

Middle right: Sgt Marian Domagała of 238 Squadron –

another Polish victor under the British sky.

(Author's collection)

Bottom left: Another trio: Sgt Józef Kwieciński, Sgt Stanisław Duszyński and Sgt Jan Budziński in June 1940. All of them had served in 4 Pulk Lotniczy (4th Air Regiment) at Toruń before the war. Sgt Kwieciński joined 145 Squadron, and was killed on 12 August 1940. Sgt Duszyński flew with 238 Squadron and was posted missing on 11 September 1940. Only Sgt Budziński survived the war, with two and half victories scored during the Battle of Britain whilst flying with 605 Squadron.

(J. Budziński)

Bottom right: P/O Michał Stęborowski of 238 Squadron also claimed destruction of e/a on 8 August 1940.

(J. Zieliński)

Polish Spitfire pilots during the Battle of Britain. Almost all of them were given nicknames from their British friends.

Top left: "Sneezy" - F/O Henryk Szczęsny. *(W. Matusiak)*

Top right: "Osti" or "Post" – P/O Piotr Ostaszewski in front of his Spitfire I of 609 Squadron. *(W. Matusiak)*

Middle left: "Breezy" – F/O Stanisław Brzezina who flew with 74 Tiger Squadron. *(J. Zieliński)*

Centre: "Big Enough" – P/O Zbigniew Oleński flew with 234 and 609 Squadrons, scoring a kill and a probable in the former. He had been a test pilot in Poland before the war. During the Battle he prepared a comprehensive report on good and weak points of the Spitfire and filed it to RAF authorities, which resulted in his immediate posting to RAE Farnborough. After the war he worked at A.V. Roe, assiting in the Vulcan bomber programme, among others. *(Author's collection)*

Bottom left: "Novi" – P/O Tadeusz Nowierski of 609 Squadron.
(G/Cpt S. Wandzilak)

Bottom right: "Zura" – P/O Janusz Żurakowski also flew with both 234 and 609 Squadrons. In 1944 he became a test pilot, first at the AAEE, and after the war he became a test pilot at Gloster, and subsequently at Avro Canada. *(Author's collection)*

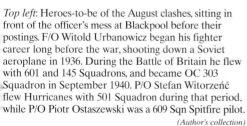

Top left: Heroes-to-be of the August clashes, sitting in front of the officer's mess at Blackpool before their postings. F/O Witold Urbanowicz began his fighter career long before the war, shooting down a Soviet aeroplane in 1936. During the Battle of Britain he flew with 601 and 145 Squadrons, and became OC 303 Squadron in September 1940. P/O Stefan Witorzeńć flew Hurricanes with 501 Squadron during that period, while P/O Piotr Ostaszewski was a 609 Sqn Spitfire pilot.

(Author's collection)

Top right: The tail of Horst Tietzen's Messerschmitt 109E during the painting on of his 17th victory bar on 15 August 1940. In this combat F/O Mieczysław Rozwadowski was killed and F/O Stefan Witorzeńć badly shot up. The latter would take his revenge a few days later, downing a 5./JG51's Bf 109E (probably that of Lt. Hans-Otto Lessing) on 18th. *(Author's collection)*

Middle left: P/O Paweł Zenker before the war. He flew Hurricanes in 501 Sqn in the Battle, but was

killed before August was out. *(J. Zieliński)*

Middle right: Hurricane I R4105/SD-U at Hawkinge. This particular aircraft was flown by P/O Zenker on 18 August 1940 when he destroyed a Messerschmitt Bf 109, believed to have been the 5./JG51's Bf 109E-3 of Hptm. Horst Tietzen (an ace with 27 kills to his credit).

(RAF Museum P017391)

Bottom left: The "County of Gloucester" Squadron Intelligence Officer interviews Sgt Antoni Głowacki after a combat. The background is formed by the latter's lucky Hurricane I V7234/SD-A, which he used to destroy a Ju 87 and damage a Do 215 on 15 August 1940, and to claim five more kills on 24th.

(Author's collection)

Bottom right: The end of the 10./LG 1 Ju 87 Stuka which, chased by Sgt Antoni Głowacki on 15 August, hit RT cables and crashed at Shorncliffe Crescent at More Hall. *(Author's collection)*

Top left: Two Poles, P/O Stefan Witorzeńć (far left) and Sgt Antoni Głowacki (crouching, fourth from right), among 501 Squadron pilots at Hawkinge. Note a 615 Sqn Hurricane in the background. From left to right: P/O Stefan Witorzeńć, Sgt Sidney Anthony Hollingsworth Whitehouse, Sgt Tony Pickering(?), Intelligence Officer, Sgt Paul Caswell Powe Farnes, Sgt Antoni Głowacki, Sgt Robert Chippindall Dafforn, P/O Kenneth Norman Thomson Lee and F/Lt George Edward Bowes Stoney (KIA on 18 August 1940). *(Author's collection)*

Top right: P/O Franciszek Kozłowski, often confused with Sgt Antoni Głowacki in group photos of 501 Squadron personnel. *(Author's collection)*

Bottom left: Polish pilots in the company of their 32 Squadron comrades at the end of August 1940. Left

to right: P/O Jan Piotr Pfeiffer (nicknamed "Fifi"), F/Lt John Bernard William Humpherson, F/O Peter Melvill Gardner, F/Lt (Acting S/Ldr) Michael Nicholson Crossley, F/O Douglas Hamilton Grice, P/O John Francis Pain (Australian). Sitting left to right: F/O Allan Francis Eckford, P/O Karol Pniak ("Cognac") and P/O Bolesław Andrzej Własnowolski ("Vodka"). *(Author's collection)*

Middle right: Sgt *Tony* Głowacki who became an ace in a day on 24 August 1940. He claimed five enemy aircraft during five sorties that day.

(Author's collection)

Bottom right: P/O Stanisław Skalski was another successful Polish pilot of 501 Squadron.

(Author's collection)

b *c* *d*

Top left: Very young P/O Franciszek Surma became a fighter ace serving with nos. 151, 607, 257, 46, 242 and 308 Squadrons. Sadly he was killed on 8 November 1941. *(RAF Museum)*

Top right: Damaged Hurricane I P3320/DZ-Y in No. 1 Civilian Repair Unit at Cowley. On 18 August 1940 P/O Franciszek Czajkowski shot down a Messerschmitt Bf 110 when flying this mount. *(Author's collection)*

Middle left to right:
a. P/O Franciszek Czajkowski was the most successful Polish pilot of 151 Squadron, claiming one Messerschmitt destroyed and two probably destroyed. *(J. Zieliński)*

b. Pre-war photo of P/O Feliks Gmur of 151 Squadron who was shot down on 30 September 1940. *(Author's collection)*

c. F/O Mieczysław Rozwadowski of 151 Squadron destroyed a Bf 109 on 15 August 1940, but was killed during the same combat. This is a pre-war photo. *(Author's collection)*

d. P/O Gustaw Radwański was a successful Hurricane pilot of 151 and 56 Squadron. *(Author's collection)*

Bottom left: P/O Janusz Maciński was with 111 Squadron and was shot down on 4 September 1940 flying one of the first examples of Hurricane II in service. *(Author's collection)*

Bottom right: Hawker Hurricane I V7434/DZ-R of 151 Squadron was flown by P/O Gustaw Radwański on 14 September 1940. *(via A. Thomas)*

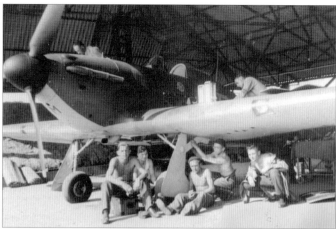

Top left: 303 (Polish) Squadron's first victor, F/O Ludwik Paszkiewicz, shot down a Messerschmitt 110 during the unit's training sortie on 30 August 1940.

(T. Drecki)

Top right: Hurricane V7235/RF-M was Paszkiewicz's lucky mount and he used it during most of his sorties.

(Author's collection)

Middle left: S/Ldr Zdzisław Krasnodębski, the Polish OC 303 Sqn, resting in the shade of a dispersal hut. He would be shot down and badly burnt on 6 September 1940.

(Author's collection)

Middle right: A team of fighters who began the war in September 1939 and still fought on a year later in the Battle of Britain. Left to right: Sgt Stanisław Karubin, P/O Wojciech Januszewicz, P/O Mirosław Ferić and Sgt Eugeniusz Szaposznikow.

(Author's collection)

Bottom: No. 303 Squadron personnel photographed in September 1940. In the middle (wearing Mae West) is F/O Witold Urbanowicz posted to command the Squadron in place of Krasnodębski.

(Author's collection)

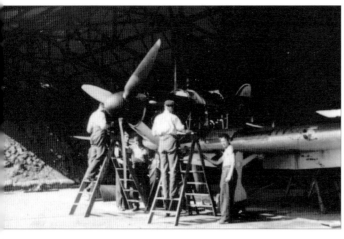

Top left: Another lucky Hurricane I V7242/RF-C under maintenance of 303 Squadron M Flight. This aircraft helped Sgt Eugeniusz Szaposznikow in becoming a fighter ace.
(Author's collection)

Top right: F/O Arsen Cebrzyński of 303 Sqn was shot down on 11 September 1940 and died in hospital eight days later. *(Author's collection)*

Middle and bottom left: Shot up Hurricane I R4175/ RF-R, after landing at Northolt on 6 September 1940. This airplane was usually flown by Sgt Josef František. *(Author's collection)*

Middle right: Sgt Josef František, the Czech ace, standing by the Hurricane I V7389/RF-S. *(Author's collection)*

Right: Tail of Oblt. Gerhard Schöpfel's Messerschmitt 109E displaying his claims. One of the bars stands for a 303 Squadron Hurricane downed on 6 September 1940.
(Author's collection)

Top left: Trio of 303 Squadron sergeants during early September 1940. Left to right: Sgt Michał Brzezowski, Sgt Stefan Wójtowicz, and Sgt Eugeniusz Szposznikow. *(Author's collection)*

Top right: Polish groundcrew posing in front of the Hurricane P3939. Although 303 Squadron did not use national insignia on their Hurricanes, contenting themselves with the "Kościuszko" unit badge, they left the red-and-white checkerboard on this ex-302 Squadron aeroplane. *(Author's collection)*

Middle and bottom right: Heavy losses on 5,6 and 7 September brought replacement aircraft and Hurricane I V6665/RF-J was one of them. The aircraft displays a red band around the rear fuselage which still puzzles RAF historians, and was one of two aircraft in this unit marked in a similar way. *(Author's collection)*

Bottom right: F/O Wojciech Januszewicz of 303 Squadron was shot down three times: on 6 and 26 September, and eventually on 7 October 1940 when he was killed. *(Author's collection)*

Top left: 303 Squadron personnel awaiting His Majesty King George VI on 26 September 1940.

(Author's collection)

Top right: The King with F/O Witold Urbanowicz, the Polish OC 303 Squadron (on the left) and F/Lt Athol Stanhope Forbes, one of the British Flight Commanders (on the right). *(Author's collection)*

Middle left: F/Lt John Alexander Kent (Canadian), with F/Os Walerian Żak and Witold Łokuciewski in front of the dispersal hut at Northolt. *(Author's collection)*

Middle right: The King shaking the hand of P/O Mirosław Feric. Next to the latter is P/O Jan

Zumbach, F/O Bogdan Grzeszczak, P/O Wojciech Januszewicz, and F/O Zdzisław Henneberg.

(Author's collection)

Bottom left: A colourful group of characters: Sgt Tadeusz Andruszków (with flying gear) with ground personnel of 303 Squadron. Next to Andruszków is F/O Hughes (intelligence officer) and F/O Wiórkiewicz, technical officer of the squadron (wearing officer's hat). Sgt Andruszków died in combat the day after the King's visit. *(Author's collection)*

Bottom right: Sgt Jan Kowalski, who shot down a Bf 109 the day the King visited the Polish Squadron.

(Author's collection)

Top left: Another trio of 303 Squadron Battle of Britain heroes. Left to right: Sgt Kazimierz Wünsche, Sgt Stanisław Karubin and Sgt Eugeniusz Szaposznikow. The latter two became fighter aces during the Battle of Britain. *(Author's collection)*

Top right: Hurricane I P3700/RF-E. This aircraft was abandoned by Sgt Kazimierz Wünsche following a dogfight on 9 September 1940. *(Author's collection)*

Middle right: Hurricane I V7504/RF-G in which Sgt Stanisław Karubin claimed his first victory over Britain. He shot down a Bf 109E-1 of 4/JG 53's Uffz.

Karl Vogel near Beachy Head on 30 August 1940.
(P. Paszkowski)

Bottom left: Remnants of P3120/RF-A destroyed by a bomb during an attack at the Northolt aerodrome on 6 October 1940. *(Author's collection)*

Middle lower right: Sgt Antoni Siudak who was killed in this accident. *(Author's collection)*

Bottom right: P/O Jan Kazimierz Daszewski called *Joe*. *(Author's collection)*

Top left: Two fighter aces of 303 Sqn: at left is P/O Jan Zumbach nicknamed *Johann* by his friends and at right P/O Mirosław Ferić called *Ox* (of Swiss and Bosnian parentage, respectively). Thanks to Ferić's memoirs and the unit chronicle he started, we now have a detailed history of this most successful Polish fighter squadron. *(Author's collection)*

Top right: The gallery of aces continues, left to right: P/O Zdzisław Henneberg, F/Lt John Alexander Kent and F/O Marian Pisarek (the latter somehow often mistaken for Ferić, even though there was no physical resemblance between them!). *(Author's collection)*

Middle left: 303 Squadron pilots, left to right: P/O Jan Kazimierz Daszewski, Sgt Mirosław Wojciechowski (standing), F/O Ludwik Paszkiewicz, P/O Witold Łokuciewski, F/O Wacław Łapkowski, sitting in front of a Northolt dispersal hut. *(Author's collection)*

Middle right: S/Ldr Witold Urbanowicz, who downed 15 enemy aircraft during the Battle of Britain. *(Author's collection)*

Bottom: The legendary personal aeroplane of S/Ldr Urbanowicz: the Hurricane P3901/RF-E and her groundcrew. Various accounts tell that this mount had under its cockpit the inscription "We do not beg for freedom, we fight for it". *(Author's collection)*

Top: Famous propaganda picture of 303 Squadron pilots, left to right: P/O Mirosław Ferić, F/Lt John Alexander Kent, P/O Bohdan Grzeszczak, P/O Jerzy Radomski and P/O Jan Zumbach in the background, P/O Witold Łokuciewski, F/O Zdzisław Henneberg, Sgt Jan Rogowski and Sgt Eugeniusz Szaposznikow.

(Author's collection)

Middle left: 303 Squadron emblem with an inscription chalked on to comemorate 126 victories credited to the unit pilots. *(Jan P. Koniarek)*

Middle right: Groundcrew posing in front of the aircraft adorned with the "126 downed Adolfs" emblem. *(Author's collection)*

Bottom left: S/Ldr Witold Urbanowicz, S/Ldr Ronald Gustave Kellett, F/Lt John Alexander Kent and F/Lt Athol Stanhope Forbes after decoration with the Virtuti Militari Cross, the highest Polish military award *(Author's collection)*

Bottom right: S/Ldr Witold Urbanowicz, F/O Jan Zumbach, P/O M. Ferić and F/Lt Zdzisław Henneberg decorated with DFC by AVM William Sholto Douglas *(Author's collection)*

b

c

d

Top left and right: P/O Witold Józef Głowacki of 605 Squadron was shot down on 24 September 1940 over the French coast. German propaganda showed him near the wreck of his Hurricane I P3822/UP-P which fell near Albermuse. Sadly, he survived the dogfight and the parachute jump, but died in a German hospital. *(Author's collection)*

Middle left to right:
a. F/O Marian Duryasz flew with 213 Squadron. *(Author's collection)*

b. P/O Tadeusz Nowak of 253 Squadron. *(Author's collection)*

c. Sgt Szymon Kita of 253 Squadron. *(Author's collection)*

d. F/O Włodzimierz Samoliński of 253 Squadron, killed on 26 September 1940. *(Author's collection)*

Bottom left: Sgt Szymon Kita and Sgt Konrad Muchowski (second and third from the right) in 85 Squadron. *(via A. Thomas)*

Bottom right: P/O Władysław Różycki of 238 Squadron. *(A. Rozycki)*

a   *b*   *c*   *d*

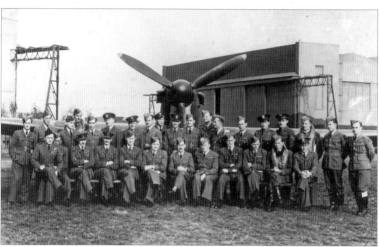

Top left to right:

a. P/O Czesław Główczyński was badly burnt during a training flight and spent weeks in hospital whilst his 302 Squadron colleagues were in the thick of fighting during August and September 1940.

(C. Główczyński)

b. On 15 September 1940, one of the greatest victorious days of 302 Squadron, F/Lt Tadeusz Chłopik shot down a Do 17, but then was killed himself. *(S. Bochniak)*

c. On 24 August F/O Stanisław Chałupa claimed the first purely Polish victory of 302 Squadron.

(J. Zieliński)

d. S/Ldr Mieczysław Mümler, the Polish OC 302 Squadron. He had commanded the Poznań-based fighter *Dywizjon* (a larger unit than the RAF Squadron) in 1939. By the time he took command of 302 Sqn, he had three and three shared kills to his score. *(Author's collection)*

Middle left: 302 Squadron at Northolt. Standing, left to right: P/O Bronisław Bernaś, P/O Władysław Gnyś, P/O Stanisław Łapka, P/O Edward Pilch, F/O Wacław Król, F/O Jan Czerny, Sgt Antoni Beda, P/O Jan Maliński, Sgt Antoni Łysek, Sgt Wilhelm Kosarz, Sgt Marian Wędzik, P/O Aleksiej Żukowski, Sgt Antoni Markiewicz, P/O Stanisław Chałupa, P/O Zbigniew Wróblewski, Sgt Eugeniusz Nowakiewicz, P/O Włodzimierz Karwowski, P/O Stefan Kleczkowski, Sgt Jerzy Załuski. Front row,

left to right: P/O Jerzy Czerniak, F/Lt Franciszek Jastrzębski, P/O Peter E. G. Carter, F/Lt James N. W. Farmer, F/Lt J. A. Thomson, F/Lt Piotr Łaguna, S/Ldr William A. G. Satchell, S/Ldr Mieczysław Mümler, F/Lt William Riley, F/O Julian Kowalski, P/O Tadeusz Czerwiński, P/O Antoni Wczelik.

(Author's collection)

Middle right: F/O Julian Kowalski, victor over the aircraft pictured below. Known as "Roch Kowalski" (a character from a popular Polish novel), he would eventually rise to command 302 Sqn, and then 131 Wing (which included this squadron) at the time of D-Day landings. *(J. Zieliński)*

Bottom: Remnants of the Junkers 88A-1 Werk Nr 2151 at Culford School, Bury St Edmunds, shot down on 19 September 1940 in combat with 302 Squadron. *(Author's collection)*

Top left: P/O Tadeusz Czerwiński posing by his Hurricane II Z2773/WX-T. Not to be confused with two other Polish fighters of the same name (F/O Andrzej Czerwiński and W/O Bronisław Czerwiński), he would lose his life in 1942, while OC 306 Sqn. At the time of his death he had four kills to his credit, of which two were scored in the Battle of France, and one in the Battle of Britain. *(Author's collection)*

Top right: F/Lt Franciszek Jastrzębski, one of the most experienced pilots of the "City of Poznań" Squadron, failed to return from a patrol on 25 October 1940. *(Author's collection)*

Middle: 302 Squadron pilots at Northolt, left to right: P/O Tadeusz Czerwiński, P/O Bronisław Bernaś, P/O Marceli Neyder, unk, P/O Władysław Gnyś, unk, Sgt Norbert Nastorowicz, P/O Władysław Kamiński, Sgt Marian Wędzik, P/O Ryszard Narucki, P/O Stanisław Łapka, Sgt Antoni Łysek, Sgt Stanisław Markiewicz. *(Author's collection)*

Right: Stanisław Łapka of 302 Squadron. *(Author's collection)*

a   *b*   *c*   *d*

Top left to right:
a,b,c. P/O Jan Borowski, Sgt Stefan Wapniarek and P/O Aleksy Żukowski were all killed during one disastrous flight of 302 Squadron on 18 October 1940.
(Author's collection)

d. Sgt Wilhelm Kosarz lost his life during an unexpected dogfight, when bounced by Messerschmitts of II./JG 26 on 8 November 1940. *(Author's collection)*

Middle left: Left to right: Sgt Eugeniusz Nowakiewicz, P/O Władysław Kamiński, Sgt Antoni Łysek, P/O Jan Maliński, W/O Leon Zamiara (one of the most precious ground crew persons in 302 Squadron), P/O Zbigniew Wróblewski and P/O Stanisław Łapka

in front of a Hurricane I WX-A. *(Author's collection)*

Middle right: F/O Marian Pisarek, S/Ldr Piotr Łaguna, P/O Jerzy Czerniak, P/O Tadeusz Czerwiński, P/O Stanisław Łapka at Northolt in 1941.
(Author's collection)

Bottom: Sgt Antoni Łysek, P/O Stanisław Łapka, W/O Paul Harding (Intelligence Officer), Sgt Eugeniusz Nowakiewicz, P/O Włodzimierz Karwowski, P/O Jan Maliński, P/O Władysław Kamiński. The trio of Łysek-Łapka-Kamiński downed a Ju 88 on 28 March 1941.

(Author's collection)

b

c

d

Top left: The Duke of Kent with 302 Squadron pilots. Right to left: Sgt Marian Wędzik, P/O Jan Maliński, Sgt Marian Rytka, Sgt Antoni Beda. Sgt Rytka was shot down over France on 21 May 1941 and managed to rejoin his unit within a few days. *(Author's collection)*

Top right: Left to right: Sgt Marian Rytka, F/O Julian Kowalski, Sgt Antoni Łysek, Sgt Marian Wędzik, P/O Marceli Neyder. *(Author's collection)*

Middle left: P/O Włodzimierz Karwowski on the wing of a Hurricane I WX-R. While flying with 302 Sqn he added a kill and a shared damaged to his score of two shared destroyed from the Battle of France.
(Author's collection)

Middle right: P/O Edward Pilch, who was killed on 20 February 1941 during a training flight. At the time of his death he had two and one shared kills to his credit.
(Author's collection)

Bottom left to right:
a. Włodzimierz Karwowski. After his tour with 302 Sqn he would command a flight in 316 Sqn, and would then become OC 306 Sqn later in the war.
(Author's collection)

b. P/O Zygmunt Kinel was shot down and killed on 8 May 1941, but not before he shot down a Bf 109.
(Author's collection)

c. Sergeant Jan Palak claimed victories in both 302 and 303 Squadrons during the Battle of Britain.
(Author's collection)

d. Sgt Marian Wędzik, who shared a Ju 88 shot down on 16 February 1941 with P/O Edward Pilch.
(Author's collection)

Top left: P/O Paweł Niemiec of 17 Squadron. While flying with that unit he scored one and one shared destroyed plus one and one shared damaged.

(S. Bochniak)

Top centre: P/O Marian Chełmecki of 17 Squadron. His official score in that Squadron was two kills and a shared damaged. *(G/Cpt S. Wandzilak)*

Top right: P/O Tadeusz Kumiega of 17 Squadron. On 29 October 1940 he shared (with Sgt Hogg) in destruction of the Bf 109E-4 Werk Nr 5794 "black 1+" of 8./JG26's Fw. Conrad Jäckel, which crashed at Tillingham. *(S. Bochniak)*

Middle: Wreck of the Hurricane I P2794/YB-E which crashed on 11 November 1940 killing its pilot, Sgt

Hogg. P/O Marian Chełmecki flew this aircraft on 1 and 9 November 1940, his lucky days when he claimed a Ju 87 destroyed and Do 17 damaged.

(RAF Museum)

Bottom left: Sgt Józef Jeka being decorated by Gen. Władysław Sikorski, C-in-C Polish Armed Forces. During the Battle Jeka flew with 238 Sqn, amassing four and one shared victories plus a damaged.

(Author's collection)

Bottom right: The Polish team of 249 Squadron, left to right: Sgt Michał Mirosław Maciejowski, P/O Jerzy Solak, P/O Henryk Skalski, and Sgt Stanisław Brzeski with Pipsqueak, the 249 Squadron mascot.
(Author's collection)

Top left: Karol Pniak (far right) among S/Ldr Stanford Tuck's pilots after their victory over Regia Aeronautica on 11 November 1940. *(Author's collection)*

Top right: F/O Jerzy Popławski, one of the Polish fighter aces, flew with 111 and 229 Squadrons.
(Author's collection)

Middle left: A section of 257 Squadron led by S/Ldr Tuck in V7296 DT-Z. The aircraft V6873/DT-O was flown by P/O Franciszek Surma in November 1940, and later in January by two other Poles – F/O Włodzimierz Łazoryk and P/O Jan Pentz.
(Author's collection)

Middle right: P/O Zbigniew Nosowicz, who scored a probable and a damaged with 56 Squadron also operated from North Weald as 257.

(Author's collection)

Bottom left: Brothers-in-arms, P/O Zbigniew Janicki (Polish) and P/O Karel Mrazek (Czech) in 46 "Uganda" Squadron. Janicki flew with this squadron from November 1940 till January 1941. *(RAF Museum)*

Bottom right: Sgt Romuald Gadus in the cockpit of 501 Squadron Hurricane I V6750/SD-O in early 1941.
(K. Chołoniewski)

Top left: Pilots of 615 Squadron posing in front of Hurricane V7598. P/O Stanisław Czternastek was killed in this aircraft in a mid-air collision on 5 February 1941. *(Author's collection)*

Top right: P/O Stanisław Czternastek who joined 32 Squadron during the Battle of Britain and then 615 in late 1940. *(Author's collection)*

Middle left: North Weald Station Commander, W/Cdr Beamish (with his pipe), flanked by his Polish pilots of 249 Squadron. Left to right: Sgt Michał Mirosław Maciejowski, Sgt Mieczysław Popek and P/O Jerzy Solak. *(Author's collection)*

Middle right: Bronisław Wydrowski piloted the airplane which collided with P/O Czternastek's Hurricane on 5 February 1941. He survived the crash and later flew with 302 and 234 Squadron. *(Author's collection)*

Bottom left: Emblem of 32 "International" Squadron displayed on one of its Hurricane IIs in early 1941. *(Author's collection)*

Bottom right: F/O Jan Falkowski amongst other pilots of 32 Squadron in late 1940. The future fighter ace scored his only victory in 32 Squadron when he destroyed an He 111 on the night of 16 January 1941.

b *c* *d*

Top left to right: Polish fighter pilots flying Spitfires in RAF Squadrons:

a. P/O Jan Rogowski from 74 Squadron in early 1941.
(Author's collection)

b. P/O Walenty Krepski died on 7 September 1940, flying a 54 Squadron Spitfire. *(Author's collection)*

c. Sgt Józef Szlagowski was in 234 and 152 Squadron.
(Author's collection)

d. P/O Jerzy Godlewski who flew Spitfires in 72 Squadron. *(Author's collection)*

Middle: 303 Squadron pilots a few months before conversion to Spitfires. Picture taken at Leconfield at the end of 1940. Among Battle of Britain veterans

there are some new faces of the pilots who joined this unit in November. *(Author's collection)*

Bottom left: P/O Włodzimierz Władysław Mudry, one of two Poles flying with 79 Squadron during the Battle of Britain. Later he moved to 316 Squadron.
(Author's collection)

Bottom centre: Hurricane I W9129/RF-W – one of the Hurricanes taking part in the offensive sweep over France and the low level attack on JG 26 aerodrome on 22 January 1941. *(Author's collection)*

Bottom right: S/Ldr Wacław Łapkowski came back home with HT cable wrapped around the tailwheel of his Hurricane on 22 January 1941. *(Author's collection)*

Top left: A group of 302 and 303 Squadron pilots photographed at Westhampnett on December 1940. Left to right: F/O Bohdan Grzeszczak, S/Ldr Piotr Łaguna, P/O Jan Kazimierz Daszewski, F/O Zdzisław Henneberg, P/O Ryszard Narucki, P/O Mirosław Ferić, P/O Stanisław Łapka, P/O Edward Pilch.
(Author's collection)

Top right: Three successful Sergeants of 302 Squadron (left to right): Eugeniusz Nowakiewicz, Antoni Łysek and Marian Wędzik. *(Author's collection)*

Middle left: P/O Jan Maliński who shared a Ju 88 shot down on 4 March 1941 with Sgt Łysek and F/Lt Kowalski. *(Author's collection)*

Middle right: P/O Marceli Neyder, P/O Wacław Król and P/O Bronisław Bernaś who, on 13 March 1941, chased a Ju 88A-5 of 4.(F)/122 that subsequently failed to return to its base. *(Author's collection)*

Bottom left: Sgt Marian Domagała was shot down by German fighters led by Hptm. Joppien on 8 May 1941.
(Author's collection)

Bottom centre: S/Ldr Piotr Łaguna discussing technical matters with W/O Leon Zamiara. *(Author's collection)*

Bottom right: Hptm Joppien of JG 51 who, together with Fw Erwin Flieg, shot down S/Ldr Piotr Łaguna and Sgt Marian Domagała on 8 May 1941. *(Der Adler)*

Top left: 308 Squadron pilots: P/O Stanisław Wandzilak, P/O Jerzy Tadeusz Skibinski, S/Ldr Walerian Jasionowski, and P/O Bogdan Muth(?).
(G/Cpt S. Wandzilak)

Top right: P/O Władysław Bożek claimed his first success on 26 March 1941. *(Author's collection)*

Middle left: Sgt Mieczysław Parafiński, the first victor of 308 Squadron. *(SHAA)*

Middle centre: P/O Grudziński and P/O Franciszek Kornicki. The former missed his great chance to shoot down 308 Squadron's first Jerry, due to the engine failure of his Hurricane. *(S/Ldr M. Cwynar)*

Middle right: Sgt Jan Kremski who claimed a Ju 88 probable on 26 March 1941, shared with P/Os Bożek and Surma. *(G/Cpt S. Wandzilak)*

Bottom left: P/O Ryszard Koczor was killed on 4 December 1940, the first loss of 308 Squadron.
(G/Cpt S. Wandzilak)

Bottom right: P/O Ryszard Wolski with the squadron mascot, a Scottish terrier called Jumbi. Wolski died in an accident on 11 January 1941. *(G/Cpt S. Wandzilak)*

Top left: 607 Squadron hosted many Poles who then formed the backbone of 316 Squadron. This is a Hurricane I from the period when they were trained. *(Author's collection)*

Top right: Sgt Aleksander Popławski was the only Polish loss in 607 Squadron. He was killed on 11 April 1941 during a combat mission. *(T. Kopański)*

Middle left: Upon leaving 607 Squadron they joined 303 (Polish) Sqn for a short while. Left to right: F/O Wieńczysław Barański, P/O Bogusław Mierzwa, P/O Aleksander Klemens Gabszewicz, P/O Tadeusz Sawicz and F/O Zygmunt Wodecki during training at Northolt. *(Author's collection)*

Middle right: P/O Bohdan Anders. He shared in 316 Squadron's first victory, claiming an He 111 with Gabszewicz. Their victim eventually crashlanded in Ireland. *(Author's collection)*

Bottom left: F/Lt Wacław Wilczewski of 316 Squadron. He crashlanded in his Hurricane I W9231/SZ-L on 17 May 1941 close to a sports ground crowded by Sunday game watchers. *(Author's collection)*

Bottom right: Remnants of Wilczewski's Hurricane I W9231/SZ-L. Unbelievably, he escaped unscathed. *(Author's collection)*

Top: 316 Squadron aircraft clearly displaying the Polish national insignia. A red-white checkerboard painted on the nose, under the exhaust ejectors, this position being characteristic for all their subsequent aircraft as well. *(T. Góra via R. Stachyra)*

Middle left: So-called "Three Kingfishers" in 316 Sqn, left to right: Sgt Romuald Gadus, Sgt Tadeusz Dobrucki and Sgt Paweł Gallus. Like the officers, they too had passed through 607 Squadron. Gallus was an exception, having served with 3 Squadron RAF during the Battle of Britain. *(Author's collection)*

Middle right: P/O Tadeusz Hojden (shown here in a photo taken during the Battle of France) was killed in an accident while on a training flight on 27 March 1941. He was one of three pilots lost by 315 Squadron that day. *(G/Cpt S. Wandzilak)*

Bottom left: Arguably the least fortunate PAF fighter pilot of 1940-1942. After many accidents on Caudron CR.714 Cyclones in France, followed by Hurricanes and Spitfires of 315 Squadron in Britain, P/O Eugeniusz Fiedorczuk met his death in a Spitfire of that unit on 15 August 1942. *(T. Drecki)*

Bottom right: Hurricanes of 315 Squadron soon after this unit was formed. These Hurricanes had Polish national insignia painted on the fuel tank cover in front of the cockpit. *(J. B. Cynk)*

Top left: The first crew of 307 Squadron to claim e/a destroyed (an He 111 on 12 April 1941): the pilot Sgt Kazimierz Jankowiak (left) and the gunner Sgt Lipiński (right) posing in front of the Boulton Paul Defiant N3437/EW-K. Late April 1941. *(Jerzy B. Cynk)*

Middle left: Another view of the same aircraft, showing the code letters EW of 307 (Night Fighter) Squadron. *(Michael Payne)*

Top right: Sgt Jerzy Karais posing in front of the same aircraft at Exeter. He was the air gunner in the crew of Sgt Kazimierz Jankowiak. They claimed an He 111 damaged exactly a month before the Squadron's first kill. *(Chris Goss via Michael Payne)*

Bottom left: F/O Maksymilian Lewandowski of 307

who damaged e/a in March and April 1941, flying a Defiant. Later he became OC of this sole Polish night fighter unit. *(Jerzy B. Cynk)*

Bottom centre: F/O Gerard Ranoszek was also a 306 Squadron pilot when he claimed e/a damaged during the same night. Later Ranoszek moved to 307 Squadron and flew night fighters until the end of the war. Eventually his personal aircraft would sport four swastika kill markings. *(Author's collection)*

Bottom right: F/O Władysław Nowak of 306 Squadron was the first pilot of a Polish day fighter unit to claim destruction of e/a by night, on 11 May 1941. *(Author's collection)*

Top left: 306 Squadron pilots, left to right: Sgt Marcin Machowiak, Sgt Stanisław Wieprzkowicz, S/Ldr Tadeusz Rolski, Sgt Jan Śmigielski. *(Author's collection)*

Top right: Left to right: F/O Władysław Nowak, Sgt Jan Śmigielski, Sgt Władysław Otto Pudrycki and Sgt Leon Kosmowski (on the ground) in front of a Hurricane I displaying the 306 Squadron badge – a flying duck. *(Author's collection)*

Upper middle left: 306 Squadron pilots resting in front of the dispersal hut. Right to left: P/O Petruszka, P/O Marian Skalski, P/O Władysław Różycki and F/O Stanisław Słoński. *(Author's collection)*

Middle left: Inside the dispersal, seated right to left: P/O Marian Skalski, P/O Stanisław Zieliński, P/O Petruszka, P/O Zdzisław Langhamer, P/O Józef Żulikowski, Sgt Jan Śmigielski. At the dart board is Sgt Józef Jeka, and to his left: Sgt Marcin Machowiak(?), F/Lt Kennard, Sgt Leon Kosmowski, S/Ldr Tadeusz Rolski. *(Author's collection)*

Middle right: Sgt Henryk Pietrzak and Sgt Brunon Kroczyński of 306 Squadron sitting on the Spitfire wing. *(via W. Matusiak)*

Bottom: Hurricane Is of 306 Squadron with Polish national insignia painted in a position that was distinct for that unit. *(Author's collection)*

Top left: P/O Matej Pavlovic, another Czech fighter pilot who served and died in 303 (Polish) Squadron. *(via W. Matusiak)*

Top right: Spitfire II P7859/RF-V – the aircraft was lost on 20 April 1940 with its Czech pilot. *(via W. Matusiak)*

Middle left: The succesful team of 15 May 1941 sweep over France: P/O Bolesław Drobiński, P/O Wiktor Stanisław Strzembosz, P/O Matej Pavlovic, unknown (ground crew), Sgt Marian Bełc, unknown (ground crew). *(via W. Matusiak)*

Middle right: P/O Stefan Paderewski. *(via W. Matusiak)*

Bottom: Lady R. Smith-Bingham, who became the Godmother of 303 Squadron on 17 February 1941, among squadron pilots. Standing left to right: F/O Mirosław Ferić, F/O T. B. Simm (British Intelligence Officer), F/O Zygmunt Wodecki (Medical Officer), S/Ldr Wacław Łapkowski, P/O

Witold Łokuciewski, F/Lt Tadeusz Arentowicz (B Flight Commander), F/O Jan Zumbach, F/Lt Witold Żyborski (Sqn Adjutant), F/O Jan Kazimierz Daszewski, F/O Wojciech Kołaczkowski, F/O Wiktor Strzembosz, F/Lt Wacław Wiórkiewicz (Engineering Officer), F/O Bogdan Grzeszczak, F/O L. Marsh (English Teacher). Seated in the middle by the side of Lady Smith-Bingham is S/Ldr Henneberg (OC 303 Sqn). Bottom row, l to r: P/O Bogusław Mierzwa, F/O Zbigniew Kustrzyński, S/Ldr Jerzy Jankiewicz, F/O W. Wittels (British Intelligence Officer). *(via W. Matusiak)*

Top left: On 15 May 1941 a pair of 303 Squadron fighters met a Ju 52/3m over France and duly shot it down. F/Lt Jerzy Jankiewicz was one of the two victorious Polish pilots. *(via W. Matusiak)*

Top centre: Sgt Wacław Giermer who shared in downing the Ju 52/3m of Transportstaffel 1 Fliegerkorps with F/Lt Jankiewicz. *(via W. Matusiak)*

Top right: Generaloberst Ulrich Grauert, a high-ranking Luftwaffe officer killed in the Ju 52/3m downed on 15 May 1941. *(Der Adler)*

Middle: Spitfire II P7786/RF-C of 303 Squadron photographed on 4 April 1941 with Sgt Giermer in

the cockpit. The same pilot flew it on 15 May 1941 when the Ju 52 was downed. Earlier, on 11 March, the same Spitfire was flown by F/O Arentowicz when he and Sgt Popek downed a 77 Squadron Whitley, fortunately without casualties. *(via W. Matusiak)*

Bottom left: P/O Ryszard Malczewski flew Hurricane IIs in 601 Squadron. On 22 May 1941 he claimed a Junkers 52 probably destroyed shared with P/O Donald B. Ogilvie. *(Author's collection)*

Bottom right: In May 1941 601 Squadron changed its Hurricane I's to II's. One of Mk. I's in the picture was flown by P/O Ryszard Malczewski prior to his first victory. *(RAF Museum)*

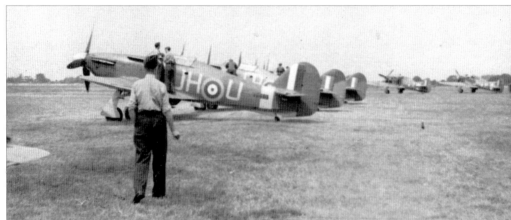

Top left: Sgt. Tadeusz Baranowski – the co-author of 317 Squadron's first victory.   *(S. Bochniak)*

Top right: F/O Paweł Niemiec receives congratulations from S/Ldr Stanisław Brzezina for 317 Squadron's first victory. In the background is Sgt Brzeski, another notable fighter pilot of this unit. F/Lt Henryk Szczęsny stands at far right.   *(S. Bochniak)*

Middle: Hurricane Is of B Flight 317 (Polish) Squadron at Ouston. April 1941.   *(Author's collection)*

Bottom left: 317 Squadron Hurricane I showing its code letters JH and the Polish red-white checkerboard insignia under the cockpit. White name HESIO just above the checkerboard was a nickname of Henryk Szczęsny and appeared on most of his personal aircraft.   *(Dr Jan P. Koniarek)*

Bottom right: P/O Ludwik Martel was flying Spitfires with 54 and 603 Squadrons during the Battle of Britain. Posted to 317 Squadron he had to revert to the obsolete Hurricanes.   *(S. Bochniak)*

In 303 Squadron's diary the day was summarised as follows:

> "This day should be regarded as truly historic, as the Squadron has exceeded the mark of one hundred enemy aircraft shot down . . ."

Next day P/O Mirosław Ferić added to the chronicle:

> "Today we received tragic news, namely that F/O Paszkiewicz Ludwik and Sgt Andruszko [sic] were found. Andruszko had his chest shot through, and a head injury from a cannon shell. 'Paszko', probably killed in his cockpit, fell on southern coast of England and was half-burnt. This was during the morning combat, after the take-off at 9.00 hours on 27 September 1940, when we achieved some 10 victories . . ."

Next day F/O Marian Pisarek became B Flight Commander after the death of F/O Paszkiewicz.

28 September 1940

The main event of the day associated with Polish fighters began about 2.30 pm, when a German formation consisting mainly of Bf 110s approached Southampton. They were engaged off Selsey Bill by three Hurricane squadrons: 213, 238 and 607, all with Polish pilots. Among the Poles only P/O Władysław Różycki of 238 Squadron claimed a victory – the destruction of a Bf 110 over the Isle of Wight. 213 Squadron claimed two Bf 110s destroyed and one damaged. RAF claims were paid for with the loss of six aircraft and five pilots, not including any Poles. On the other hand, Luftwaffe reports failed to confirm the claims, as no Bf 110's were lost on this occasion.

At Speke, the 308 Squadron Officer Commanding, S/Ldr Stefan Łaszkiewicz, crash-landed in Miles Master N8010 due to engine failure and was taken to a hospital, having suffered injuries. He was replaced temporarily by F/O Wiórkiewicz. This accident, together with a lack of flying instructors caused delay in training, and the unit diary reported:

> "The rate of our training is very slow due to lack of equipment and lack of confidence in our flying among the Englishmen, the latter slowly vanishing. Lack of command of English language causes many problems, but everybody is working on it, learning at the moment the most important phrases."

29 September 1940

Decreased activity by the Luftwaffe over Britain gave a break to the exhausted defenders; shortage of serviceable aircraft was also significant. Amongst several reported actions by RAF fighters, only one resulted in an aerial victory for a Polish pilot. A pair of 234 Squadron Spitfires were ordered to intercept a lone aircraft which turned out to be a Bf 110, and was attacked by them five miles south of Exmouth. In his report F/O Żurakowski described this action:

> "I was Blue 2 ordered to Falmouth. I saw anti aircraft bursts but no aircraft. I proceeded to Plymouth. Again saw anti aircraft burst and the enemy aircraft in

front proceeding North East. I chased it and attacked from starboard beam and fired one burst of five seconds. I then broke away and enemy aircraft turned South East. I followed it joined Blue 1 and two minutes later Blue 1 attacked from astern and I attacked afterwards from starboard rear. I saw both engines smoking and then enemy aircraft disappeared into clouds."

Both Janusz Żurakowski, flying the Spitfire I N3191, and his leader, P/O Dewhurst, in X4424, claimed a Messerschmitt *Jaguar* probably destroyed. Their victim seems to have related to the only Bf 110 lost by the Luftwaffe that day, a II./ZG 26 aircraft that crashed at St Aubin aerodrome in France, although none of the crew was hurt.

30 September 1940

The last day of September 1940 was summarised by P/O Radomski, one of the 303 Squadron pilots:

"We take off twice after lunch – nothing. In the afternoon we take off with results, namely F/O Urbanowicz shoots down two Me 109s and a Do 215. Karubin a one-o-nine, and Bełc a Do 215. I damaged a one-o-nine south of the Channel. I was hit, again, but landed safely."

The flight, that ended so safely for P/O Radomski, began about 1.10 pm when a dozen of 303 Squadron's Hurricanes joined 1 RCAF Squadron and 229 Squadron in a "big wing" formation. The Polish Squadron pilots that took part in this engagement were as follows:

P/O Mierzwa	V7235/RF-M	
F/Lt Forbes	P3089/RF-P	
Sgt František (Czech)	L2099/RF-O	
P/O Zumbach	V7503/RF-U	
Sgt Bełc	P3217/RF-S	
Sgt Kowalski	L2029/RF-Q	
S/Ldr Kellett	N2460/RF-D	Red 1
Sgt Karubin	V7504[51]/RF-G	Red 2
F/O Urbanowicz	P3901/RF-E	Yellow 1
P/O Ferić	V6684/RF-F	
P/O Palusiński	V6681/RF-B	
P/O Radomski	P3663/RF-H	Yellow

The formation flew over Dungeness at 14,000 ft and then spotted about 30 Do 17 bombers flying in close formations of nine aircraft, escorted by Bf 109s. This force was on its way back to France. Although other squadrons of the wing were not attacking, 303 Squadron gave chase. Red Section engaged the fighters, although Sgt Karubin was the only pilot of this section to claim enemy aircraft destroyed. He recorded it:

---

[51] Listed as V7505 in 303 Squadron Operations Record Book. That erroneous serial number very often appeared in this document, but in fact such aircraft never flew in this unit.

"After climbing to 22,000 ft I noticed a formation of enemy bombers in one large formation and Me's in loose formation of 2's. I attacked one Me from below firing two short bursts. Enemy aircraft began to smoke, then burst into flames and fell earthward through the clouds. Next I chased the bomber formation towards the coast, but could not get within reach. I saw two enemy bombers break formation and dive to earth."

It is probable that Sgt Karubin, who had recently returned to the Squadron after a short spell in hospital, had shot down Uffz. Karl Vogel of 4./JG 53 near Beachy Head. Vogel's Bf 109E-1, Werk Nr. 6384, marked 'white 3 and bar', crashed, and the German pilot was taken prisoner.

Now the Yellow Section led by F/O Witold Urbanowicz entered the fray and its leader later reported:

"Our Squadron attacked the bombers from behind and above. After the second attack two enemy aircraft broke away from their formation. One smoking fell into the sea. The other was attacked by our fighters and also fell into the sea smoking . . ."

This latter bomber was attacked by P/O Radomski who recalled:

"One enemy aircraft broke formation and I fired a short burst at his cockpit, then another at the left motor, which stopped. I again fired several bursts, and after the last the other machine also stopped. Whilst firing a Spitfire joined me, but after the left engine had stopped flew off. Enemy aircraft fell into the sea about 15 miles from Dungeness.

"During the battle aircraft behaved normally and instrument readings were normal. Returning to Northolt after action, suddenly after what seems to me to be an explosion in the engine, the whole aircraft began to tremble, and smoke, and flames issued from the exhaust, so thick was the smoke in the cockpit that I was unable to take any readings from the instruments. As I was over the Channel at a height of about 25,000 ft I decided not to jump. I closed the throttle, turned out the petrol, and switched off the engine and side slipped as smoke was blinding me. I glided and side slipped as far as the coast and landed on shingles without my undercarriage. From the moment of switching off my engine, petrol, smoke and flames continued to issue from exhaust."

In the meantime, F/O Urbanowicz attacked another Do 17 that was making its way to France very slowly; he did not observe any results from his three short bursts. After that the bomber was unexpectedly joined by two protecting fighters. F/O Urbanowicz described it.

"Thinking that they were ours I joined them in order to attack the bomber together. Getting close to them I discovered that they were two Me 109's protecting the bomber. From a distance of 50 yards I fired a burst at one of them. Next I fired a longer burst at the other Me 109, who did not smoke or burst into flames, but immediately dived headlong into the sea. I again attacked the bomber from a distance of 30 yards to the rear, and fired once more without result. I continued the attack and the enemy aircraft which was now over France, made as if to land, hit the ground with its right wing and burst into flames. None of the crew came out."

Probably his prey was the Do 17Z of 8./KG 2, U5+BS, which crashed and burnt at Bertincourt with all the crew on board.

The rest of the squadron did not claim any damage to enemy aircraft. All, except P/O Radomski, were back at Northolt and ready for the next action. Soon the ten remaining serviceable aircraft were airborne.

"A" Flight

S/Ldr Kellett	N2460/RF-D
Sgt Karubin	V7504/RF-G
F/O Urbanowicz	P3901/RF-E
Sgt Szaposznikow	P3120/RF-A
P/O Palusiński	V6681/RF-B

"B" Flight

P/O Mierzwa	V7235/RF-M
Sgt Bełc	P3217/RF-S
P/O Zumbach	V7503/RF-U
Sgt František	L2099/RF-O
F/Lt Forbes	P3089/RF-P

These Hurricanes left Northolt about 4.40 pm with orders to patrol the base area. Soon the order changed and they were told to join 229 Squadron and 1 RCAF Squadron, which had taken off about 15 minutes earlier. Climbing at full boost, the Flights became separated, and neither was able to join the wing. In the Brooklands area "A" Flight was broken up by Bf 109s, of which F/O Urbanowicz destroyed one. Pilots reported:

"In this area were 150 to 200 Me 109s and 110s and odds were too great. Cloud cover alone saved heavy casualties."

"B" Flight made towards some bombers going south east near Croydon. Then, in the words of the Squadron Operations Record Book:

"Sgt Bełc broke away to protect Hurricane pilot baled out and being attacked by Me's and after seeing him safe never rejoined Flight" (going straight back to Northolt).

Sgt Bełc must have been protecting 229 Squadron pilot, P/O L. B. R. Way who baled out unhurt, and would return safely to Northolt. Some publications quoted the name of Sgt Bełc among the casualties of the day, but this seems to have resulted from a misunderstanding of the above note, as no document seems to confirm this, and he and his aircraft would take part in combat during the next few days.

The remaining four Hurricanes of B Flight were dived upon by Me 109s when they were four or five miles away from the bombers. The Flight was broken up and, after inconclusive dog-fights everybody returned to Northolt.

Sgt František was the only pilot who did not follow his leaders:

> "As I had difficulty in starting up my engine I took off on my own. After taking off I flew in a South East direction, wishing to join up with my Squadron. Flying above the clouds I noticed a large number of planes and at that moment six Me 109's made to attack me. I looped in order to meet them, but they formed a circle and I circled within theirs. One enemy aircraft came out of line slightly and I fired a burst. Enemy aircraft began to circle to earth. I followed and again fired from the left side. Enemy aircraft burst into flames and fell to earth. I then fired at another in the circle, and saw him smoke, but falling into clouds myself I could not find them again, and returned to Northolt."

He claimed one Bf 109 destroyed and one probable, one of two pilots of 303 Squadron to claim a victory during this scramble.

The now almost customary "tea-time" scramble (recorded the ORB) led 609 Squadron to a second engagement over Swanage, with a mixed raid of about 100 aircraft. The squadron was outnumbered and outmanoeuvred, and only three pilots were able to get to grips with the enemy. These were P/O D. M. Crook, who probably destroyed one Bf 109 in what he described as an enjoyable dog-fight, F/O Tadeusz Nowierski, who claimed a Bf 109 destroyed and damaged another, and P/O Noel Agazarian who was detached from his squadron in a chase with a fighter. It is believed that the Polish pilot, flying the Spitfire I R6961/PR-P, shot down Bf 109E-4 W.Nr.4861 of 5./JG2, which crashed at Sydling St Nicholas, killing Gefr. Dollinger. Nowierski reported:

> "I was flying Green 2 and on orders from the leader Green section went to investigate six bogeys. They were Me 109s. I attacked a Me 109 from astern and gave him a short burst (1 sec. 100-50 yards). I gave him another burst (3 secs.) at the same range. White smoke came from the e/a and then very thick black smoke and he started to dive steeply. I noticed another Me 109 on my right and attacked him from astern. I gave him one burst (2 sec. 200-150 yards). White and black smoke came from e/a. I broke away to the left and after a few seconds I saw a man come down in a parachute which did not open. The parachute seemed to be fouled by a cord half way up the canopy. This was about 10 miles NW of Portland."

David Crook, the Green Section leader, described the combat:

> "[...] I was still under the impression that these machines were Hurricanes, but as we got nearer I recognised them as Me.109s and shouted to Novi accordingly. We both attacked together and he opened fire on the last one on the line and shot it down almost immediately. I don't think they ever saw us till we opened fire, as we dived on them out of the sun.
>
> "[...] The rest of the squadron has not been in action, and so Novi and I were the only lucky ones. He had shot down two of the Me.109s, and the pilot got out of the second machine and tried to open his parachute. One of the rigging lines fouled it, however, and it only opened slightly, and the unfortunate German

therefore continued his drop with scarcely any reduction in speed, and was killed. Novi, bloodthirsty as ever where Germans are concerned, recounted this story to us with great relish and a wealth of very descriptive gestures."[52]

After this action Nowierski landed at Middle Wallop in a shot-up Spitfire. The Squadron diary summed up the extent of damage in the following words:

"Few minor holes in R6961 (Flying-Officer Novo) fixed with patching technique."

238 Squadron Hurricanes, which usually accompanied 609 Squadron during interceptions, joined the fray when the raid was near Portland, claiming four aircraft shot down, one probable and one damaged. Two airmen of this unit in their enthusiasm to became involved, collided in the air near Shaftesbury, their Hurricanes becoming the unit's only losses. Sgt Józef Jeka (Polish) involved in the pursuit of a Bf 110, attacked but had to leave it smoking 20 miles south of Portland, claiming only a damaged.

Several incidents haunted 302 Squadron on 30 September. P/O Wapniarek, after coming back from a patrol, reported the failure of the airscrew pitch mechanism, while Sgt Jerzy Sergiusz Załuski, whilst taxiing in Hurricane I P3925 ran into the parked P3924/WX-Y, causing damage to both aircraft. The pilot was, fortunately, unhurt.

1 October 1940

303 Squadron's good luck continued, when nine Hurricanes were airborne about 1.15 pm to patrol the Kenley-Brooklands area, together with 1 RCAF Squadron. The pilots were:

"A" Flight

F/Lt Kent	V6681/RF-B
P/O Ferić	N2661/RF-J
Sgt Szaposznikow	P3120/RF-A[53]
F/O Henneberg	V7504/RF-G
Sgt Siudak	N2460/RF-D

"B" Flight

Sgt Palak	P3217/RF-S
F/O Pisarek	V7503/RF-U
Sgt František	V7235/RF-M
Sgt Wojciechowski	P3089/RF-P

After rendezvousing with the Canadians over the aerodrome, they proceeded to patrol at 20,000 ft over North Foreland. F/Lt John Kent, the only victorious pilot of 303 Squadron that day, described his efforts in his combat report.

---

[52] F/Lt D. M. Crook DFC, *Spitfire Pilot*.

[53] In this particular action 303 Squadron Operations Record Book gives the erroneous serial number V6681, the same as that which F/Lt Kent flew during the same sortie! During the next sortie Sgt Szaposznikow flew P3120/RF-A, while other pilots used the same aircraft as listed above. The other possibility is V6684/RF-F.

"After being vectored around, we were eventually told that there was a large formation of bombers and fighters to the East of us. We met many e/a Me 109's above, on a level, and below us. I saw enemy aircraft long way below us in vics of three, and assumed that they were bombers. Expecting No. 1 Canadian Squadron to engage the higher fighters, I dived down."

"In doing so", he continued the story in a more colourful manner, in his memoirs, "I outdistanced my own squadron, and at the same time failed to see that the Canadians had turned away to meet an attack from some more German fighters which I had not seen. The leader of the squadron, being on a different frequency, could not tell me what he was doing and the Poles, being somewhat excited, forgot their English and could not tell me either. It came as a distinct shock, therefore, when just as I was closing with the enemy, which I had now recognised as 109s in an unusual formation, a stream of tracer bullets streaked past just above the top of my cockpit canopy. I immediately broke right; I did this as nine people out of ten – I am speaking of pilots, of course – will turn left if suddenly told to turn. An attacking pilot subconsciously expects his target to turn in that direction and when it does not he is, for a spilt second, upset. He does, of course, recover extremely rapidly but there is that split second of hesitation which can make all the difference between death and survival. In this instance I discovered that I was all alone with a mass of enemy fighters. I could not dive away as they would easily catch me before I could reach cloud cover, which was many thousands of feet below. I had, therefore, no alternative but to stay and fight. I kept in a steep right-hand turn with enough rudder on to keep the machine skidding while various 109s attacked, though none succeeded in hitting me. When the tracer stopped flying past I straightened up and, as four of the enemy passed close in front of me, I opened fire and the rearmost one went down with smoke pouring out of it. The Germans started to mill around above me while I circled, watched and waited and at this point the Controller called me and asked if I had engaged the enemy yet! I replied, 'No, but I think they are going to engage me at any moment and – here they come!'"[54]

The mastery of Kent's flying and tactics allowed him to survive the encounter with the Luftwaffe *Experten* of JG 26. F/Lt Kent claimed one Messerschmitt Bf 109 destroyed and one probable in his lone combat, for which he was later awarded a DFC. He finished his report in the following words:

"I counted 38 of them, which would mean that there had been 40 at the outset."

Later, flying along the coast west of Dungeness, he attacked a lone Messerschmitt which hid in clouds. One of the two Messerschmitt attacked by Kent – the first, "smoking furiously", or the second which "went down with the engine in flames" – was certainly the Bf 109E-1 of 4./JG 26 which fell burning at Balmer Down, Falmer with Uffz. Blüder still in the cockpit. Pilots of II./JG 26, who were attacked by a single Hurricane, claimed two Hurricanes destroyed in this action but in fact all the pilots of the Polish unit were back at Northolt.

A few hours before 303 Squadron engaged enemy fighters over the North

---

[54] Kent, *One of the Few*.

Foreland, some bombers arrived over Portsmouth. A few squadrons, including nos. 607 and 238, were scrambled to interrupt their attack. Sgt Józef Jeka was among the pilots of 238 Squadron. Whilst his comrades engaged and claimed the destruction of three enemy aircraft, Jeka had to save his life, breaking off and landing his Hurricane P3219 which had been damaged in the combat.

302 Squadron's Operations Record Book also mentions an aircraft damaged in the hands of a Polish pilot:

> "Weather fine. Flying. P/O Karwowski obliged to force land at Bramcote after Patrol. Port gun cowling torn loose. Pilot uninjured. Aircraft Cat. 2. Aircraft No. L.8359."

A small mystery surrounds this entry, as the serial number mentioned actually belonged to a Miles Magister assigned to the unit. P/O Włodzimierz Karwowski in fact had flown Hurricane I P3931/WX-V, but there is no trace of this accident in other documents and possibly this entry reflects the incident of 15 September, already described. The accident to Miles Magister L8359 occured three days later.

2 October 1940

The morning *Freie Jagd* Messerschmitts of JG 53, intercepted by Spitfire Squadrons, brought great success for 603 Squadron. The unit's pilots claimed destruction of four aircraft, and in addition two as probable and two damaged. Their losses amounted to a single Spitfire, and a wounded pilot, P/O P. G. Dexter who baled out over Croydon. One of the damaged aircraft was claimed by P/O Ludwik Martel, who had taken off from Hornchurch in his Spitfire X4274[55] XT-P at 9.20. He described his encounter in the combat report:

> "When on patrol with 603 Squadron I saw one Me 109 coming underneath from the starboard quarter, the squadron being 1000 ft below me. I dived and made a stern attack and saw glycol smoke came out of the Me 109 which took evasive action. I then saw two Me 109's in my mirror so I half rolled and dived."

He landed back at Hornchurch at 10.37.

The only other RAF unit involved in fighting that day was 66 Squadron, which claimed one Bf 109 for no loss. Pilots of JG 53 claimed four Spitfires shot down during the morning combat, and actually lost four Messerschmitts, including those of Olt. Walter Radlick, *Gruppenadjutant* of III./JG 53, and Olt. Walter Fiel, *Staffelkapitän* of 8./JG 53.

4 October 1940

During one routine training flight S/Ldr Piotr Łaguna of 302 Squadron, with F/Lt Thomson as passenger, force landed in Miles Magister L8359, damaging the aircraft. The landing was due to the port wing fuel tank being emptied, and an air lock forming in the fuel pump, which then failed to feed the fuel from the other tank.

---

[55] Identity of the Spitfire according to his personal flying log book. Some documents quote it as X4272, but the latter machine (one of the early cannon-armed Mk Is) was not delivered to 603 until the beginning of October, while P/O Martel had flown X4274/XT-P since late September, according to his log book.

5 October 1940

After two days of bad weather the Luftwaffe resumed its fighter and fighter-bomber offensive. Polish 303 Squadron was airborne four times that day, but only during the morning patrol did they have an occasion to meet the enemy. The "scrambled" sections of this unit were as follows:

S/Ldr Kellett	V7504/RF-G	Red 1
P/O Ferić	V6681/RF-B	Red 2
P/O Radomski	V7244/RF-C	Red 3
F/O Henneberg	V6684/RF-F	Yellow 1
Sgt Siudak	N2460/RF-D	Yellow 2
Sgt Karubin	P3901/RF-E	Yellow 3
F/O Pisarek	V7503/RF-U	Blue 1
P/O Mierzwa	L2026/RF-Q	Blue 2
Sgt Bełc	V7235/RF-M	Blue 3
F/O Januszewicz	P3892/RF-T	Green 1
Sgt Wojciechowski	P3089/RF-P	Green 2
Sgt Palak	P3217/RF-S	Green 3

Followed by 1 RCAF Squadron aircraft, they met the enemy about 11.05 am, in the Rochester area. S/Ldr Kellett, leading the Polish Squadron, recalled:

"There was a cloud layer at 25,000 ft and from time to time Me 109's came out of it. We saw about seven altogether and I led the Squadron to attack them in line astern. I got in a good burst from in front and on the quarter of one Me 109, and I saw pieces fall off the engine and starboard wing root. Enemy aircraft turned right, and dived under me. I could not follow it owing to the big dog fight which had developed, involving about 100 aircraft."

After a short combat with Bf 109s of JG 3 that appeared out of the clouds, about 15 twin-engined Bf 110s of 1. and 2./ErpGr 210, escorted by Bf 109s of JG 53 *Pik As*, appeared ahead. These aircraft were on their way to bomb West Malling airfield and Becton gas works. P/O Mirosław Ferić, flying as wingman to S/Ldr Kellett, described it thus:

"As Me 110s were above us, we began to climb. I then noticed an Me 110 break away from the circle, and diving made towards the sea, smoking slightly, but maintaining a very high speed. I chased the enemy aircraft and catching up with him about seven miles from the coast fired a burst from a distance of about 20 yards into his cockpit. Enemy aircraft immediately dived into the sea."

The only ErpGr 210 Messerschmitt 110 lost over sea was the aircraft coded S9+FH, piloted by the *Gruppenkommandeur*, Oblt. Weimann.

In the meantime, the Yellow Section leader, who had been the first to engage the Bf 109s, soon returned to the combat area, after a fruitless attempt to pursue one. F/O Zdzisław Henneberg noted:

"I climbed to my former height and after a short while I noticed near the coast a defensive circle of Me 110's. Above them were flying several Me 109's. I attacked a Me 110, but after firing two bursts I observed a Me on my tail. Evading enemy aircraft I chased a Me 110 making towards the coast and began to fire from a distance of 250 yards. After firing two bursts enemy aircraft right engine burst into flames and dived straight for the sea. I was then attacked by three Messerschmitt 109's and evading them returned to Northolt."

It seems probable that the Messerschmitt 110 that F/O Henneberg claimed as destroyed, was in fact that which P/O Ferić finished off over the Channel.

Like his leader, Sgt Karubin first engaged a Bf 109. His victim

"burst into flames and smoking fell to earth in the region of Kent."

After that, Sgt Karubin had to evade another Bf 109, and in the ensuing dog-fight fired a short, well aimed burst.

"Enemy aircraft smoking slightly made off."

The events in the air were seen from quite the opposite point of view by Uffz. Wilhelm Ghesla, a 1./JG 53 pilot who was shot down, probably by one of the Polish fighters, although the Canadian and 501 Squadron pilots also filed claims after this sortie.

"We were again in a raid against London, at an altitude of 8,000 metres, when we were attacked unexpectedly by several Hurricanes coming out of clouds. One hit the oil cooler of my machine. I executed a bunt at once, in order to leave the danger and get to a safe place. I levelled at 4,000 metres and headed for Dover.

"Soon after that I heard another loud noise in my machine, I was shot at again, but could not see by whom. After this second attack my 'Me' was so damaged that I had to look for a suitable place to land. I soon found a meadow and started approach for an emergency landing. I had to unfasten the parachute harness, to be able to leave the aircraft immediately, but by mistake I undid my seat belts. After the second attack I lost my reason. That was why, during the belly landing, I hit the instrument panel with my head."

Willi Ghesla in Bf 109E-4 Werk Nr. 1804, 'white 10', crash landed near Aldington, as did another pilot of 1./JG 53, Lt. Zeiss in Bf 109E-4 Werk Nr. 1564, 'white 3'. He tried to help another Messerschmitt which had a Hurricane on its tail, but was attacked himself, and forced to bale out of his machine, which crashed and burnt at Sheerlands Farm, Pluckeley. Probably one of them was included in the claims of the day's record breaker, – Sgt Antoni Siudak, who claimed two Messerschmitt Bf 109s destroyed and a Bf 110 shared destroyed:

"I saw enemy aircraft being attacked by Spitfires. Me 110's after being attacked formed a circle. I attacked a Me 110 from the rear and slightly to the left, and a Spitfire attacked the same Me from the rear and slightly to the right. I fired two bursts, enemy aircraft burst into flames, and fell to earth near Ashford burning on the ground. I immediately attacked an Me 109 which flew close to me, and fired a long burst. Enemy aircraft broke up into bits and fell to earth also near Ashford. I then attacked another Me 109 which fled towards the sea. I fired a burst and enemy aircraft fell into the sea smoking off Littlestone near a boat. Being short of ammunition and petrol I landed at Gravesend."

The enemy aircraft which broke up and fell near Ashford, could have been that flown by Lt. Zeiss, but the Bf 110 shared with a Spitfire was almost certainly an aircraft of 1./ErpGr 210 which crashed at Millbank Place near Ashford.

F/O Marian Pisarek, leading Blue Section, attacked the defensive circle of Bf 110s, firing at one of them. He later wrote:

"The result of this attack I did not see, but according to Sgt Bełc enemy aircraft began to smoke, and broke away, probably damaged. I pulled out of my dive and turned and attacked a Me 110 from the rear and above. Firing several short bursts I saw enemy aircraft begin to smoke, one engine stopped and enemy aircraft fell into the sea. I was then attacked by Me 109 which I evaded and returned to Northolt."

Sgt Bełc, mentioned in Pisarek's report, claimed a Bf 110 which crashed near Lympne. The Polish sergeant noticed that one of the crew managed to bale out, but there is no record of a Bf 110 crashing in this area. Sgt Jan Palak also mentioned in his report an aircraft which crashed near Lympne. He claimed one Bf 109 destroyed and one Bf 110 damaged:

"I attacked one Me 110 firing a short burst, enemy aircraft began to smoke. I did not see what happened as I was attacked by two Me 109's. I turned and attacked the enemy aircraft firing two bursts from the rear. Enemy aircraft burst into flames and dived to earth in the neighbourhood of Lympne."

The only loss by 303 Squadron in this battle was F/O Wojciech Januszewicz, who was shot down by a Bf 109 near Stowting. He was leading the rear section, from which only Sgt Palak had a well documented encounter with the enemy. Nobody saw what happened to Januszewicz, who was an experienced fighter pilot. Three days after the outbreak of war in September 1939, he had been posted to command 111 *Eskadra Myśliwska 'Kościuszkowska'*[56], when its commanding officer was wounded in action. He led this unit until the end of the 1939 campaign, and was credited with a Bf 110 and two Ju 87s shot down. Later, in France he commanded the Polish flight of GC II/7, flying Dewoitine D.520s. At the end of the French campaign he flew, with a group of other Polish pilots, from Perpignan to Africa, ferrying fighter planes of his unit. In Britain he was with 303 Squadron from the very beginning.

About the same time as 303 Squadron was fighting with Bf 109s and 110s in the Dover area, 603 Squadron engaged other Messerschmitts with good results. Pilots of this unit claimed one Bf 109 destroyed, one probable and one damaged. The confirmed success was described by its Polish victor, P/O Ludwik Martel, flying the Spitfire I X4348/XT-R:

---

[56] 111th 'Kościuszko' Fighter Squadron. 303 (Polish) Squadron RAF was heir to the traditions of that unit.

"When on patrol with 603 Squadron I saw a circle of Me 109's, and one Me 109 left the circle and started to climb and I dived on him and made a beam attack, firing for about three seconds. The Me 109 took evasive action by skidding and I attacked again with slight deflection firing the remainder of my ammunition from 200 yards. The Messerschmitt went up and then dived gently into the sea. I saw him crash into the sea about 6 miles East of Dover."

Almost two hours later another Polish pilot, F/O Henryk Szczęsny, flying Spitfire II P7363, was on patrol with two other pilots of 74 Squadron. They spotted a Do 17, and claimed the only victory of the day for that unit. Szczęsny wrote:

"I was Green 3 in 74 Squadron, when we sighted Do 215. Green Leader and two attacked e/a first. I attacked him in a dive towards the sea. I opened fire at 250 yards and continued to fire all my ammunition in to his engines and fuselage. There was no return fire and e/a was burning port engine. I pulled away at 1000 ft and e.a. was still diving in flames towards the sea at approximately 300 mph. I broke away to port and did not see e/a fall into sea on account of haze at sea level."

All the section pilots shared in the claim for this Do 17 about 30 miles east of Harwich. They lost the bomber in the haze, but 2./KG 3 lost one such Dornier which crashed and burnt out at Hamme, with all the crew on board. It seems therefore that the attack by the pilots was effective and that their victim failed to reach its base.

Some of the Poles had less luck during other encounters. P/O Władysław Różycki of 238 Squadron, based at Chilbolton, described one of the combats in his personal diary:

"Combats continue in various parts of Southern England, and usually at large heights. I receive relatively much mail from friends in various parts of England. I learn that many of ours have been killed. But this does not depress or discourage me. I have always felt much better in the air than on the ground. I am always joyful, and especially when I can see the sea of aircraft, against which we set off for this friendly gathering. Just on one day I felt sorrow, disappointment, pity. When I found myself among fifteen enemy aircraft, and intended to attack the nearest one, the machine guns failed me. I cried in the air and on the ground. My English friends were sad, too, when they saw my bitterness."

His unit lost one pilot wounded in action over Shaftesbury, who had to force-land at Shoreham airfield during the first patrol of the day.

Whilst undertaking one of the first flights by 307, the Polish night fighter squadron, Sgt Jerzy Malinowski, flying with LAC Ostrowski, damaged Defiant L7035 whilst landing. The port undercarriage leg failed on the runway, but fortunately, neither airman was hurt.

Continuing this series of misfortunes, another Polish pilot, F/O Tadeusz Nowierski of 609 Squadron, had to abandon his Spitfire I, N3223/PR-M, during the afternoon. This had nothing to do with air combat, as 609 was off-duty that day, resting after the exhausting engagements of the previous night, when a rather rowdy farewell party was held by their departing CO.

Novi's accident was described in detail by D. M. Crook:

"That afternoon we took off to do some practice flying, and when we came in to land again and put our undercarriage down, only one of Novi's wheels would come down and the other remained locked obstinately in the raised position. Try as he would, he was unable to move it. This meant that it was very dangerous to land, as one wheel would hit the ground and the Spitfire – still doing about 75 m.p.h. – would then somersault towards the missing wheel. I called him up on the R.T., and told him that he must not land but instead climb up and bale out.

"I was flying very close to him, and we climbed up to 5,000 feet over Salisbury Plain, and then Novi opened his sliding hood, took off his flying helmet, undid his harness and prepared to abandon ship. However, he seemed to experience some difficulty in getting out of the cockpit into the slipstream, and finally he turned the machine over onto its back, and dropped neatly out of his seat. The Spitfire promptly dived into the corner of a small wood and burst into flames. Novi, after fumbling for his release cord, opened his parachute, and a few minutes later he dropped into the middle of a hen run, to the consternation of the poultry.

"People seemed to spring up from all over the place and rush towards him, and so I circled the spot for a few minutes, as I thought that, with his rather broken English, he might be mistaken for a German parachutist. But everything was O.K. We sent out a car to collect him, and half an hour later he was in the mess again, none the worse for his experience, except for a bruised arm. The machine that he had been flying was not a very good one – it was rather old and slower than the new ones – so we were all very grateful to him for writing it off!"[57]

6 October 1940

The most effective Polish fighter pilot from the previous day, Sgt Antoni Siudak, had little time to celebrate his victory. On 6th, about 1.15 pm, he was killed during a bombing attack on RAF Northolt. A single bomber sneaked over the airfield and dropped bombs near a Hurricane of 303 Squadron – P3120/RF-A[58]. The explosion killed three airmen, including one pilot – Siudak – and two others were wounded. Two more aircraft suffered damage, including Hurricane P3217/RF-S.

Hurricanes of 229 Squadron were alerted immediately, but they failed to catch the raider.

Antoni Siudak had been a career airman in the Polish Air Force before the war. During the French campaign he had served in the Polish GC I/145 Squadron, based at Lyon-Bron, flying Caudron CR.714C1 Cyclone fighters, and later in GC I/8 on Bloch MB.151C1s. He was also one of three pilots attached to the special flight for the protection of the Polish Government residence at Angers. After his arrival in Britain, and conversion onto RAF aircraft, he began his service in 302 Squadron, from which he transferred to 303.

---

[57] F/Lt D. M. Crook DFC, *Spitfire Pilot*.

[58] Often erroneously quoted as "RF-D" due to a misspelling in one of the 303 Sqn documents. This aircraft had carried the individual letter A since its arrival on 7 September 1940. No information about P3120 appears in the 303 Squadron ORB after 2 October 1940. On 10 October V6808 arrived as the replacement for this aircraft and it became the new RF-A. The aircraft coded D (N2460) arrived on 30 September 1940 and continued its service up to the end of the year. For more details see Appendix 3.

7 October 1940

303 Squadron Operations Record Book recorded the early morning sortie:

"Patrol over Thames Estuary – No contact made."

This contradicts another note in the same document:

"1 Me. 109 destroyed"

added by the name of P/O Palusiński (N2661/RF-J). This mysterious claim does not appear in any official Fighter Command document, nor any other 303 Squadron papers.

The second patrol brought more definite success for the unit. Taking off at 13.15 were:

S/Ldr Kellett	P3901/RF-E	
P/O Palusiński	N2460/RF-D	
Sgt Szaposznikow	V7244/RF-C	Red
F/O Grzeszczak	V6684/RF-F	
P/O Ferić	V7504/RF-G	
P/O Radomski	V6681/RF-B	
F/O Pisarek	V7503/RF-U	Blue
P/O Mierzwa	P3089/RF-P	
Sgt František	R4175/RF-R	
Sgt Bełc	L2099/RF-O	
Sgt Palak	P3383/RF-T	

These 11 Hurricanes followed 1 RCAF Squadron to patrol the Kenley-Brooklands area.

When the fighters from Northolt arrived over London, they sighted more then 50 Bf 109s (some incorrectly identified by the Polish pilots as He 113[59]) flying north east at 25-30,000 ft. German fighters dived in five aircraft sections from above, attacking the Canadian squadron first. Ten aircraft attacked 1 RCAF and others went for 303 Squadron which was flying behind, and then, continuing their dive, they tore away from the Hurricanes, flying south. 303 Squadron tried to follow them, but without result. During this manoeuvre another formation of Me 109s was sighted flying west, which tried the same trick. After the diving attack these Messerschmitts flew south, too. This time F/O Pisarek caught one and claimed it shot down over the Channel, as did Sgt Szaposznikow. The latter described this event:

"We met a formation of Me 109 flying below us. Then immediately below us I saw three Me 109, followed by two more. I attacked, and after firing one burst, enemy aircraft climbed. I followed and firing two bursts, enemy aircraft began to smoke but evaded me. I then met two Me 109's over the coast. I attacked one, and firing a burst saw enemy aircraft dive. I fired from a distance of 150 yards, but there was no sign of smoke or flame, although the enemy aircraft fell into the sea just off Brighton.

---

[59] Mentioned in 303 Squadron personal combat reports.

"I noticed today that, whereas in previous combats enemy aircraft dived towards the earth when attacked, they now climbed, easily leaving the Hurricane behind."

Sgt Bełc began to circle with one Bf 109:

"Me began to smoke and the right side of the engine burst into flames. Enemy aircraft dived straight towards the earth, and disappeared beneath the clouds. The place of its crash would be South West of Redhill."

In this action the Canadians claimed one Bf 109 shot down by F/O Lochman, but at a cost of one Hurricane. On the way home, P/O Mierzwa of 303 Squadron landed his Hurricane P3089 at a decoy landing ground at Borstal, Chatham. Subsequently trying to take off, he crashed and damaged his aircraft. The unfortunate pilot was brought from Detling to Northolt by car.

The next sortie by 303 Squadron, at 3.30 pm, was uneventful.

More action was seen by Sgt Zygmunt Klein of 152 Squadron, when a dozen Spitfires intercepted 30 Junkers 88s. The squadron took off from Warmwell at 3.27 pm:

P/O Holmes	R6964
Sgt Wolton	P9391
P/O Bayles	R6643
P/O Hall	R6608
Sgt Shepperd	R6607
P/O Cox	R6763
P/O Marrs	R6968
P/O Williams	X4381
Sgt Szlagowski (Polish)	L1048
Sgt Kearsey	X4550
Sgt Akroyd	K9882
Sgt Klein (Polish)	P9386

They met German bombers proceeding north west at 17,000 ft with a cover of Bf 110s behind and 1,000 ft above.

"The Messerschmitt 110's were in line astern and from time to time the leaders of each line turned round and formed a defensive circle. The circle then broke up and Messerschmitt 110's made up with their bombers again."

When the Spitfire squadron intercepted in line astern and attacked the bombers, the Junkers 88s turned south between Lyme Regis and Exeter. The fire of the first three Spitfires failed to produce results. Yellow Section was more successful, when Sgt Shepperd (Yellow 1) forced one Junkers to drop its bombs and the crew to bale out. P/O Hall (Yellow 2) force-landed at Sutton Scotney, while P/O Cox (Yellow 3) damaged one bomber. The Blue Section, including Sgt Szlagowski[60] attacked Bf 110s

---

[60] No. 152 Squadron ORB mistakenly describes Sgt Klein's action as that of Sgt Szlagowski. There is no evidence of any combat success of Sgt Szlagowski that day. The Personal Combat Report of Sgt Klein states that he was flying as Green 2 and attacked Messerschmitt 110s.

before they managed to make a defensive circle and P/O Marrs (Blue 1) shot one down. Unfortunately, Sgt Szlagowski failed to gain sufficient height as he could not get his oxygen turned on. The Green Section leader, P/O Williams, made two successful attacks on bombers, and when Messerschmitts approached, dog-fights ensued. Sgt Klein stated in his combat report.

"I was Green 2 on patrol with the Squadron at 18000 ft. Enemy sighted flying NW. We were about to attack the bomber formation when I saw 3 Me 110s about 3 miles behind the bomber formation. I climbed into sun, and waited until they turned back when I attacked the starboard a/c. I fired 3 bursts at close range, broke away and climbed back into sun. White smoke was issuing from both engines and e/a was losing height. I attacked again but had to break away before opening fire as there were two 110s on my tail. I did not observe any return fire."

Two Spitfires crash landed and nine others landed back at Warmwell at 16.40. Sgt Klein landed to refuel at Middle Wallop and was back home a few minutes after his colleagues. All of them described the Bf 110s (which came from III./ZG 26) as painted white from the nose to the cockpit. Sgt Klein's victim was probably one of two Bf 110s which, attacked five miles from Swanage, crashed nearby. One, coded 3U+BT, was down at Hart Hill, Stoborough near Wareham, killing its crew, while the other, 3U+JT, force-landed near Corfe Castle. However this engagement failed to prevent Yeovil from attacks by the rest of the formation which reached their target a few minutes later, and bombed it from about 17-18,000 ft.

56 Squadron, based at Warmwell and flying Hurricanes, was also sent up to intercept the bombers flying towards Yeovil. The Hurricanes took off at 3.30 pm, a few minutes after 152 Squadron, and (obviously) there was a Polish airman among the Punjab Squadron pilots:

F/Lt Brooker	V7510
F/O Wicks	V7508/US-N
P/O Nosowicz (Polish)	V7505
Sgt Robinson	P3862
Sgt Nicholls	P3514
P/O Higginson	V7509/US-S
Sgt Whitehead	N2712/US-M
Sgt Smythe	P3055/US-P
Sgt Hillwood	N2386/US-U
P/O Maxwell	P3866/US-V

The squadron reached 19,000 ft before attacking the bomber formation, consisting of Ju 88s of II./KG 51, and an escort of Bf 110s of II. and III./ZG 26. Six miles south east of Yeovil, the Hurricanes attacked from the sun. P/O Zbigniew Nosowicz attacked a Bf 110 head-on, then turning onto its tail. After his first, well aimed burst the Messerschmitt turned back towards the sea, emitting smoke. Nosowicz then chose another Bf 110, first neutralizing the rear gunner, but he was then attacked by other Messerschmitts himself, and was not able to finish off his prey.

In total, the pilots of 56 Squadron claimed damage to three Messerschmitts, with four others probably destroyed. The Polish pilot claimed one of each category. The cost was one Hurricane lost, its pilot baled out wounded.

About 3.40 pm 605 Squadron was also scrambled. The formation of ten Hurricanes left Croydon for the third time that day. The day, described as "very fine" in the squadron's Operations Record Book, ended with total claims for seven destroyed and four damaged. The squadron, while flying at 27,000 ft, was in a good position to bounce some Bf 109s.

Sgt Wright	V6786
P/O Foster	V6783
Sgt Jones	V7506
F/O Passy	P3022
P/O Parrott	V7468
S/Ldr McKellar	P3308
P/O Forde	V6755
Sgt Ralls	L2014
Sgt Budziński (Polish)	P3965

Some of the pilots encountered four Messerschmitts flying 1,000 ft below. S/Ldr McKellar claimed one shot down and Sgt Wright, F/O Passy and Sgt Budziński shared one. Sgt Wright described this in his combat report:

"No 605 squadron at 26,000 ft SE of Biggin Hill, sighted four Me 109's approaching from ahead, below and to port. Yellow 1 (Sgt Wright) and Red 2 (Sgt Budziński) each fired a short deflection burst at one of them, which broke away downwards from the others and continued to dive away for home, apparently undamaged. Red 3 (F/O Passy) and Red 2 (Sgt. Budziński) then fired at it from astern, Red 3's windscreen being sprayed with glycol from it. It than dived again steeply and was fired on by Yellow 1, Red 2 and Red 3, it then turned, lost height and speed, and crashed in a large plantation with a lake, 2 miles North of it, thought to be near Cranbrook. (Confirmed by Green 1 and Yellow 2)

"I wish this destroyed Me 109 to be credited equally between myself, Red 2 and Red 3.

"E. W. Wright Sgt."

This shared Messerschmitt was that flown by Uffz. Lederer of 4./LG 2 and was the last victorious combat for Sgt Jan Budziński during the Battle of Britain. Budziński then suffered from meningitis and consequently was out of service for a long time. Later he served in training units and years later he recalled that, had the sickness not caused the loss of his hearing, there is no doubt he would either have become an ace or died (or both?) . . .

At the same time as the squadrons mentioned above engaged the enemy in the area south of London, 238 Squadron was scrambled and directed further west to intercept the bombers that headed for Yeovil. At about 4.30 pm the unit claimed four enemy aircraft, one Ju 88 being claimed by a Polish pilot, Sgt Józef Jeka in Hurricane L1889. 601 Squadron also took part in the interception over Yeovil. Seven Hurricanes from this unit were sent to defend the Westland works at Yeovil. Pilots were:

F/Lt Clyde	P3230

Sgt Taylor	V6632
F/O Riddle	V6630
F/O Mayers	R4218
P/O Whitney-Straight	P3675
F/O Jankiewicz (Polish)	P3831
P/O Aldwinkle	V6666/UF-J

The encounter near Bridport with 25 Ju 88s of II./KG 51 escorted by Bf 110s of II. and III./ZG 26, was described as follows by F/O Jerzy Jankiewicz:

> "I was Blue 2. Took off Exeter at 15.45 and climbed in the direction of Yeovil. When N of Axminster e/a were sighted heading south between Beaminster and Bridport; enemy fighters appeared to be flying in line astern at 15,000 ft numbered about 20. Below them were about 20 bombers some flying in sections of three, others singly, and others in pairs. Bombers were in no particular formation. We were flying at about 11,000. Estimated speed e/a 200-210 mph."

Jankiewicz fired a few short bursts into a Bf 110 from 400 yards, closing to 50 yards. He hit it, claiming it as damaged. In total, the Luftwaffe lost seven Bf 110s of ZG 26 and two Ju 88s of II./KG 51 during this raid. RAF pilots reported one Bf 109 destroyed, at least four Ju 88s destroyed and three damaged, and seven destroyed (exact match!), six probably destroyed and six damaged twin-tailed aircraft – Bf 110s and Do 17s.

8 October 1940

303 Squadron lost its ace Czech pilot Sgt Josef František, on this date. A patrol of a dozen Hurricanes over Biggin Hill was uneventful. On the way back to Northolt, František's Hurricane, R4175/RF-R, suddenly left the formation. The pilot did not answer calls and the aircraft crashed at Cuddington Way, Ewell, Surrey. Possibly the oxygen system had failed, and the talented pilot lost consciousness being killed in the crash.

10 October 1940

P/O Władysław Różycki in his lucky Hurricane P3618 took part in the last encounter of 238 Squadron with the enemy during the Battle of Britain. The Polish pilot was one of two pilots to claim Bf 109s damaged. In the same combat P/O R. F. T. Doe was shot down, and baled out of his Hurricane P3984. Różycki described the subsequent days in his diary:

> "Last days of the month were bearable, as we commenced flying over the Channel again, but without encounters. Weather very variable. Mostly very warm . . ."

11 October 1940

On this date a rotation of two Polish squadrons took place. 303 Squadron left Northolt and moved to Leconfield, to take a rest after the exhausting fighting, and become a combat training unit. F/Lt Kent wrote in his memoirs:

> "It was with a very proud record that No. 303 Squadron left Northolt, the place

of its rebirth. In six hectic weeks, perhaps the most important in our history, the Squadron had destroyed 126 enemy aircraft for the loss of only eight pilots killed although a much greater number had suffered wounds of greater or less severity. It was a record unrivalled by any other squadron."

The unit was replaced by another Polish Squadron, 302. The stay of this latter unit at RAF Northolt was summarised in Combat Diary, RAF Station Northolt, in these words:

"This Squadron was most unlucky during their stay, losing pilots through flying accidents as well as high operational losses."

But 302 Squadron pilots were not the only ones to suffer flying accidents. P/O J. J. Solak, who served in 249 Squadron, damaged Hurricane V6728/GN-Z during the day, whilst landing at North Weald after one of his first local flights. P/O Solak, together with Sgt Michał Mirosław Maciejowski, known as Miki, had been in that unit since the end of September. P/O George Barclay mentioned in his memoirs the arrival of Jerzy Solak in the Gold Coast Squadron:

"We got a Polish officer today – he seems a very good sort and speaks good English. He was in a Polish fighter squadron at the start of the war, but never fought as they were so short of aircraft. His name is George Solak – the George part in Polish sounds like 'Jersey' so he has been christened that already! We had all sorts of discussions on the war, the Air Force, etc., yesterday with the Wing Commander [Victor Beamish – author], Jersey, the CO and the pilots."

12 October 1940
Sgt Józef Biel of 3 Squadron damaged Hurricane R4077 while landing at Wick at about 5.35 pm. This is the only trace in official documents of service of at least two Polish pilots in 3 Squadron RAF late 1940.

14 October 1940
F/O Marian Duryasz of 213 Squadron had troubles while landing at Tangmere at about 5.50 pm. During a patrol over base the view through the windscreen was obscured by ice, so the pilot had to place his head out of the cockpit for a better view while approaching to land. The stream of air blew off his goggles and Hurricane V6541/AK-I struck the ground before the pilot could see what was happening. During this heavy landing the undercarriage collapsed and the aircraft was damaged.

Chapter Five

THE BATTLE REACHES ITS TWILIGHT PHASE

15 October – 31 December 1940

"We fought together through the great offensive of 1940 and I then knew that the pilots of 303 were not only of the best, but also would see me through any troubles. In the month of September 303 was on top – no Squadron in the Empire could equal the courage and skill of our pilots. Together we have seen good days and bad but as English and Polish we shared them. Although I say goodbye to 303, they know that they have won for Poland a special place in the hearts of people in the British Empire. We will continue to fight alongside our gallant Polish allies until we regain Poland and restore freedom to Europe."

S/Ldr Ronald Kellett, on leaving no. 303 Sqn in mid-December 1940

15 October 1940

The first major action by 302 Squadron within the Northolt Wing took place exactly one month after its first victorious combat in Bader's Duxford Wing. This was summed up in the Squadron Operations Record Book:

"One Me 109 destroyed by 'A' Flight at 10.15 hrs. Attack delivered over Canterbury at 25-16,000 ft. One Me 109 destroyed over Maidstone at 15.00 hours."

On the morning of 15 October 302 and 229 Squadrons were on patrol in the Canterbury area at an altitude of 20,000 ft when they were attacked by two separate formations of Bf 109s. In this action the Northolt Wing claimed to have shot down three Bf 109s and one probable, with the loss of five of its own aircraft. Sgt Wędzik of 302 Squadron and S/Ldr Banham, who led the whole formation, were wounded.

The full list of 302 Squadron pilots and aircraft taking part in this patrol is as follows:

S/Ldr Satchell	P3812/WX-L	
Sgt Łysek	P3205/WX-E	
F/Lt Łaguna	P3085/WX-A	
P/O Wróblewski	V6744/WX-C	
Sgt Kosarz	P3935/WX-D	
P/O Maliński	R2684/WX-B	
F/Lt Riley	P3923/WX-U	Blue 1

F/O Czerwiński	V3751/WX-Q	Blue 2
Sgt Wędzik	P2752/WX-R	Blue 3
P/O Pilch	V7417/WX-T	
Sgt Markiewicz	P3930/WX-X	
P/O Król	P3931/WX-V	

F/Lt Riley, who claimed one Me 109 destroyed, was the only victor of 302 Squadron, and he described his efforts:

"When we were at about 21,000 ft we were ordered onto Easterly course and saw a large enemy formation (about 70) flying North about 4000 ft above us. We continued to climb but could not intercept, and they continued North. Our Squadron went into defensive circle climbing slightly, to deal with odd pairs of enemy aircraft which were diving down for a quick attack and climbing above us again. Blue 3 was shot down by one of these attackers. Blue 1 and Blue 2 tried to catch the attacker but he escaped. Later a large enemy formation passed above at about 26,000 ft flying South West but did not attack. Another enemy formation of about 30 dived towards us from North and Blue 1 attacked formation, selected one Me 109 and fired a 3 sec burst at 50 yards. Immediately after I fired a 1 sec burst at Me 109 from 25 yards, which crossed his nose. He then took evasive action and in neither case had time to watch for results. Blue 1 later rocked aircraft laterally and two Caleb aircraft joined him and then continued patrol. No further enemy aircraft seen."

Sgt Marian Wędzik, mentioned in Riley's report as Blue 3, was shot down and his Hurricane P2752/WX-R crashed at Chatham. The Polish pilot managed to bale out from the burning aeroplane and saved his life. S/Ldr Jack Satchell, leading the unit force landed Hurricane P3812/WX-L, when his aircraft ran out of fuel unexpectedly; he came down in a field on the Slough Building Estate. After closer examination of his machine it was found that his petrol tank was holed and the gauges shot through. After refuelling, S/Ldr Satchell flew back to Northolt. Another 302 Squadron pilot was less lucky, P/O Jan Maliński in R2684/WX-B force landing in a very rough field with the undercarriage up, through engine failure.

The afternoon patrol brought another claim for a Bf 109 shot down. The combat report of P/O Król, giving the time as 4 pm, provided some details:

"Interception of the Me 109 took place at 20 000 ft. There were approximately 100 Me 109's at 25 000 ft. In spite of their passing over us, we were not attacked, and they only started to attack when we got into a defensive circle having gained a certain amount of height. Suddenly I saw a Me 109 attack another Hurricane which was about 300 yards on my port beam slightly below. I did a beam attack on this Messerschmitt, getting in one burst of ½ second at about 150 to 100 yards range owing to being attacked myself by another Messerschmitt. I had to take evasive action doing steep turns. On orbiting I saw a parachute open. Later I joined up with Caleb leader, S/Ldr Satchell and turning I noticed four Me 109's flying towards us in line astern from above and in front. Each aircraft about 100 yards behind the other. We were at 20 000 ft while the Me's broke away. After turning I noticed that the pilot had baled out and that he was not wearing his 'Mae

West'. I returned to base with Caleb Leader, but owing to lack of fuel I had to land at White Waltham where I refuelled. Landing at Northolt at 16.30 hours."

The apparent similarity of these actions, as described in the reports of both F/Lt Riley and P/O Król could indicate that in fact both took part in the same engagement. Further, the information that one of "A" Flight's pilots had destroyed a Bf 109 contradicts F/Lt Riley's report. Disorder in 302 Squadron's papers again provides contradictory information. The only certain thing is that F/Lt Riley and P/O Król both reported actions against Bf 109s, which in each case ended in shooting down one enemy fighter. The casualties of the day are certain, too – one aircraft lost, two force landed. In addition, one Hurricane was damaged during the late afternoon patrol. Four pilots of 302 Squadron – Sgt Łysek, F/Lt Łaguna, P/O Wróblewski, and Sgt Kosarz made a few short patrols. One of these patrols ended with an accident, when Sgt Wilhelm Kosarz, flying the Hurricane P3935/WX-D, was on his way back to base as the weather suddenly deteriorated. In clouds and mist Kosarz's aircraft struck a balloon cable and went into a spin, but the pilot was able to recover, and landed normally at Heston airfield.

Further south about noon several units engaged *Freie Jagd* Messerschmitts from JG 2, Polish pilots marking their presence in at least two units. 609 Squadron was called to intercept:

> "a new-style raid of Messerschmitt fighter-bombers stepped up in tiers from 16,000 to 30,000 ft near Southampton"

stated the squadron ORB. The Spitfires were attacked by Bf 109s, and being in a very unfavourable position were ordered to break away, and were rather fortunate to destroy some of the invaders. They were credited with two Bf 109s and one Bf 110. The former were claimed by P/O Noel Agazarian and F/O Tadeusz Nowierski. The single 110 was reported by F/O J. C. Dundas.

D. M. Crook wrote:

> "At about 10,000 feet there was some cloud, and as soon as we got above this I looked around and above, and saw many thousands of feet above us at least thirty Messerschmitt 110s, accompanied by a lot of Me.109s. [...]
>
> "We were in a hopeless position, a long way below them and outlined against the white cloud underneath us. However, we continued to climb, in the hope of somehow managing to get in one attack, and all the time we watched the Messerschmitts like cats, as sooner or later they would obviously drop down on us. Altogether rather an unpleasant few minutes.
>
> "It was very difficult watching them, as they were almost in the sun, and the glare was awful.
>
> "Suddenly I saw two Me.109s just behind John's [Dundas – author] Spitfire [...]
>
> "I immediately shouted on the R.T., 'Look out, Messerschmitts, they're coming down'. I have never seen the squadron break up so quickly. [...]
>
> "[...] When the squadron broke up and dived away, both Noel [Agazarian – author] and Novi stayed up there with the Me.109s – a very cool and risky thing to do, since they were in such a hopeless position. However, like some other audacious schemes, it worked. [...]

"Novi was also attacked, but managed to shoot down another 109, which crashed near Bournemouth. When the machine was near the ground, the pilot got out and just managed to open his parachute in time, but landed very heavily and lay on the ground, probably winded by the fall. Novi circled round and said afterwards, in his rather broken English, 'I circle round, bloddy German lies down, he is dead. O.K. But I look again, he is now sitting up, no bloddy good.' He was very disappointed; in his opinion the only good Germans are dead Germans."

Nowierski, flying R6961/PR-P, reported:

"I was Green 3. The squadron was attacked by Me 109's and we split up. A few minutes later I saw an Me 109 slightly above me and opened fire from astern. He went into a left hand spin and pieces fell off the machine. He disappeared into cloud and I lost him but F/O Oleński followed him down and saw him crash. The pilot did not get out and was lying or sitting with his parachute near the crash (believed between Milton and Lymington)."[61]

The most probable victim of the Polish pilot fell at Everton near Lymington, where Gefr. Alois Pollach of 4./JG 2 crashed in Messerschmitt Bf 109E-1 (Werk Nr.3279, 'white 10') and was taken prisoner. Also Fw. Hellriegel of I./JG 2 was taken prisoner, his Messerschmitt Bf 109E-4 (Werk Nr. 1588, 'white 8') crashing at Bowcombe Down near Newport. This aircraft was claimed by P/O Noel Agazarian, flying Spitfire I X4539. Probably the same aircraft was attcked by another Polish pilot taking part in this engagement. P/O Bolesław Własnowolski, who a month earlier had been transferred from 607 to 213 Squadron, reported his action over the Isle of Wight:

"I was Blue 3 when we were attacked from the rear by enemy aircraft. I turned to the right, climbing, and then to the left to get the sun behind me. I saw 2 Me 109s one a long way off, one below me. I approached the one below me and shot at him about 5 or 6 short bursts from astern and above. I do not think enemy pilot saw me. After my attack he did a stall turn away and then vertically dived to the ground. Smoke was pouring from his engine. I circled looking for him but did not see him again."

Everything happened at an altitude of 23,000 ft over the centre of the Isle of Wight at about 12.45. Fw. Hellriegel's Messerschmitt Bf 109E-4 was the only one to crash on the island.

16 October 1940

Flying training for the personnel of 308 Squadron began with accidents for its Officers Commanding. Following the Polish OC, S/Ldr Stefan Łaszkiewicz, who crashed on 28 September, S/Ldr Davis, the British OC, died in an accident two days after the arrival of the Hurricanes to Speke. Davis hit barrage balloon cables near the aerodrome, while flying P3399. Both his wingmen, P/O Erwin Kawnik and Sgt Władysław Majchrzyk, miraculously missed the cables and landed safely at Speke. Davis and his aircraft spun from less than 200 feet, crashed and burnt. This fatal crash

---

[61] F/Lt D. M. Crook DFC, *Spitfire Pilot.*

did not end 308 Squadron's bad luck. That same day F/Lt Young, one of the British flight commanders, landed with the undercarriage up, damaging another Hurricane, V6859.

17 October 1940

This day was not a good one for 302 Squadron. About 9.20 am a dozen of the squadron's Hurricanes were airborne to patrol over Biggin Hill at 25,000 ft. "No contact made", the very common note in the ORB at this time, was accompanied by sad information about the death of Sgt Jerzy Sergiusz Załuski. On the way back he crash landed at Colliers End; his Hurricane, V7417/WX-T, hit the ground and turned over, and the pilot was crushed to death in the cockpit. Later the aircraft was transported to Northolt, and after repair was back in service.

Late in the afternoon, about 4.20 pm, a dozen Hurricanes were again on duty. Similarly to the morning patrol, whilst returning from the Biggin Hill area, they sustained non-operational casualties. F/Lt Jan Czerny got lost and landed in a field, slightly damaging his Hurricane V6753/WX-Z. After finding out his position, he took off and was back at Northolt only a little later than the other members of his unit. However, P/O Stanisław Kleczkowski also force landed near Sittingbourne due to lack of fuel. His aircraft – Hurricane V6735/WX-M – was damaged, but the pilot was unhurt.[62]

18 October 1940

About 3 pm two squadrons of the Northolt Wing, including 302, were airborne to patrol the Maidstone area. The 302 Squadron team was as follows:

F/Lt Jastrzębski	P3923/WX-U	Blue 1
P/O Wapniarek	P3872/WX-R	Blue 2
P/O Żukowski	V6571/WX-Q	Blue 3
F/O Carter	P3931/WX-V	Green 1
P/O Bernaś	P2918/WX-Y	Green 2
P/O Borowski	P3930/WX-X	Green 3
F/Lt Thomson	V6865/WX-L	Red 1
P/O Karwowski	P6744/WX-C	Red
S/Ldr Mümler	P3538/WX-J	Red
F/Lt Wczelik	V6860/WX-B	Yellow 1
Sgt Nowakiewicz	P3205/WX-E	Yellow 2
F/O Kowalski	P3085/WX-A	Yellow 3

The weather was getting worse and cloud cover hid enemy bombers as well as freelance Messerschmitts. According to a report, about 3.31 pm the wing, with 229 Squadron led by 302, was advised that two enemy aircraft were approaching from the south, but these were not seen. After that 229 Squadron broke away and later engaged an enemy aircraft claimed as damaged. During almost an hour long patrol 302's "A" Flight soon found a good target for their guns. Sgt Eugeniusz Nowakiewicz described [62] this event:

---

[62] The information about Kleczkowski's forced landing is included in the ORB narrative (Form 540) under the heading of 26 October 1940. However, this does not match the aircraft listings (Form 541), as that day Kleczkowski was not flying at all. The last mention of him in Form 541 is included under the heading of 17 October, with a note Forced landed Sittingbourne.

"I was flying Yellow 2, and after about an hour flying Red 1 attacked a Ju 88, shooting at and receiving very heavy fire from the rear upper gun turret. I attacked after Red 1 from ¾ above and a beam behind. The e/a was painted such a dark green colour that it was scarcely possible to see the black crosses. I was unable to see the effect of Red 1's attack, and with my first attack I got in a burst of two seconds, opening fire at about 250 yards, closing to 100 yards and I did not encounter any fire whatsoever in the e/a either in my first or second attack, and I supposed that the gunner was put out of action in the first attack by Red 1. I noticed no result at all from my first burst and I attacked a second time from above and behind, opening fire at about 150 yards, closing to about 30 yards, getting in a burst of 3 seconds. I broke away to starboard, climbing and I noticed two persons from the Ju 88 crew jump out, and their parachute open. Once more I noticed no fire from the Ju 88. The e/a continued in a gentle glide earthwards, and after a few seconds disappeared into clouds, lost from view. The R/T worked very well indeed. The attack took place at 15,000 ft."

"(The rest of this pilot's report does not affect the combat, and has therefore not been translated.)"[63]

Both wingmen of F/Lt Thomson, who led Red Section, attacked the bomber unsuccessfully. One of them reported that he saw a Bf 109, flying above the bomber, and as soon as the squadron attacked the Ju 88, this aircraft

"made a steep turn about 360 degrees and disappeared in the cloud. One Hurricane was seen to go after this supposed Me 109."

Most of the claims reported by fighter pilots during that misty day were not confirmed by the RAF authorities, and the 302 Squadron pilot had to content himself with one Ju 88 probably destroyed, despite two of the crew baling out of the bomber which he had reported. The two Flights of the Polish unit then became separated, although it is not clear at which point, as the Composite Combat Report stated –

"After the attack the Squadron reformed and Yellow 2 Sgt Nowakiewicz states that he was the last aircraft in the Squadron, and that he counted ten aircraft besides himself."

This would appear to mean that one of the 302 Squadron pilots followed the Messerschmitt which disappeared in the cloud. No members of "A" Flight reported chasing an enemy fighter, while most of the "B" Flight pilots would not be able to report anything because of a disaster which struck later, as will be recounted.

F/Lt Thomson led the unit back to Northolt after fixing the position of the squadron, which he found to be about 30 miles from base. Probably he lost the last three sections – Blue, Green and Yellow – when descending to investigate another enemy aircraft at 5,000 ft, which was reported immediately after this fixing of his position. In spite of the bad weather, all of the "A" Flight pilots reached Northolt aerodrome, but "B" Flight found itself under the clouds, and getting lost in the mist.

---

[63] Reports of 302 Squdron pilots, as well as other Polish units, were originally written in Polish and then translated by Intelligence Officers. Almost all 302 Squadron reports preserved at the Public Record Office are duplicated in Polish and English versions.

The last part of the Composite Combat Report concerning the subsequent tragedy states as follows:

"Blue 1 landed at Cobham with 1 gallon of petrol.

"Blue 2. P/O Wapniarek crashed at Cobham (An eye witness states he saw 4 aircraft flying overhead very low in and out of cloud – one of those aircraft detached itself and seemed to shut off its engine, and a moment later came out of cloud, and crashed, catching fire immediately.)

"Blue 3 – P/O Żukowski is still missing. Crashed and killed near Detling.

"Green 1 F/O Carter and Green 3 – P/O Borowski crashed at Kempton Race Course within 200 yards of each other.

"Green 2 – Landed at Langly."

P/O Stefan Wapniarek crashed at Nutwood Farm, Thames Ditton, and was killed. F/O Edward Carter baled out of his aircraft at 50 feet, but his parachute did not open and he was killed on hitting the ground; P/O Jan Borowski, who had joined 302 Squadron the day before, posted from 5 OTU, was killed and burnt in his aircraft which dived steeply into ground at high speed; P/O Aleksiej Żukowski died in a crash at Harp Farm, Boxley near Detling, when his fuel ran out. Only P/O Bronisław Bernaś survived a crash landing.

Neither of the two surviving "B" Flight pilots reported chasing a Messerschmitt, but P/O Żukowski's crash site was far (more then 30 miles) away from the rest of the "B" Flight casualties. This could indicate that he expended more fuel than the others when attacking the Messerschmitt and got lost after the combat. Even if he damaged the Bf 109, he did not live to report it.

23 October 1940

Turnhouse-based 607 County of Durham Squadron maintained flying training, and during one routine flight on 23 October, F/O Juliusz Frey, who would later become flight commander in 316 Squadron, made an unfortunate landing, causing damage to Hurricane I P3962. This Auxiliary Air Force unit was one of those which had hosted many Polish airmen since September 1940.

308 Squadron also suffered damage, when its British Commanding Officer, following a local flight landed with undercarriage retracted at Kinver near Stourbridge. S/Ldr Morris escaped unhurt but Hurricane P3452 was damaged.

24 October 1940

The chain of unfortunate accidents continued. 303 Squadron history recorded:

"No encounters with the enemy. Moreover, intensive training continues, due to posting in of new, non-operational pilots."

During a dog fight practice P/O Jan Bury-Burzymski, flying Hurricane I V6807/RF-R, crashed and was killed. The same day F/O Marian Pisarek damaged his Hurricane I, V7384/RF-H. When he was back from operational patrol over base due to failing light, he was not able to see the windsock and overshot Leconfield runway. Pisarek's accident, who was well known for his perfect eyesight, was annotated by Officer Commanding:

"No training in dusk landings has been given in this country to the pilots of squadron."

25 October 1940

The day brought more losses amongst Polish airmen and their aircraft.

Sgt Kazimierz Waśkiewicz of 306 Squadron, a very experienced pilot on older types than the Hurricane, "faced with too many knobs" in the cockpit during his first solo flight forgot to lower his undercarriage and belly landed at Church Fenton. Aircraft number L1771 was sent for repair, but it was recommended that the pilot be posted to fly bombers.

308 Squadron, also undergoing intensive flying training on Hurricanes at Baginton, lost one of its aircraft when P/O Feliks Fryderyk Szyszka forgot to switch over fuel tanks, and was forced to land in a field, damaging Hurricane I V6914. The pilot was unhurt.

A similar accident happened to one of the Polish pilots of 229 Squadron, based at Northolt. P/O Józef Gil also force landed his Hurricane I N2607 due to lack of fuel. The pilot was unhurt, but the aircraft suffered damage classified as Cat. I. Several Polish airmen served with this unit, which shared its base initially with 303, and later 302. They were P/O Józef Gil, P/O Mieczysław Gorzula, P/O Edmund Jereczek, P/O Jerzy Popławski and P/O Stefan Stegman.

302 Squadron made three operational sorties from Northolt during the day. A morning patrol at about 9.20 am was undertaken by a dozen aircraft, but F/Lt Franciszek Jastrzębski failed to return. He was last seen flying his Hurricane V7593/WX-V towards France. Jastrzębski had spotted some Bf 109s in the distance and tried to intercept them, followed by his section. Neither of his wingmen, Sgt Antoni Markiewicz and P/O Bronisław Bernaś, could keep pace with their leader, and left him alone somewhere over the Channel. Jastrzębski was presumed missing.

Other units involved in combat with German fighters during the early morning hours included three Spitfire squadrons. Whilst 41 and 66 Squadrons claimed some victories in their engagements, 603 Squadron suffered heavy losses. One of the three unfortunate pilots of this unit was P/O Ludwik Martel, who was shot down near Hastings by a Bf 109 while flying Spitfire II P7325/XT-W.

Wounded, he lost consciousness for a while. Then he realised he was flying his Spitfire out of clouds in an inverted position. There was a large hole in one wing, and the engine was dead. He managed to recover from the dive immediately above the ground, and crash-landed in a field.

He later recalled that the first thing he noticed in the vicinity was a windmill, which made him believe that in his unconscious flight he had somehow reached Holland, and would now be taken prisoner. Fortunately, this was proved wrong as soon as a patrol of rather elderly Home Guards arrived. Suffering from his wounds, and not speaking good English at that time anyway, Martel was unable to communicate with them, while their aircraft recognition was obviously far from satisfactory, and so he spent quite a while under guard, mistaken for a German. Finally an officer arrived, and identified him correctly. After his wounds were dressed he was taken to a hospital where, in his fever, he threatened to shoot a German airman admitted there at the same time (no doubt proving to the medical staff, the wild hatred Polish airmen were believed to have for their Luftwaffe adversaries). Eventually Martel spent ten days in the hospital, returning to operations with 603 Squadron by 6 November.

About the same time as the Spitfires were engaged over Hastings, Sgt Michał Mirosław Maciejowski of 249 Squadron became separated from his unit, also engaged in fighting Bf 109s. The Polish pilot got lost during the combat and made a perfect landing near Colchester in his Hurricane I V6692/GN-O. He was later led back to North Weald by F/O Lofts in a Miles Magister.

P/O Stanisław Piątkowski of 79 Squadron based at Pembrey crashed near Carew Cheriton in his Hurricane N2708 after a routine patrol over Linney Head. He and Sgt Włodzimierz Mudry, had arrived with 79 Squadron on 11 September 1940 while it was based at Biggin Hill. Except for the incident on 25 October, in which Piątkowski was killed, Poles failed to mark their presence in the unit. However, Donald Stones in his memoirs recalls Sgt Mudry as a very colourful character:

"We had two artists in the Squadron now. John Parker, who was already established as the keeper and illustrator of our unofficial Squadron diary, and Sergeant Mudry, one of three newly acquired Polish pilots . . ."

". . . Parker and Mudry decorated the walls of our mess with exciting drawings in coloured chalk of near-nude chorus girls and caricatures of aerial battles in which 79 Squadron always came off badly. Of the girls, one magnificent specimen with much leg and what we call an air-cooled chest, wore only a short pair of black French knickers, attached by drawing pins to the wall. A visiting VIP of high rank fell into the trap and through unendurable curiosity, casually lifted the knickers, to be confronted with a card bearing the message: 'You have a dirty mind. Put 2s 6d in the beer kitty.'"

26 October 1940

As on the previous days, several accidents occured in Polish units under training. Sgt Bronisław Kościk of 303 Squadron based at Leconfield crash-landed Hurricane I V6681/RF-B due to engine failure, and the aircraft was sent to a repair unit. P/O Jerzy Tadeusz Skibiński of Pembrey-based 308 Squadron following a cross country flight damaged Hurricane I V6536 whilst landing, and Sgt Kazimierz Waśkiewicz of 306 Squadron force landed with the undercarriage up three miles from Shrewsbury, damaging Hurricane I L1717. This latter pilot was sent back to an Operational Training Unit for more training.

On the other hand, the day brought more success for the Northolt-based 302 Squadron. 24 Hurricanes from this unit and 229 Squadron took off at about 11.00 am with orders to patrol the Croydon area. The following pilots and their aircraft took part in this sortie:

F/Lt Czerny	P2918/WX-Y
P/O Chałupa	V6941/WX-W
P/O Gnyś	P3872/WX-R
P/O Pilch	V6923/WX-U
Sgt Markiewicz	V6942/WX-S
P/O Król	P3877/WX-T
S/Ldr Satchell	V6865/WX-L
Sgt Kosarz	V6860/WX-B
F/Lt Thomson	V6744/WX-C
F/O Kowalski	P3935/WX-D
S/Ldr Mümler	P3538/WX-J
P/O Czerniak	P2717/WX-H

This eventful sortie, which ended with a chase as far as Boulogne, was described by

Sgt Antoni Markiewicz, who claimed a Bf 109 probably destroyed:

"I was flying as Blue 3 at 10 000 ft and suddenly noticed an Me 109 flying alone. It disappeared into thick cloud, and later came out above it on the port bow. I therefore broke away from my Section and using clouds as cover I went after him managing to get into attacking position, slightly above and parallel with the e/a. I opened fire at 200 yards with a beam attack giving him a burst of 3 seconds. The e/a was taken by surprise and zoomed very steeply. I noticed intense black smoke issuing from the starboard wing centre section. After executing a loop e/a turned on its back and went down out of control. I now gave him another burst of 1 second from 120 yards. The e/a went into cloud. I saw him continuing his dive to earth. I then suddenly noticed two other Me 109's on my port bow about 1000 ft below me. In proceeding to the attack I became conscious of tracer being fired at me from 3 Me 109's on my starboard bow at about 600 yards distance. I saw the burst which passed my tail unit, took evasive action and escaped into cloud.

"When preparing to attack the above two mentioned Me 109's I noticed through a gap in the clouds an aerodrome where about 25 to 30 Me 109's were stationed. I saw one Me 109 land and two others take off. I returned to base landing at 13.00."

Markiewicz had probably caught Bf 109E-1 Werk Nr. 6180, piloted by Ofw. Werner Kaufmann from 4./JG 53 by surprise. Kaufmann, shot down into the sea, was later rescued by the *Seenotdienst*. S/Ldr Satchell, leading both Hurricane squadrons, damaged one Bf 109 east of Boulogne harbour. His victim escaped into cloud, but just before this Satchell noticed some parts of the Messerschmitt falling off.

27 October 1940

One of the largest actions by the Luftwaffe in the last stage of the Battle of Britain was the launching of a series of simultaneous attacks against London, Liverpool, and Coventry. 17 Squadron based at Debden, after a month of rest, had an opportunity to engage the enemy. The squadron took off about 9.30 am and P/O Paweł Niemiec, who claimed a Do 17 shared damaged with Sgt Griffith in the ensuing combat, described his action:

"I was on patrol with the squadron weaving above, when I was given vector 090 degrees and when about 500 yards away from the Squadron following vector I saw a twin-engine aircraft below me. I dived down, and when above the a/c I circled in and saw the crosses on fuselage. I attacked him as he went into cloud, diving from above, giving a short burst at about 300 yards. I broke away upwards and saw another Hurricane attacking. I then dived from above astern, firing a 3 to 4 second burst, coming in very close, we were then both in cloud and I lost the e/a."

According to his report they delivered their attack somewhere over Eastchurch on the Isle of Sheppey. The international team from 17 Squadron taking part in this engagement was as follows:

F/Lt Bayne	V6759
P/O Wissler	V7570

P/O Ross	P3894
P/O Kordula (Czech)	V6791
Sgt Cameron	V7241
Sgt Bartlett	V6553/YB-J
Sgt Griffith	P2972
Sgt Stevens	V7408
F/O Niemiec (Polish)	P2794/YB-E
P/O Kumiega (Polish)	V6743
F/O Pittman	V7500/YB-D

Another claim by a Polish pilot on this day was made by P/O Piotr Ostaszewski-Ostoja, flying with 609 Squadron. The unit ORB recorded:

"Green Section (F/O T. Forshaw, P/O P. A. Baillon and F/O P. Ostaszewski) pursued and fired upon an elusive enemy bomber, believed He 111 or Ju 88 near Andover with uncertain results. The enemy aircraft was believed by the controller to have been shot down, but this report was not confirmed. Baillon received return fire which damaged his oil system compelling him to bale out near Upavon. His machine landed near C.F.S. and burned up. Green 1 highly praised the vectoring of the duty Controller, again F/Lt Fieldsend. These recent bouquets for the Operations Room were no doubt appreciated coming, as they did, after a long series of brickbats."

The day ended with a landing accident at Leconfield, at about 6.30 pm, when Sgt Marian Bełc damaged Hurricane I V7401/RF-G. Patrolling section had been ordered to Pancake but owing to the drome being bombed aircraft were not able to land correctly. During the approach Bełc failed to level out at sufficient height and his undercarriage collapsed.

28 October 1940

The day began before dawn with an accident in 307 Squadron, when Sgt Stanisław Grondowski's Defiant N1560 crashed during landing. It was the first serious accident causing damage to an aircraft since this unit had been formed.

Several single Luftwaffe bombers attacked different targets during the morning. One of these was intercepted by P/O Franciszek Surma of 257 Squadron. Surma, flying Hurricane I P3893, claimed damage to a He 111 between Romney and Folkestone about 11 am:

"I was Red 2, of the leading section of 257 (Burma) Squadron. We were following 249 Sqn., when we were ordered to look for an enemy bomber. While searching over Ashford area, I lost my squadron in the clouds. When I came out of cloud I saw seven planes of either 249 or 257 Squadron, which I intended to follow, when I saw a twin engined aircraft flying in their direction below them. I went to investigate and saw the crosses on the wings so I dived down onto him, but could not attack head on as it was too late. I zoomed up and made an astern attack. When I was about 300 yards behind the e/a, a He 111, the rear gunners opened fire from below.

"I gave them one short burst to unnerve them. When I was 150-200 yards behind the e/a's tail on the port side I gave a 3-4 secs. burst at the cockpit. I passed over him and then fired at the starboard engine from about 80 yards.

"He continued to fly level and I gave him another burst of about 4 secs, from about 100 yards at the starboard engine. Seeing no result I followed the attack up with another burst at the starboard engine. I noticed a small explosion from the engine and saw grey smoke pouring out. At this time, the aircraft lurched to the right, and as I passed him, a piece of aircraft flew by my plane, almost hitting me.

"We went into cloud at about 4500 ft. I levelled out, came out of the layer and searched above and below. As I came below cloud I saw that I was directly above the coastline. I looked for the e/a without being able to find it."

29 October 1940

Late in the afternoon RAF North Weald, which housed 46, 249 and 257 Squadrons, was attacked by *Jagdbomber* Bf 109s from II./LG 2. One of two Polish pilots from 249 Squadron who was at readiness, P/O Jerzy Solak, described this surprise attack in his memoirs:

"On 29 October the weather near the airfield was quite good, vertical visibility very good, but horizontal was reduced by a slight haze. Operations room ordered us to take our places in the cockpits, as radar stations had found some targets, but they soon lost them off their screens. Our squadron was prepared, waiting to scramble. The same was done by the neighbouring squadron [257 – author], taking place for take-off at our side and at right angles to our left.

"Suddenly I was startled, and from the corner of my eye I saw bomb explosions on the other side of the aerodrome, one of which blew a part of the mess up! A red flare was fired – signal for the squadrons to scramble. We started up our engines immediately, and everybody started their take-off runs at full throttle. The same was done by the pilots of the other squadron . . . I just thought – how many of us will collide? I had no time to consider this, as I kept on the port side of my section leader, so I looked to starboard, I could not see those taking off to my port. All I wanted was to get airborne.

"Explosions on the ground! We are airborne . . . I see bombs falling, still in the air . . . I bend down in the cockpit . . . Explosions on both sides... Explosion on my starboard very close . . . The Hurricane flying to my starboard disappears in a cloud of dust and smoke, mine is thrown up, the leader goes on. I can hear rattle on my wings and fuselage . . . End of the aerodrome, a field R/T underneath, and explosion on one side . . . The tent is thrown up to our height, like paper! The leader waves his wings and goes down steeply, his machine has failed. I am alone.

"I make a steep turn and head back towards the bomb blasts, where Messerschmitts play. I can see a melee of aircraft, and have to be careful to avoid any of them getting on my tail. I can see a Messerschmitt above, and a Hurricane behind him. But now a foursome of Germans dive after a Hurricane. I pull the machine as if for looping, and start a long burst from my machine guns, sending it in front of the Germans' noses . . . My Hurricane stalled with no speed, but the Messerschmitts scattered away to all sides. Like partridge – I thought for a moment.

"When I regained control of the machine, I found myself close to a German who was running away eastwards. Estuaries underneath us, visibility deteriorated. I was slowly gaining on him at full throttle, positioning myself under his tail . . .

Quite calm and quiet, I fired a long, well aimed burst . . . The German pulled the machine up vertically, and then went down, and with a trail of smoke he disappeared in the ground haze over the estuaries.

"I turned back to my airfield, joined the circle of aeroplanes that awaited a landing strip to be marked among the bomb craters. After a dozen minutes or so I landed safely. At our dispersal a Hurricane was burning laying on its back, the guard room at the entrance to the aerodrome, rebuilt four times, I think, had disappeared. This place was now occupied by a large hole. A fire fighting vehicle was on its back! I taxied to my pen carefully. Fitters cheered over my victory. Sadly, the burning Hurricane was the starboard wingman in our section."

Fortunately F/O Keith Temple Lofts, the pilot of the crashed Hurricane mentioned in this account, was unhurt and his aircraft, V7627, was only damaged. Presumably the Messerschmitt attacked by P/O Solak returned to its base at Calais-Marck only slightly damaged. One of JG 2's Messerschmitts, Bf 109E-7 Werk Nr. 2032, crash-landed at Wissant due to damage in combat over North Weald. Three others never returned to France and fell victim to Hurricane pilots of 249 and 257 Squadrons. One of the claims was made by another Polish pilot of the Hyderabad Squadron, Sgt Michał Mirosław Maciejowski, flying Hurricane I P3463/GN-L. His combat report stated:

"I followed F/Lt Barton as he was attacking one of a formation of five enemy aircraft at about 4000 ft. Two of the formation separated and I pursued them. They dived into cloud and I cut through cloud and found myself 50 yards behind both of them. I gave one of them a 5-10 seconds burst, astern attack, and it immediately burst into flames and fell to earth about 200 yards from the sea-shore on land, where I saw it burning. I could not tell whether it was by the river Blackwater or river Crouch. There were some small boats nearby. I gave the second one about 5-seconds burst but I then lost it in the clouds."

His victim was Obfw Josef Harmeling from 4./LG 2. Harmeling's Bf 109E (Werk Nr. 5593, black triangle[64] + N) crashed at Langenhoe Wick, and the wounded pilot was taken prisoner.

During this surprise attack on North Weald 257 Squadron suffered the largest casualties. P/O Franciszek Surma, one of the Polish pilots of that unit, was shot down by a Messerschmitt Bf 109, probably that flown by Oblt. Schöpfel, the *Gruppenkommandeur* of III./JG 26, who reported that his victim, shot down at 3,000 ft, managed to bale out. P/O Surma's aircraft, P3893, crashed at Bobbingworth near Matching, and the pilot indeed saved his life by baling out. 257 Squadron lost another aircraft, in which the pilot was killed when caught during take-off.

The Messerschmitts returning from North Weald were then met by 17 and 46 Squadrons, which had taken off earlier from Stapleford. Among the ten pilots of 17 Squadron were three Poles:

F/Lt Bayne	V6759
P/O Wissler	P3894

---

[64] In line with all *Jagdbomber* aircraft in II./LG2, the fighter carried the triangle emblem and a code letter. For some reason many publications refer to this Bf 109 as "3X+N". Perhaps the German word *Dreieck* (triangle) was somehow mistaken for *Drei X* (3 X).

P/O Leary	P3061
Sgt Sewell	V7570
Sgt Cameron	V7241
F/O Niemiec (Polish)	V6553/YB-J
Sgt Hogg	V7500/YB-D
P/O Chełmecki (Polish)	P3868
Sgt Bartlett	V7658
P/O Kumiega (Polish)	V6743

P/O Tadeusz Kumiega, together with Sgt Hogg, claimed one Bf 109 shot down over Foulness. This was the first success for the young Pole and the only victory for 17 Squadron that day. He described his combat thus:

> "Myself and Sgt Hogg were weaving behind the squadron when on patrol over North Weald at 25 000 ft. When I saw below me a single Me 109 at about 19 000 ft I dived and attacked him from astern quarter firing a 2 seconds burst at 100 yards range. As I broke away upwards, Sgt Hogg made astern attack range 250 yards, burst 2 seconds. I then made another quarter attack from 300 yards with burst of 1½ seconds. The Me 109 climbed very fast and gained on us. We saw glycol smoke pouring from it. Then the e/a dived and Sgt Hogg caught him just as he went into cloud and fired a 1 second burst at 400 yards. I overtook the e/a turned and made another quarter attack at 80 yards range with a 2 second burst. Sgt Hogg gave several more short bursts. The e/a then turned over on his back and the pilot jumped while his a/c was upside down."

Fw. Conrad Jäckel of 8./JG 26 baled out of Bf 109E-4 (Werk Nr.5794, black 1 and bar). The aircraft crashed at March House Farm at Tillingham, where the Luftwaffe pilot was taken prisoner.

At the same time squadrons based south of London were also busy. Eight Hurricanes of 253 Squadron got airborne about 5 pm, together with 501 Squadron from Kenley, and were ordered to patrol the Kenley-Brooklands area at 15,000 ft. Polish pilots were in both units. 253 Squadron:

F/Lt D. Woodley	V7608	
Sgt Moore	V7301	
P/O Nowak (Polish)	V6637	Blue 2
P/O Greenwood	V7499	
Sgt Allen	V7466	
Sgt Kita (Polish)	V6815	
Sgt Kopecky (Czech)	P5172	
P/O Marsland	V7606	Green 1

The squadron, flying as one section of four with a section of two astern, with two aircraft weaving, climbed to 21,000 ft and then altered formation to three pairs in shallow vic with two aircraft weaving. 501 Squadron was attacking some Messerschmitts at 15,000 ft in the vicinity of Dover, when 253 Squadron sighted two formations of nine Bf 109s at 28,000 and 30,000 ft altitude. The former, to the west, was flying in a wide fan, while the latter was in two lines abreast of five and four astern. The squadron was at 27,000 ft and circled beneath both formations, whilst 501

Squadron engaged and dispersed the Messerschmitt 109s at 15,000 ft. Both formations above then turned south east and east. As it was impossible to engage either formation, the Squadron split into pairs, to hunt for isolated enemy aircraft.

P/O Marsland attacked a Bf 109 travelling south. After his attack the Messerschmitt rolled and was last seen by the British pilot at a height of 300 ft. Horsham Observer Corps later reported that a Bf 109 crashed at the time of the engagement.

One of the Poles, P/O Nowak described his efforts:

> "Leader gave orders to go down and in diving I lost my leader. I was searching for the Squadron when I sighted 1 Do 17 at 200 feet with a Spitfire circling at 1000 feet apparently without ammunition. I delivered a line astern attack on enemy aircraft firing a six second burst with two further attacks after which enemy aircraft went out to sea near Rye. I followed and some 15 miles out when enemy was losing height I delivered a fourth attack from ³/₄ to line astern. Enemy aircraft crashed in sea and I returned to base."

No twin-tailed aircraft was reported by the Luftwaffe as lost over the sea, although two Bf 110s and one Do 17P crashed at their bases following combats or "routine domestic flights".

Apart from these successes and losses, Polish units under training also suffered some losses during the day. P/O Włodzimierz Miksa of 303 Squadron was hurt in an accident at Leconfield, flying Hurricane I P3206/RF-X, while F/Lt Walerian Jasionowski of 308 Squadron damaged Hurricane I L2092. The latter noted in his diary:

> "12.30 hrs I land at Wittering aerodrome. Too long run downhill, poor brakes. I crash the aircraft against a wall at butts. Morris [308 Squadron OC] referred the matter to No. 9 Group."

302 Squadron, the only Polish fighter unit actually on operations at this time also, had a bad day. F/Lt Jan Czerny collided with another aircraft, flown by F/Lt James Thomson; Czerny landed in his Hurricane V6923/WX-U at White Waltham with a broken airscrew and with the undercarriage up. F/Lt Thomson's Hurricane, P3085/WX-A, was cut in half by Czerny's airscrew. Thomson had to bale out and was slightly injured on landing. An investigation stated that error of judgement on the pilot's part had caused the accident. The same day F/Lt Thomson was posted to RAF Northolt Station HQ 'non effective due to sickness'.

30 October 1940

This was another day full of accidents caused by fuel shortages.

P/O Bolesław Własnowolski, serving with 213 Squadron, got lost and force landed near Amberley, damaging his Hurricane I P3641/AK-P. This seems to have been his personal aircraft, which he had flown almost continuously since 24 September 1940. It is interesting that the other Pole in the same unit, who lost his life in combat on 11 September 1940, Sgt Wójcicki, had also usually flown the aircraft coded P. Was it 'P for Polish'?

The other Polish pilot forced to make an emergency landing was Sgt Michał Mirosław Maciejowski of 249 Squadron, based at North Weald. Following a long chase after Messerschmitts over the Channel, Sgt Maciejowski was back over Britain when his fuel ran out. He landed his Hurricane I V6685 perfectly at Stoney Field, Blackford Farm, near Herstmonceux, about 1.20 pm. Despite his aircraft being clearly marked with blue-white-red roundels, the local police took him for a German, although he tried to explain his nationality in his very rough English. His adventure had a happy ending, however, and after filling his tanks with petrol he returned to base, where his comrades described how they had claimed one Bf 109 destroyed, one probable and one damaged.

Less lucky was the crew of 307 Squadron Fairey Battle R7411 on their way back from Digby to Kirton-in-Lindsey at night. After about ten minutes flying from the base the cooling system failed. Glycol was pouring into the cockpit and both airmen decided to abandon the aircraft. P/O Kazimierz Kazimierczuk and Sgt Mieczysław Adamiecki, baling out at low altitude and in mist, landed so badly that both broke both their legs.

31 October 1940

This proved to be another day of unfortunate accidents amongst night fighter pilots. Sgt Bronisław Malinowski, who volunteered to fly Hurricane Is in 43 Squadron, rather than perform the role of a Defiant pilot (without any forward-firing guns) in 307 Squadron (his original posting), force landed at Chirnside, Berwick in P3357, due to engine failure, but suffered no injuries although slightly damaging the aircraft.

Another accident happened to Sgt Juliusz Bilau from 307 (Night Fighter) Squadron. When he was climbing to the cockpit of his aircraft, he slipped on the wing, fell, and broke his leg. This accident had occured even without starting the engine! Later the unfortunate pilot remarked that he had "no air accident in his whole career, and now, trying to get airborne . . ."

1 November 1940

Polish pilots of 213 Squadron, P/O Bolesław Własnowolski and F/O Marian Duryasz, had already received postings to 302 Squadron, with an opportunity to take some leave before moving to the Polish unit. The same day, when both were prepared to go for their well earned holiday, the newly arrived S/Ldr D. S. McDonald placed them on readiness, due to shortage of pilots. F/O Duryasz, subsequently replaced by one of his British colleagues, was on the way to the administration huts to arrange the paperwork, when suddenly enemy aircraft appeared over the airfield. He watched the show performed by Bf 109s of I./JG 2 and Hurricanes of all the Tangmere-based squadrons, during which P/O Własnowolski was killed. The pilots of 213 Squadron who rushed to engage the *Freie Jagd* Messerschmitts about 3 pm were as follows:

S/Ldr McDonald	AK-K
F/O Clark	AK-F
Sgt Adair	AK-H
P/O Kearsey	AK-E
F/L Kellow	V6866/AK-D
Sgt Snowden	AK-C
F/O Sizer	AK-X
P/O Własnowolski (Polish)	AK-V
Sgt Barrow	AK-J
P/O Bouchart	AK-W

Własnowolski was shot down in combat with a Bf 109 over Stoughton, and his Hurricane I N2608/AK-V crashed some nine miles north of Chichester.[65] During his service with the RAF he had been credited with five victories.

Opportunities to meet large formations of Luftwaffe bombers were becoming rare due to the autumn weather. Patrols over the southern part of England were frequently fruitless and uneventful. On 1 November during an afternoon patrol, 501 Squadron pilots spotted some aircraft flying in the far distance, but they would not even get close. During this sortie Sgt Mieczysław Marcinkowski separated from the formation of fighters and suddenly dived into the sea. The cause of the tragedy was never ascertained, but the most probable reason seemed to be freezing of the oxygen system in his Hurricane V7405, common in the type, which caused the pilot to lose consciousness. He had arrived with 501 Squadron only a few weeks before his death, previously serving in 151 Squadron. He joined P/O Stanisław Skalski, the only Polish pilot to serve in the former unit at the end of the year. Soon, more Poles arrived here, as well as with another 'international' squadron, 32. In the latter unit a large group of Polish fighters arrived after the Battle of Britain and at the beginning of 1941, preparing themselves ultimately to become the backbone of newly established Polish Air Force squadrons. They were: P/O Mieczysław Waszkiewicz, P/O Wilhelm Śniechowski, F/O Olech Antoni Kawczyński, P/O Gerard Karol Ranoszek, Sgt Leon Kosmowski, P/O Michał Kolubiński, P/O Janusz Marciniak, P/O Tomasz Rzyski, P/O Zdzisław Radomski, F/O Jan Jakubowski, P/O Stanisław Szmejl.

Following a training formation flight on 1 November 1940 P/O Wilhelm Śniechowski slightly damaged his Hurricane P3351 while landing at Acklington. Cause of accident as stated in accident report – mishandling.

Sgt Stefan Wójcik of 307 night fighter Squadron, damaged his aircraft while landing at Kirton-in-Lindsey. His Defiant N1704, flying too fast to land properly, finished its landing run amongst parked aircraft; both N1704 and another Defiant, N1696, were damaged.

3 November 1940

In 32 Squadron F/O Jan Falkowski, while flying P3351, damaged his aircraft as had P/O Śniechowski a couple of days before, while P/O Mieczysław Waszkiewicz, blinded by glycol fumes and unable to see the ditch and fence in front of him, crashed his Hurricane R4216 at Wooperton. Both pilots were unhurt.

Sgt Bolesław Olewiński of 111 Squadron was less fortunate. His unit, after the exhausting combats of the Battle of Britain, moved north, to Scotland. Even there fighters from the Treble One Squadron found targets for their guns. On 3 November single Luftwaffe bombers dropped bombs over Aberdeen, causing a lot of damage. A section from 111 Squadron consisting of P/O Kellett (V7237), Sgt Wallace (P2979) and Sgt Bolesław Olewiński (V6560) took off from Dyce, heading to the Peterhead area, and there they managed to intercept the Heinkel 111H-3 Werk Nr. 3171 of I./KG 26. First they attacked the enemy bomber over Moray Firth, and followed it out to sea. After a 30 mile chase all three fighters severely hit the bomber. During his

---

[65] The place of Własnowolski's death was commemorated by the owner of the land, Mr Ronald Langmead, who in 1997 raised a memorial with an inscription HE DIED DEFENDING BRITAIN, POLAND AND FREEDOM.

second attack, the Hurricane flown by Olewiński was hit by return fire and immediately crashed in the sea. The rest of the section fired all their ammunition and left the bomber at an altitude of 400 feet. Smoking badly from one engine, it finally reached the Norwegian coast, and crashed at Hevdland, killing all four of Uffz. Josef Mendler's crew. Nevertheless, the RAF fighters were credited only with a He 111 damaged.

5 November 1940

While P/O Wilhelm Śniechowski continued the series of accidents in 32 Squadron, this time force-landing at Acklington and damaging his Hurricane P3460, other units with Polish airmen engaged *Freie Jagd* Messerschmitts.

Hurricanes from Northolt, 302 and 615 Squadrons, were attacked by three Bf 109s in the Maidstone area (the official report states that 302 Squadron was engaged by 'He 113s'). One of the pilots tried to fire some bursts from long distance but without apparent results.

At another airfield in the London area, P/O Stanisław Skalski of 501 Squadron damaged his Hurricane I V7614, the results of the accident being assessed as Category I.

The only combat loss among the Poles on 5 November took place when Hurricanes of 238 Squadron patrolled over the Bournemouth area and were bounced by Messerschmitt Bf 109s from I./JG 2 "Richthofen". Two RAF pilots were forced to crash-land and two others baled out. One of the latter was Sgt Józef Jeka (Polish) who was wounded, his Hurricane I V7535 crashing at Sturminster Marshall.

6 November 1940

On this date P/O Jerzy Popławski from the Northolt-based 229 Squadron, force landed at Streatley, damaging his Hurricane P3898. He separated from the rest of his squadron while flying in cloud. He soon got lost and due to fuel shortage his engine cut. Popławski decided to land with wheels down and ran into soft ground although able to see very little through the misted windshield. The aircraft was found with slight damage in a field near Streatley, Beds.

7 November 1940

About noon nine aircraft of 249 Squadron took off to intercept large forces of enemy aircraft coming towards the Thames Estuary. P/O's Barclay and Crossey then joined the formation abandoning patrol duty over their base. When they arrived in the area of the Thames Estuary they saw a convoy being attacked by Ju 87s which were escorted by Bf 109s. Later on, W/Cdr Beamish, the OC RAF North Weald, joined the battle. 249 Squadron pilots taking part in this encounter were as follows:

P/O Neil	V7627
P/O Thompson	V6958/GN-D
Sgt Smithson	V6798
P/O Maconnell	V6855
Sgt Maciejowski (Polish)	V6534/GN-P
F/Lt Barton	V7538/GN-T
F/O Wells	P3463/GN-L
Sgt McNair	P3579/GN-Y
Sgt Palliser	V7677/GN-N
P/O Crossey	V7600/GN-C

| P/O Barclay | V6692/GN-O |
| W/Cdr Beamish | V7507/GN-B |

Sgt Michał Mirosław Maciejowski described his efforts in this engagement:

"In position Yellow 4 after patrolling the Thames Estuary e/a were sighted attacking convoy. The squadron dived to attack and split up. I sighted 5 enemy 109's attempting to bomb the convoy; they eventually split up into pairs leaving one straggling in the rear. I attacked the single e/a from behind and above, pouring into him from very close range approx. a 6 sec. burst. The e/a made no attempt to escape and burst into flames. The pilot did not jump. E/A crashed in flames in the sea about 8 miles north-west of Margate."

He claimed one Bf 109E destroyed over the Thames Estuary. In total 249 Squadron claimed four destroyed and four probables.[66]

Late afternoon, about 4.45 pm, 302 Squadron took off from Northolt to patrol the Guildford area. The patrol was uneventful, until Sgt Antoni Łysek had to force land at Woodley, Reading, due to an oil leak and consequent low pressure in the oil system of his Hurricane V6734/WX-K. The pilot was unhurt.

On 7 November 1940 307 Squadron moved to Jurby and 306 Squadron moved from Church Fenton to Ternhill, damaging one of its aeroplanes on the way. Three days before, 306 Squadron, the third Polish-manned fighter unit, had become operational. Only two pilots of the nucleus of 306 Squadron had taken part in the Battle of Britain – F/O Stefan Witorzeńć (flying previously in 501 Squadron) and Sgt Józef Jeka (who had been in 238 Squadron).

8 November 1940

The infamous Junkers 87 dive bomber, which had suffered heavy losses during the Battle, and had last been seen on 18 August, had appeared again on 1 November. 17 Squadron had engaged these on 1st, and again on 8 November. Between 4 and 5 pm on this latter date Ju 87s of StG 3 and LG 1 attacked two convoys in the Thames Estuary. There the Hurricanes of 17 Squadron met them. In the ensuing battle RAF pilots claimed 15 enemy aircraft destroyed, six probably destroyed and two damaged, although in fact only three Stuka dive bombers were reported lost and one badly damaged. 11 Group Headquarters telegraphed to 17 Squadron:

"Group Commander sends special congratulations to 17 Squadron on their outstanding success this afternoon when they destroyed thirteen dive-bombers in spite of a heavy fighter escort and without loss to themselves of pilots or aircraft."

The victorious team was as follows (claims in brackets):

F/Lt Bayne	V7542	(1-1-0)
Sgt Stewart	V6751	(1-0-2)
P/O Leary	P3061	(2½-½-0)

---

[66] More details of this and subsequent engagements involving Sgt Maciejowski and the squadron can be found in *249 at War* by Brian Cull (Grub Street, 1997).

Sgt Sewell	P3894	(0-2½-0)
F/O Niemiec (Polish)	V6759	(1-0-0)
Sgt Cameron	V7570	(1⅕-1-0)
F/Lt Harper	V7408	(0-0-0)
W/Cdr Farquhar	P3623	(2-0-0)
Sgt Griffith	V7500/YB-D	(2½-0-0)
Sgt Bartlett	V7658	(1-1-0)
P/O Chełmecki (Polish)	P2792	(1-0-0)
Sgt Hogg	P3868	(1½-0-0)

P/O's Marian Chełmecki and Paweł Niemiec described this engagement:

"I was weaving above squadron when we dived to attack Ju 87's. The squadron wheeled to port, and I saw 3 Ju 87's below me to the right of the squadron. I dived to attack the right-hand a/c of the 3, and gave it a 4 seconds burst from vertically above. I attacked again from astern quarter with a 2 second burst , and the e/a rolled over and went into the sea. I also saw another of the Ju 87's crash into the sea after being attacked by another Hurricane. I then saw a Me 109 at about 600 ft just above me, and climbed to attack it, but lost it in the haze. I got the leader's order to return to base if not engaged, and did so.

"Chełmecki – Yellow 3, Flight A, Sqn 17"

"I was following Blue 2 and saw him attacking 2 Ju 87's. I saw 2 more Ju 87's on my right at about 50 feet above sea level and attacked them from astern, firing a long burst, after which one of them turned away to the right, and went down to 10 feet over the sea. I then attacked again from astern quarter crossing over for another quarter attack from the port side, and again from the starboard. After that the e/a turned over and went into the sea. I noticed no return fire at any time. I was then looking for the rest of the squadron when I saw an Me 109 following a Ju 87 at 300 feet. One Hurricane had just turned away from the Junkers and it was wallowing badly at about 50 feet. I gave the Me 109 a 2 seconds burst at 400 yards closing to 300 yards from the port beam, but observed no effect. I heard Rider Leader order all a/c not engaged to return to base, and did so, having used nearly all the ammunition.

"Niemiec – Green 2, Flight B, Sqn 17"

302 Squadron undertook three patrols during the day. In the second one, about 1.10 pm, two dozen Hurricanes of 302 and 615 Squadrons left Northolt, and soon met the enemy. The pilots of the Polish unit were:

F/O Wczelik	V6860/WX-B
Sgt Kosarz	P3538/WX-J
Sgt Nowakiewicz	P3935/WX-D
P/O Karwowski	V6744/WX-C
P/O Wróblewski	V6694/WX-G
P/O Kleczkowski	V6865/WX-L
Sgt Beda	P3877/WX-T
F/Lt Farmer	V6942/WX-S
P/O Sporny	P6753/WX-Z

Sgt Markiewicz	R2687/WX-X
F/O Czerwiński	P3785/WX-R
Sgt Rytka	V6941/WX-W

The formation of fighters, flying at 20,000 ft, was bounced by Bf 109s of JG 26. These, flying some 5,000 ft above, picked the last section for their attack. Sgt Wilhelm Kosarz was shot down and killed, while Sgt Eugeniusz Nowakiewicz, was wounded, and crash landed at Detling. The third victim of the Messerschmitts, F/O Antoni Wczelik, force landed at Tunstel with the radiator shot up. 302 Squadron documents recorded sarcastically that the leader of 615 Squadron, who led the whole group, failed to notice the attack and the combat behind him.

Sgt Nowakiewicz described this combat in his report:

"We took off at a strength of two Squadrons, our Squadron following 615 and we were climbing the whole time until we got over South London. The weaving section was attacked by Me 109's. I did not see Sgt Kosarz attacked but a few seconds after he went down in flames two Me 109's attacked me from behind. In the ensuing dog fight I got down to 10 000 ft and the e/a disappeared. Whilst looking for my squadron I saw F/Lt Wczelik in aircraft WX-B and joined up with him. We both started climbing. We patrolled the length of the Channel at about 30 000 ft and I saw several formations of Me 109's at a considerable height above us. When my petrol had got down to about 15 gallons we started for home, diving. Whilst loosing height I acted as a weaver for F/L Wczelik doing S turns behind him. Coming through thin layer of clouds I straightened up because I did not think S turns were necessary any more. At this very moment I felt a burst of fire. My cockpit filled with smoke, oil and glycol, blinding me. I smelt burning. At the moment of noticing the strike F/Lt Wczelik did a steep turn to the right and through this escaped being shot down. I undid my straps, having opened the cockpit and got ready to jump, but could not because I saw two Messerschmitts very close to me, so I put the aircraft on its back and dived very deeply; two Messerschmitts accompanying me down. When it was already too late to jump the Messerschmitts stopped pursuing me and I did a half roll which righted the aircraft and was just able to land in a field. As my straps were undone I cut my head on the Perspex."

F/Lt Wczelik had been looking around very carefully on his way home:

". . . I saw four aircraft at about 30,000 ft flying from West to East. Still gliding I noticed that No. 2 was doing S turns behind me. The moment these four aircraft disappeared from view having passed me I saw in my mirror several aircraft diving at me from behind, so I did a very steep turn to the right and in an endeavour to face them head on, but as at this moment an aircraft got on my tail and fired I did a few more steep turns losing height the whole time. After a considerable number of turns I no longer saw any aircraft, but felt that there was something behind me, which I took to be my No. 2 so I straightened up and began flying straight and level. Looking in my mirror I realised what was going to happen to me as I saw a Yellow nose closing in on me. I did a steep turn, but already there was smoke issuing from my cockpit. After my first turn I saw the enemy aircraft at a distance of about 1500 yds go past me. It was probably a Me 109.

"I forced landed at Detling with my radiator damaged through bullets."

After this battle between Messerschmitts and the Hurricanes of 302 and 501 Squadrons, Obfw. Roth and Obfw. H. Hofmann of 4./JG 26, reported shooting down two Spitfires each, while Hptm. Adolph, the *Gruppenkommandeur* of II./JG 26, claimed his 15th victory over Tonbridge. This would appear to have been Sgt Kosarz of 302 Squadron, although Sgt Groves of 501 Squadron was also lost. During this encounter P/O Stanisław Skalski flying V6723, of 501 Squadron, claimed the destruction of a Bf 109 shared with others.

Another victim of JG 26 fighters during the day was P/O Stanisław Tarkowski of 605 Squadron who, flying the morning patrol in Hurricane N2646/UP-O, was downed by *Hauptmann* Schöpfel of III./JG 26. The Polish pilot later described this event in his memoirs:

". . . loudspeaker announces: 'Squadron at readiness!' I put the letters in my boot and ran across the garden to my Hurricane UP-O. The ground crew were waiting already, one helped me don my parachute, while another started the engine. In a few minutes we were airborne in a formation of three. It was 9 am, at 10 000 feet the sky was beautiful and cloudless. At that time I did not understand English well enough to follow various pilots' remarks, so I concentrated on pre-set rules and regulations. I was flying at the rear and my duty was to warn the others about the enemy, and of course to keep up with the leader. I did not fancy the situation much, as all too often while guarding others a pilot would fall victim to an enemy strike from behind. And above all this every 15 seconds I had to transmit a signal to the ground control to fix our position. In such a situation these signals at 15 second intervals deprived me of radio contact with the others. We were told to climb higher and higher. The engine of my Hurricane worked at full throttle, the unheated cockpit was becoming colder and colder, and despite the warm clothes my legs were becoming numb. We were crossing 27 000 feet already, when the voice in my headphones shouted: 'Bandits below and at our altitude!'" I had 29 000 feet already when enemy machines in formation of pairs appeared from the east. They looked like shiny silver fish in water. I noticed one closer to me, I pushed the button of my guns – shots were fired, engines roared, as pilots wanted to squeeze the necessary power out of them . . ., when suddenly a loud bang – and the whole front of my aeroplane disappears, fire engulfs at the cockpit. In the wink of an eye I perform the bale out procedure strictly by the book. I am almost blinded by the choking smoke, I open the cockpit, but fire strikes from starboard, so I am in a turn – I think. I start to panic, I cannot bale out in such a position. No, no – I do not want to die here! Blinded, panicked, I must have kicked the stick – sudden jolt and . . . nothing more . . ."

Tarkowski lost consciousness, then regained it at 16,000 ft and opened the parachute. He landed safely at Sissinghurst Court, although the local inhabitants had to extricate him from a tall tree, initially mistaking him for a German. Soon everything was explained, his burnt face was dressed, and after a copious dinner washed down with many a glass, he returned to his unit. Tarkowski must have set an altitude record, baling out at 25 000 feet, where there is not enough oxygen in the air to breathe.

In another Auxiliary Air Force Squadron, P/O Zbigniew Oleński of 609 had an interesting incident during one of his patrols, as described in the unit chronicle.

"P/O Oleński in X4560 [PR-H] burst a tyre on take off. He made a good landing after completing his flight but unfortunately hit a soft patch – probably a filled in bomb crater – and turned completely over. Pilot undamaged, aircraft beyond unit capacity for repair. P/O Bisdee who owned the aircraft was on leave. He would have been peeved had he witnessed the proceedings. The aircraft was nicely decorated with his family crest, a Fleur de Lis with the usual trimmings and motto, plus of course his score in Swastikas. The poor old signwriter will be in demand again."

9 November 1940

The day brought another victory for a Polish pilot flying with 17 Squadron. Late in the afternoon a section of Hurricanes (P/O G. E. Pittmann V7500/YB-D, Sgt Griffith P2972 and P/O Marian Chełmecki P2794/YB-E) met a Dornier 17 of 5/KG 3 south west of Aldeburgh[67]. Both P/O's Pittman and Chełmecki fired at the bomber until they had spent all their ammunition. The damaged Do 17Z-3 Werk Nr. 2891 crashed during forced landing at Antwerp, killing Lt. Heinrich Hattwig and his crew. Chełmecki described:

"I was Yellow 3 on convoy patrol when I saw AA fire from a destroyer, and we dived towards the bursts. We saw 2 a/c, one of which I recognised as a Do 17. I followed Yellow 1 and attacked the e/a alternately with him. I made five attacks from astern quarter, giving 3 to 4 seconds bursts at about 250 yards range in the first four attacks and at about 150 yards in the last. When I finished attacking, I saw some white smoke from the port engine.

"Yellow 1 went on with his attacks after I had finished my ammunition and returned towards base. There was intense and accurate fire from the rear top gun through my attacks, but I was not hit."

10 November 1940

Sgt Tadeusz Dobrut-Dobrucki of 607 Squadron damaged Hurricane I P2565 during landing at Turnhouse due to having only one wheel locked up. The pilot was unhurt. "Pilot had not been instructed at 5 OTU (Aston Down) to always pump 'unlock solid' prior to landing" stated the accident report.

Sgt Zaniewski of 308 Squadron crashed Hurricane P3891 on the way from Baginton to Worcester. He failed to find his way home almost inexplicably in ideal conditions and over a short distance. "Pilot has little ability in map reading or compass courses" – said accident report. He was unhurt in a forced landing, but the aircraft was badly damaged.

11 November 1940

Under the date 11 November 1940 P/O Marian Chełmecki wrote in his log-book: "very lucky convoy patrol". He reported shooting down one Bf 109, giving more details in his combat report:

"I was weaving above and behind the Squadron on convoy patrol when we sighted

---

[67] Or five miles east of Aldeburgh, according to Chełmecki's report!

a sky full of Me 109's from 8,000 to 15,000 ft. I followed the Squadron as it dived, and turned left in order to look out behind. At this moment when at about 6,000 ft 2 Me 109's came at me head on from below. The one on the right was firing at me, and I turned slightly to the left and attacked the other head on with a three seconds burst at 75 yards.

"As I broke away I saw black smoke coming from him and I then climbed above cloud at 5-6000 ft and saw a Hurricane with an Me 109 on his tail. I followed them through the clouds, where I lost the Me 109. I saw another Hurricane dive straight into the sea, and did not see the pilot get out. I then returned to where a dog fight was going on, and while doing so was attacked by 4 Me 109's. Two Spitfires came along and attacked them, and returned to the convoy, I then heard Rider Leader tell all who were not engaged to return to base."

The rest of Chełmecki's unit, also heavily engaged, claimed five enemy aircraft destroyed and five probables for the loss of only one pilot – Sgt Hogg. The pilots involved in this action were:

F/O Pittman	V7500/YB-D
Sgt Griffith	P2972
Sgt Bartlett	V7658
P/O Chełmecki (Polish)	V6553/YB-J
Sgt Hogg	P2794/YB-E
S/Ldr Miller	P3176
P/O Wissler	V7570
P/O Ross	V6759
Sgt Stewart	P3894
Sgt Cameron	V7241
F/O Niemiec (Polish)	V6791

While 17 Squadron were fighting the Bf 109 escort for Junkers 87 that were attacking ships in the Thames Estuary, 257 Squadron (also based at North Weald) prepared to intercept a bomber formation which, unexpectedly, turned out to be Italian BR.20s escorted by CR.42s.

Ten Fiat BR.20M bombers of 43° *Stormo BT*, accompanied by 42 Fiat CR.42 and 46 Fiat G.50 fighters, covered by some Bf 109s, intended to raid the British coast from bases in Belgium, but bad weather had caused the Messerschmitts and Fiat G.50s to turn back to their airfields. Only the bombers, escorted by CR.42 biplanes, reached Harwich. P/O Karol Pniak, flying the Hurricane I V7296/DT-Z was the only Polish pilot taking part in 257 Squadron's engagement with the *Regia Aeronautica*; he claimed one Fiat BR.20:

"I attacked enemy bomber (No. 7 in formation) from below and behind from the distance of 200 yards. I gave him 1 burst four seconds long. Just after enemy plane began to smoke and fire, he turned over on his back and dived straight into sea. One of the enemy crew baled out with parachute. I attacked another enemy bomber and gave him two 4/5 second-long bursts. He began to smoke and glided to the coast.

At the same time another of our fighters fired at him. We followed him until he force landed in the wood near Woodbridge. I was in Blue Section as No. 2."

This famous combat by S/Ldr Robert Stanford Tuck's unit, led by F/Lt Peter Blatchford, resulted in overclaims substantially exceeding the actual loss of three Italian bombers and three biplane fighters. In total RAF fighter pilots from 46 and 257 Squadrons claimed nine Italian bombers destroyed and one damaged plus four CR.42 destroyed, three probables and one damaged.

13 November 1940

After moving to Ternhill and starting patrols in the area between Birmingham and Liverpool, 306 Squadron soon met the enemy in the air. On 13 November at night a section of 306 Squadron pilots, F/Lt Hugh Charles Kennard, P/O Bohdan Bielkiewicz and P/O Edward Jankowski, took off to patrol over Coventry. After receiving a message regarding one enemy bomber flying in the vicinity of Birmingham, they found this and shot it up. All three lost sight of the intruder when it hid in clouds, trailing black smoke, ten miles west of Worcester. Probably the three pilots attacked He 111P-4 Werk Nr. 2994 of 5./KG55, which landed on its own airfield substantially damaged; its rear gunner died of wounds. P/O Bohdan Bielkiewicz was hit by accurate bursts of fire from the gunner and landed in damaged Hurricane V6950/UZ-T at Ternhill. He later described the damage:

"port wing: two bullet holes at the bottom. Fabric on top and bottom torn. One large hole on the port side of the fuselage immediately aft of the engine. Throttle lever shot through. Starboard wheel tyre shot through. An anti-armour shell stuck in the pilot's seat."

The success of this trio was widely commented upon by the airmen of the unit. The Medical Officer, F/O Apolinary Wiktorczyk, later wrote in his memoirs:

"Another Scramble, on 13 November 1940 caused less excitement than usual. People were getting used to it. It took Bodzio [Bielkiewicz] to land like a stuntman with wide open gun ports that were usually patched over, to make everybody realise that something had happened. Then the excited Bodzio jumped out of his cockpit and described the encounter: Operations guided them well – they saw the Junkers from far away, but in spite of full throttle the distance was shrinking very slowly. Bodzio was the first to get to it. Gunners fired fiercely in response, shot his machine up, and holed one of his tyres, but soon the Jerry was hit with a burst. However, the heavily armoured Junkers managed to hide in clouds. It probably did not make it to Germany. Sadly, Bodzio would not enjoy his success for long. A few days later a quiet cemetery saw the modest grave of the first 306 Squadron pilot killed on English soil."

P/O Bohdan Bielkiewicz was in fact killed in an accident on 13 February 1941, three months after the first victory.

Poles undergoing training in the Aldergrove-based 245 Northern Rhodesia Squadron, marked their presence by several flying accidents. Although some undertook a few patrol flights, their duty was training in the main. In November the

Northern Rhodesia Squadron was joined by F/O Jerzy Orzechowski, F/O Tadeusz Koc, F/O Jan Wiśniewski, P/O Władysław Szczęśniewski, Sgt Stanisław Brzeski, Sgt Bronisław Kościk and Sgt Franciszek Prętkiewicz. All of them were ex-307 Squadron Defiant pilots who did not want to serve as 'gun-bus drivers' and had asked for re-posting to day fighter units. They were posted to RAF day fighter units under training and would not find their way to Polish fighter squadrons until early 1941. On 13 November both Sgt Kościk and P/O Szczęśniewski damaged their Hurricanes in accidents at the airfield. Kościk damaged P3385 during landing, breaking the undercarriage, while Szczęśniewski ran his P2906 into a lorry.

An accident in 307 Squadron on the Isle of Man also occured when F/Lt C J Donovan and S/Ldr G C Tomlinson damaged Defiant L1682 during landing at Jurby. Both of the aircrew were unhurt.

14 November 1940

P/O Władysław Różycki ended his career with 238 Squadron during a flight to Chilbolton on 14 November, when he crashed his personal Hurricane P3618. He reported the accident to his Commanding Officer in a very official way:

"Sir

"I have the honour to submit the following report.

"On 14/11/40 I crashed Hurricane P3618 near Stockbridge as a result of engine failure. I took off from Blandford en route to Chilbolton, where I was to deliver the aeroplane, it having forced landed originally as a result of enemy action. There was nothing unusual during the flight until I got to Stockbridge flying at 1000 ft, when the engine suddenly developed very violent vibrations and the airscrew merely ticked over. There was a lot of white smoke pouring out of the engine and exhaust and into the cockpit which made it very difficult for me to see. I switched off the petrol and found myself about to crash on the side of a hill. I levelled out and skidded about 40 yards on the belly of the aeroplane. I got out and found the engine was on fire. An A.A. patrolman came to my assistance and extinguished the fire.

"I have the honour to be your obedient servant, Sir

"W. Różycki"

Almost a week later P/O Różycki was transferred to 306 Squadron based at Ternhill.

Meanwhile, on 14 November G/Cpt Vincent, Officer Commanding RAF Northolt, flying the Hurricane V6694/WX-G of 302 Squadron was attacked by two Bf 109s, and was forced to land the shot up aircraft at Kenley. This encounter took place in the Deal area at 19,000 ft, when Vincent was leading a patrol of two Hurricane squadrons (229 and 615) over a convoy. Other pilots of the Northolt Wing claimed three Bf 109s probably destroyed and one damaged. It is believed that Vincent was a victim of Hptm. Joppien from JG 51.

15 November 1940

P/O Czesław Gauze took part in a patrol by 605 Squadron Hurricanes, flying V6951. They left Croydon, and in the Canterbury area intercepted "fifty-plus bandits crossing the North Foreland, heading north".

After the RAF pilots spotted the formation, the Messerschmitts suddenly turned south. At the same time another group of Bf 109s arrived in the area and 605 Squadron found itself between two fighter formations of II./JG 53 and Stab./JG 26. In the ensuing battle 605 Squadron lost two aircraft, one of which was credited to *Oberstleutnant* Adolf Galland of JG 26. P/O Gauze (Polish) lost his life, while Sgt Jones baled out safely.

17 November 1940

About 9.15 am 17 and 257 Squadrons took off to patrol the Harwich area. They met a raid by Bf 110s of ErpGr 210, escorted by JG 26 Bf 109s. While 257 Squadron engaged the 109s, 17 Squadron attacked the twin-engined fighter-bombers. F/Lt Bayne and Sgt Cameron shot down one Bf 110 whilst the squadron's Polish pilot shared another with a Czech pilot of that unit. Both P/O Paweł Niemiec (Polish) and P/O F. Kordula (Czech) claimed the Bf 110. P/O Niemiec, flying Hurricane V6759, wrote:

> "I was following Blue 1 when we sighted Me 110 and Me 109 on our right, and we turned to attack, coming in behind the Me 110's – As we were flying into the sun, it was difficult to see, but I got in a 2 seconds burst at one of the Me 110's in the rear section at about 300 yards range. I did not observe the result of my attack owing to the sun. I broke away left, and saw the Me 109's above and behind, and two of them coming down to attack and firing their guns, but at very long range. I got in a long burst from below at one of them at about 300 yards range, but again saw no result. I then saw a/a fire over Harwich and flew towards it, but saw no e/a. I joined up with a returning Hurricane and came back to base."

Later the Intelligence Officer of 17 Squadron noted:

> "two Me 110's seen by searchlight post F.F. 35 at Butley crossing the coast in flames at 2000 ft and losing height rapidly – After consultation with other pilots ½ share is credited to F/O Niemiec."

Again, 17 Squadron had overclaimed. They reported four destroyed and two damaged, whilst Luftwaffe reports recorded the loss of three Messerschmitt 110s only.

18 November 1940

P/O Stefan Stegman of 229 Squadron was involved in a taxying accident at Northolt. Following undercarriage collapse due to "drome surface extremely bad where accident took place" his Hurricane V7645 was slightly damaged.

19 November 1940

During convoy patrol performed by 303 Squadron P/O Włodzimierz Miksa was forced to land near Preston, damaging his Hurricane L2099/RF-O. His log-book makes no mention of an incident that day, but accident report stated that aircraft tipped on nose. Miksa made the mistake of flying at 150 ft this height being unable to pick up suitable land marks when petrol was quickly running short. Further comments said: "Few Poles have developed air sense in bad weather and are also bad at map reading. Steps are being taken to provide instruction in reco subjects."

22 November 1940

Training in 308 Squadron at Baginton was not free from accidents, either. Sgt Tadeusz Adam Krieger damaged his Hurricane I V6936 whilst landing at Baginton. Following his first solo flight on this type, the pilot was so excited that he failed to check undercarriage lights and it collapsed on landing.

23 November 1940

302 Squadron now left RAF Northolt and moved to Westhampnett.

Also on this date P/O Wilhelm Szafraniec, who was serving with 56 Squadron, died following a mid air crash with P/O Guest. Although Guest's Hurricane P2910 was lost, the pilot survived the accident unhurt, unlike the Polish pilot who lost his life in V7569.

24 November 1940

Wing Commander Oliver from 9 Group HQ arrived at Baginton to visit the newly-formed 308 Squadron, and to see how the Polish pilots were processing with their training. OC 308 Squadron wrote in his report:

> "Training rate is poor due to small number of instructors: three, who are at the same time are flight and squadron commanders, so apart from training have a lot of different work. Mist and rain more and more frequent at this period, also make rapid training difficult. It is difficult to quote the expected time of completion of training, but considering that adverse weather might stop flying entirely for a prolonged period, I take into account that the squadron does not attain operational capability before early spring!"

W/Cdr Oliver certainly never expected the surprising event which occured during a training flight in which he took part. Later he described this sortie:

> "After break up to practice Squadron formation, I noticed smoke trace over Coventry at 15.15 hours. Climbed in formation with Sgt Parafiński and Sgt Grudziński. Warned section to turn on oxygen and at 20,000 ft over centre of Coventry sighted either Junkers 88 or long nosed Blenheim. Grudziński had broken away as he had no oxygen. Parafiński and myself pursued enemy north of Coventry for five minutes up to 26,000 ft when enemy turned due South, and commenced shallow dive. I had been at gate for over five minutes, and Parafiński was drawing ahead. Enemy was silhouetted against the sun, and I wanted to be certain of identity before opening fire. Parafiński then delivered a quarter attack. I fired three bursts from long range, and the enemy turned sharply beneath me. I dived to get on his tail, but blacked out, and found enemy some distance further south with Parafiński still attacking, smoke appeared from starboard engine, and I then easily closed range to 50 yards. The starboard engine caught fire then the whole fuselage burst into flames and he turned on his back, and dived into the ground crashing in a sheet of flame near a large castle."

This kill was credited to Sgt Mieczysław Parafiński, who shot down the Junkers 88A-5 Werk Nr. 451 4U+HL z 3.(F)/123, which fell near Gloucester, killing the crew. It was the first victory for 308 Squadron.

Although bad weather had not prevented an effective attack and the loss of a Luftwaffe bomber, it also caused the loss of a Hurricane, when Sgt Romuald Gadus, flying Hurricane I V7223 of 607 Squadron, crashed due to bad weather at Scot's Gap, 8 miles west of Morpeth. The pilot was unhurt, but the aircraft which struck the stone wall on landing was reported to be Cat. C.

26 November 1940

This day was distinguished by many incidents in 306 and 308 Squadrons, as well as other units with Polish pilots.

Sgt Józef Derma of 308 Squadron, after a training flight, landed at Baginton in thick haze and crashed in Hurricane V7025, breaking an undercarriage leg. Accident report stated that he failed to use throttle correctly and is intended to be posted to non-operational flying for three months. Later he was sent to 5 BGS and then to Ferry Pool. He did not join operational unit until early 1942.

A 306 Squadron section, consisting of S/Ldr Douglas Scott, F/O Stefan Witorzeńć, and P/O Bohdan Bielkiewicz, took off for a training flight which the leader ordered to keep tight. Just over the edge of the airfield their path was crossed by an Anson, flying at some 100 ft. Both Scott's wingmen broke off to prevent a mid-air crash. Unfortunately, the leader did not notice the approaching aircraft and collided with it. Both fell at the edge of the Ternhill aerodrome; Scott, extricated from the wreck of Hurricane V7533, was badly injured and never returned to operational flying in Fighter Command.

Sgt Ludwik Mirończuk of 307 Squadron force landed Defiant N1624 near Jurby airfield. The pilot escaped unhurt from the accident, and explained later that the engine failed suddenly; closer investigation by technicians failed to confirm his statement.

In another squadron now flying by night, 43, Sgt Wacław Giermer force landed three miles south of Usworth, unable to reach the aerodrome. His Hurricane P3527 suffered damage but he was unhurt himself. Years later he recalled this accident:

> "During a patrol sortie I noticed that the engine started to overheat, and before I had time to find the nearest aerodrome, glycol started to boil, and white smoke started to come out of both sides of the engine, and I was forced to land. I saw a small field ahead and brushed the ground wheels-up. As my harness was rather loose, I banged my head on the rubber cover on the gunsight, and cut my forehead above one eye. A flame appeared in the engine. Fortunately the fire was not big, being concentrated around the engine. Main tanks in wings were undamaged. I unfastened my harness, but could not jump out of the cockpit quickly, as my parachute harness, oxygen and radio systems caught. Fortunately I landed by an AA post and the soldiers ran to me with shovels and put the engine fire out with soil."

About 16.45 a section of 65 Squadron took off from Turnhouse for flying practice. Spitfires were flown by P/O Finucane (P9454), F/O Szulkowski (R6987) and Sgt Lowson (X4233). Only P/O Finucane returned home at 18.50. Sgt Lowson baled out over Glamis, Angus, and his aeroplane crashed. While F/O Szulkowski's Spitfire crashed on landing after dusk, hitting an RT pole near the aerodrome.

152 Hyderabad Squadron ORB recorded on this date:

> "While on patrol in the afternoon Sgt. Pilot Klein, one of our Polish pilots was

reported missing. After some time a message was received that he had crash landed near Torquay owing to lack of petrol. He was unhurt and his plane not so badly damaged as might be expected. His companion in the patrol flight missed him first while near Portland. It was a great relief to all when the news arrived that Sgt. Klein was safe. It was quite dark when this news was received."

Sgt Zygmunt Klein landed his Spitfire I L1048 two miles north of Torquay. Unfortunately, two days later further reports of his being missing would prove to be correct.

27 November 1940
Sgt Włodzimierz Mudry of 79 Squadron had begun his service with this unit at the beginning of November. At that time pilots of the Madras Presidency Squadron based at Pembrey were involved mostly in patrolling the coast and the base. One scramble gave them hopes of a kill, when on 27 November P/O Stones (P6957) and Sgt Mudry (V7115) were sent off about 2.15 pm to intercept an unidentified aircraft. Much to their regret, though, the machine turned out to be a Hawker Henley. These fruitless patrols and the boredom of waiting were sometimes interrupted by well remembered events as described by Donald Stones:

"Sergeant Mudry, who was a bit gullible, was persuaded to climb on to the roof of our hut while we all snoozed inside, near the tortoise-stove glowing with almost incandescent coke, and put a Very light cartridge down the chimney. The result was most impressive. The cartridge exploded, the stove lost its lid and stocking-doo, the hut was filled with red smoke, while hot cinders flew in all directions and small fires started. Oddly, no one was killed or injured. No hut was ever more quickly evacuated. Mudry was grounded for two days . . ."

Even more disappointing was the ending of a patrol flown by P/O Petruszka of 306 Squadron. His Hurricane L1717 caught fire in mid-air and he had to abandon the aircraft, which crashed three miles south of Shrewsbury; the pilot escaped with some burns.

28 November 1940
A day of fighter aces! It began as a great day for the Luftwaffe *Jägers* from JG 2 led by *Major* Helmut Wick, as they claimed British aircraft shot down in each of their patrols over Britain although it ended with the death of their commander. Polish fighter pilots, flying Spitfires, were involved.

But before that, about 3 pm, 249 Squadron flying Hurricanes had encountered JG 26 fighters allowing another Luftwaffe fighter ace to claim a victory. Obstl. Adolf Galland shot down P/O Wells, and none of the other 249 pilots managed to engage his Messerschmitt. Only Sgt Michał Mirosław Maciejowski, flying his usual Hurricane I V6855, reported one Bf 109E probably shot down near Maidstone, but this claim was not confirmed by RAF authorities and does not even appear in any official Polish Air Force papers.

"A day of great activity, of victories but also of sad losses." – recorded 152 Squadron's ORB. "In the early afternoon P/O Hancock while on patrol engaged a Me 109 and after a long chase last saw it with its port engine on fire and in a bad way heading for France. He was quite certain that it never could have reached the French coast, but did not actually see it crash into the sea.

"Later in the afternoon the Squadron made contact with a large force of Me 109's in the vicinity of the Needles. Many dog fights took place. P/O Watson was killed. It appears that his plane was badly hit as it was pouring out smoke. He was seen trying to bale out by P/O Cox but the parachute failed to open and his body and plane were found just south east of Wareham. When found the parachute had a large rent in it and it is thought it must have caught in some part of the plane before it opened. P/O Watson's death has been a great sorrow to the Squadron as he was a most popular Officer. However, P/O Marrs brought down one Me 109 for certain and he thinks it was the one that attacked P/O Watson. He saw the hostile aircraft making for France and gradually overtook it and gave it some good bursts of fire. The airman baled out and P/O Marrs saw the hostile aircraft blow up. P/O Marrs did a fine piece of work and almost certainly avenged the death of his friend P/O Watson. And lastly Sgt. Pilot Klein one of our Polish pilots is missing. Nothing has been heard of him since he took off with the Squadron except that P/O Holmes during the battle caught sight of a Spitfire upon which he saw what appeared to be a bright spark. This plane spun three or four times. F/O Holmes then lost sight of the plane as he was hotly engaged with enemy aircraft. This was over the sea and it appears as if we have lost a very gallant pilot and ally."

It is interesting to note that Lt. Julius Meimberg, the *Staffelführer* of 4./JG 2, recalled that during that combat he fired a short burst at a Spitfire which then entered a spin, although it showed no traces of being hit. He thought the pilot must have been knocked unconscious, or perhaps dead, as the Spitfire spun down until it hit the sea. Meimberg also recalled a bright flash of light sparking off the Spitfire canopy at every turn in its spin. It therefore seems that the spinning Spitfire seen by P/O Holmes must have been the one attacked by Meimberg, and may well have been that flown by Sgt Klein's P9427. Officer Commanding 152 Squadron, stated in his report dated 9 February 1941:

"This NCO was posted to No. 152 Squadron on 5/10/40. He took on flying duties at once and flew continuously with this Squadron until he was posted missing on 28/11/40. He fought in two combats and assisted in the destroying of 2 enemy aircraft on his first fight. He did not return from his second fight.

"Sgt Klein was very popular with the officers and airmen of his Squadron. His flying was well above average, and his flying discipline was excellent.

"The Squadron was very sad to loose this popular Polish NCO.

"Signed: W. D. David[68], F/Lt, Commanding No. 152 (Hyderabad) Squadron"

Amazingly, some information about Sgt Klein's last combat is provided by 609 Squadron's Operations Record Book.

"F/Lt Dundas was heard by the controller (F/Lt Fieldsend) and by his C.O. to say over R/T. 'I've finished an Me 109 – whoopee!', to which Robinson was heard to

---

[68] See the authobiography of this officer, *Dennis "Hurricane" David*, published by Grub Street, 2000.

reply 'Good show, John!', after which nothing further was heard or seen of Dundas, although Robinson tried persistently to speak to him over R/T. P/O Baillon also failed to return. There were no other claims or casualties except Żurakowski's machine [X4165 – author], which had a shell hole through the port mainplane.

"152 Squadron was also engaged at the same time and place, and it is considered possible that either one of their pilots, Sgt Klein (Polish) or Dundas may have been responsible for bringing down the German ace – Major Wick who was reported in the German press to have been killed in action at the time off Isle of Wight and that his friend had immediately disposed of the British pilot who brought down Major Wick's Messerschmitt. On the other hand there is much 'Wishful thinking' that Dundas may have gone in for another cross-channel hun-hunt and landed safely on the wrong side of the water."

Up to this day there remains some dispute as to who was responsible for downing the Luftwaffe fighter ace, F/Lt Dundas, P/O Marrs or Sgt Klein?

During night flying practice in 307 Squadron, F/O Józef Tański taxied his Defiant N1683 into the fence around the runway, causing damage to the airscrew.

30 November 1940

The Polish Air Force lost two of its Sergeants however serving in RAF fighter units, both killed in accidents. Sgt Wilhelm Sasak of 145 Squadron based at Tangmere was flying Hurricane I P3704 when the aircraft caught fire in the air. He tried to force land about one mile south of Chichester, but crashed and was killed. Sgt Franciszek Prętkiewicz of 245 Squadron based at Aldergrove, dived into the ground near Cushendall, Co. Antrim in his Hurricane I R4079 during dog fight practice. He had made only three operational sorties with the unit.

1 December 1940

On 1 December 1940 at about 10 am, Sgt Szymon Kita took part in a patrol with nine other pilots of 253 Squadron. Flying the Hurricane P3678, he was shot down near Falmer, Sussex by a Bf 109 of I./JG 3. He escaped unhurt, and later described that day in his memoirs:

"Sunday, not a cloud in the sky, only the sun shining blindingly. 11.00 hours – the squadron takes off to patrol Brighton. Altitude 25,000 feet. I am the last in the group, I cover the whole formation. Operations room is silent. Over Brighton we wheel to port – I stay some 300 metres behind the squadron. We are almost over the sea shore. I look around, but the sun makes observation difficult. Suddenly I see in front of me traces of machine gun bullets. I make an evasive action and a sudden turn to port. In front of me, perhaps 200 metres away, I can see a German Me 109 fighter. All I have to do is to aim a bit, my heart accelerates, and the thought 'got you, bastard!' crosses my mind. From such distance I cannot miss, after the first burst some pieces of metal fall off and a trail of smoke pours . . .

"The same moment something jolted my aeroplane, something hit it. I saw holes on my starboard wing, I can see another German nearby. At first I thought – I will have another one! I make a tight loop, I blacked out for an instant . . .

Puffs of smoke poured from the engine of my Hurricane, and when I looked around the cockpit, I saw red blood streaming from my right arm, above the elbow. I could feel no pain, just dark flakes started to whirl before my eyes. I switched off the magneto and petrol. I told operations that I was going to bale out. I pull the canopy release, but it refuses to move. I repeat my attempt, but get no result. This is the end – I realise. Grey shroud obscures my sight, and I fade into unconsciousness. . ."

In spite of his temporary unconsciousness, Kita levelled out just above the ground and force-landed, hitting some trees which reduced the speed of his crashing Hurricane. Some people who watched the crash, extracted him from the cockpit just before the aircraft exploded. After this accident and convalescence, Sgt Kita flew with 287 (Anti-Aircraft Co-operation) Squadron, and later in air delivery units and flying schools.

The Messerschmitt shot up by Sgt Kita in this encounter was never claimed by him, and there is no evidence of any loss by JG 3 that day. The next encounter by his unit, almost two hours later, also ended with two Hurricanes destroyed without any casualties among enemy aircraft.

About noon the Spitfires of 74 and 92 Squadrons based at Biggin Hill patrolled the coast in bright clear weather. The only pilot to find a good target was F/O Henryk Szczęsny (Polish) who, flying the Spitfire II P7363, claimed the destruction of a Bf 109E:

"I was Red 3 of 74 Squadron ordered to patrol Canterbury area at 27,000 ft. When over Dover area I sighted nine Me 109's at 32,000 ft, circling in from the sea. Fighters climbed to 32,000 ft. I then saw one enemy aircraft diving to attack on our fighters.

"Red 1 turned to attack enemy aircraft and I also attacked and closed to e/a before Red 1. I closed to 250 yards and gave a four seconds burst closing to 150 yards. E/a emitted white smoke from starboard near fuselage and dived into the sea about 10 miles NE from Dover. I then returned to base."

2 December 1940

A pair of 609 Squadron Spitfires flown by F/O's Noel Agazarian and Tadeusz Nowierski (Polish) attacked:

"a twin-engined twin-tailed enemy bomber of uncertain type (Me 110 or Do 17Z) 5 miles south of Southampton without certainty of results until the aircraft was reported to have crashed on the beach at Thorney Island, where ground observers stated that it had been brought down by two Spitfires. The local A. A. also claimed it as a victim (they nearly brought down Agazarian, it appears). After due investigation this enemy aircraft was credited to 609 Squadron, and shared between the above-named pilots, bringing their respective totals of enemy aircraft destroyed to: Agazarian – 6, Nowierski – 5½."

This was recorded in 609 Squadron's Operations Record Book, but the enemy bomber attacked by both pilots appears to have been the Do 17 W.Nr.3618 7T+KL of KüFlGr 606 which in fact crashed at Brest, killing all of Lt. Helmut Anders' crew.

Just before noon 74 and 66 Squadrons were sent to intercept some *Freie Jagd* Messerschmitts over Dungeness. The pilots of 74 Squadron fought with Messerschmitts of I./JG 53, eventually claiming two destroyed, one probable and one damaged, F/O Henryk Szczęsny in Spitfire II P7363 being responsible for the single damaged. As he stated in his report, 74 Squadron attacked more than seven Bf 109s at about 11.40 in the Dungeness-Dover area:

> "I was No. 3 of Red Section flying about 26,000 ft over Dungeness-Dover area. I saw to my right and below about 7 Me 109's returning home. Squadron Leader dived on to them and I followed him and saw behind the formation one Me 109. I dived onto him and opened fire at a range of 400 yards closing to 50 yards, head on. The enemy aircraft dived steeply and I saw black smoke coming from his fuselage after three bursts. I broke off to another attack and lost sight of the first enemy aircraft."

During training flights in 307 Squadron, Defiant L7035 overshot the runway at Jurby on 2 December 1940. The pilot, Sgt Jan Mikszo, had not seen the landing strip due to oil on his windscreen from a cracked oil pipe, and landed too fast. He touched down mid-way along the runway and finished the run against a wall surrounding the airfield. The pilot was unhurt, but the gunner, Sgt Stanisław Kondras, suffered a cut on his face.

4 December 1940

308 Squadron suffered its first casualty, losing P/O Ryszard Koczor. A section led by F/Lt Wiórkiewicz flew into a balloon barrage in bad weather. P/O Koczor hit a balloon cable and his Hurricane V7071 suffered severe damage. Still losing height, the pilot circled round the airfield, but just above the runway the aircraft lost speed and spun in, killing its pilot. This was not to be the only accident with balloons in the Coventry area. The next occured a few days later, during a training flight by Red Section on 7 December in thick haze. The telegram to 9 Group HQ said:

> "After having done two or three circuits over Austin Works, balloons were rapidly let up and forced aircraft to climb fast in order to avoid fouling balloons."

Even this failed to cause closer co-operation between Baginton-based fighter squadrons and the ground defences.

5 December 1940

During sweeps by Luftwaffe fighters over Britain on this date, two Polish fighter pilots added to their scores.

Sgt Michał Mirosław Maciejowski took part in a sweep over Southern England and claimed the only victory as his when 249 Squadron, together with 253, had a short encounter with Messerschmitts. The 249 Squadron pilots taking part in this encounter were as follows:

P/O Maconnell	V6958/GN-D
Sgt Maciejowski (Polish)	V6614/GN-B
F/Lt Lofts	V6561/GN-A

Sgt Palliser	V6565
P/O Neil	V6854/GN-F
P/O Crossey	V7600/GN-C
Sgt Evans	V6798
F/Lt Barton	V7538/GN-T
F/O Cassidy	V6692/GN-O
Sgt Mills	V6534/GN-P
P/O Solak (Polish)	V6635
Sgt Stroud	V7677/GN-N
W/Cdr Beamish	V6728/GN-Z

Maciejowski described his efforts in the report:

"Having patrolled Maidstone with the Squadron, West South towards Dungeness, I saw about 5 Me 109's about 2000 ft above us, we being at about 19 000 ft. We formed a circle going lower and lower, while the enemy followed us down.

"Two Me 109's dived and attacked. I turned left out of formation and I saw one Hurricane shot down. The Me. which had shot it down diving steeply, pulled upwards and climbed. In this climb he passed before me and I gave him two short bursts, as he was climbing almost vertically before me. He went into a spin and crashed into the sea about 500 yards from the sea shore."

The Hurricane, attacked by the Messerschmitt which was claimed shot down by the Polish pilot, was Sgt Stroud's V7677/GN-N. Its pilot was able to bale out. In fact none of the attacking Messerschmitts led by Hptm. Hermann Friedrich Joppien, I./JG 51 *Gruppenkommandeur*, was lost. The leader of the German formation claimed shooting down a Hurricane (i. e. Sgt Stroud) and was back in France without a scratch.

The Hurricanes expended considerable fuel on the long patrol and in flying a defensive circle, so when the Messerschmitts turned back to France, almost all 249 pilots had to land before reaching North Weald. Sgt Palliser force landed damaging his Hurricane, whilst others landed at Hornchurch, Redhill, or Rochester.

Another big battle with Messerschmitts, this time of JG 26, brought a victory claim by F/O Henryk Szczęsny. A dozen Spitfires of 74 Squadron left Biggin Hill about 2.10 pm, together with 92 Squadron, to patrol the Maidstone area at 15,000 ft. Later both units were directed towards Dover. Being already in the vicinity of Dover, 74 Squadron were ordered below cloud and at approximately 15,000 ft they met 16 Bf 109s coming out of clouds over Folkestone. The squadron attacked and in the ensuing fight the Spitfire pilots claimed eight enemy aircraft destroyed and one damaged. F/O Henryk Szczęsny, flying Spitfire II P7363, claimed the destruction of one at about 3.30 pm:

"I was Red 3 when Squadron sighted about 20 Me 109's. I attacked one enemy aircraft and climbed to deliver astern attack. Closed to 300 yds, giving a 2 second burst. E/a did a steep right hand turn and white smoke came from enemy aircraft. I gave another 5 second burst and e/a did a half roll and black smoke came from (e/a) fuselage. I closed to 150 yds. range and gave another short burst. Enemy aircraft dived and spun into sea. Pilot of e/a did not bale out and is believed to be killed or injured. Position of crash 8/10 miles SSE from Dover."

6 December 1940

P/O Franciszek Surma of 257 Squadron force landed near Clacton, Essex, out of petrol after a long patrol. His Hurricane I V7052, flown by him on many occasions, was damaged, but he escaped unhurt.

7 December 1940

Sgt Stanisław Karubin, one of the fighter aces of 303 Squadron, damaged his Hurricane during a training flight. Nothing more is known about this accident.

8 December 1940

On 8 December pilots of 306 Squadron trained at attacking in a dive. During one such mock attack Hurricane I P3938 flown by P/O Kazimierz Rutkowski caught fire and the Polish pilot had to force land. He selected a field at Beatton and immediately after landing left the cockpit of the burning aircraft. He was then taken to hospital for closer examination of severe burns, which required prolonged medical treatment.

Sgt Bronisław Malinowski of 501 Squadron crashed in Hurricane I R4101/SD-I at Wye near Ashford, while he fainted. After repair, this aircraft would be allocated to 306 Squadron.

10 December 1940

A three aircraft section from 302 Squadron, led by F/Lt John F. Finnis (recently posted in from 229 Squadron) was on patrol in the area south of Bognor. The section comprised:

Sgt. Łysek	P3867/WX-F
F/Lt Finnis	V7045/WX-A
P/O Łapka	P2717/WX-H

About 10.10 am they received an order to investigate an unknown aircraft, which turned out to be a Junkers 88. Finnis attacked twice and during the chase out to sea both P/O Stanisław Łapka and Sgt Antoni Łysek got in several bursts. The Junkers began to smoke and lose height, but due to bad weather all three 302 pilots then returned to base, Finnis claiming one Ju 88 probably destroyed.

After a training flight, F/O Mieczysław Jakszewicz of 307 Squadron landed his Defiant N1699 at Jurby and retracted the undercarriage while on the ground by mistake, instead of operating the flap retraction lever.

11 December 1940

A day significant only for two incidents.

P/O Tadeusz Kumiega of 17 Squadron was wounded in an accident, damaging Hurricane I P3023 Cat. II during a forced landing at Martlesham Heath.

F/O Witold Łokuciewski of 303 Squadron damaged his Hurricane I V6577/RF-P. No details of the accident are known.

12 December 1940

During a patrol near Middle Wallop, P/O Zbigniew Nosowicz of 56 Squadron collided in mid-air with the aircraft flown by P/O Marston. Marston's Hurricane, V7510, crashed, killing its pilot, but Nosowicz managed to nurse his damaged P3870 to the airfield, where he crash landed, suffering severe injuries. After medical treatment he was posted to 316 Squadron for operational duties, and subsequently resumed operational flying.

15 December 1940

During routine training with 308 Squadron, Sgt Muth damaged a Miles Magister when he taxied it into a battery trolley. Next day the same pilot caused damage to another aircraft of 308 Squadron!

16 December 1940

Sgt Muth was again in trouble when he damaged Hurricane V7048. After take off he failed to switch on the fuel tanks and the engine cut suddenly, forcing a landing at Wellesborne which ended with the aircraft standing on its nose. The accident was qualified as pilot carelessness and in December a report by 308 Squadron's Polish OC stated:

> "The Squadron has 25 operational pilots, the rest finishing their training. Sgts Muth and Derma have displayed such a low level of flying that the English OC of the Squadron requested his authorities to post them away from the Sqn.
>
> "The flying programme calls for a thorough training, which puts much stress on navigation and air fighting. At present theoretical foundations are laid for night flying."

A few days earlier 43 Squadron had moved from Usworth to Drem; its Polish pilot P/O Andrzej Malarowski, was on a patrol on this date when the engine of his Hurricane I R4227 cut and he was forced to abandon the aircraft, baling out. The aircraft sunk in the sea one mile off the Isle of May, Firth of Forth.

A friend of the unfortunate pilot, then Sgt Wacław Giermer, described the event in his memoirs:

> "When escorting the torpedo-damaged battleship which showed a significant listing and steamed slowly, P/O Malarowski baled out. An escorting warship fished him out, and it took two weeks before Malarowski was back with us. He told us he had a good time on the ship. The sailors washed his clothes, the food was good, and he had a vacation."

18 December 1940

S/Ldr Tadeusz Rolski, the Polish Officer Commanding 306 Squadron, while seated in Hurricane I V7865, was hit by a taxiing aircraft piloted by an English pupil pilot. No more information concerning this accident at Ternhill is known.

21 December 1940

The British crew of 307 Squadron Miles Master N8009 was interned in Ireland on 21 December 1941, when P/O Covington and P/O W. A. Proctor (the squadron engineer) on their way from Ringway to Jurby had to force-land in the neutral country.

The interned aircraft received Irish Air Corps number 96 and was almost ready for its first flight in new colours when a crack was discovered in its main spar, so it was relegated to ground instructional duties.

20 December 1940

F/O Czajkowski of 303 Squadron force landed at Sand Hutton near York; during this landing the undercarriage of his Hurricane V6684/RF-F struck some ledge (as stated in the accident report) and the aircraft stood on its nose.

23 December 1940

Defiant N1641 of 307 Squadron crewed by P/O Stanisław Szabłowski and Sgt Jan Broda, undershot its landing by about 150 ft and hit a wall in front of the runway at Jurby airfield. Due to the impact, the wings of the aircraft broke off and leaking fuel caused the aircraft to catch fire. Both airmen were injured. P/O Szabłowski did not lose consciousness until medical staff had performed the surgical removal of a flying instrument switch from his head. The aircraft was damaged beyond repair.

24 December 1940

S/Ldr Rolski, Polish Commanding Officer of 306 Squadron, described Ternhill airfield in his memoirs:

> "Tern Hill Station was not fully equipped at that time. In particular it did not have the so-called VHF homing, to guide the pilot on the right course, which resulted in serious navigation problems. After going down through clouds with low cloud ceiling, it was difficult to locate our own airfield, and the Welsh mountain ridges nearby endangered the aircraft flying in clouds or mist. That was how one of the instructors and deputy commanders, F/Lt Tennant, was killed. Coming out of clouds at night, he levelled too low and hit the ground, dying instantly, even though he was quite a good pilot."

Thus 306 lost a Flight Commander and one of the Hurricanes (V6992), which crashed at Hopton, Devon.

The day was important for one of the Polish pilots of 609 Squadron. Squadron Routine Orders of the Officer Commanding of the Warmwell-based unit included the following passage:

> "His Majesty the King has been graciously pleased to approve the award of the DFC to: F/O Tadeusz Nowierski."

27 December 1940

P/O Mirosław Orzechowski force landed with the undercarriage up at Acklington and damaged Hurricane P3829 of 607 Squadron, based at Turnhouse near Edinburgh.

28 December 1940

The day after F/O Orzechowski's accident, F/O Wiśniewski of 245 Squadron ended his scramble in Hurricane N2594 with the aircraft standing on its nose due to mishandling.

29 December 1940

P/O Józef Gil of 145 Squadron crashed in Hurricane I V7230 at East Dean during low flying practice. The pilot was injured and the aircraft damaged. He had previously served with 229 and 43 Squadrons; after leaving hospital he would be posted to 53 OTU at Heston to convert to Spitfires.

Chapter Six

BY DAY AND BY NIGHT

1 January – 31 March 1941

"Having completed many night patrols I came to the conclusion that scoring a kill at night is a matter of chance only, as to spot a machine further than 300 metres is very difficult, and even once spotted it is lost during a turn. I had a case where, while in the operation room, I guided F/O Janus onto over 11 aeroplanes, but all passed him by. There are frequent cases of pilots flying through the turbulence of German aircraft without seeing the latter; and even regardless of the fact that they take the pills for improved night vision[69]."

S/Ldr Jerzy Orzechowski, OC 308 Sqn

March 1941

9 January 1941

The day was marked by many accidents of Polish airmen in different RAF Squadrons. P/O Stefan Stegman of 229 Squadron damaged Hurricane I V7674, when he overshot during landing at Hawarden; P/O Włodzimierz Miksa of 303 Squadron belly landed at Hillingdon, damaging Hurricane I V6815/RF-J; and P/O Bronisław Wydrowski of 615 Squadron damaged Hurricane I V7339 during a forced landing at Kenley, upon return from one of the first offensive sweeps over France.

615 Squadron (County of Surrey) was reinforced by Polish airmen in December 1940. These were – P/O Franciszek Kornicki, P/O Mieczysław Grudziński, F/O Stanisław Czternastek, F/O Mieczysław Gorzula and P/O Bronisław Wydrowski. Some of them would continue to fly the KW-coded Hurricanes until May 1941.

One flight of the Polish night fighter 307 Squadron was detached to Squires Gate. The five detached crews included the Officers Commanding – S/Ldr George Tomlinson and his Polish equivalent, Stanisław Grodzicki. The same evening two aircraft at readiness were scrambled to patrol the Formby area. After a 45-minute patrol both returned to the airfield, but the crew of P/O Roman Smok and Sgt Zygfryd Blachowski, flying Defiant N3315, had trouble during landing. The landing

---

[69] Capsules with vitamin A, the lack of which in the wartime food could lead to degraded vision when in inadequate lighting.

lights of Squires Gate were still unserviceable and they taxied into a ditch, slightly damaging the aircraft.

10 January 1941

Immediately after midnight an 9/10th, 307 Squadron Defiants began patrolling the Formby area. Hourly patrols, ordered by Speke Operations Room, were provided by aircraft of 96, 312 (Czechoslovak) and 307 Squadrons. At the end of their patrol the crew of S/Ldr Stanisław Grodzicki and F/O Lech Karwowski successfully landed at Squires Gate. The other crew failed to receive its homing due to R/T failure and probably became lost. When fuel was exhausted, Sgt Antoni Joda decided to land on a flat strip of beach near Barmouth. However, the place chosen by the pilot of Defiant N3401 proved not to be a beach, but a flat strip of sand covered by water three feet deep. During landing the aircraft hit the water surface and immediately flipped over. Both airmen failed to get out of the aeroplane, and drowned. The next day, a rescue team got under water and found the body of the gunner, Sgt Wiktor Gandurski, still in the cockpit. Both bodies were finally recovered on 13 January, and buried at Blackpool two days later.

The only success by a Polish pilot on this date is linked with the first RAF operation code-named *Circus*. W/Cdr Victor Beamish, who led the North Weald-based 242 and 249 Squadrons, providing forward support cover, described this in a BBC broadcast on 4 January:

"We pressed on towards our objective but there was not a sign of German fighters coming out to intercept us and stop the bombers from reaching their target. The sky was empty except for our great formation, waiting and watching above the bombers, ready to pounce if anybody did attempt to interfere with them. The only man who had luck on that outward journey was a Polish sergeant pilot . . ."

The pilot mentioned by W/Cdr Beamish was Sgt Michał Mirosław Maciejowski, flying Hurricane V6614/GN-B, who described his efforts in his combat report:

"I was on the sweep patrol in the neighbourhood of St. Inglevert aerodrome and got temporarily separated from my section when I saw five Hs 126 in line at the corner of what I have since verified through photographs was Guines-La Plage aerodrome. I came down to between 200 and 300 feet and machine gunned the line of aircraft but did not have time to observe the result. I saw two Me 109's at about 300 ft flying NNW climbing. I climbed to 1000 ft and then attacked the rear Me giving him one long and two short bursts from about 150 yards from behind and above slightly from the right hand side. It turned steeply and dived vertically towards the ground as if the pilot had been hit and I saw it hit some trees. My throttle had jammed full open and as the other Me 109 was climbing steeply, I was unable to follow so I came down to ground level and made for the coast which I crossed between Cap Gris Nez and Boulogne. As I was approaching the coast, I was fired on by machine gun posts and Bofors, and from ships as I was crossing almost at sea level. My throttle was still jammed so I came over Hornchurch and switched off the ignition and landed. I later returned to North Weald and landed at 15.15 hours."

The Messerschmitt claimed by Sgt Maciejowski, which presumably crashed near Guines-La Plage airfield, is an uncertain victory[70], because the only known loss among the Bf 109s that day happened too far south west, when a JG 2 pilot force landed at Bernay airfield.

The day ended with P/O Waszkiewicz of 32 Squadron damaging his Hurricane I V6927 at Middle Wallop during landing.

11 January 1941

S/Ldr Tadeusz Rolski of 306 Squadron force landed his Hurricane I V7165/UZ-W at Cosford, inflicting damage qualified as Category A.

F/O Wacław Łapkowski of 303 Squadron damaged his Hurricane I W9129/RF-W, also qualified as damage Cat. A.

On 11 January 1941, late in the evening Sgt Ludwik Mirończuk of 307 Squadron had another incident, causing damage to two aircraft. During taxiing he ran his Defiant N1699 into the parked N1684. Mirończuk was then called to report to F/Lt C. J. Donovan, who said: 'Hitler has a good ally in yourself!' The same night the Polish night fighter squadron was ordered to move from Jurby to Squires Gate, but due to bad weather did not arrive there until 23 January. Here they joined the flight that had been detached to this airfield on 9 January.

Due to shortage of flying instructors in 308 Squadron based at Baginton, F/O Witalis Nikonow from the Central Flying School at Cardiff had arrived there on 28 December 1940. Less than two weeks later, on 11 January 1941 he was killed in a flying accident. One of the 308 Squadron pilots described by his Officer Commanding in the monthly report as "flying below average" took off in Master I N7955 for a training flight, in company with F/O Nikonow. After blind flying practice, whilst on the way back to base, P/O Jerzy Wolski lowered the undercarriage and the aircraft lost speed. The Master entered a spin and crashed at the edge of the airfield, killing both Wolski and Nikonow. (The latter had had a similar accident in Poland, when a PWS 10 monoplane fighter trainer he was flying lost speed on approach. He had broken both legs and spent a long time in hospital before he was posted back to flying duties.) After the crash the Polish Officer Commanding, Jerzy Orzechowski wrote:

> "In this connection I have an idea to introduce dual checks for those pilots who had had serious accidents, in order to verify whether they do not repeat the same errors in a given phase of flight. I have encountered similar checks in British units."

12 January 1941

The day proved important for all the Polish pilots in 609 Squadron. The Officer Commanding of the Warmwell-based unit announced:

> "The Polish Embassy has been pleased to award the Polish Cross Class V for Meritous Service to: F/O Tadeusz Nowierski, F/O Ostaszewski, P/O Żurakowski, P/O Oleński."

---

[70] According to the official PAF scoreboard, this victory has been categorised as an air-to-ground kill, rather than air-to-air one. This was probably caused by the fact that Maciejowski's dogfight started with a strafing run across the aerodrome, and he then described the Messerschmitt as "destroyed on land" (to stress that it did not fall into the Channel), which was mistaken for "destroyed on the ground".

13 January 1941

In 306 Squadron, Sgt Henryk Pietrzak while landing Hurricane UZ-P, struck the wreck of a Master and damaged his own aircraft.

14 January 1941

P/O Władysław Chciuk of 308 Squadron force landed at Wittering in Hurricane I P3598, in unspecified circumstances.

16 January 1941

Activity by Luftwaffe aircraft over Britain was again very low. Single bombers sneaked over the Isles, under the cover of clouds. In total, RAF fighter pilots claimed two enemy aircraft: one destroyed and one damaged, for the loss of three of their own aircraft and two pilots – a very unprofitable balance. The only confirmed claim was credited to a Polish pilot with 32 Squadron. F/O Jan Falkowski, flying the Hurricane II Z2984, wrote his report (in Polish) which was sent to the Polish Senior Liaison Officer at Fighter Command HQ. The victory was a historic achievement for it was the first night victory by a Polish Air Force pilot.

"Report from a combat sortie of 16 January 1941

"RAF Middle Wallop

"32 Sqn F.

"First of all I have to stress that night combat is incredibly difficult due to lack of special glasses that would facilitate spotting the enemy, and because the amount of searchlights is extremely high, while their results negligible, as for reasons unknown to me the searchlights catch the enemy only very seldom.

"I had patrolled that night for a while and could see nothing, eventually searchlights caught one of the enemy machines returning from bombing. I saw that from far away, and sped towards the e/a at full throttle. After a while I got quite close and then the searchlights lost the e/a, but I no longer needed their assistance as I could see the silhouette clearly ahead of me. I came in so close that I was only a dozen meters or so apart and I opened fire. The result was immediate, as within seconds the e/a smoked and fell crashing into the Channel. From my observations I concluded that this was a Heinkel 111, although it is very difficult to come close and identify precisely. On my way back to the aerodrome my engine suddenly started to choke, and in spite of all sorts of attempts came to a halt. There was no aerodrome nearby, and my altitude was decreasing rapidly, so reluctantly I decided to bale out. During the jump my parachute caught on the cockpit, and eventually when I managed to free myself, the fin crushed my leg just above the ankle. Upon my parachute landing I was taken to the hospital where I still remain. My leg has been set and is in plaster now, I hope that within weeks I will be able to resume successful combat against the enemy. For the glory of Poland.

"Jan Falkowski por. pil.

"P.S. I should like to stress that I had flown many day and night sorties in this skadron[71] patrolling the Channel area, but I never submitted any reports as I had no encounters with e/a during these sorties."

---

[71] Original spelling in Falkowski's report.

However, the Luftwaffe did not lose any He 111s that night, and perhaps the aircraft shot up by Falkowski took effective evasive action, although a single Heinkel 111H-2, Werk Nr. 2710 of 5./KG 53, only managed to reach the other side of the Channel where it crash landed at Staden due to damage by RAF fighters. The report written by Falkowski at the hospital circled from one office to another, until PAF and RAF authorities confirmed this victory. Additionally his report was supported by an account of an eyewitness, Mr H. Pycroft from North Hayling, Hants.:

> "Near about eight o'clock I heard Machine Gunning. Looking up towards North West I saw a flash and the engine stopped of one of the planes and I heard it rushing down towards the sea due South when I heard an explosion, I ran in to my wife, when we heard another plane come down North West of us, we stepped outside the house thinking someone might bale out and subsequently heard Mr. Falkowski calling and I am very pleased to have been able to render him service."

21 January 1941

That day 315 Squadron was formed officially at Acklington, as the fifth Polish day fighter unit in the RAF.

P/O Bogusław Mierzwa of 303 Squadron damaged Hurricane I R4081/RF-O in unspecified circumstances.

22 January 1941

303 Squadron moved on 3 January 1941 to its former base at Northolt, and was back on operations. The first *Mosquito* operation performed by the unit proved to be one of the most spectacular actions of early 1941. Just before noon seven of the unit's aircraft took off from Northolt to Hawkinge. After refuelling, six of them were airborne about 20 minutes after noon. This *Mosquito* over France was later described in the Polish language press printed in Britain:

> "Polish airmen of a famous pursuit squadron have distinguished themselves again in a magnificent achievement – a daylight attack against German aerodromes in Northern France.
>
> "Six Polish pilots in Hurricanes flew twice to the French coast, reaching the river Somme. They attacked and destroyed aircraft at aerodromes, dispersed a military column on a road, machine gunned German troops . . .
>
> "During the first mission, one of the pilots commenced an attack, diving and firing at a group of small motor boats encountered near the French coast, on the way to the aerodrome at Le Touquet. At the airfield he saw 5 Messerschmitts and fired at them from machine guns. On his way back he encountered strong AA fire, and manoeuvred until he spent all his ammunition at the machine gun posts."

After an hour all six aircraft were back, and about 3 pm they were ready for another trip to France. The report of this action recorded:

> ". . . after passing Dungeness they went south. Cloud extended about 40 miles from the English coast 10/10th at 3000 feet. F/Lt Henneberg signalled to carry on and the pairs scattered. As there was no more cloud to the south F/Lt Henneberg changed course eastwards, where he saw clouds continuing. He and

F/O Grzeszczak flew on a course 120 degrees and then 140 degrees. Cloud was at 3500 feet from the coast. They flew for six minutes in cloud on a course of 160 degrees. They left cloud at 4000 feet over France in an unknown position and came down to ground level. They saw nothing on the roads or the railways. They changed course to 90 degrees and after ten minutes search saw an aerodrome in course of construction about 20 miles inland. There were huts and rollers and concrete building plant. The two pilots attacked and a green light was fired from the aerodrome. There were machine guns and probably 20 mm flak posts which returned their fire. They fired at the huts and flak posts. They saw men in German Air Force uniforms running away from the runways and huts into fields. From the centre of the aerodrome F/Lt Henneberg saw small red tracer shells passing him. This aerodrome was on a low hill and may have been Quoeux. After this, they flew westwards and saw a railway station on the coast. As there was only an engine in the station they did not fire. After circling up to 4000 feet F/Lt Henneberg lost F/O Grzeszczak in the clouds and returned alone to Northolt, landing at 16.30 hrs. F/O Grzeszczak landed at Redhill and damaged his aircraft on an obstruction. He is unhurt, and his report will be sent later.

"The second pair F/O Gabszewicz and P/O Mierzwa after leaving F/Lt Henneberg on the second sortie vectored 90 degrees and flew in clouds at 3500 feet for 8 minutes. They saw a gap in the cloud and flew along roads for about ten minutes in several directions at ground level. On a road which appears to be that from Maningheim to Desvres they saw a convoy of about 30 dark green covered military lorries proceeding north west about 200-500 yards apart so they zig-zagged among them firing bursts at the lorries. Some stopped, and men in German Air Force uniform jumped from them into ditches. On approaching a village probably Desvres they heard small repeating cannon fire coming at them and climbed into clouds. F/O Gabszewicz lost P/O Mierzwa. He flew at 3000 feet at 340 degrees and in a hole in the cloud (over Boulogne) encountered much light and heavy flak. An Me 109 flew over him at 6000 feet and in the opposite direction without apparently seeing him. At the coast he saw fishing boats and a floating platform 60' by 20' 300 yards from the shore with a black round tower with a mast on it. He then returned to Northolt. P/O Mierzwa landed at Hawkinge.

"Of the third pair, P/O Łapkowski landed at Hawkinge and P/O Strzembosz landed at Lympne, the latter with his aircraft slightly damaged . . .

"Leaving Hawkinge at 15.20 hours in the company of the other four aircraft of the flight, they flew south over the Channel and split into pairs off the French coast. Cloud base about 2000 feet and whilst flying in the cloud the French coast was crossed in the Boulogne area. Over land, they came down from 2000 feet to 1500 feet below cloud and searched for an objective. An aerodrome was noticed on which two Me 109's were taxiing into position to take off. This aerodrome is believed to be near Auxi le Chateau."

The following is P/O Łapkowski's account:

"I dived and opened fire at 400 yards range at two aircraft and noticed the one on the right fall on its wing. I continued, and fired at gun positions and saw the gunners abandon their post. I then pulled out of the dive, turned slightly left and attacked three or four Me 109's dispersed amongst trees on the fringe of the aerodrome. At the end of the attack, I noticed something in front of me, pulled up sharply and cut through an electric overhead cable, a length of which wrapped itself round parts of my aircraft and deadened the controls climbing for height. A.A. fired at me continuously. I climbed right through clouds, finding the top at about 7000 feet and returned to Hawkinge at 16.00 hours."

P/O Strzembosz's account:

"I dived and attacked the two Me 109's, after my No. 1 opened fire at about 600 yards, I noticed that one was lying on its wing and the other was standing motionless. I then fired at gun posts which apparently returned my fire as bullets splintered the windscreen and damaged the port wing. I held on as long as possible and in pulling away, I caught the tip of my starboard wing in the sandbags around the gun posts, the collision breaking a small piece off the wing. I then went on to fire at the e/a dispersed amongst the trees and at this moment noticed a large flash followed by smoke coming from No. 1's aircraft, and also noticed smoke coming from the trees where he had been firing, and at the same time, saw A.A. bursts, immediately behind his aircraft. I then took cover in cloud, and flew West. Coming down below cloud, I was still over land and flying very low I noticed a number of soldiers waving to me from the ground, so I greeted them with a good burst and flew low over the sea back to England, and, as visibility was bad, I landed at the first available aerodrome which was Lympne at 16.00 hours."

P/O Łapkowski's aircraft had about 25 yards of seven-strand eighteen gauge bare copper wire wrapped round it. The radiator, airscrew and tailplane were damaged. P/O Strzembosz's aircraft received damage to the starboard wing tip. Bullet holes were in the port wing and the fractured windscreen. This action was described by the 303 Squadron Intelligence Officer and forwarded to Fighter Command. P/O Łapkowski and P/O Strzembosz had attacked an airfield north of Abbeville at Crecy where I./JG 26 Messerschmitts were based. This Luftwaffe unit lost one Bf 109, probably the one shot up by P/O Łapkowski as described in his combat report. Fhr. Friedrich Graf von Uiberacker, was wounded in his Bf 109E-7 Werk Nr. 4147 on the ground.

The lucky six of that day was:

F/O Łapkowski	W9129/RF-W
P/O Strzembosz	R4081/RF-O
F/O Gabszewicz	V7466/RF-S
P/O Mierzwa	V7182/RF-U
F/Lt Henneberg	V7183/RF-J
F/O Grzeszczak	V7499/RF-D

and F/Lt Brinsden flying the Hurricane V7606/RF-A, who took part in the noon attack only. F/O Gabszewicz preserved a cutting of the press account of that sortie entitled 'Daylight raid of Polish airmen to Northern France – splendid performance of 6 pursuit pilots', in his diary, with a personal annotation by the pilot:

"That was the sortie that gave me the most emotion and satisfaction."

This was to be one of the unit's last combat sorties on Hurricanes, as that day it took delivery of its first Spitfires, the first Polish squadron to begin converting to the type.

After this mission F/O Gabszewicz started to prepare tactics for a similar attack on German Army Headquarters in Paris. He suggested using three Spitfires with auxiliary tanks, but this propaganda mission project was not approved by the RAF authorities, due to lack of long range Spitfire fighters, and to the possibility of civilian casualties. Similar actions would prove extremely successful during the later stages of the war, using Mosquito fighter-bombers.

23 January 1941

When finally the weather cleared, it allowed the move of 307 Squadron's aircraft and supporting Harrows transport from Jurby to Squires Gate. On the way mist over the Blackpool area got thick, and landing at Squires Gate became risky. Despite that, one of the three aircraft reached the aerodrome without trouble. However, F/O Jerzy Antonowicz, flying Defiant N3439, force landed near Southport, but after the mist cleared he took off and landed at Squires Gate. The last aircraft, N3320 of Sgt Jan Mikszo, force landed at Ormskirk, sustaining some damage.

1 February 1941

When landing at High Ercall, P/O Jan Artur Czapiewski of 306 Squadron rolled off the runway and stood Hurricane I V6986/UZ-Z on its nose.

P/O Mirosław Orzechowski of 607 Squadron damaged Magister T9874 while landing during a snow-storm.

2 February 1941

During strafing training at a sea range Sgt Antoni Markiewicz of 302 Squadron, flying Hurricane V6753/WX-Z, had an accident, described by the pilot:

"On the eve of a 'Mosquito' mission to France we (mjr Łaguna, ppor. Król, Karwowski and myself) flew on strafing training over the sea. The idea was to practice moving focused fire from one point to another, this being rather useful over France, when strafing airfields.

"About six miles from the shore, after dropping a smoke buoy into the sea we attacked it in turns strafing it.

"During the final phase of my attack, focusing on aiming I realised I was too low, and started pulling up immediately. Unfortunately, it proved too late, and the machine, moments before regaining level flight, sank during pull-up, and hit water with its bottom, seriously damaging the radiator and the propeller. After several bounces on the sea surface I managed to get back into the air and take off again. After making a turn towards the shore I started to gain height, at the same time preparing to bale out. Glycol was pouring from the damaged radiator, covering my face and eyes, while the damaged propeller started to shake so violently that the engine was about to break off or seize. Asked about what had happened – I replied that I had hit water. At an altitude of some 800 meters, when I was back over land, the engine seized – the propeller came to a halt. I decided to land at once. Doped up by the fumes of the hot liquid I started to weave right before reaching the field I had selected to land. Some 20 metres above ground just before final approach I lost consciousness altogether.

"I later learned that on hitting the ground with a wing I was thrown out of the cockpit, suffering serious bruises. The Hurricane was broken completely, falling apart at the cockpit, the tail falling on top of the nose. According to eyewitnesses of the accident, I escaped on all fours from the site of the crash. I regained consciousness in the hospital.

"My friends say that one has to be born lucky to be so fortunate. Indeed, if I had not been thrown out on the first hit against the ground – the next moment I would have been smashed up by the broken fuselage which shattered the cockpit."

The pilot, slightly injured, was taken to the Royal West Sussex Hospital, and did not take part in the *Mosquito* operation.

Sgt Dobrucki of 607 Squadron damaged Hurricane P3161 when taxiing his aircraft – he ran into a hole covered by the snow and the aircraft flipped onto its nose.

3 February 1941

F/Lt Young, the British night flying instructor of 308 Squadron, got lost during a weather test, flying Hurricane I V7502, and landed with undercarriage retracted at Whitle Ford near Stoney Stansford. After the accident it was found that he still had fuel for more than half an hour's flying.

4 February 1941

Two Defiants of 307 Squadron were damaged during landing at Squires Gate. One was flown by F/O Jan Krzyżanowski and the other by P/O Marian Piwko.

5 February 1941

Operation *Circus* No. 3 proved disastrous for 615 Squadron, and for Polish airmen of that unit. A dozen Hurricanes left Kenley with orders to join 1 Squadron and rendezvous with Blenheims over Rye at 12.30 pm. 615 Squadron's composite combat report said:

"Two formations of aircraft were sighted moving across Channel about 10 miles ahead. S/Ldr Holmewood took the aircraft to be the bombers and attempted to catch them up but was unable to gain much distance. French coast was crossed over Hardelot at 12,000 ft when near Colomber, Green 2 P/O Wheeler saw one Yellow nosed Me 109 diving to attack Blue 2 Sgt Jenkins. Some pilots reported other Me 109s but no further attacks were made on our aircraft."

Sgt Jenkins was lost, probably crashing near St. Omer, while P/O Wheeler attacked the Messerschmitt but without apparent results. When the squadron recrossed the French coast, it was attacked by a larger formation of Messerschmitts. Four Bf 109s were pursued by two Hurricanes of 615 Squadron. Some others attacked two single Messerschmitts without positive results.

"One pilot reports seeing the Hurricane pilot down in sea off South East coast. He circled and tried to ring Control but could obtain no reply."

Probably he saw a pilot of either 1 or 56 Squadrons, which lost one pilot each.

"After Squadron had crossed English coast near Dover two Polish pilots of Green

Section, P/O Wydrowski and P/O Czternastek collided in mid air and P/O Czternastek was killed."

P/O Bronisław Wydrowski, flying Hurricane V6618, baled out and was sent to Marine Hospital with severe injuries. F/O Stanisław Czternastek's Hurricane V7598/KW-U crashed at Appleton Farm, Marlon near Dover, killing its pilot.

6 February 1941

The day brought several accidents in 308 Squadron. After a combat training flight, P/O Wandzilak was forced to land due to engine failure, alighting on hard terrain near Leamington, miraculously without damage to the aircraft, V6861.

This accident earned him two different entries in his flying logbook:

"In accordance with 9 Group letter, reference 9 G/C.503/73/PR, dated 25.2.41, the accident involving Hurricane V6861, piloted by P/O Wandzilak was due to 'disobedience' on the pilot's part on 6.2.41.

"Jerzy Orzechowski

"Squadron Leader

"O.C. 308 Polish Squadron"

"Irrespective of the decision of 9 Group, as O.C. of the Squadron I herewith append my own remarks. Whilst landing Hurricane V6861 on the 6.2.41, the pilot displayed great presence of mind and considerable flying skill. He landed in a confined space on very uneven ground. Surrounded by high trees, from which it would have been impossible to take off. After flying very low over trees with a stopped engine, P/O Wandzilak let down his undercarriage and landed without damaging his machine, a very creditable achievement in the circumstances.

"Squadron Leader Jerzy Orzechowski

"O.C. 308 Polish Squadron"

The same day 308's British OC, S/Ldr Morris destroyed Hurricane V6939 when he force-landed at Coint Farm, four miles south of Warwick. The aircraft skidded into a lodge and caught fire. He later reported that "the aircraft was abandoned unserviceable by previous pilot", who reported an oil pressure system malfunction, but he took off, only to end up in hospital. The Polish OC of 308 Squadron, S/Ldr Orzechowski, wrote:

"I have discussed immediately my remarks about the two accidents with pilots and the Engineering Officer, ordering technical inspection of all machines. No faults were found in other machines."

This was the second British OC that the Squadron lost in an accident[72]. Thus S/Ldr Jerzy Orzechowski became the sole commander of the unit.

F/O Eugeniusz Ebenrytter of 307 Squadron landed at Squires Gate in his Defiant N3432 with undercarriage up, and damaged it.

9 February 1941

Sgt Hegenbarth of 308 Squadron during his first night training flight, damaged a

---

[72] As mentioned before, S/Ldr Davis was killed in an accident on 16 October 1940.

wingtip of the Hurricane. The aircraft was serviceable again within 24 hours. His OC wrote a report about this accident:

"The cause consisted in very difficult weather conditions under which the pilot made his first night flight. Night flying is made at Bramcote, under command of F/Lt Young. Several times I have brought to the attention of S/Ldr Morris that the way F/Lt Young conducts night flying leaves much to be desired. He is a very reckless and tactless officer, who has no idea of night flying, and often commits stupidities."

10 February 1941

Exactly a month after the first *Circus* operation, Sgt Michał Mirosław Maciejowski, who had become the hero on 10 January, again claimed a victory over a Bf 109E. This time 249 Squadron took part in operation *Circus* no. 4. Maciejowski's unit was one of four squadrons protecting six Blenheims of 139 Squadron flying to bomb the docks at Dunkirk. The 249 Squadron team was as follows:

Sgt Maciejowski (Polish)	V6614/GN-B	Red 2
F/Lt Lofts	V6945	
P/O Crossey	V7600/GN-C	
Sgt Brzeski (Polish)	R4178	Blue 2
W/Cdr Beamish	V6817	
F/Lt Neil	V6854/GN-F	
F/O Lewis	V6582	Yellow 2
Sgt Palliser	V6565	Red 4
Sgt Davidson	V6728/GN-Z	
P/O Davis	V7171	
Sgt Mills	V6655	
S/Ldr Barton	V7538/GN-T	

Just over the target Bf 109s of IV./JG 51 and I./LG 2 attacked the escorting Hurricanes. In the first attack P/O Davis of 249 Squadron was shot down and wounded. After a successful bale-out he became a PoW. Maciejowski, who claimed a Messerschmitt, described his efforts:

"I was Red 2. I was flying 1000 ft higher than the leader who was at 14 000 ft. I saw 3 Me 109 attacking the formation below me. I dived down and did a steep climbing turn and delivered a ³/₄ stern attack with deflection with a long burst of 5 or 6 seconds. The e/a turned on its back immediately and the pilot baled out although the aircraft had given no sign of injury. I then looked around and saw a dog-fight a long way above me but as I could not reach them, I dived to 700 ft and returned home."

Most probably Uffz. Karl Ryback of I./LG 2 was Maciejowski's victim. His Bf 109, "White 3", crashed into the sea and the pilot was killed, although Sgt Maciejowski saw him bale out. At the same time the other Polish participant attacked another Messerschmitt:

"I was Blue 2. I attacked a Me 109 at 16 000 ft and while he was taking evasive action another Me 109 dived on me and I was forced to break away. I found myself just out to sea beyond Dunkirk and saw a merchant vessel of about 3000 ton about 1½ miles West of Dunkirk. I dived on it from 4000 ft and machine gunned it from 500 ft but did not observe any damage, nor did I see any sign of life on board.

"I then climbed to 4000 ft and saw a Me 109 and a Hurricane having a dog-fight 1000 ft below me. This Hurricane was W/Cdr Beamish. I dived with boost and made astern attack on the e/a from above, giving a long burst for 5 seconds breaking off at the same level at a distance of 150 yards, then immediately made for the coast, losing height rapidly – emitting fire and smoke. Then reached the beach and crashed about 500 yards inland. I then rejoined my squadron and returned home with them."

Sgt Stanisław Brzeski, who described this action with details, probably attacked the Messerschmitt flown by Lt. Adolf Steckmeyer of II./JG 51, although Sgt Palliser also claimed a Bf 109 which he shot off some Hurricane's tail.

Even though Brzeski had destroyed a German observation balloon in September 1939 over Poland, this 109 was his first German aeroplane confirmed destroyed. He would go on to become an ace, eventually scoring seven and three shared confirmed victories, two probables and one damaged. On the other hand, Sgt Maciejowski became an ace in this sortie, claiming his fifth Bf 109 destroyed while flying in 249 Squadron. By the end of the war he would reach a total of ten and one shared victories, nine of them being single-engined fighters. Interestingly, both Polish victors of this combat would end the war as PoWs, although neither would be shot down by the Luftwaffe – Maciejowski baled out after his wingman collided with his Spitfire in August 1943, while Brzeski fell to AA fire in May 1944.

13 February 1941

The weather conditions on 13 February were described by 306 Squadron's Officer Commanding, Tadeusz Rolski:

"A haze remained over the aerodrome. When you looked at it from below, or directly from above, it looked quite innocent. But knowing personally all sorts of hazards hiding in such hazes, I decided to take off myself for a test. Just as well I did. When approaching to land I noticed that when I looked at the haze at an angle, it seemed completely non-transparent. When you were landing, you looked at this angle, a flat approach could end tragically. I warned the pilots, to start the approach rather high and close to the aerodrome, thus making sure they would land rather steeply. Unfortunately, not all of them were able to use my advice in practice."

About 8.30 pm P/O Bogdan Bielkiewicz crashed in his Hurricane P3069/UZ-Y and was killed, when his aircraft hit trees near the airfield. That same night Sgt Wawrzyniec Jasiński crashed another of the unit's Hurricanes; his V6946/UZ-Q also hit a tree, but this time the pilot was only injured.

308 Squadron also undertook night flying training. P/O Stanisław Wandzilak, flying Hurricane I V7027, returning from one such flight, approached too high, and being at 100-200 ft he opened up again. However, the engine cut and he overshot

Bramcote runway; the undercarriage and airscrew of his Hurricane were damaged.

Before these night flying accidents a notable incident happened during the day in 609 Squadron. F/Lt Forshaw and F/O Tadeusz Nowierski (Polish), while patrolling over Swanage, saw what they took to be a friendly aircraft on account of its yellow roundels. The OC, 609 Squadron wrote:

> "Nowierski began to practice attack and then saw crosses on the wings. Notifying Forshaw, who did not hear him, he then carried out 4 genuine attacks until he had exhausted his ammunition, enemy's reaction being to dive. Pieces flew off enemy aircraft (believed Ju 88) after second attack, but since Nowierski did not see it enter the sea, the enemy aircraft is only claimed as damaged. Return fire experienced three times from top gunner, once from lower, but slight damage to Spitfire probably due to abrupt breakaway. The incident was mentioned in BBC 1 o'clock news."

This incident happened between 5 and 5.40 pm, when the section of Spitfires (X4471/PR-R and X4773) was on patrol. The only Junkers bomber reported by the Luftwaffe as attacked by RAF fighters was Ju 88A-1 W.Nr.4176 of KGr 806, which crashed at Caen with all three crew wounded. Also 53 Squadron however, based at Thorney Island, reported that Blenheim IV R3679 returned damaged beyond repair.

A few days earlier, on 8 February 1941, Officer Commanding 609 Squadron wrote a 'Report on Polish Pilots' and summarised Nowierski's claims as five enemy aircraft destroyed himself and a half in a section, plus two enemy aircraft damaged. His opinion regarding Nowierski, who had been in the unit since 5 August 1940, was:

> "A very good and reliable pilot. His enthusiasm and keenness to fight and his unfailing cheerfulness on the ground all combine to make him a very great asset to the squadron."

Despite this opinion, Polish authorities would later downgrade some of his claims, and Nowierski would never be officially acknowledged as a fighter ace in the PAF.

14 February 1941

This misty day saw a tragic accident in 302 Squadron. Spitfires of 610 Squadron approaching Northolt crashed into Hurricane P3867/WX-F which was being maintained by two ground crew members. AC2 Przybyłowicz, sitting in the cockpit, was killed, and LAC Gintrowicz, an armourer working on the wing, was severely injured.

Sgt Jan Palak of 303 Squadron damaged one of the first Spitfire Is delivered to his unit while converting from Hurricanes, when he force landed the Spitfire R6700/RF-X due to lack of fuel, after he had got lost.

15 February 1941

P/O Bolesław Drobiński had been posted to the Spitfire-equipped 65 Squadron from 7 OTU on 12 August 1940. His service there continued without incident, until on 15 February 1941 he landed at Tangmere at night and overshot the landing strip, taxiing into soft ground and damaging his Spitfire II P7829. The Polish pilot was injured in this accident. At about that time Drobiński was transferred from 65 to 303 (Polish) Squadron, as he later described:

"In mid-February 1941 por. Witold Urbanowicz came to Tangmere as, in his capacity of the Polish Liaison Officer to Fighter Command, upon giving up command of 303 Squadron, he reviewed the Polish pilots who still flew with British squadrons. After a short conversation with me he announced that I would soon obtain posting to no. 303 Squadron. I replied to Urbanowicz that I would prefer to be posted to another unit. 'No. 303 is all aces, and I'm afraid I will not be able to keep up with them', I said. Urbanowicz laughed, and said – 'You should not be afraid, lieutenant. Quite the contrary, the squadron is converting to Spitfires and you can help them with your experience'."

So Drobiński left 65 Squadron, and joined the 'Kościuszko' Squadron at the beginning of March 1941. By early July he would score six victories, becoming the top-scoring Polish Spitfire pilot.

Polish pilots of 257 Squadron did not achieve much success, but on 15 January 1941 F/Lt Łazoryk was scrambled from Honnington, ordered to intercept an He 111 flying at 7,000 ft. The Polish pilot in his Hurricane V7607 attacked the enemy aircraft, but after exhausting all the ammunition, he saw the enemy bomber escape, smoking slightly. No claim was reported.

16 February 1941

A few minutes after midnight a section of 307 Squadron Defiants took off from Squires Gate to patrol the Formby area. After the patrol both aircraft reached the aerodrome area but were unable to land due to the presence of German bombers nearby. After Squires Gate cancelled the bombing alert the Defiants landed, but mist impeded visibility of the landing lights. As he was taxiing P/O Antoni Alexandrowicz hit a steamroller left near the runway, damaging Defiant N3402. Both the pilot and his gunner, Sgt Kazimierz Osieleniec, luckily escaped unhurt. The other aircraft of the section was also damaged during taxiing, when it hit a lamp-post. The crew of Stanisław Grodzicki also escaped unhurt.

A 302 Squadron section of P/O Edward Pilch (P3877/WX-T) and Sgt Marian Wędzik (P2918/WX-Y) took off about 11.00 am to patrol the Northolt area. About noon the Operations Room received an echo from two enemy aircraft coming in to the Tangmere area from the north. The 302 Squadron Hurricanes, flying at 8,000 ft, began to close in on the enemy.

"Flying as Blue 2 with P/O Pilch leading we received an order from the Controller at about 12.00 to fly on a vector of 015 degrees and then 350 degrees at 12 000 ft. After a certain time I saw an e/a approaching from Arundel about 2000 ft above emerging from cloud. P/O Pilch did a steep turn of 180 degrees and at the same time I followed him and we began to chase the e/a which was flying South but had not yet seen us. After a while the e/a must have seen us because the pilot began doing violent zig-zags, at the same time trying to gain height which enabled us to catch him up. I flew on the right hand side 500 yards behind and above so that when e/a did a right hand turn I dived and gave him a burst, 3 short bursts at about 300 yards breaking away to the right. After my bursts I noticed smoke coming from the port engine. The e/a did a left turn away from me when Blue 2 attacked him and I saw an explosion which was probably the port petrol tank. After this the e/a went into a dive over the Channel about 15 miles over the coast.

I did not attack further as it was unnecessary and my engine was overheating and I was short of fuel. I landed at Westhampnett 12.35. – Sgt Wędzik M."

17 February 1941

During formation flying training one of three 307 Squadron aircraft taking part crashed, killing its crew. This happened about 3 pm when Defiant N3314 with Sgt Kazimierz Bocheński and Sgt Kazimierz Frąckiewicz aboard, being at 1500 ft, left the formation and began to make aerobatic figures. First it pulled up and then entered a spin, making turns. None of the accompanying pilots received any warning from the diving Defiant crew. The aircraft hit the ground almost vertically. It is believed that the pilot had lost consciousness.

18 February 1941

This day brought the last victory for a Polish pilot in 249 Squadron. Sgt Stanisław Brzeski reported strafing Bf 109s on the ground during a *Rhubarb* mission over France. A few days later the three Poles, Solak, Maciejowski and Brzeski, moved to 317 Squadron, while some time after this Sgt Popek went to 303.

20 February 1941

Four aircraft of 302 Squadron took off for a dog-fight practice over base at 20,000 ft. One of the pilots, P/O Edward Roman Pilch flying Hurricane R2687/WX-X, suddenly dived into ground from 15,000 ft. The others noticed that his aircraft began smoking and burning just above the ground. P/O Pilch was killed in the crash near Arundel. The cause of the accident was never definitely explained.

22 February 1941

317 Squadron was officially formed at Acklington.

23 February 1941

316 Squadron was officially formed at Pembrey; the last new fighter squadron of the Polish Air Force was born. Soon the nucleus of personnel for the unit arrived, posted from 303 and 607 Squadrons and from the Polish Depot at Blackpool.

During operational flights in 307 Squadron P/O Eugeniusz Przysiecki, flying a Defiant, hit the tail unit of another aircraft (N3339) in which F/Lt Lumsden was flying ahead of him. The British officer, sensing the impact, opened up, ending his flight on a beach near Blackpool.

W/O Przybylski of the Service Ferry Pool was ferrying aircraft to 317 Squadron at Acklington, but upon landing, Hurricane I V7316 flipped onto its nose, resulting in damage to one of the first aircraft for the unit newly formed just the previous day. This aircraft was later repaired, and flew with the squadron, receiving the code letter K.

24 February 1941

P/O Jan Zumbach of 303 Squadron force landed Spitfire IA R6977/RF-C at Colney, London due to lack of fuel.

74 Squadron's Operations Record Book reported:

"Sgt Morrison missing on return from patrol. Sgt Jan Rogowski (Polish) forced landed near Eastbourne and admitted to Princess Alice Memorial Hospital, Eastbourne with scalp wounds – detained. Nothing further to record."

The Polish pilot who got lost and force landed in his Spitfire II P7559, had joined 74 Squadron on on 9 February.

A Defiant crew of 307 Squadron, F/Lt Jerzy Antonowicz and Sgt Stanisław Sadawa, received an order to patrol over Liverpool. Their take-off ended suddenly, surprising all personnel present at Squires Gate at that time. The roar of Defiant N3375's engine ceased suddenly, and the aircraft disappeared at the end of the runway. One of the witnesses, P/O M. Lewandowski, described that when he reached the place where he expected to see a fatal crash, he saw the aircraft lying with broken undercarriage, entangled with some canvas, and a demolished truck nearby. It turned out that the Defiant hit a truck driven across the runway by LAC W. Short, who was killed in the accident. The port wing of the aircraft was damaged and the undercarriage leg was stuck in the remains of the truck. The crew were unhurt.

25 February 1941

On 25 February a dozen Spitfires of 303 Squadron took part in a Circus operation over Dunkirk. Rendezvous with Blenheims was over Canterbury. The chronicle of the unit described this:

> "From this area the Squadron headed in the direction of Calais. Here it encountered accurate and strong AA fire. Then the OC saw five Me 109s that were flying South below the Squadron and some 5 miles ahead. At the same time the OC saw an air combat inland. So he headed in that direction. When he arrived there, the fighting aircraft were already lower and hiding in clouds. Therefore there was no chance to join in the combat. The Squadron headed back for England. When crossing the French coast the AA fire proved so intensive that it had to be avoided. At one instant Sgt Wojciechowski felt a strong shudder in his aeroplane, and when he looked back in his mirror, he saw a Me 109 following him, and the ragged rudder of his aeroplane. Sgt Wojciechowski turned to port and flew into clouds, hiding from the enemy. Upon landing it was found that the aeroplane had a completely smashed rudder, both mainwheel tyres shot through, five holes in the port wing and one hole in the fuselage."

Sgt Mirosław Wojciechowski had escaped fire from a Bf 109 that probably belonged to JG 51, and returned to Northolt in his damaged Spitfire I N3108/RF-P. Other pilots who took part in this mission were as follows:

"A" Flight

S/Ldr Henneberg	R6975/RF-A
P/O Daszewski	X4481/RF-G
Sgt Wűnsche	P9555/RF-D
F/Lt Arentowicz	R6763/RF-B
P/O Zumbach	R6996/RF-E
P/O Ferić	X4770/RF-H

"B" Flight

F/Lt Łapkowski	X4344/RF-R
Sgt Wojciechowski	N3108/RF-P
Sgt Bełc	R6972/RF-N

P/O Łokuciewski	P9519/RF-M
Sgt Palak	N3122/RF-Y
Sgt Pavlovic	N3285/RF-J

26 February 1941

The first victorious pilot of 308 Squadron, Sgt Mieczysław Parafiński, lost his life in mysterious circumstances during a combat training flight with P/O Witold Retinger. The 308 Squadron Officer Commanding described this accident in which Hurricane I V7073 crashed at Guisborough:

> "Sgt Parafiński stayed for a while longer with his leader at an altitude of 23,000 ft, but then got lost at an altitude of 18,000 ft. P/O Retinger searched for his wingman in vain for 40 minutes and then landed at his aerodrome. Witnesses of the accident said they saw a Hurricane aeroplane about 3.15 pm coming out of a loop and flying on its back, and then the aeroplane entered a steep dive from approximately 8,000 ft and crashed into the ground. The pilot was killed on the spot. The aeroplane completely wrecked. The cause of the accident: the pilot probably lost consciousness at high altitude. Possibility of oxygen system failure."

28 February 1941

F/O Władysław Nowak of 306 Squadron damaged Hurricane I V6948/UZ-R when landing at Ternhill. The aircraft flipped onto its nose while taxiing in a cross wind, but the accident report states "Pilot carelessness".

2 March 1941

The 303 Squadron chronicle stated:

> "From 27 February 1941 until 4 March 1941 operational sorties continued over English territory, but without events, training flights are also made."

During one training flight F/O Wojciech Kołaczkowski damaged Spitfire IA P9519/RF-M during a landing at Northolt.

3 March 1941

F/Lt Younghusband of 308 Squadron damaged his Hurricane I V7053 whilst taking off from Hawarden, when the undercarriage collapsed.

4 March 1941

On 4 March in the early morning individual Luftwaffe reconnaissance aeroplanes appeared over England. One of them was intercepted by pilots of 302 Squadron; the three pilots and Hurricanes were:

F/Lt Julian Kowalski	V6744/WX-C	Red 1
Sgt Antoni Łysek	V3207[73]/WX-A	
P/O Jan Maliński	V6860/WX-B	

---

[73] The number V3207 appears in 302 Squadron ORB, but this number was in fact in a batch allocated to Airspeed Oxfords and never used. WX-A at that time bore serial V7047, but probably the correct number was P3204 (WX-E).

F/Lt Kowalski described this flight in his combat report:

"I took off as Red 1 with orders to patrol St Catherine Point at 17 000 ft. Having arrived in position and reached the given height I was told that an e/a was approaching from the North West. After about three minutes searching I saw one bomber to the West of Isle of Wight diving at an angle of about 45 degrees Southwards. I recognised it to be a Ju 88. At the same moment I saw three Spitfires very high to the North of the e/a. During the next two minutes I did a stern attack from slightly to the port side and got on his tail and having closed to 150 yards, gave him two bursts. I then closed to about 100 yrds and got in three more long bursts. After these last bursts the e/a lost speed and I was able to approach to within 50 yards when I fired the rest of my ammunition. I saw that my shooting was accurate because bits of the e/a's wings between the fuselage and engine flew off. Being unable to fly any longer through lack of ammunition I broke away beneath him to allow Red 2 and Red 3 to attack. The e/a slowly descended at about 140 mph. Red 3 now attacked from head on and after his second attack I saw two Spitfires attacking the e/a from each beam. I flew back to base having told the other two pilots that I was out of ammunition. During my attacks on the Ju 88 I received fire from 3 mg's and one cannon the latter being situated on the left hand side of the rear gunner's turret facing the tail. I landed at Westhampnett at 11.35."

The damage to this Ju 88 was eventually credited to three 302 Squadron pilots and three pilots of 152 Squadron Spitfires (P/O Rowlands, P/O Miller and Sgt Short). The Junkers 88, Werk Nr. 0520 of 3.(F)/121, despite the damage inflicted by the RAF fighters, managed to reach the other side of the Channel and crashed during landing at Dinard. It was seriously damaged, but the crew was unhurt.

5 March 1941
Sgt Marek Słoński of 315 Squadron force landed Hurricane V7188/PK-X at Acklington. The pilot was unhurt.

7 March 1941
P/O Stefan Stegman of 229 Squadron, flying Hurricane I V7042 on patrol, force landed in mist near Penrhos. Investigation stated that had he waited, within ten minutes after his unfortunate landing the mist disappeared.

8 March 1941
P/O Aleksander Ryszard Narucki crashed at Westbourne in one of 302 Squadron's new Hurricane IIs, Z2499. The engine suddenly stopped during a routine training flight and the pilot was forced to belly land. He was unhurt.

9 March 1941
P/O Ryszard Nartowicz of 607 damaged Hurricane I V6962 when landing at Drem on return from patrol.

10 March 1941
303 Squadron Spitfires took part in a sweep over Calais. First they moved to Hawkinge and from that airfield 11 aircraft proceeded over France.

Before action commenced, Sgt Mieczysław Popek damaged Spitfire IIA P8040/RF-D during landing, when he hit the airscrew of another aircraft. S/Ldr Zdzisław Henneberg crashed his Spitfire IIA P7821/RF-A on take-off; this aircraft, flown by the 303 Squadron commanding officer, had been with the unit less than a week.

The mission over France in company with 601 Squadron Hurricanes in fact brought no contact with enemy aircraft.

11 March 1941

This was an unfortunate day for RAF personnel. S/Ldr Gillam, while landing at Preston, crashed Hurricane UZ-X, borrowed from 306 Squadron, which he had commanded from December until the beginning of March.

An interesting story related to S/Ldr Tadeusz Halewski who served with the Servicing Ferry Pool. He was ferrying an unarmed ex-Canadian Hurricane, number 311, when he was attacked by an unknown aircraft (probably friendly). He took violent evasive action and escaped into cloud. With an overheating engine, the cockpit filled with vapour and he had to force land.

The same day Polish pilots of 303 Squadron mistakenly attacked an RAF aircraft. The story entitled 'Little mistake' in the 303 Squadron history provides the details:

"After take-off the section is guided from the ground, by the Operations Room. After several vectors the patrol was directed south-west. Suddenly the controller told the section commander about an enemy aircraft at an altitude of 10,000 ft. The pilots saw the aeroplane immediately above clouds, and attacked it in turns. It proved to be an English aeroplane, though, which in spite of several bursts fired at it did not suffer any damage. The section was sent further south, and then back to base. Real enemy was not encountered."

The RAF Northolt Combat Diary gave a less glamorous account of the encounter's results:

"12.31

"Three aircraft of 303 Squadron vectored onto a bandit by Operations, fired at a Whitley, and damaged it. There were over 100 .303 strikes on the Whitley, which had ten men on board, but nobody was injured."

The section consisted of F/O Jan Zumbach, flying Spitfire II P7524/RF-G, F/O Tadeusz Arentowicz in P7786/RF-C and Sgt Mieczysław Popek in P7858/RF-H. Only the latter two shot at the Whitley, T4337 of 77 Squadron, flown by Sgt James on paratroop training. The Whitley pilot reported that on the way from Boscombe Down to Topcliffe he was attacked by a friendly fighter, but

"fighter pilot gave aircraft no chance to identify itself".

12 March 1941

307 Squadron, taking part in patrols over Liverpool Bay, made seven sorties throughout the night. Some Defiant crews reported German bombers seen in excellent visibility, but only one managed to catch one. The pilot of Defiant N3739 reported his story:

"I received an order for patrolling the line George South at 14,000 ft. I took off at 21.50 hrs. It was a moonlit night, and visibility was good. After patrolling the line for 10 minutes I noticed above Garn an enemy aircraft He 111 against a background of white cloud in a South East direction 3,000 ft below, and at 600 yards in front of me.

"I warned my air gunner and dived to 150 feet below the He 111 and 50 yards from his right side. The air gunner gave a burst of about 3 seconds. Simultaneously the lower rear gunner of the enemy aircraft returned fire with a short burst, but failed to hit the Defiant. I saw the bullets of my air gunner entering the central part of the enemy aircraft fuselage. I consider that the He 111 was damaged. After delivering the attack I turned right to make another attack but whilst flying below the enemy aircraft, I lost sight of him. The speed of the He 111 was about 180 m.p.h.. My air gunner was Sgt Karais."

The Defiant crew claimed damage to the He 111. It was one of 316 Heinkel 111s and Junkers 88s of KG 26, KG 27, KG 51, KG 55, KG 76, KGr 100 and KGr 806 taking part in that night's offensive with Liverpool as the main target. Among them was the crew of Fw. Gűnther Unger linked by some publications with this 307 Defiant claim. Although Poles reported a He 111 damaged, Fw. Unger of III./KG 76 was flying a Junkers 88 which received a direct hit by AA fire which caused fire on board and this forced the German crew to bale out. None of the reports written by captured German airmen mention any encounter with an RAF night fighter, so it seems that the victim of Sgt Kazimierz Jankowiak/Sgt Jerzy Karais escaped undamaged.

About midnight four air gunners of 307 Squadron, on leave in Blackpool, returned on foot to Squires Gate, asking to join the crews at readiness and hoping to repeat the successful combat of Jankowiak and Karais. The first aerial victory by the Polish night fighter unit reversed 9 Group's decision to disband the unit. Two days before the night blitz over Liverpool, W/Cdr Stefan Pawlikowski, Polish Liaison Officer at HQ Fighter Command visited the unit to which 9 Group HQ raised several objections:

"1) Polish pilots, both in attitude and character are not suited to night fighter duties, 2) Language problems of pilots in air communication on the R/T are so big that even placing a Polish officer at the Ops Room is not going to solve the question, as he also has too limited vocabulary to control an aeroplane in the air, 3) Pilot's discipline is poor, 4) Instrument flying ability is less than that of British pilots, 5) Still a high number of aircraft damaged are being recorded. Conclusion: 307 Squadron should be re-equipped with single-engined aeroplanes and transferred for day fighter duties!"

13 March 1941

302 Squadron based at Westhampnett made several patrols in sections from the early morning. The Squadron Operations Record Book recorded:

"One Ju 88 damaged by 'A' Flight, Blue section. Attack was delivered at 27 000 ft over Selsey Bill. Enemy aircraft on being attacked dived to sea level. After several bursts from Blue section the enemy aircraft speed was reduced by 50%. Section returned to base through lack of petrol and ammo. Information later received from HQ 11 Group states that the plots on this e/a ceased in such a manner as to suggest that it had crashed into the sea and was therefore claimed as having been destroyed."

A few pages earlier in the same document, the names of the "A" Flight section P/O Karwowski in Z2386/WX-C, Sgt Nowakiewicz in Z2523/WX-G and P/O Wróblewski in Z2667/WX-E, which took off at 3.20 pm, are given an interesting annotation:

"Yellow section patrol Bembridge. One Ju 88 damaged by Aircraft 1 and 2."

During offensive operations that day the Luftwaffe lost two Ju 88s of which one was linked to a claim by 504 Squadron, and the other to Polish pilots of 302 Squadron. Both enemy aircraft belonged to 4.(F)/KGr 121. The Ju 88A-5 Werk Nr. 0419 coded 7A+LM failed to return and the crew of Uffz. Egon Schmidt was presumed lost. The other Junkers, Werk Nr. 0408, badly damaged by RAF fighters, returned with one of the crew killed. Probably this second Junkers was damaged by F/Lt Rook and Sgt Haywood of 504 Squadron. Hurricane V6812 piloted by Sgt Haywood was damaged by return fire and the rear gunner of the latter bomber claimed the destruction of an attacking 'Spitfire'. But what exactly happened to the Junkers Werk Nr. 0419 and who was the author of that victory?

The apparent victory by Nowakiewicz and Karwowski, is listed as damaged in the 'Victories of Polish Fighter Pilots in Great Britain from 19.7.1940 – 31.12.1942' statistics sheet, set up by the Polish Liaison Officer to HQ Fighter Command, dated 11 February 1943. The same document, under the same date, credits one Ju 88 damaged to another trio of 302 Squadron pilots. One of them, P/O Marceli Neyder, described this engagement in the 302 Squadron chronicle:

"There was a readiness and there was a 'scramble' like many before. Date: 13 March 1941. I am with Bronek Bernaś in the section of Wacek Król, on his starboard. Blue section, altitude 20 000 ft. Patrol over an island in the Channel. Weather beautiful, 16:00-17:00 hrs. After 30 minutes order: return to base and land. We start to lose height. Suddenly another task.

"Altitude 30 000 ft, new point over the Channel. We climb up. Vector 180. Then: 'Attention, at your altitude 5 miles to port, e/a approaching from the south." I drag a bit behind. After a while I see him on the horizon. Long fuselage, wide cockpit, surely a Do 215. Never mind that at a closer distance I can see a single fin. That's unimportant. The large black cross on the fuselage is what matters.

"I turn by 180 degrees. Wacek has reported he can see. The Jerry continues north, at approximately 28 000 ft. We are in the sun. I have a slight height advantage. I start to close in on him to 500-600 m. Suddenly he noticed me. He makes a sharp turn to port and dives at a steep angle. I am the closest, Wacek right behind me, Bronek is a bit behind – his machine is the weakest. In dive I come closer, fire a few short bursts, the upper gunner returns fire. He fires poorly, his tracers pass at least one metre above my cockpit. At the same time Wacek teases the belly gunner. I get down to the water. I have moved entirely to the tail. From a distance of some 250 yards I make my presence felt. The gunner no longer replies. The Ju 88 has good speed, we can hardly close in. Wacek seems not to fire, but keeps guard to port. Above the water my armoured glass covers with mist, I fire without seeing, looking through the side window to check the effects. The rounds are well placed. The Jerry squirts weak white smoke every now and then, his speed decreases, but I have no ammunition. I break starboard, up a bit. Bronek has also closed in, and he, too, has used up all his ammunition. Wacek is floating about very close to him, his lasts bursts seem to be very well aimed. But his ammo is also up, and the Jerry still flies on. We do not have much fuel left, so we are not going to follow him to France. Wacek swears violently into his microphone. We go back. In a while information from the ground: 'That b . . . rd is not going to fly any more. He crashed into the Channel some 20 miles off shore. O.K."

"Pity we could not see that. It would be much more joyful. It turned out later that I had three rounds in my wings, quite harmless.

"I still do not understand, however, why I said over the R/T that it must have been a Do 215. The first thought was stuck firmly in my mind. This cost me a bottle of whisky in the bar, but it turns out that this liquid fails to dissolve my shame. I still turn red at the memory."

The action described above clearly matched the first note in the 302 Squadron ORB and the Composite Combat Report from that day signed by P/O J. Jokiel. Both documents mentioned that the Ju 88 was damaged by the Blue Section (usually "B" Flight!). That day the Blue Section consisted of P/O Bronisław Bernaś (Z2350/WX-W), P/O Wacław Król (Z2485/WX-U) and P/O Marceli Neyder (Z2423/WX-V), and it is most probable that this trio was responsible for the loss of Ju 88A5 7A+LM piloted by Uffz. Egon Schmidt. The action was monitored at the Operations Room of 302 Squadron. Extracts from the Ops log were preserved in the 302 Squadron chronicle.

"16:38   – Hallo, Gerbox Blue I! Bittle calling. Pancake.

                 – OK, Bittle!

                 – Hallo, Gerbox Blue I! Bittle calling. New orders. Patrol Jardam, Angel 19.

"16:40   – Hallo, Bittle! Is that the cape?

                 – Hallo, Gerbox Blue I! That's the cape.

                 – OK, Bittle!

"16:42   – Hallo, Gerbox Blue I! Climb higher, Angel 25.

                 – OK, Bittle! 25.

"16:43   – Hallo, Gerbox Blue I! Now bandit is coming straight at that cape. From south. Vector 180.

                 – OK, Bittle! 180.

                 – Hallo, Gerbox Blue I! Coming straight at you!

                 – OK.

"16:44   – Hallo, Gerbox Blue I! Look south, Angel 30, 5 miles from you, look!

                 – OK, Bittle!

"16:45   – Turns north-east.

                 – Hallo, Bittle! I can see him!

                 – Hallo, Gerbox Blue I! You've got to get him!

                 – Hallo, Bittle! I go after him.

"16:48   – Hallo, Gerbox Blue I! Don't let him go! Turns port! Let him out of the sun and get the bastard!

"16:49   – Hallo, Bittle! We are still in the sun, I have him in front of me. He is going towards the land! We close in to him! I start to fire!

"16:50   – Hallo, Gerbox Blue I! Hit him! If your gunsight fails get close and
          hit the barrel, the engine!
"16:52   – Hallo, Bittle! He's got speed, damn!
          – Hallo, Gerbox Blue I! Dive and shoot! Open full boost and hit!
"16:55   – Hallo, Bittle! He reduced speed, but I'm out of ammo!
          – Hallo, Gerbox Blue II! You hit him, but save your ammo!
"16:56   – Hallo, Bittle! Gerbox Blue II answering! I'm out of ammo!
          – Hallo, Gerbox Blue III! You get him!
          – Hallo, Bittle! We might strike him. I fire closely. He dives steep!
"16:58   – Hallo, Gerbox Blue III! Look out for your ammo!
          – Hallo, Bittle! I'm out of ammo, starboard guns jammed. He's got
          armour, damn it . . ."

So it seems that the Ju 88 of 4.(F)/121 Werk Nr. 0419 was shot down by 302
Squadron's Blue Section, while the pair Nowakiewicz-Karwowski did not score
anything, or perhaps fired at the Junkers later shot down by the 504 Squadron pilots.
Unfortunately, up to now I have not found any documents describing details of
Nowakiewicz's and Karwowski's victory. No combat report, no entry in the 302
Squadron chronicle . . .

Thus, although in all probability the only victory of 302 Squadron that day was
scored by the Bernaś-Król-Neyder trio, many publications (based on 302 Squadron's
Operations Record Book[74]) do not even mention their names. The error of a clerk,
who entered the information "One Ju 88 damaged by Aircraft 1 and 2" by the names
of Nowakiewicz and Karwowski of A Flight, plus the disorder in 302 Squadron
documents, still obscure the true picture of that day's efforts.

As stated in the 609 Squadron chronicle, it was

"supposed to be an unlucky day – the 13th".

Sgt Mercer damaged an aircraft, after he forgot to lower the undercarriage for landing,
and a Polish pilot had some technical troubles while still in the air:

"P/O Oleński in P7835 became the first victim of the new idea, the jettison hood.
The hood, according to the book, jettisoned itself when the necessary 'string' was
pulled. This hood did it without any string pulling but somehow still remained
attached to the aircraft. It commenced to break up and P/O Oleński was busy
catching portions of perspex which fell in his lap, meanwhile continuing to retain
the main part of his hood. He returned with only one or two pieces deficient, a
good show. His homily on how the thing should work requires translating from
the Anglo-Polish into King's English!"

14 March 1941
On the night of 13/14 March a section of 308 Squadron Hurricanes flown by P/O
Bożek and P/O Kudrewicz was on patrol, taking off from Baginton. While they were
gone, Bramcote was bombed and they had to land at Baginton, completely

---

[74] Easily available both at the Public Record Office, Kew and the Polish Institute and Sikorski
Museum in London.

unprepared for receiving aircraft at night due to lack of runway lights. About midnight they were ordered to land with wheels up but both landed successfully with extended undercarriage, saving the aircraft.

That same night 307 Squadron Defiants at Squires Gate were at readiness, expecting increased activity by German bombers, similar to the nights before. German mine-layers appeared over the Irish Sea, but hourly patrols by Hurricanes and Defiants based at Squires Gate brought no contact. Shortly before 10 pm five aircraft of 307 Squadron commenced a patrol over Liverpool. That night again Liverpool was one of the main targets for Luftwaffe bombers. Five more Defiants were airborne about midnight. This time one of the crews was lucky. Its pilot later reported:

> "I received an order to patrol line West of Liverpool Beacon at 20,000 ft and took off at 23.42 hrs. It was a moonlit night, without clouds and visibility was good.
>
> "At 00.50 hrs. my air gunner, Sgt Niewolski, noticed an enemy aircraft and told me to 'turn left'. As he was sitting facing the tail he realised his mistake and corrected his order to 'turn right'. After a turn I saw within 50 yards from my port, slightly behind, and 60 ft above a twin engined aircraft without lights. At this moment my gunner opened fire. The first burst was one second and the second burst three-four seconds. The enemy aircraft made a violent turn to the left and my gunner gave him a third burst. The enemy aircraft made a steep dive and I saw bullets enter nose and right engine of enemy aircraft and I consider him as probably destroyed. I followed him but lost sight of him.
>
> "I reported the attack by R/T to Sector and continued patrol for another 10 minutes."

The report was written and signed by F/O Maksymilian Lewandowski, who flew that night with Sgt Marian Niewolski in Defiant N3439. They attacked an aircraft flying in a south-easterly direction towards Liverpool above the coast line. The unidentified twin-engined aircraft, claimed as probably destroyed, was later downgraded to damaged only. A single Stab./KG 55 Heinkel 111, coded G1+HA, landed at Le Bourget near Paris with one man killed and one wounded, following a combat over Liverpool. Another aircraft coded G1+GS, with three of the crew wounded, also landed at Le Bourget. A third aircraft of III./KG 55 crashed at Cherbourg, with one of the crew members killed and three others wounded. It is believed that one of these three He 111s was shot up by the Polish Defiant while on patrol "west of 'Point George'".

15 March 1941

On 15 March after a night patrol, P/O Stanisław Wielgus of 308 Squadron while landing at Baginton, bounced on a high part of the aerodrome and sank where the field went downhill. His Hurricane V6858 lost its undercarriage, and the propeller blades were bent. The pilot escaped unhurt.

Sgt Marek Słoński of 315 Squadron repeated his achievement from 5 March, damaging the port wing of the same Hurricane I, V7188/PK-X, while taxiing after a successful landing. Three days later (on 18th) his unit became operational and moved to Speke, to take part in convoy patrols over the Irish Sea.

18 March 1941

S/Ldr George Tomlinson was posted to HQ 9 Group and left 307 Squadron. Thus

S/Ldr Stanisław Grodzicki became the sole Officer Commanding of the only Polish night fighter unit.

19 March 1941

About 1 pm a patrol of 609 Squadron Spitfires over the Channel was attacked by Bf 109s. The unit chronicle recorded:

> "P/O Ogilvie P7830 and Żurakowski P7600 while on patrol were pounced on by 6 Me 109s, with 6 more in position behind them in case the first 6 missed. However, using their skill and their ammo they escaped, the only damage sustained being a shot through P/O Ogilvie's port main plane. One Me 109 was observed to be in difficulties but was not claimed."

Sgt Leon Kosmowski was returning from a night patrol about 20.10 in his Hurricane I V6950/UZ-F, and upon landing at Ternhill his undercarriage suddenly collapsed during taxiing. The accident investigation committee found that wear and tear of a wheel leg was the cause. The aeroplane was sent back to Rolls-Royce Ltd and converted to a Hurricane IIA Trop.

151 Squadron saw its first Defiant sortie by a Polish night fighter crew comprised of P/O Stanisław Reymer-Krzywicki and F/O Kazimierz Bokowiec; they were flying Defiant N1793. Both would continue to fly in 151 Squadron until 2 May, when they moved to 23 Squadron, to convert onto Havoc heavy night fighters.

20 March 1941

Sgt Marian Domagała of 238 Squadron force landed at Wimborne. He was flying a new Hurricane II Z2331 and got lost after his wireless failed to operate. The landing without a drop of fuel left was successful, and the pilot escaped unhurt.

P/O Franciszek Kornicki of 315 Squadron also force landed at Speke in his Hurricane I V7675/PK-M, when returning from patrol.

22 March 1941

Sgt Bronisław Kościk of 317 Squadron had an unfortunate experience, when he hit a man when taking off in Hurricane I V6534 from Acklington. In trying to avoid killing this person, he altered the course of his aircraft and damaged it.

P/O Zbigniew Janicki of 213 Squadron force landed at Castletown when his Hurricane V7019/AK-S "failed to operate correctly".

23 March 1941

Sgt Wacław Giermer of 303 Squadron damaged Spitfire II P7590/RF-F, when whilst taxiing at Northolt he hit another aircraft.

24 March 1941

S/Ldr Stanisław Brzezina, Officer Commanding 317 Squadron, damaged Hurricane I W9226 during taxiing. He collided with Blenheim V5380, causing damage to both aircraft.

25 March 1941

A lone low flying Junkers 88 made a surprise attack on Northolt airfield with machine gun fire breaking only a couple of windows. More damage was sustained by Spitfire II P8038/RF-W when P/O Wojciech Kołaczkowski of 303 Squadron damaged it while taxiing at Northolt. The extent of the damage was categorised as Cat. 1.

316 Squadron based at Pembrey was declared operational. F/O Aleksander Gabszewicz described the first operational flights in this unit:

"Almost all our operational sorties were flown over sea. In early 1941 large convoys sailed to British ports from America. Some ships sailed to Liverpool, Bristol and Swansea, while the tankers, full of petroleum, oils, or petrol, were directed to Milford Haven, at the south-western cape of Wales, where enormous tanks, both on the ground and underground, were situated. It was therefore quite natural that 316 Squadron was used for protection of these convoys.

"We took over this duty from Coastal Command, far away in the Atlantic Ocean, and carried the ships to the ports of Milford Haven and Swansea. This was a monotonous task, not to say a boring one. But this duty required much effort from the pilots. On average every pilot flew no less than four operational sorties a day, this totalling to 5-7 flying hours daily."

26 March 1941

Lectures regarding German tactics and the successes of 303 Squadron in the Battle of Britain that F/O Witold Urbanowicz had given to 308 Squadron on 2 March 1941 bore fruit when a few weeks later pilots of this unit had the opportunity to encounter the enemy in the air. On 26 March 1941 308 Squadron sections were scrambled five times in a day. The first section of F/O Moszyński (V7049), P/O Bożek (V7177) and P/O Surma (V6999) took off about 9.10 am. They returned to Baginton after an hour long fruitless patrol. The next patrol by P/O Bożek (V7177), P/O Surma (V6999) and Sgt Kremski (P2855) was more lucky, shooting down a Ju 88. The chronicle of 308 Squadron described the attack that took place near the airfield:

"After the first attack the aeroplane jettisoned its bombs between Leamington and the aerodrome, and then at an altitude of 300 m flew over the aerodrome, attacked all the time by our 'Hurricanes'. It was a special feature of the combat that the whole Sqn and British station personnel watched it from the ground.[75]"

Probably the enemy aircraft attacked by 308 Squadron pilots was Junkers 88A-5 Werk Nr. 4259 F1+FP of II/KG 76 carrying the crew of Lt. Otto Peper. P/O Bożek continued the story:

"After identifying the enemy I attacked him from the back, slightly from below, and fired a burst from some 150 yards. The gunners started to fire and stopped immediately. The Ju 88 hid in a cloud for a moment, but as this was a small one, I saw him immediately as he dived steeply.

"I attacked him from the port from above, and fired a rather long burst from a distance of some 200 yards. Then I saw pieces falling off the starboard side of the e/a. The e/a levelled out and I attacked it from behind, I fired a short burst and exhausted my ammunition. During my second and third attack nobody fired at me. I accompanied him flying for a long while.

"The e/a was flying very slowly smoking and very low, more or less on vector

---

[75] 308 Squadron Chronicle.

140 from Baginton going slightly to the south. Meanwhile I signalled the Operation room, giving the situation and the position of e/a and asked for a fresh machine with ammunition to be sent. After a while I turned back to the aerodrome due to lack of fuel."

The next section consisted of F/L Kosiński, P/O Wandzilak and Sgt Kowala and took off at 3.20 pm. Then P/O Szyszka, Sgt Piątkowski and P/O Wielgus were airborne about 4 pm. The last trio that day, airborne at 5 pm, was led by OC 308 Squadron, S/Ldr Orzechowski, who flew with P/O Kudrewicz and Sgt Hegenbarth.

The same day 307 Squadron moved its 15 Defiants to Colerne near Bristol. Sgt Antoni Skiba damaged his aircraft slightly after landing at the new airfield, but real trouble was experienced by the echelon which was bombed and strafed by German Bf 109s and Ju 88s at Gloucester railway station. Fortunately, no member of the personnel was hurt.

27 March 1941

315 Squadron pilots took part in formation flying practice and simulated attacks at 25,000 ft. Two Hurricane sections were airborne about 10 am. The sections of "B" Flight were as follows:

F/Lt Szulkowski	V7188/PK-X	Blue 1
P/O Fiedorczuk	R4122/PK-S	Blue 2
Sgt Paterek	V7187/PK-W	Blue 3
F/O Woliński	P3936/PK-Z	Green 1
P/O Hoyden	V7656/PK-V	Green 2
Sgt Zaniewski	P2974/PK-P	Green 3

After 15 minutes from take-off Sgt Zaniewski returned to the airfield due to high oil temperature in his Hurricane. Eventually only two aircraft from those listed above would return to Speke.

Whilst they were practising in the air, the Operations Room changed their duty and called them for an operational patrol. P/O Tadeusz 'Rumun' Hoyden, together with F/O Kazimierz Woliński chased an unidentified aircraft, but without apparent effect. On the way back they were vectored erroneously by the Operations Room and the former, descending due to lack of fuel, crashed into the sea, while Woliński ditched in the sea near some vessels, and was rescued by their crews. Hoyden was presumed missing. Blue Section lost two pilots when Sgt Edward Paterek collided in the air with his number 1, F/Lt Władysław Szulkowski. Only P/O Fiedorczuk returned from the operational patrol to base.

28 March 1941

Yellow Section of 302 Squadron was scrambled about 11.21. The three Hurricanes taking part in this patrol were as follows:

P/O Władysław Kamiński	Z2342/WX-F
P/O Stanisław Łapka	Z2668/WX-H
Sgt Antoni Łysek	Z2806/WX-E

P/O Władysław Kamiński described his efforts in the 302 Squadron chronicle:

"We received our task, to patrol Shoreham below cloud. Easier said than done, 'below cloud'. After take-off, we made a few rounds, but with that low cloud base, so that flying below them was almost impossible, Łapka asked operations to allow going above the clouds. We started to gain height, until we were at some 9,000 ft. Meanwhile we were given vectors 100, 180, 200, 260 and eventually 290 degrees, with the warning that we would encounter a German bomber on that course, coming straight at us. A little shudder! At the same time we received a order to give full throttle. All this part of the sortie lasted some 20 minutes, when scanning the clouds below I noticed to our port below us a bomber that had already passed our leader, going as forecasted, exactly on the opposite course, and moving in the layer of thin cloud like below a spider's web. I alerted the section leader over the R/T, giving its precise position, and telling him to follow me towards the target. But the leader acted quickly, broke violently down and followed him. Łapka started to circle it like a wasp in order to find whether he was not one of ours. Perfect camouflage, apparently the same as that of British machines, failed to give positive identification, so he called us: 'do not fire, he's a friend'. Soon, however, he noticed a swastika on the tail and commenced attack from behind, from starboard, firing a burst. This made me approach head-on, and attack him 3/4 from the front, firing a short burst. Łysek attacked behind me, also from the same direction. But the Jerry went into clouds and disappeared. This was at an altitude of 2-3 thousand ft, not far from St Catherine's Point. In view of the above we continued on his trail, and divided in such a way that two of us flew above the clouds, and I went in the cloud-free corridor that continued along the whole cloud layer. I paid close attention so that he could not cross this corridor and get into the other cloud layer, as then the chance to get him would be slight. Those clouds continued like an endless sea to France. But he did not show up . . .

"During the chase operation ordered us to switch the R/T buttons from A to B and from B to A so that with a few more like this we could become organ players. We were soon given new data from operations, specifying his short distance from us, and we were told to give full throttle again.

"At one point I saw the Jerry again, and attacked him head-on from above again. I pushed 'fire', firing a burst from a close distance. He was similarly attacked from behind by Łapka and Łysek. During which, when coming in to attack, as instructed by Marian Duriasz, our operations controller, I told him we had the Jerry and were dealing with him; this time he was at a lower altitude. We attacked him again, jumping at him from various sides, but soon he disappeared in clouds again. We entered clouds after him, each one of us 'gating' as he could, Stasiek was close to hitting the water, and we climbed above the clouds again. It was a bit sad that we still failed to finish him off, but we refused to lose our faith, and continued in the same direction stubbornly, controlling any cloudless space. Soon the clouds became weaker, we went down a bit, and then the Jerry appeared for the third time, flying very low, at some 50 metres. Spotting us, he started to jettison all his bomb load into the sea, leaving fountains of water rising high into the sky. I thought: drop it, drop it you bastard, nothing's gonna help you now, anyway. After he jettisoned his bombs he tried to change his course, and started to steer away from the previous one. But we were there. We made such a merry-go-round around him that the Jerry was stupefied. He threw to starboard and port, but that was the end of it for him. I started to close in on him from rather far away, quite flatly from starboard, and he started to fire at me with a cannon. I moved onto his tail, and his lower gunner opened heavy fire, but the rounds were hitting the water below me. Closing in to 200 metres in such a manner, I attacked him from the port, and opened fire, aiming at the port engine. I kept firing for a few seconds, closing in to 50 metres, and had to break not to collide with him. The upper gunner fired at me, but in vain. Then Łapka and Łysek attacked him. After this attack my colleagues noticed that his port engine started to smoke, and oil appeared on the sea surface. I soon spotted him below me, ditching in the sea, performing the manoeuvre in quite a skilled way. I reported to operations that we had shot the bastard down, and he was in the sea, and that I was waiting until the crew left the cockpit. I made three circles above him, and waited for them, but they refused to come out. Soon the nose started to sink, and four crooks come out slowly, sitting on the wing looking around. I can take my revenge now, gangsters! I waited, circling them, until they moved to 'readiness' and formed a line-up, whence I flew above them firing from all guns. Noticing from the boiling water that my fire was somewhat short of them I took slight deflection, and then I saw lights among them like candles on a tomb. Łysek, who descended after me, maintained he could see nothing but floating boots. We had to turn back, as our section was called out, so we could not stay there until the end of the funeral. I wanted to call: 'Auf wieder sehen Fritze' on the R/T, but I realised they were already gone. It was time to return to our section. All this happened 15 miles south of Beachy Head. Moments later we were congratulated on behalf of Fighter Command, of the Group, and of the Station Commander, on the R/T.

"Upon our way we had another surprise, namely that the cloud base went down to the ground. We were told to return as fast as possible. Łapka got us down perfectly and we arrived back while the clouds were at tree-top height. We tried to go in line astern, but even that was not possible. So we broke and went above the clouds again, and then returned, and I found the aerodrome safely and touch down. Soon they, too, returned, and we started relating our impressions. As I am rather pessimistic in my views, my friends started to put forward two reservations: first, whether we had not shot down a British aeroplane, and second, that apparently after we left it took off again and fled. I agreed that both were possible, after all it is hard to be optimistic in these pessimistic times."

The pessimist version of events did not materialise, and the Junkers 88A-5 coded 3Z+EN, of II./KG77, really ditched in the Channel. Ofw. Hohndorf's crew was lost and the Polish team scored a confirmed victory. The most pleased at the outcome was the section leader, who added to Kamiński's recollections:

"I have never seen such close fitting co-operation in a trio before. No orders were necessary. 'Pessimist' – excellent, Łysek – formidable.
"St. Łapka (The lord and master of the Yellow Section – trio of rascals)"

30 March

Sgt Wieprzkowicz of 306 Squadron force landed in Hurricane UZ-F due to an unexpected rise in oil temperature and the possibility of fire.

Chapter Seven

GETTING THE UPPER HAND

1 April – 2 June 1941

"For the first time since the squadron was formed, on 11 May a scramble of the Sqn was ordered. Even though some of the pilots were at the so-called 30 minute readiness and were in the Officers Mess, it took the squadron just 12 minutes to head in formation from over its aerodrome towards Cornwall, where 40 German aircraft were reported to have broken through some 15 miles inland. The eagerly awaited encounter failed to take place, though, as the Germans, seeing several squadrons awaiting them, preferred to head back for the French coast. For a while now they have avoided encounters during daytime, as these usually end with scores of 1:5 in our favour."

316 Squadron chronicle

1 April 1941

Just after 3 pm three Heinkel 111s belonging to KG 27 took off from Tours for their last sortie that day. The Heinkels, coded 1G+HH, 1G+LH and 1G+CH, in vic formation crossed the French coast over Brest and then headed into St George's Channel. They found some vessels of a convoy off Pembroke and prepared to attack. Ofw. Ernst Lorra, flying Heinkel 1G+LH, aimed at the motor tanker *San Conrado* (7,982 tons) and hit it in the first run. The defensive fire from the accompanying ships was heavy and Lt Heinz Grau, the navigator of the bomber, was badly wounded. In the meantime, Hurricanes of the Polish 316 Squadron arrived over the convoy.

As April Fools Day 1941 began, nobody in 316 Squadron had expected the most exciting combat since the squadron was formed. F/O Aleksander Klemens Gabszewicz recalled that day:

"The morning of 1 April promised a beautiful spring day. That day P/O Bohdan Anders was assigned to my section. In the morning, with beautiful weather, we protected a convoy of four tankers that approached Milford Haven. From 14 hours on the weather started to deteriorate suddenly and low clouds appeared over the sea, and about 16 hours it began to rain slightly. Our next take-off was planned for 17.45 approximately. Immediately after take-off the leader of the patrol, who was over the convoy at that time, informed us that the tankers were slowly entering Milford Haven. It took us some 20 minutes to get from Pembrey aerodrome to

Milford Haven. The weather was bad. Low cloud with base at 1,000 ft, or even lower over land, and the rain. We approached the Haven from the sea. Visibility very poor. Two tankers were already inside the Haven, the third was just passing the entrance, and the fourth one was waiting for its turn in the open sea, one mile from the Haven. We met the patrol that we were replacing. We waved our wings, they left, while me and Anders started our patrol duty. We flew low over the Haven. We turned south and flew out to sea. We reduced our altitude to 500 feet. The weather was deteriorating rapidly. We flew further out to sea. Suddenly I heard in my radio the voice of Tadeusz Nowierski: Operations Room! Olek! An unknown aircraft approaching from the south!"

F/O Gabszewicz described his later actions in his personal combat report:

"Some minutes later I found myself over the convoy (south of Pembroke) and saw one of the ships burning. A few seconds after I saw three e/a. Heinkel 111, flying below me. I cried 'Tally Ho' and attacked them. The cloud level over the sea was about 4000 ft. and over the land about 150 ft. The attack took place at about 1200 ft. I attacked five times . . .

". . . After the first attack the right engine was on fire and much smoke was seen. The right leg of the undercarriage sprang away. The frame of the right side of the pilot cabin and engine mask were shot into many pieces and flew in all directions. The rear and below gunner ceased fire. After being damaged the e/a took the nearest direction towards the coast, loosing gradually its height from 1200 ft. to 300 ft. when it reached clouds about 130 ft. thick. Probable landing place should be within 2-3 miles radius of Pembroke or Milford Haven."

P/O Bohdan Anders was following F/O Gabszewicz all the time, and he also attacked another He 111 with a short burst, but shortly after the bomber disappeared in the clouds.

The pilot of the Heinkel 111H-5 marked 1G+LH attacked by the Poles faced a difficult decision. The commander was badly wounded, dinghies were riddled with bullets, and although the burning engine was put out by the fire extinguisher, the other engine, overheating, would not allow them to reach France. The options were: ditching in the sea, coming down in Britain, or forced landing in Ireland. About 7 pm the bomber crossed the Irish coast, and force landed in a field at Ballyristeen, ending up with the aircraft's nose going through a low earth bank. No one was injured in the crash landing. The crew was interned at the Curragh Internment Camp.

P/O Bohdan Anders marked his shared victory in the official chronicle of his unit with these words:

"1st Day of April 1941 I will always remember as the most pleasant in my life, because during my first combat sortie in 316 squadron I contributed to shooting down an aircraft."

After analysing the action, F/O Gabszewicz noted:

"Enemy tactics:
    (i) Low torpedoing and bombing attack. This makes observations of e/a. by our

Observer Posts and the sending of messages by the post, very difficult. Visibility of the aircraft from above, because of exceedingly good camouflage of upper planes, was also very difficult.

(ii) When one aircraft of the enemy section is attacked, two other enemy aircraft gain altitude, one on either side and rear gunners fire into the attacker.

Deduction.

(i) Patrolling aircraft should not fly higher than 2000 ft. especially during bad weather conditions, when observations become difficult.

(ii) The pilots used as convoy assistance, should be fitted as soon as possible with dinghies."

The chronicle of the 1st Polish Fighter Wing was started on 1 April 1941 with the following entry:

"On the 1st day of April 1941 the first Polish wing was formed at Northolt operational station. By orders of the English authorities, kpt. pil. Urbanowicz Witold was appointed OC of the Wing. The first Wing comprised nos. 303 'Warsaw/Tadeusz Kościuszko' and 306 'City of Toruń' fighter squadrons."

2 April 1941

306 Squadron moved to Northolt, where it joined 303 (Polish) and 601 Squadrons.

Pilots of 308 Squadron received news that was entered in the official chronicle of the unit:

"On 2 April the Sqn OC announced to the pilots that he had received orders from Fighter Command to re-equip the Sqn from 'Hurricanes' to 'Spitfires'. The news was received by pilots with real enthusiasm as, even though the 'Hurricane' was a nice aeroplane, at this time in the war, given the requirements of the day, it was now 'an elderly gentleman' . . ."

3 April 1941

P/O Witold Łokuciewski of 303 Squadron was wounded in a landing accident which also damaged his Spitfire II P7989/RF-U.

P/O Stefan Stegman of 316 Squadron, flying Hurricane I V6735/SZ-B, overshot the runway at Pembrey. This accident was mentioned in the unit chronicle:

"Our airfield is very wet, and take-off and landing can usually only take place on special concrete runways, placed along the prevailing wind directions. During rain it is slippery, and the machine rolls on in spite of braking. P/O Stegman learnt that clearly, as he was only stopped by the ditch at the end of the runway. Fortunately, only the starboard wing was damaged, and the propellers bent."

4 April 1941

That day the Polish President, Władysław Raczkiewicz, visited and inspected the newly formed 1 Polish Fighter Wing at Northolt, accompanied by the US Ambassador to the Polish Government in exile, A. Drexel Biddle. They were welcomed at Northolt by AM William Sholto Douglas (AOC Fighter Command) and AVM Trafford Leigh-Mallory, (AOC 11 Group).

308 Squadron Officer Commanding, S/Ldr Jerzy Orzechowski, reported in April:

"In connection with re-equipment of the squadron from Hurricanes to Spitfires I carry on with conversion training of pilots on Spitfires. On average pilots have 2 hours for circuits, 2½ hours for formation flying, and an hour each for attacks and aerobatics. The squadron has 15 Spitfires. At the same time I continue training the rest of pilots in night flying, using Hurricanes."

On 4 April S/Ldr Orzechowski was at Kirton-in-Lindsey to collect aircraft for his unit from 65 Squadron. During take-off the engine of Spitfire I X4388 suddenly cut, and he force landed, damaging the airscrew and port undercarriage leg.

5 April 1941

A Polish crew of a 255 Squadron Defiant, Sgt Józef Feruga and Sgt Władysław Serafin, damaged their aircraft, N3321, during a night forced landing at Kirton-in-Lindsey.

During routine training flights by 317 Squadron a section comprised of P/O Solak (T9530), P/O Sikorski (V6545/JH-H) and Sgt Biel (V6552) was ordered to intercept a Ju 88 sighted by a trawler crew. The three fighters arrived in the reported area but failed to catch the bomber. However they stayed over the Farne Islands area, expecting other enemy aircraft. A situation where the Operations Room changed training flights into operational patrols very often occured, and P/O Tadeusz Szumowski described this in his diary:

"Our task was to patrol convoys along the coast from the Tyne to the Firth of Forth. We never saw a German, but were constantly in peril from the guns of the ships we were there to protect. We had coloured signal rockets so that the ships could identify us but they seemed to have decided to be safe rather than sorry and opened fire. We had to fly very low over them so that they could see the recognition marks below our wings before they could be induced to accept our support and this made life hazardous. The coast was rocky and unfriendly in the extreme and offered no opportunity for a forced landing if one should become necessary and there was little comfort to be gained from the idea of ditching in the grey heaving waters of the North Sea."[76]

6 April 1941

This date proved to be lucky for a Polish pilot with 56 Squadron. The "international" section of this unit, consisting of P/O Gustaw Radwański (Polish), flying Z2636/US-U, and F/O Jaroslav Himr (Czech) in Z2575/US-L, was on a convoy patrol. Radwański described it in his memoirs:

"It happened over a convoy, close to the Thames Estuary. An area well known to us, where we knew every mast sticking out of the water. It would be an exaggeration to say that the masts were becoming less numerous thanks to our flying, but it is a fact they were not increasing in their numbers.

---

[76] Tadeusz Szumowski, *Through many skies – The flying days of one Polish pilot*, Highgate Publications (Beverley) Ltd. 1993.

"One day a long convoy steamed on, somewhere northwards, and I and Jarek were flying above it. After a while Jarek went above the clouds, a thin layer of which hung at about 2,000 feet. I stayed under the clouds.

"I circle the convoy for I do not know how long, thinking of sweet nothing. Suddenly I see that the entire artillery of the ships is firing at the clouds. The next moment a Dornier 17 leaves the cloud and speeds at me. It was going to the other side of the convoy straight at me, obviously focused on some bigger ships for its bomb.

"I made a rapid turn backwards, which could even look suspicious at first glance. I gained some altitude in this turn, and facing the Dornier again, as it offered itself kindly, I performed a beautiful – or so I thought, at least – head-on attack from above. Giving it proper deflection, I fired a long burst, keeping the trigger button until the long silhouette with glass nose and black crosses on its wings passed before my eyes. I pulled my machine in a sharp wingover, in order to make another attack from the tail, but the Dornier was disappearing in cloud, trailing a long white tail like a comet.

"'Glycol' I thought, partly satisfied. 'I have shot through the radiator, he might fail to return'. I turned back to the convoy. A great circular spot was visible on the water near the ship – a trace of the bomb which must have caused 'several casualties, some fatal' – among fish.

"I hung around the convoy for a while and, unable to communicate with Jarkiem on the radio, returned home. There was a lot of joy, as at that time encounters over England seemed to be limited to memories of the Battle of Britain.

"Meanwhile, Jarek had landed and, knowing nothing, started to reproach me that I did not join him in the clouds. But Francois, a Belgian, stopped him with plain straightforwardness:

"'Don't be crazy, you silly fool, he got a Dornier and what exactly have you got?'"[77]

According to the 'Victories of Polish Fighter Pilots in Great Britain from 19.7.1940 – 31.12.1942' statistics sheet, P/O Radwański was credited with a Do 17 damaged. Two Heinkel 111s of KG 27 returned to France damaged by gunfire, and possibly one of them was shot up by the Polish pilot. Radwański, who had been in 56 Squadron since 14 October 1940, would soon be posted to 302 Squadron, leaving the Punjab Squadron in May.

The same day P/O Eugeniusz Fiedorczuk of 315 Squadron damaged Hurricane I P2974 during a landing at Speke.

7 April 1941

Between 1st and 6th April 302 Squadron was based at Tangmere, and on 7th it moved to Kenley. Its arrival was watched and approved by the station commander W/Cdr John Peel, who had flown with Poles in 145 Squadron. 302 Squadron Intelligence Officer, P/O Jan Jokiel, described the landing of the Hurricanes:

---

[77] Jaroslav Himr did not claim any destroyed enemy aircraft during his service in the RAF. Awarded a DFC, he joined 313 (Czechoslovak) Squadron and became its OC in June 1942. During 1943 he eventually claimed 2-0-1 victories, while still commanding that unit, but was missing in action on 24 September 1943.

"According to the orders of the OC I informed the Station OC about the ambitious plan of the 302 Squadron pilots who had decided to land at Kenley in flight formations of 9 aircraft, in three-aircraft sections. When I told him John Peel stressed that Kenley aerodrome was small, the landing runs short, ending with a steep slope, but that he knew the high skills and great ambitions of my colleagues, and was therefore sure that the whole show would prove very impressive . . .

". . . No. 302 Squadron arrived at Kenley on time, and raised great interest among the English, who were able to appreciate the precision with which the formation approached the aerodrome. The interest turned into the admiration of numerous pilots, when the entire formation landed painlessly on the very short landing runs. And yet, none of the Polish pilots of no. 302 had ever landed at Kenley before!"

A pair of Spitfires from the Manston-based 74 Squadron were on a *Rhubarb* sortie over France, which the Polish participant described in his combat report:

"I was Blue 2, ordered to patrol Dover in company with Blue 1 (P/O Howard) at 09.25 hours 7.4.41.

"Whilst over Dover we were warned of 'Bandits' and vectored to France and when 3 miles inside French occupied territory 2 Bandits were seen. One enemy aircraft opened fire on me. I R/T'd to Blue 1 – 2 Bandits in sight – and I immediately went into cloud as one e/a was on my tail.

"When I emerged from cloud e/a was in front of me. I followed him and opened fire at 150 yards with two 3 second bursts. Enemy aircraft immediately half rolled and dived vertically into ground.

"I was by now 200 feet from ground and circled to miss A.A. fire and returned to Base, Manston at 10.25 hours."

Sgt Jan Rogowski, flying Spitfire II P8199, thus claimed one Bf 109 destroyed three miles off Cap Gris Nez. His section commander claimed the destruction of another Messerschmitt.

Late at night P/O Stanisław Reymer-Krzywicki and F/O Kazimierz Bokowiec, a 151 Squadron crew of Defiant N1792, force landed at Melton Mowbray when their R/T failed to operate. The 151 Squadron Operations Record Book commented on this accident:

"Reymer out of gas and forced landed in a field and got away without damaging his aircraft to any great extent. A good effort."

9 April 1941

P/O Tadeusz Sawicz became hero of the day, claiming the second victory for the Pembrey-based 316 Squadron. He described this in his report:

"At 09.00 hours on 9th April 1941, I took off together with P/O Anders as No. 2 to patrol line Linney Head – Skomer Island, and was on the line at 09.10 hours. Near Milford Haven about 09.45 hours I saw A.A. fire from warship about 3 miles west of St. Ann's Head. The shells were bursting at approximately the same height as my aircraft, 1000 ft. I then observed a bomber flying very low in the direction of one of the ships; I did not at once recognise the aircraft as hostile owing to the poor visibility and in addition thought the enemy aircraft must be flying higher on account of the height of the A.A. bursts.

"I realised, however, that the aircraft was a Heinkel 111 at the moment a bomb was dropped on the ship. I at once dived and attacked the enemy aircraft from the rear, giving it a long burst of 1½ seconds from about 150 yards, and saw flames issue from the fuselage and the starboard engine. I gave it 3 more short bursts – total 1½ seconds – and the enemy aircraft crashed into the sea and sank. Two of the crew were picked up by a warship lying in the vicinity of the engagement. P/O Anders did not need to become engaged."

F/O Sawicz, flying Hurricane I P3926/SZ-P, together with P/O Bohdan Anders, R4178/SZ-T, engaged Heinkel 111H-3 Werk Nr. 3328, coded V4+CH, of III./KG 40. Sawicz shot this down near St Anne's Head, and the crew of Lt. Ludwig Rebensdorf was rescued by a nearby vessel, and taken prisoners.

The 316 Squadron chronicle mentioned that F/O Sawicz, after his return to Pembrey, told his story and said that a destroyer also shot at the enemy aircraft, so he was not certain whose the victory was.

"The captured German crew left no doubts whatsoever, stating that they were downed by an aeroplane. An English officer who interrogated the Germans, sent a gift for F/O Sawicz, consisting of German aircrew badges, taken off the collar of one of the Germans."

The letter from the Interrogation Officer, R.A.F. Station, Pembroke Dock, dated 16 April 1941, stated:

"Reference your Intelligence Combat Report, Form F. of the 10th April, Ops. A.I. and Composite Combat Report, relating to HE.111 attacked by Flying Officer Sawics [sic!] of No. 316 Polish Squadron, Aircraft are enclosed herewith as souvenirs for the pilot.

"It is regretted that no German buttons could be sent as the tunic is a working one and only has bone buttons. It is hoped that this souvenir, though small, will serve its purpose, particularly as the German Observer himself pulled them off his tunic and handed them to the Interrogation Officer for presentation to the Royal Air Force Pilot.

"Needless to say, it was not possible to tell him the nationality of his victor, who, it is hoped, will claim many more victims."

Answering the letter, P/O Sawicz wrote:

"I wish to thank you for the souvenirs of the combat which you very kindly procured for me and which will always remind me of my first success in England.

"I only hope that as a result of future combats, which I shall do my best to make as successful as my first, there will be no survivors from whom souvenirs can be obtained."

The straightforward F/O Sawicz, very popular among his friends, was nicknamed

Szczur (Rat) by his comrades. One day the squadron artist adorned Sawicz's aircraft with an emblem showing a rat holding a swastika in its hands. Unfortunately, the emblem did not survive long, and no picture of it is known to have existed.

The following days of operational patrols by 316 Squadron pilots were fruitless, but brought many accidents. The newly formed squadron shared RAF Pembrey with 79 Squadron and the diary of the Polish unit recalls lodging with the Madras Presidency Squadron with a sense of humour:

> "Some of the Englishmen cannot be counted among our best friends, for example the OC 79 Squadron, who for unknown reasons, always finds something to complain about us – this might have something to do with competition, in which we fare better, as our pilots, in spite of large number of sorties and sometimes even tiny breaches of flying discipline – such as bouncing the airfield – do no damage to the equipment, while his personnel does not always end such flights without damage. So the result between 79 Squadron, and our no. 316 in terms of damaged aeroplanes during April is 1:7 in our favour."

10 April 1941

During the night of 9/10 April the home base of 307 (Night Fighter) Squadron was bombed by a single enemy bomber flying very low. Although Defiants of that unit were available, the Operations Room did not scramble them! The bombs did not cause much damage, however, and no one of the personnel was injured. Later on 10 April 307 Squadron lost two airmen in an accident. About 3 pm the crew of Defiant N3390, consisting of Sgt Maksymilian Frychel and Sgt Jan Edward Dziubek (a fitter), were air testing a new R/T. On the way back, somewhere between Colerne and Charmy Down, at an altitude of 800 ft, another aircraft suddenly crossed their course. Avoiding a collision, the pilot pulled the Defiant up and the aircraft entered a spin. They crashed three miles north west of Bath at Rooks Manfield, and were both killed.

Sgt Stanisław Widlarz of 308 Squadron damaged one of the last Hurricanes with the unit. During practice flying, the engine of Hurricane I V7053 suddenly stopped, and the pilot had to force land at Baginton with undercarriage partially retracted; he escaped unhurt.

11 April 1941

F/O Henryk Skalski of 249 Squadron, flying too low in Hurricane II Z2450 on a local practice, struck high tension cables, and force landed with the undercarriage retracted near Colchester. The pilot was injured.

Another accident occured further north, with the Drem-based 607 Squadron. Poles had flown in this unit since September 1940, but the only casualty among them was Sgt Aleksander Popławski, who was killed on 11 April when his Hurricane P3425 crashed into sea and sank five miles off Dunbar, probably due to engine malfunction.

12 April 1941

On Good Friday night (11/12 April) the Luftwaffe launched raids on Bristol, Avonmouth and Portishead. As in the Liverpool area, that had been bombed during March, 307 Squadron again had the opportunity to intercept German bombers. Defiants began their patrols about 10 pm and made six operational flights in their sector. Fifteen minutes after 1 am the crew of Defiant N3315, Sgt Kazimierz

Jankowiak and Sgt Józef Lipiński, took off to patrol at 12,000 ft. The pilot later reported:

> "I was vectored onto a course 180 degrees and ordered up to 15,000 ft. I was then informed by R/T that a bandit was in front of me and on my port side. After cutting through the layer of cloud and climbing to 15,000 ft I saw, at 1.35 hrs., the silhouette of a twin engine aircraft without recognition lights. I could not at once recognise this aircraft which was just above the clouds at about 40 degrees on my port side and 1000 yards in front."

The aircraft, later described by the Polish airmen as having: "dark colour above surface of wings – with white markings not recognised by pilot or gunner as crosses", was a Heinkel 111P-2 belonging to 9./KG 27 piloted by Uffz. Leo Roth. The Defiant pilot continued:

> "I turned towards the aircraft giving full throttle and diving to get into a good position to attack. At this moment I recognised aircraft to be Heinkel 111 flying in an opposite direction to mine. I immediately made a sharp turn to the left and circled completely round the Heinkel 111 keeping him on my port side at a distance of 80 yards, while I kept 100 feet above. My air gunner Sgt Lipiński opened fire whilst I was passing the Heinkel starboard wing and continued whilst I flew past his nose and until I reached his port side. I noticed pieces of fuselage falling off the Heinkel and also a series of small explosions in the centre part of the fuselage, giving off small flashes in all directions. The Heinkel went into a steep dive and disappeared into the clouds. I returned to Colerne where I landed at 2.35 hrs."

The pilot claimed the Heinkel as probably destroyed, but a few minutes after this action the Operations Room at Filton received a report from an observation post that the enemy bomber had fallen near Sherborne, Dorset. After closer examination of the wreck, HQ 10 Group sent to 307 Squadron a technical report and a piece of the wing of the bomber, Werk Nr. 2002, coded 1G+HT. The trophy was proudly exhibited above the door of the "A" Flight dispersal hut.

Following this success, came tragedy for 303 Squadron's Commander. During the afternoon six aircraft of that unit left Northolt and landed at Hawkinge in preparation for a *Rhubarb* sortie over France. Fifteen minutes before 5 pm the Spitfires took off and headed off in three pairs. They were as follows:

1 pair

F/Lt Łapkowski	P7859/RF-V
P/O Waszkiewicz	P8079/RF-M

2 pair

F/Lt Kustrzyński	P7962/RF-A
S/Ldr *Dzidek* Henneberg	P8029/RF-P

3 pair

F/Lt *Szpak* Arentowicz	P7746/RF-B
F/Lt *Ox* Ferić	P7858/RF-H

All six aircraft crossed the English coast at Dungeness and then headed towards three separate targets. The third pair crossed the French coast west of St Valerie, and proceeded to the road between Le Treport and Abbeville. They appear to have missed the aerodrome at Abbeville and therefore continued their flight along a road leading to Auxi-le-Chateau. From there they flew north west, to the Abbeville-Hesdin road. As nothing of interest could be seen they made for the coast again south of Montreuil. They then appear to have found Waben aerodrome on which some dummy Bf 109s had been placed. They experienced some inaccurate machine gun fire and afterwards proceeded to the coast, south of Berck-sur-Mer aerodrome. In the town they noticed a car park with many dilapidated vehicles. A large building caught their attention and a number of army motor transport vehicles well camouflaged with netting, which were attacked. F/Lt Ferić described this in his usual manner:

> "Szpak made about five passes, strafing the trucks. Myself, I followed him around, strafing the spots where machine gun flashes blinked. This is terribly unnerving, though. Your forehead covers with sweat. Then, as if that was not enough, I can see two Messerschmitt 109s above us. I call Szpak on the radio. We climb up, but it seems they never spotted us, as they flew on, disappearing in the mist. This was after the third pass over the town. Then we returned to our target."

After that, the Poles continued strafing an R/T station and some cable pylons. After generally demolishing the area very close to the JG 53 aerodrome, and exhausting their ammunition, both returned safely to Northolt.

F/Lt Łapkowski and P/O Waszkiewicz reached Le Touquet aerodrome. The former flew over the dispersal on the south east side of the airfield and attacked barracks in front of which there were a group of soldiers who immediately fell to the ground. He then attacked the dispersal south west of the aerodrome and hangars, firing at a large aircraft (possibly Ju 52) and two or three other transport aircraft standing nearby. His attack was then directed at buildings and works in progress as well as some soldiers nearby. Near the hangars, where the aircraft stood, something started to burn and the pilot noticed smoke and flames.

His wingman first noticed a machine gun position on the fringe of the aerodrome and fired at it, but did not observe any results. Flying along the runway, P/O Waszkiewicz attacked a working party and a building in the course of erection. A further machine gun post was then fired at, and the pilot noticed a large flame shoot up, which indicated that possibly he had hit the ammunition. His final attack was launched at another working party, after which he joined F/Lt Łapkowski and both returned to Northolt. On the way back all heard the voice of F/Lt Kustrzyński saying: 'Dzidek in the sea' meaning that their Squadron Leader had crashed into the Channel.

Long before that the pair led by S/Ldr Henneberg had found themselves over woods at Crecy-en-Ponthie, leaving the cloud cover in which they had flown all the way from the French coast. After flying low over the wood, they struck an aerodrome north of Crecy, which appeared to be Maitenny-Duriez. Here they noticed approximately a dozen Dornier or Heinkel bombers with the ground crew working nearby. S/Ldr Henneberg flew right along the row firing all the time and then proceeded to look for the aerodrome at Berck-sur-Mer. Although he failed to find it, he flew north and saw a railway station and a large field west of Berck, and a large building like a hangar near the station. The camouflage of this building was very good, and from its corner some gunfire was directed at the leader's aircraft. F/Lt Kustrzyński proceeded to attack this gun position which suddenly ceased firing. After that he joined his leader, climbing up for cloud cover, to cross the French coast. There F/Lt Kustrzyński noticed that S/Ldr Henneberg's aircraft had received a direct hit and was emitting white smoke or fuel from the wing. About 15 miles off the British coast the engine of the Spitfire flown by Henneberg stopped and he subsequently ditched in the water. Kustrzyński circled and saw his leader appear on the surface. After fixing the crash position he tried to call base, but he needed to climb to 10,000 ft to receive a positive response from Northolt.

About 5.35 pm three sections of "B" Flight, 302 Squadron, Hurricanes were sent south east of Dungeness to search for S/Ldr Henneberg. Sgt Rytka separated from the other aircraft and noticed an object that looked like a pilot's head, but his attempts at direction were not properly understood by a rescue boat. Because Rytka's R/T was not working well, P/O Kinel repeated the information regarding the pilot in the sea to the Station. When the weather deteriorated all six aircraft of 302 Squadron returned to base.

S/Ldr Henneberg, a Battle of Britain veteran, and a very popular Squadron OC, was never found.

13 April 1941

From early in the morning, 303 Squadron pilots were out searching over the Channel, still hoping that S/Ldr Henneberg might somehow have survived the night in cold water. About 9 am one of the pairs taking part in the search was warned of German fighters. Soon after this warning, nine Messerschmitt 109s jumped them out of the clouds and S/Ldr Wacław Łapkowski's Spitfire II P7567 was hit by a cannon shell, the pilot being wounded in the head. Łapkowski's wingman, P/O Wiktor Stanisław Strzembosz, flying P8079/RF-M, was also attacked, his aircraft being damaged. Luckily, the pilot was not hit, and after firing some bursts towards the escaping Messerschmitts he returned, protecting his leader until the latter landed at Hawkinge in a barely controllable aircraft.

15 April 1941

306 Squadron based at Northolt exchanged its Hurricane Is for Mk IIs. The remaining Mk Is were ferried to Squires Gate.

While Polish day fighter squadrons patrolled the British coast without any notable incident, 307 had a busy night. Its Defiants made ten operational sorties that night, and during one of these, about 10.35 pm, the crew of Sgt Jan Wisthal and Sgt Jan Stengierski spotted an enemy aircraft which fired at them. Unfortunately, the gunner was blinded by searchlights, and was not able to fire. After passing a coded signal, the searchlight was turned off, but the enemy was not seen again.

16 April 1941

After midnight another 307 crew made contact, when F/O Maksymilian Lewandowski and Sgt Mieczysław Zakrocki, flying Defiant N3490, met an He 111; Max Lewandowski wrote in his report:

> "I took off at 0.15 hours. There were no clouds, visibility was very good and there was moonlight. During the patrol I was vectored several times and whilst flying on

a course of 210 degrees at 12,000 ft I saw He 111 at 30 degrees on my port side 300 yards in front and 150 ft above me. He 111 was flying in the same direction as Defiant. I approached to the starboard side of Heinkel for a beam attack at 50 yards and 150 ft below him. After my air gunner gave two bursts of one second each at about 01.10 hrs to the front part of the enemy aircraft return fire was observed from lower gunner's position of He 111. At the same time He 111 dropped its nose violently but straightened out again and began to lose height flying at about 160 m.p.h.

"Second attack was delivered on the enemy aircraft whilst I was passing behind it from his starboard to his port side. My air gunner gave a burst into air gunner's position of enemy aircraft and apparently silenced him for the rest of the combat. A short explosion then occurred under port wing of He 111 between the fuselage and his port engine.

"Third attack was made whilst enemy aircraft was coming down with a speed of about 150 m.p.h. A number of short bursts was given from both sides of enemy aircraft at a distance of 20-40 yards at 100 ft below him. This attack lasted about 5 minutes and I saw clearly that Heinkel took no defensive or evasive action whatsoever. Attacks ceased about 5000 ft because all the ammunition was exhausted. I saw rounds of fire from my air gunner grouped on the front and central part of the fuselage. As I was approaching to sea I decided to break away and to ask for vector to base. I landed at Colerne at 01.40 hrs. I consider the He 111 was probably destroyed."

The most probable victim of Lewandowski was Heinkel 111H-3 Werk Nr. 6937 of 1./KGr 100, coded 6N+MH, which was attacked by a night fighter over the Bristol Channel and returned to base with much damage.

All squadrons of the Northolt Wing took part in Circus no. 9. 306 and 601 Squadrons were part of the close escort to six 21 Squadron Blenheim bombers. After the formation rendezvoused over Northolt at 4.45 pm, all aircraft crossed the English coast over Beachy Head and headed to attack Berck-sur-Mer airfield. Pilots of the 306 Squadron Hurricanes taking part in this operation were as follows:

S/Ldr Rolski	Z3153/UZ-A
P/O Jankowski	Z2965/UZ-B
F/O Witorzeńć	Z2969/UZ-F
Sgt Śmigielski	UZ-C
F/O Zieliński	Z2922/UZ-H
Sgt Pudrycki	Z2973/UZ-G
F/Lt Zaremba	Z2884/UZ-Z
Sgt Pietrzak	Z2338/UZ-U
F/O Słoński	UZ-S
Sgt Kroczyński	UZ-R
P/O Różycki	Z2970/UZ-X
Sgt Jasiński	UZ-Y

P/O Różycki, flying Z2970/UZ-X, wrote in his diary after the mission:

"The day was specially nice for me, as I had a chance to be over France. We flew escort to a flight of bombers. We were issued pistols and explosives to destroy the aircraft should we be forced to land in enemy territory. On the way back a combat took place with two more of our Squadrons. I saw a machine fall into the sea close to our coast, and a life boat set out to the rescue."

"I really have no words to express my joy to be back in fighting again. Today I only saw Messerschmitts and an aerodrome over the sea, that was the target of our attack today – Le Touquet[78]. I also have no words to express my appreciation for the two Wing Commanders who participated in the mission. I have already seen one of them with his head bandaged and his uniform in blood, as he resumed his duties rapidly after being shot down. I know nothing about the other. I was told he is missing.[79]"

Three of the highest ranking officers of the Northolt Wing were wounded in this engagement (two of them mentioned in Różycki's diary) – G/Cpt McEvoy (the station commander) and W/Cdr Manton (the Wing OC) were both slightly wounded, as was 601 Squadron's commanding officer. The Northolt Wing Combat Diary mentioned that 601 Squadron was engaged by Messerschmitts near the British coast and S/Ldr O'Neill destroyed one of them, while F/Lt Whitney-Strait claimed another damaged. However, the main German effort was aimed at 303 Squadron's Spitfires. The top cover was attacked by the JG 53 Messerschmitts seen by Różycki. The Bf 109s waited for a favourable moment, then attacked out of the sun. Lt Franz Schiess wrote of this interception:

"Over Dungeness the Englishmen make a gentle right turn and the outer man on the right becomes a little detached. The *Kommodore* draws close to this Tommy and opens fire from about 50 metres. The Spitfire at once tilts to the left and dives vertically, trailing a long white banner. The *Kommodore* immediately pulls up to the right, leaving me free to attack. I close on the Spitfire before last, but as I prepare to open fire he sees me and hauls his aircraft sharply around to the right. I aim a little ahead of him and open fire. I see hits in the fuselage and the cockpit and then the Spitfire rolls to the right and drops away."

The Polish squadron lost two pilots – P/O Mierzwa (in P7819/RF-S) and P/O Waszkiewicz (in P8039/RF-R), while the Spitfire of P/O Strzembosz (P7385/RF-P) was damaged. Almost certainly one or two of them fell victim to Lt Schiess and his *Kommodore* – Maj. Günther von Maltzahn. Later, 303 Squadron's Spitfires were also engaged by some pilots of JG 51 led by Maj. Mölders.

The 303 Squadron team were as follows:

F/O Jankiewicz	P7786/RF-C
Sgt Wünsche	P8040/RF-D
F/O Grzeszczak	P7858/RF-H
Sgt Szlagowski	P8085/RF-H
P/O Paderewski	P7746/RF-B
Sgt Popek	P7962/RF-A

---

[78] In fact Berck-sur-Mer, not Le Touquet.
[79] At that time W/Cdr Manton was in hospital.

F/O Kołaczkowski	P8038/RF-W
Sgt Wojciechowski	P7546/RF-T
P/O Strzembosz	P7385/RF-P
P/O Waszkiewicz	P8039/RF-R
P/O Łokuciewski	P7524/RF-G
P/O Mierzwa	P7819/RF-S

17 April 1941

303 Squadron was ordered to patrol the Kenley area in two aircraft sections. During one such patrol, P/O Stefan Paderewski in Spitfire II P7746/RF-B collided with his wingman. Fortunately, both pilots were unhurt and Paderewski's Spitfire suffered more damage than that flown by Sgt Jan Palak – P8073/RF-Z. Another section of 303 Squadron very nearly attacked an aircraft which turned out to be a Blenheim.

Sgt Stanisław Widlarz of 308 Squadron overshot Bramcote airfield and his Hurricane I V6990 hit a fence and crashed. Another pilot of this squadron enjoyed more luck, as indicated by the following entry in the logbook of P/O Stanisław Wandzilak, made by his superior:

> "On the 17-4-41 P/O Wandzilak averted a forced landing with possible damage to the machine by his skilful piloting. The glycol pipe broke, and, when the pilot noticed the high temperature and the leakage of glycol, he switched off the magneto and managed to return to the aerodrome. The incident took place about 10 miles from the aerodrome but the pilot landed safely and, after the damaged pipe had been changed, the machine was fit for further flights.
>
> "J. Orzechowski,
> "Squadron Leader – O.C. 308 Polish Squadron"

The incident, which involved Spitfire I X4172, would find an ironic epilogue barely two weeks later.

P/O Wilhelm Śniechowski of 32 Squadron, now based at Carew Cheriton, encountered a strong cross wind when landing Hurricane II Z2642, which pushed the aircraft into a bomb crater.

18 April 1941

The last Polish pilot in 249 Squadron, F/O Henryk Skalski, hit another aircraft during formation flying and damaged his Hurricane II Z2695. The pilots were unhurt.

P/O Różycki of 306 Squadron wrote in his diary:

> "I flew with kpt. Zaremba as escort to a Hudson to Martlesham Heath. The Duke of Kent flew in this aeroplane. At 5 pm we took off back to our base. The weather on the way not too good. Visibility very poor. Nevertheless I feel more satisfied when I have to work under more difficult conditions."

Różycki was flying his usual Hurricane II, Z2970/UZ-X and F/Lt Zaremba UZ-Z.

20 April 1941

303 Squadron Spitfires left Northolt about 10.25 am for *Sphere* operations. It was intended to carry out a sweep over Le Touquet, St Omer, Dunkirk and Dover at an

altitude of 27,000 ft, the maximum height at which condensation trails would not form. The three pairs of Spitfire IIs which crossed the French coast south of Le Touquet were as follows:

F/O Kołaczkowski	P8038/RF-W	Blue 1
Sgt Palak	P8079/RF-M	Blue 2
P/O Łokuciewski	P7546/RF-T	Green 1
Sgt Pavlovic	P7859/RF-V	Green 2
P/O Daszewski	P8041/RF-E	Black 1
Sgt Wünsche	P7858/RF-H	Black 2

F/O Kołaczkowski, who led the formation, described the encounter with Messerschmitts which occured when the six Spitfires were over Le Touquet:

"Initially I could see nothing interesting, so I started turning slightly to port, in order to strictly follow the curve that Szpak had drawn for me on the map with his finger. Then I spotted two tiny dots slightly higher and to port. The dots grew in my sight and approached us with great speed. Just in case I turned towards them and then I recognised them as two Messerchmitts. The Jerries must have disliked our manoeuvre, as one of them went straight up, and the other dived on us. Facing the, let me say, eternal enemy, I felt my fighting spirit rise up, and gave my first order on the radio to my men, that is to Antek and Wűnsche, to take care of the lower Kraut, while I and the rest followed the other, upper one. The upper Messerchmitt tried to attack us from behind from the sun, and to achieve that he circled us in a wide curve. This manoeuvre failed, though, as my foursome, stretched in a starboard arch, performed narrower circles, having him in front all the time. My attempts to get on the Messerschmitt's tail were also fruitless, as every time I closed in, the Jerry pulled up, using the advantage of his aircraft at this altitude. We made more than a dozen circles like that, without success for anybody. During which I spotted four Me 109s coming towards us from below. I announced that on the radio to my four, and turned into them. The first two Messerschmitts started firing at me, and immediately after their bursts they went underneath me in a wingover. The next two turned, preventing me from firing a burst. During all this Tolo got separated from my pair and from then on everyone fought for themselves . . ."

P/O Witold Łokuciewski, called Tolo by his friends, noticed the attacking Messerschmitts at the same moment. His wingman, Sgt Matej Pavlovic (Czech) was immediately shot down and killed by the Messerschmitt flown by Hptm. Hermann-Friedrich Joppien of I./JG 51. Łokuciewski, flying some 100 yards behind the formation leader, later described the attack he then made on another Bf 109:

"I made a sharp turn and noticed an Me 109 in front of me, slightly above. I went into a steep climb and gave a short burst. The Me 109 dived down and I followed him and gave a long burst from a distance of about 150 to 200 yards. A trail of black smoke was left behind the Me 109 as it was falling to the ground. This Me 109 crashed just on the French coast, or just off. I did not see him actually crash since I was attacked by three Me 109's and I had to take evasive action."

When Łokuciewski returned to Northolt he claimed one Messerschmitt destroyed. His probable victim, a Bf 109E-1 of 3./JG 51, crash landed at Coquelles. P/O Jan Kazimierz Daszewski claimed a Messerschmitt damaged. His pair were ordered to engage one of the first two attacking aircraft. They followed the Messerschmitt which dived under the Spitfire formation, but then noticed another approaching from behind. Daszewski turned and attacked this, but the enemy aircraft escaped. He reported:

> "I tried to rejoin the other aircraft of my flight, which were about a mile away – when suddenly I noticed a Me 109 which approached my flight from the rear. I immediately closed in to attack, the Me 109 however noticed me and turned, so that we were flying one against the other at the same height. I aimed at him and gave a long burst of 120 rounds from 4 MG (4 MG were inactive owing to freezing oil). When the enemy aircraft passed my aircraft I saw black smoke coming from its engine. The enemy aircraft made a sharp turn and went into a vertical dive. I too made a sharp turn then, but was blacked out for a short time and lost the enemy aircraft."

As the engagement ended five Spitfires headed for home. On the way back, somewhere in the middle of the Channel, Sgt Palak noticed a twin-engined aircraft which was flying towards England at about 15,000 ft. When he dived closer to investigate it, he recognised black crosses. The bomber crew also spotted the attacking Spitfire and turned left, diving for France. With the advantage of height, Sgt Jan Palak attacked the bomber. He later reported:

> "I attacked from the rear and above, opening fire at about 300 yards and gave two short bursts. At first the rear gunner was firing at my aircraft, but stopped firing after the second burst. I continued to attack from a distance of about 100 yards and saw smoke coming out from the starboard engine. At that moment I was forced to break away because my engine suddenly stopped working for a short moment – I then tried to finish the enemy aircraft again, but could not locate it. I fired about 700 rounds. I returned to base."

At Northolt Sgt Palak reported one Ju 88 damaged over the Channel. The only twin-engined aircraft of the Luftwaffe reported as damaged that day was a Junkers 88A-1 of IV./KG 77 which crash landed at Laon-Athies. No other RAF pilot reported attacking a German bomber on 20 April, so almost certainly this was the aircraft attacked by Palak.

While landing at Northolt, the undercarriage of Łokuciewski's Spitfire collapsed, resulting in Category B damage to the aircraft. The pilot was unhurt.

Late in the afternoon, the other Polish squadron based at Northolt undertook two patrols. P/O Różycki of 306 Squadron wrote in his diary:

> "Patrol of a Flight over the Channel at 25,000 ft. We spotted six Me 109s that flew in our direction with advantage of height. I quickly warned the flight and changed course by 180 degrees. The first Me 109 closed in on me to perhaps 100 metres, but neither I nor he could fire. I saw another Me 109 approach our rears. The rest, four Me 109s, flew towards France."

After this patrol Sgt Wieprzkowicz force landed at Manston, his Hurricane coded UZ-J being slightly damaged.

21 April 1941

Although 303 Squadron was not engaged on any operational sorties, they reported an accident when F/Lt Jerzy Jankiewicz was forced to land in Spitfire II P8041/RF-E due to an oil system failure. Luckily, the pilot was unhurt.

24 April 1941

During the day RAF Colerne was visited by Her Royal Highness Queen Mary, the Queen Mother. 307 Squadron exhibited its aircraft and squadron officers were presented to the Queen. After this short visit the personnel returned to their duties, and late in the evening Defiant crews began to patrol their alloted sectors.

During one of these patrols Sgt Witold Dukszto felt the engine begin to shake. Even though the instruments indicated no faults, it stopped and the pilot decided to abandon the aircraft. His gunner, Sgt Jan Banyś, turned the turret to one side and got out, clutching the side of the fuselage, waiting for the pilot. The latter called the gunner several times on the intercom to be certain that he had baled out safely. Hearing no answer, he baled out from the starboard side of the aircraft, only to become entangled on the gun barrels. After a few seconds the pilot tore himself free, but with his Mae-West ripped. Both airmen landed safely and independently informed Colerne of the event, as a consequence of which Defiant N3391 crashed near Carlton Musgrave.

25 April 1941

Following the recent successes of the Northolt-based Polish airmen against enemy bombers and fighters, 306 Squadron pilots received an unusual order. On 25 April S/Ldr Rolski (UZ-H) and P/O Skalski (UZ-F) were detailed to shoot down a barrage balloon which had broken free from its cable. Unfortunately, no report of the 'combat' which followed has been traced!

The monthly report by the OC of 308 Squadron, signed by F/Lt Kosiński, described an accident involving P/O Wandzilak:

> "P/O Stanisław Wandzilak in a Spitfire aeroplane, while coming in to land in formation, struck with his undercarriage a machine parked at the aerodrome, resulting in an undercarriage leg being torn off. Landing on a single main wheel the machine turned and stood on its nose."

Spitfire X4184 was badly damaged.

26 April 1941

On the morning of 26 April P/O Stanisław Skalski force landed in his Hurricane IIA Z2922/UZ-H two miles south east of Eastchurch. P/O Różycki flew him from Eastchurch back to Northolt in the 306 Squadron Magister, V1089. In February 1941 P/O Różycki had written in his diary:

> "24 II – a new pilot by the name of Skalski arrives.
> "25 II a third Skalski arrived. Let us see how many Skalskis we are going to have."

Finally 306 Squadron boasted three pilots by this name – Henryk[80], Marian[81] and Stanisław Skalski[82].

Late in the afternoon the Northolt Wing, including both 303 and 306 Squadrons, was ordered to sweep over the English coast, but no incidents were reported.

The Kenley-based 302 Squadron was also ordered to patrol over the coast. Both Flights of that unit were airborne about 6 pm and headed towards Maidstone. During the patrol no enemy aircraft were reported. At 30,000 ft over Dungeness, Hurricane Z2814/WX-K flown by Sgt Tadeusz Nastorowicz suddenly made a sharp turn and began climbing very steeply. Soon afterwards the aircraft entered a dive and the pilot failed to respond to calls on the radio. Other 302 Squadron pilots lost him from sight and Sgt Nastorowicz was presumed missing, having probably dived into the sea. The mystery of his death was not resolved, and the most probable reason of such strange behaviour was loss of consciousness again caused by frozen oxygen supply, a common fault in Hurricanes. After the patrol, the rest of the squadron landed at Kenley. While taxiing, one of the Hurricane was damaged when an undercarriage leg collapsed. Sgt Bronisław Malinowski, who was in the cockpit of the damaged Hurricane Z2673/WX-Y, had checked that all controls were lit up and had not expected any such problem.

On 26 April the night fighters of 307 Squadron commenced operations from a new airfield, Clyst Honiton, very often visited by German bombers. The move from Colerne had begun two days earlier. This transfer strengthened the Exeter Sector's night fighter forces, and for nearly two years the city would be home to the Polish unit that carried the name of the City of Lwów (now Lviv in the Ukraine).The motto of both Exeter and Lwów, *Semper Fidelis* (Always Faithful), united the 307 Squadron airmen and the city's population.

During the early hours of 29 April the Polish night fighters experienced the first night visit by the Luftwaffe to their new base . . .

29 April 1941

As on previous days, aircraft of 302 Squadron were engaged in patrols over the coast and the Channel. Six Hurricanes left Kenley around 3.25 pm and about half an hour later encountered Messerschmitts. The ensuing combat was unresolved, but on the way back the engine of Hurricane II Z2342/WX-F flown by Sgt Marian Domagała started to emit white smoke. While at 27,000 ft over Dungeness, the engine stopped and, despite the pilot's attempts, remained dead. Domagała glided towards the nearest airfield, which proved to be Biggin Hill, but the speed of his aircraft was by then too low, and it stalled just before the runway. The Hurricane sustained much damage, but the Polish pilot was unhurt.

A dozen Hurricane IIs of 306 Squadron took off at 6 pm for a patrol over the Maidstone area at 30,000 ft. The pilots were:

F/O Witorzeńć	UZ-A
Sgt Kosmowski	Z3065/UZ-B

---

[80] Henryk Skalski, who had flown with 249 Sqn during the Battle of Britain, would be re-posted to 72 Sqn RAF. He would be shot down with that unit during Circus 85 on 27 August 1941, to become a PoW.

[81] Marian Skalski would be killed in a flying accident on 20 October 1941, while flight-testing a Messerschmit Bf 109F at the Air Fighting Development Unit.

[82] Stanisław Skalski would end the war as the top-scoring pilot of the Polish Air Force.

F/O Nowak	UZ-D
Sgt Pudrycki	UZ-L
P/O Żulikowski	UZ-C
Sgt Jeka	UZ-F
F/O Słoński	UZ-S
Sgt Pietrzak	Z2456/UZ-W
P/O Różycki	Z2959/UZ-T
Sgt Kosmowski	UZ-Z
P/O Czapiewski	UZ-R
Sgt Machowiak	Z2970/UZ-X

P/O Różycki wrote in his diary:

> "On the second mission, somewhere around 7 pm, we spotted four Me 109s in front of us and above. It was clear they were going to our rear. Our leader started to gain height, which resulted in the squadron significantly stretching out. At the same time he performed a turn which broke the squadron unity. After that turn there were 7 or 8 of us together. Upon return we learnt of one machine shot up with cannon and machine gun fire."

The Hurricanes, attacked by four Messerschmitts, were unable to engage their opponents, and the German fighters flew off towards the France. The tail of Sgt Marcin Machowiak's Hurricane Z2970/UZ-X was damaged.

Meanwhile in 72 Squadron Sgt Józef Biel – a Polish pilot with that unit – damaged two Spitfires when he hit P8174 while landing in P8164; both aircraft were damaged Category B.

30 April 1941
A Polish pilot with 615 Squadron, P/O Bronisław Wydrowski, damaged Hurricane I V7064 during a forced landing due to engine failure.

2 May 1941
P/O Bruno Kudrewicz of 308 Squadron damaged Spitfire I X4174 whilst making a night landing at Bramcote. The accident report stated that the landing flaps were not working properly.

3 May 1941
According to some records P/O Tadeusz Kratke and F/O Jan Wiśniewski, both of 317 Squadron, damaged their aircraft in flying accidents during training. Hurricanes R4216 and V6552 were slightly damaged, but both pilots were unhurt. According to other records, that same night 317 Squadron pilots were on patrols over the base when F/O Wiśniewski experienced further trouble . . .

4 May 1941
Just after midnight Wiśniewski had been ordered to patrol over base and the Blyth area. He undertook this patrol between 0.50 am and 1.55 am, but whilst landing, he overshot Ouston runway and damaged Hurricane I . . . V6552. It seems unlikely that by this stage of the war a worn Hurricane I would have been repaired so quickly after

its mishap the previous day. Therefore it seems that the two reports regarding F/O Wiśniewski and V6552 applied to one and the same incident.

On the morning of 4 May "A" Flight of 302 Squadron was on patrol over the Channel. During the afternoon their place was taken by "B" Flight. During this routine flight Sgt Marian Wędzik had trouble with his Hurricane Z2350/WX-W, when its engine seized and caught fire. The pilot left the burning aircraft at the last moment, baling out in thick mist. Wędzik was not certain whether he would land in the sea or on land, but eventually came down on the coastline near Dungeness, landing in a field somewhere near Hythe. His burning aircraft crashed nearby, killing a ram in the same field. Records failed to mention what use was made of the roast mutton!

The succession of accidents in Polish units was continued by 308 Squadron, when Sgt Władysław Majchrzyk damaged his Spitfire I R6963 during taxiing, while P/O Stanisław Wandzilak of the same unit landed at Baginton with undercarriage retracted, seriously damaging his Spitfire I. As if to prove the changing fortunes of war, X4172 which he was flying on that occasion was the same aircraft that he had saved so gallantly on 17 April.

Night accidents at 307 Squadron also contributed to this unfortunate day. The crew of P/O Eugeniusz Przysiecki and Sgt Jan Woźny were on patrol from 10.30 pm, and twice made contact with an enemy, who meanwhile successfully bombed their home base. After an hour and half of flying, their Defiant N1769 began to shake, indicating that the fuel was almost exhausted. Due to thick mist and imprecise vectors from the Operations Room, they searched for the airfield in vain, and when the fuel ran out Sgt Jan Woźny baled out, followed by the pilot. At the last moment they saw the lights of their own airfield, and the abandoned aircraft crashed in the middle of this. The Operations Room blamed the pilot for not descending to an altitude of 2,000 ft and for poor navigation skills. The OC 307 Squadron, S/Ldr Grodzicki, gave the unfortunate pilot the best reference however, writing in the unit chronicle:

"I have known this pilot personally for years. I have seen him navigate in mist, and I will never agree that his navigation is poor – quite the opposite, he is an excellent navigator. He did not descend lower while looking for the aerodrome, as he would have to go down to 1,000 ft to see the landing lights (they are not visible above that). On the other hand, to descend to 1,000 ft above sea means to be 200 feet below the tops of the surrounding hills. Not trusting the controllers and their fixes, he simply preferred to be safe than sorry. Concluding: in my opinion the baling out of P/O Prusiecki was the only solution.

"He should be acknowledged for taking the only sound decision, and for conducting the bale-out skilfully and quickly.

"The loss of time in finding the aerodrome discredits the Ops Room, but not the pilot."

5 May 1941

During a daylight training flight the crew of 307 Squadron Defiant N1809, F/O Mieczysław Jakszewicz and Sgt Józef Starosta, overshot the Clyst Honiton runway and damaged the aircraft.

P/O Feliks Fryderyk Szyszka of 308 Squadron, flying Spitfire I X4859, hit a transmission cable, damaging the wing of his aircraft, following which he landed safely.

Another accident, mentioned in the 316 Squadron chronicle, was the forced landing of P/O Józef Jakub Górski near St Anne's Head, where he damaged Hurricane I V6635/SZ-X.

6 May 1941

P/O Władysław Chciuk of 308 Squadron rendered Spitfire I X4477 unserviceable by a hard landing at Baginton.

Polish pilots were not the only ones to cause damage to their aircraft, for that night German bombers bombed Ouston airfield. Three aircraft were destroyed and four damaged, including some 317 Squadron Hurricanes, one of which, V7119, received a direct hit.

A Polish pilot with 72 Squadron, P/O Jerzy Godlewski, flying Spitfire II P7376, was credited with a Ju 88 damaged, shared with another pilot of this unit. Somehow, subsequent publications have attributed the claims to P/O Gregory and Sgt Gregson.

8 May 1941

A dozen Hurricanes of 302 Squadron took off from Kenley about 11.50 to patrol the Maidstone area. F/Lt Czerwiński, Sgt Rytka, F/O Kinel, P/O Neyder, P/O Król, P/O Janicki of "B" Flight were vectored to intercept Raid no. 23. At 10,000 feet the unit met six Bf 109Fs of I./JG 3 which were heading south east. Later, pilots of the Polish squadron reported:

> "The enemy aircraft are described as of a greyish blue colour with yellow noses, tapered mainplanes, with normal markings in vic formation."

Over Ashford Black Section attacked the Messerschmitts from above. F/Lt Czerwiński fired at one from 50 yards, but was then attacked himself, making a sharp turn to starboard and diving. Later he claimed this Messerschmitt as a probable. After Sgt Rytka's attack, his Messerschmitt suddenly emitted black smoke, some pieces of the wing fell off, and it dived steeply. Seeing no more results from his first bursts, Rytka attacked another Messerschmitt, but claimed only one probably destroyed. F/O Zygmunt Kinel and P/O Wacław Król each claimed a Bf 109 destroyed; in fact both must have shot at the same Bf 109F-2 Werk Nr. 5647, "Black 3", piloted by Lt G. Pöpel of 1./JG 3. F/O Kinel, flying Hurricane Z3095/WX-N, wrote in his report:

> "I took off at Kenley at 11.50 hours flying Green 1 in B Flight with instructions to patrol Tenterden area. Whilst at 10 000 ft six Me 109's were sighted travelling SE and after turn to the North we dived on them from astern. I attacked 1 Me 109 with a 70 round burst at 300/150 yards with the result that parts fell off and the pilot baled out and is, I understand, with the Ashford Police. I landed with my flight at Kenley at 13.15 hrs."

P/O Król added interesting details to this description; after his attack the enemy aircraft exploded into pieces.

"A" Flight, airborne a little later, also met aircraft from II./JG 3 near Maidstone and chased the Messerchmitts when they turned away, shooting down one of them. Bf 109F-2 Werk Nr. 5765, flown by Lt Karl Ponec of 4./JG 3, was claimed by Sgt Eugeniusz Nowakiewicz, who described the victory in his report:

"I took off from Kenley at 12.35 flying as white 2 with instructions to patrol Dover area. At 25 000 ft some 5 miles NE of Dover I as weaver sighted 3 Me 109 in vic formation flying SW and signalled my flight accordingly. They apparently did not understand my hurried signal and I turned to attack alone head-on, concentrating on 1 e/a. I delivered three further attacks from astern, chasing the e/a towards the French coast. White smoke emission was followed by black smoke and finally the e/a plunged into the sea some ⅔ across the Straits of Dover. In the meantime another Me 109 had got on my tail delivering several cannon bursts which I managed to avoid by making zig-zag fashion for the English coast. I landed at Kenley at 13.28."

"A" Flight[83] of 302 Squadron left Kenley again about 5.35, consisting of:

S/Ldr Łaguna	Z3435	Red 1
P/O Kamiński		Red 2
P/O Wróblewski	Z2806/WX-E	White 1
Sgt Domagała	Z2523/WX-G	White 2
P/O Główczyński	WX-A	Yellow 1
P/O Karwowski		Yellow 2

All six were vectored to the Dungeness area with orders to climb to 25,000 ft. P/O Główczyński and P/O Karwowski were flying 1,000 ft above, as the weavers. After 20 minutes flying P/O Główczyński had to return and force landed at Kenley with the cockpit filled with smoke caused by an oil system failure.

The remaining five saw six Messerschmitts, which attacked the Hurricanes from 30,000 ft. Prepared for the attack, the Hurricanes turned towards them, but it was too late. Sgt Marian Domagała's Z2523/WX-G, was hit in the rudder and ailerons, and spun to the ground; the pilot baled out, safely. S/Ldr Piotr Łaguna, leading the formation, was also hit, and his Hurricane Z3435 immediately began to burn; he also had to bale out. Both Hurricanes were claimed by pilots of Stab I./JG 51, Fw. Erwin Flieg and Hptm. Joppien.

After this violent engagement P/O Wróblewski joined "B" Flight, which at this moment were supporting Spitfires of 92 Squadron over Dungeness, fighting more Messerschmitts of Stab I./JG 51. In this engagement "B" Flight fought with four Bf 109s and P/O Kinel, flying Hurricane Z3098, was killed. Another pair of Messerschmitts joined the melee.

Another "B" Flight pilot, P/O Zbigniew Janicki, summarised this afternoon engagement in his logbook, and mentioned that P/O Zbigniew Wróblewski claimed a Bf 109 probably destroyed. This information was not confirmed by the Composite Combat Report of "A" Flight, although his victory is listed in the 'Victories of Polish Fighter Pilots in Great Britain from 19.7.1940 – 31.12.1942'" statistics sheet. Unfortunately, lack of records concerning the operations of 302 Squadron during May, makes more detailed description of this victory impossible.

The day, so eventful for 302 Squadron, was also a sad day for the Polish Air Force. Apart from the loss of P/O Kinel, accidents in 32 Squadron resulted in the

---

[83] It is impossible to list the B Flight pilots taking part in the afternoon sortie, due to incomplete records.

death of first Sgt Tomasz Rzyski, when he overshot the runway at Pembrey in his Hurricane II Z2413. His colleague, Sgt Kawczyński, was also killed when he failed to recover from his dive during air to ground firing training on Pembrey Sands; Olech Antoni Kawczyński died in Hurricane Z2324 which crashed into the sea.

In May and June there remained a large group of Polish pilots in 32 International Squadron. Among them were P/Os Kolubiński, Falkowski, Marciniak, Rzyski, Śniechowski, F/O Kawczyński, P/O Radomski, and F/Os Jakubowski, Szmejl. Most of them moved to Polish units during June and July 1941.

By the end of this day Sgt Jan Kremski of 308 Squadron had also suffered an accident, damaging Spitfire I X4617 (Cat. AC) due to "faulty equipment". No more detail is known.

9 May 1941

This day was very busy for 303 Squadron, as pairs of Spitfires flew convoy cover in the Barrow Deep area. The first of the sections off intercepted a twin-engined aircraft near Margate.

> "On a 'Bacon' patrol P/O Gładych fired at an unidentified enemy aircraft, but broke off because fighters approached him from behind – these transpired to be Hurricanes."

said 303 Squadron ORB. P/O Gładych flying Spitfire P7962/RF-A opened fire but without apparent result. In the following hours the whole squadron patrolled over the Maidstone area twice; during the second patrol the "A" Flight was attacked by three Messerschmitts, which then flew away, but were followed by ten more Bf 109s. Thanks to perfect leadership by P/O Daszewski, the Flight took evasive action and all six returned home unscathed.

Late in the afternoon six aircraft of 303 Squadron again made their way towards France, for a 'Sphere' operation.

> "Flak opened up at them because of smoke trails from Gravelines, and six 109's came in to attack."

recorded the RAF Northolt Combat Diary. The six pilots flying at 32,000 ft were as follows:

F/O Strzembosz	P8099/RF-V
F/O Wróblewski	P8041/RF-E
F/O Zumbach	P7962/RF-A
Sgt Szlagowski	P8085/RF-J
F/O Ferić	P8360
F/O Urbanowicz	P8038/RF-W

While over Marquise, F/O Strzembosz noticed six Messerschmitts (of III./JG 3) coming in to attack. He immediately turned west and crossed the French coast north of Boulogne, chased by the yellow-nosed Bf 109s. Over the sea the Spitfires formed a defensive circle, and zig-zagged their way to the British coast. Only three Messerschmitts attacked, the other three waited higher, barely seen through the sunshine. F/O Urbanowicz recalled this escape:

"My machine runs slower than the others. Because of this I lagged some 1,000 metres behind my colleagues. I tell Strzembosz over the R/T who is leading the patrol: 'Slower, Strzembosz', but then I see three Messerschmitts, creeping up on me from behind. Two of them on my starboard, one on my port, above. 'Messerchmitts behind', I say on the R/T. I repeat again and give full throttle, but still lag behind. The Messerschmitts are coming closer and closer towards me. I make short, sharp turns, and try to avoid the port and starboard traces of rounds aimed at me. The traces of rounds come together near my machine. I wait for a moment until the Messerschmitts come closer to me, and then make a sudden turn to starboard climbing backwards – which saves me. Two Messerschmitts jump to starboard below – me behind them, but I can see that another Messerchmitt has crept in to attack right above me. I give up those two, and turn towards the one who attacks me. We go head-on, but do not fire as it is too close, a mere several metres between us. At the same time F/O Strzembosz makes a turn towards me. The Messerschmitts must have noticed that, as they escaped downward, heading for France."

The three Messerschmitts which attacked F/O Urbanowicz were also spotted by F/O Jan Zumbach who tried to attack them:

"At one point I heard on the radio: 'Messerschmitts above to starboard'. As I was higher and trying to catch the flight, I started to look around. Indeed, I saw three Me 109s underneath me. I looked back and saw a machine rather far behind, but assuming that this was my wingman, Sgt Szlagowski, I waved my wings and started to attack the Messerschmitts I spotted. I had hardly entered a dive when something thundered through my cockpit and glass poured around. I pushed the stick away and then pulled it back. Two Messerschmitt 109s brushed me. I started calling on the radio, but it would not work. Therefore I headed back to England in wide turns. My headgear was shot through, my head scratched, my cockpit was broken as were some clocks on my dashboard, and oil was pouring somewhere. Barely had I reached the coast when glycol started to burn. Initially I wanted to bale out, but after a few minutes I felt I was losing consciousness in the smoke, so I turned my aeroplane upside down, pushed the stick slightly, and in a moment I was hanging under my parachute. Under the careful eye of my colleagues, who circled above me, I landed, and not on a high tension line, as I had anticipated, but right next to it, on the very hard English soil."

Following this busy and eventful day at Northolt, 306 Squadron made only night patrols, sending single aircraft into the air. P/O Jan Artur Czapiewski, flying Hurricane II Z2338/UZ-U, force landed after his patrol, damaging the aircraft.

The same night 307 Squadron continued its patrols over the Exeter area and, after one of these, Defiant T3999 was damaged during landing, due to brake failure. The crew of Sgt Józef Armanowski and Sgt Wiktor Sroka was unhurt.

10 May 1941
Early in the afternoon six Hurricanes of 302 Squadron were scrambled to intercept four Bf 109s (belonging to I./JG 53). One Polish pilot caught one Messerchmitt over

the Maidstone area, later describing this:

> "When over Ashford at 19.20 hrs we were attacked by four Messerschmitt 109s in sections of two. The first section attacked and dived and the latter attacked and zoomed. I managed to single out one Me 109 as it was returning to attack and delivered an 80 round burst at a distance of 200 yards afterwards chasing same for a distance of 16 miles during the course of which enemy aircraft after emitting grey smoke left a persistent trail of black smoke during the whole chase gradually losing altitude. I was unable to attack again because the sector companion of my target gradually climbed to 27,000 ft in order to dive on me if I should attempt a further attack on his companion.
>
> "I therefore climbed with him and on losing sight of my original target I returned to base at 19.50."

P/O Marceli Neyder, later one of the most skilful Polish night fighter pilots, had actually shot down Bf 109F-2 Werk Nr. 12644, "Black 2", although he was credited only with damaged. His victim crashed at Event-Plage and its pilot, Gefr. Leo Pielach of 1./JG 53 was wounded.

P/O Jan Kazimierz Maras, a Polish pilot of 601 Squadron, damaged his Hurricane IIA Z2507 when the undercarriage failed while landing at Manston. 601 Squadron had moved to Manston on 2 May, leaving only the Polish squadrons (303 and 306) at RAF Northolt. On the night of 10 May 306 Squadron carried out individual patrols over London during an extremely heavy attack by over 500 German aircraft. Four Hurricanes were airborne simultaneously, dispatched to their sectors to wait for the enemy. The first group took off at 11 pm, F/O Zieliński (UZ-A), Sgt Pudrycki (Z3065/UZ-B), P/O Jankowski (UZ-D) and P/O Żulikowski (UZ-G) returned after an hour-long patrol. In the meantime, the next four were in the air . . .

11 May 1941

This next group of four, airborne in the early hours of 11 May, were as follows: F/O Nowak (Z2969/UZ-F), F/Lt Witorzeńć (Z3162/UZ-M), S/Ldr Rolski (Z2965/UZ-K) and Sgt Śmigielski (Z3439/UZ-N). F/O Nowak, radio code *Carmen 17*, described his sortie:

> "I took off at 0020 hrs with orders to patrol London at 14 000 ft. Whilst circling north over the Thames I saw an aircraft which I recognised as a Hurricane. Shortly afterwards I saw a big aircraft flying head-on towards me on a Southerly course towards London. I did a sharp turn, but the aircraft disappeared. I received a vector of 180 degrees, and at the same time sighted another aircraft flying South to London, also head-on towards me at about 12,000 ft. I did a sharp turn but lost the enemy aircraft against the smoke of London fires. I dived to 10,000 ft and saw it again against the sky at about 150 yards away. I could not see the exhaust flames but the under part of the aircraft was lit up by the fires below. I approached to within 30 yards and saw the exhaust flames of two engines. I was then at 12,000 ft. I could not be sure of the silhouette so I turned to port and passed below the enemy aircraft, and then recognised it as a He 111. Simultaneously the enemy aircraft saw me and dived. I followed and fired three short bursts from 50-15 yards. I received fairly accurate return fire from the upper rear gun of the enemy

aircraft. I saw what appeared to be tracer bullets. The enemy aircraft began to climb to starboard, and I fired three more short bursts from 30-20 yrds. The enemy aircraft turned to port and dived. When he flattened out I dived on him and made a further attack from 40 yards closing to 10 yards in one long burst. My guns then ceased to fire and I saw that the port engine of the enemy aircraft was on fire. It was then flying South at 9000 ft and losing height. The enemy aircraft was then about 12 miles North of Beachy Head. I did not follow as I had no more ammunition and my R/T went u/s.

"I returned to Northolt and landed at 01.35 hrs. On Y service information received through 11 Group I claim this enemy aircraft as destroyed."

The Hurricane II flown by F/O Nowak had two holes in the starboard wing and two in the rudder, apparently caused by 12 mm ammunition.

The next group of Hurricanes were flown by: F/O Ranoszek (Z2968/UZ-D), Sgt Kosmowski (Z3065/UZ-B) and F/O Zieliński (Z3153/UZ-A). They finished their patrol after an hour and this time it was *Carmen 52* that had the opportunity to shoot at a German aircraft. F/O Ranoszek reported damage to a Junkers 88:

"When at 15,000 ft over North East London I saw a Hurricane very clearly by the light of a big fire, so decided to remain in the vicinity. Shortly afterwards I saw a big twin-engined bomber without lights flying from West to East in a gentle turn to port. He was then about 80/100 yards from me. I fired a short burst from port quarter and enemy aircraft continued turn to port. I fired a second burst, and when the enemy aircraft pulled up and then dived sharply to port I followed him down, firing two more bursts deflection shooting. I then remembered balloons flying at 10,000 ft and pulled out to 11,000 ft. I did not see the effect of my firing on this enemy aircraft. I climbed back to 15,000 ft and orbited.

"At about 02.30 hrs. I saw a Ju 88 against the moon 1000/1500 ft above me. It was flying straight South East. I pulled up to get behind him, and nearly ran into him; throttled back and got him in my sights. I fired two more bursts, and then my ammunition ran out. I saw things like big sparks, coming away from the middle of the enemy aircraft. I turned away to starboard and as the enemy aircraft dived I followed down to 10,000 ft, but lost sight of the enemy aircraft. I returned to Northolt and landed at 02.45 hrs.

"I claim the second enemy aircraft contacted as Damaged."

During the day another Northolt squadron, 303, made several patrols over Dover and base, and escorted a convoy near Barrow Deep. After one such patrol P/O Władysław Drecki damaged his Spitfire II P8079/RF-M whilst landing.

A pilot of 308 Squadron based at Baginton was less lucky. A pair of Spitfires flown by P/O Franciszek Surma and Sgt Widlarz were on patrol over the Worcester area when they received an order to investigate an unidentified aircraft reported in the vicinity of Kidderminster. The plotted aircraft soon turned out to be a Blenheim, so they abandoned the idea of claiming another victory for their unit. The engine of Surma's Spitfire I R6644/ZF-H overheated, and began to develop black smoke which filled the cockpit. Being over the Malvern Hills, the pilot steered the burning plane eastwards, intending to force land. The smoke decreased visibility from the cockpit, and the young Polish pilot decided to bale out. He landed safely, but his aircraft crashed near Madresfield Court, Worcs.

During the day 302 Squadron was ordered to patrol the Tangmere area. Just after take-off from Kenley, the Z2386/WX-C flown by P/O Włodzimierz Karwowski, stalled and crashed; the pilot was unhurt. All the unit's other aircraft returned to base after dusk and everybody at the airfield anticipated accidents. P/O Czesław Główczyński, landing in Hurricane Z3099/WX-B, retracted the undercarriage and damaged his aircraft. Two other Hurricanes were damaged, when P/O Aleksander Ryszard Narucki in Z3435 was hit by Z3433 flown by P/O Zbigniew Wróblewski; Narucki was killed in this accident. Night bombardment of RAF Kenley, which caused damage to another 302 Squadron aircraft (Z3095) ended this unfortunate day.

307 Squadron also lost several aircraft to a night raid on their airfield. The second wave of bombers flying over Clyst Honiton hit the dispersal area, destroying Defiant N3439 and damaging T3980, N1812 and one other.

12 May 1941

As this heavy raid on Clyst Honiton was in progress, Sgt Jerzy Malinowski and Sgt Stanisław Jarzembowski were the only 307 Squadron crew able to get airborne. Thanks to the assistance of the ground crew, especially LAC Józef Śniegowski, their Defiant N3404 took off under falling bombs dropped from low flying aircraft. Soon they found one of the raiders and the pilot later described his revenge in his combat report:

> "I sighted a Heinkel 111 against background of clouds flying South. I intercepted him when 4 miles South of Exmouth.
>
> "I made a beam attack from 300 yards away and 20 ft below – the Heinkel 111 being on my port side. At 03.30 hrs. I gave him a 1 second burst hitting the central part of the fuselage. The enemy turned in towards me and dived gradually; he did not fire at me. Keeping on the same course I flew under him and as he turned I was 40 ft below. My air gunner fired 3 short bursts in total 1 second, hitting the Heinkel in the nose. The enemy did not return any fire but turned and fell steeply to starboard losing height rapidly. I saw the Heinkel dive vertically after having rolled on to his back. I could not observe him hit the sea because I noticed a second Heinkel 111 approaching. I landed at 4.10 hours at Exeter."

14 May 1941

During this day 302 Squadron practised flying squadron formation, but whilst returning from this flight P/O Zbigniew Janicki damaged the undercarriage of his Hurricane Z2673/WX-Y during a heavy landing. The accident report excused this due to a strong wind and difficult conditions.

At Northolt one of the 303 Squadron pilots also made a heavy landing, Sgt Józef Szlagowski damaging Spitfire II P8085/RF-J at the conclusioin of a night flight.

15 May 1941

This proved to be another memorable day for 303 Squadron. Again the weather over France allowed *Rhubarbs* to be performed. F/Lt Jankiewicz checked the weather over the Channel and reported that the low level of cloud with good visibility were perfect for such operations. Half an hour before noon six Spitfires left Northolt and landed at Hawkinge for refuelling. The pilots were divided into three pairs:

1st pair

| F/Lt Jankiewicz | P8130/RF-T | Blue 1 |
| Sgt Giermer | P7786/RF-C | Blue 2 |

2nd pair

| P/O Paderewski | P8360 | Green 1 |
| Sgt Popek | P8085/RF-J | Green 2 |

3rd pair

| P/O Drobiński | P8038/RF-D | White 1 |
| Sgt Bełc | P8099/RF-V | White 2 |

All took off from Hawkinge about 12.15 pm and headed towards the French coast. The first pair crossed the coast in clouds and a few miles inland dropped to a lower altitude. Their target, Merville, was close, and Sgt Giermer, the wingman, later wrote in his memoirs:

"We dived at once some 25 metres. I stayed a larger distance from him, as we agreed that he would navigate, and I would watch the sky, so that no Messerschmitts could bounce us. I armed my guns and lit the gunsight, I was ready to fire.

"We were flying low, so as not to be detected by German radar, we also maintained radio silence.

"Not far from our target I spotted a large aeroplane on the horizon. I flew closer to F/Lt Jankiewicz, he looked at me, and I showed him the aeroplane with my hand. Jankiewicz raised his thumb, indicating he could see it. We abandoned our target and headed towards him. This was a Ju 52, large 3-motor transport aeroplane. Jankiewicz on the port side, and I underneath, we fired a burst. The port engine of the Junkers caught fire, I gave him another burst in the fuselage. After this burst from four machine guns the Junkers crashed in a great explosion on the ground.

"We left it, looking for other targets, but in pursuit of the Junkers we had gone too far in the opposite direction. There was nothing to shoot at. We flew along a road, but the road was empty. In the end I fired a burst at a high tension pylon – flash, a cascade of lights and the wires burnt."

After that both pilots of Blue Section hid themselves in the cloud cover and returned to Northolt without incidents. It was later ascertained that the Junkers shot down by Sgt Giermer and S/Ldr Jankiewicz carried *Generaloberst* Ulrich Grauert, AOC I. *Fliegerkorps*, and some officers of his staff, who were all killed. Among them were: Otlt. Heinrich Dönitz, the general quartermaster and the crew of Fw. Fritz Riewe, Ofw Bruno Schlesinger and Fh. Robert Rose. The Ju 52/3m W.Nr.5595 of *Transportstaffel/I. Fliegerkorps* crashed at Manillet near Boulogne.

The second pair of Spitfires reached Hardelot in company with Jankiewicz and Giermer, but then flew towards St Omer. When they arrived over the airfield they found no activity and no interesting targets. They then headed north to Calais and found another sleepy airfield. This time several huts and one army tank attracted the pilots' attention, P/O Drobiński giving a short burst at the huts and Sgt Bełc attacked the tank. Then they flew west to St Inglevert. This part of the operation was later recalled by the section leader:

"So, while flying I spotted an empty field and a large German aeroplane taxiing. I immediately turned and strafed the aeroplane which turned out to be a Ju 52. My burst was repeated by Bełc. I could see the aeroplane stop and turn slightly. The aeroplane must have been hit, as I observed rounds enter the fuselage and wings where the engines are. After pulling up I noticed two Me 109s with yellow noses, but right underneath me, so I could not fire at them. At first I made a wide turn, and intended to return to the aerodrome, but the field of fire of the AA defence of the airfield was excellent, completely flat country, and Bełc shouted that I was being fired upon from the ground, and that there were four Me 109s above us. So I gave up the aerodrome, and immediately after turning to port I saw a few ships out to sea, some 3-4 miles from the French coast. So I shouted to Bełc that we were going to shoot at ships, now . . ."

The convoy spotted by Drobiński consisted of Harbour Defence Boats nos. 54 and 55, which were in fact Flak-ships, plus some other vessels, of which three suffered damage. The leading ship VP1805 (ex-French S/S *Senateur Louis Brindeau*) was attacked by Drobiński from astern and showed signs of burning. Three of the crew were wounded. Later the fire was extinguished and the ship was repaired. Two of the remaining ships were attacked by Sgt Bełc. In total there were two killed and three wounded on board the minesweeper *Dirk* and on the tug *Barfleur* attacked by him. On the way across the Channel the Polish pilots subsequently made a short attack on an E-Boat, but saw no results.

The third pair, flying in the direction of Lumbres, experienced light Flak, accurate for height and direction, south of this town. South of St Omer they were fired on by machine guns from the ground, the fire being fairly accurate. On an aerodrome south of St Omer P/O Paderewski gave a four second burst at six Bf 109s in blast shelters, and Sgt Popek made an attack on what appeared to be a petrol bowser. Neither pilot observed the results of their fire.

On the return journey these pilots noticed two large goods trains at Lumbres, fully laden, and experienced further machine gun fire in this neighbourhood. Along a road leading west from the town Sgt Popek attacked a group of 12 soldiers, who immediately fell to the ground. On reaching the coast, both pilots noticed much smoke coming from the direction of the attack by P/O Drobiński on the merchant vessel.

All six returned home safely.

17 May 1941

A very serious accident happened to F/Lt Wilczewski of 316 Squadron. Due to engine failure in his Hurricane W9231/SZ-L he was forced to land. He chose a perfect landing ground – a sports field near Llanelly. Unfortunately, some people gathered at the field thought he was about to perform an aerobatic show, and thereby prevented him from landing. F/Lt Wilczewski was forced to pull the aircraft up at the latest moment, and crashed, hitting a power line pole. The aircraft fell to the ground and broke up, but the fortunate pilot survived the crash without injury.

"It could have ended in a lowered flag on our mast.", recorded 316 Squadron's chronicle. "One has to be born lucky to escape such an ordeal unscathed."

Another accident occured in 317 Squadron, when Sgt Tadeusz Baranowski damaged his Hurricane I V6695/JH-J whilst taxiing at Ouston after a training flight.

18 May 1941

On the way back from a patrol P/O Jan Kazimierz Daszewski of 303 Squadron hit a radio mast whilst landing at Northolt, damaging his Spitfire II P8325/RF-K.

19 May 1941

About 10 am a pair of 306 Squadron Hurricanes, flown by F/O Nowak (Z2969/UZ-F) and Sgt Śmigielski (Z3162/UZ-M), were sent to undertake a patrol over a convoy in the Dungeness area. While over this, they noticed four Bf 109s, and tried to engage them. The German fighters did not take the challenge, and turned back to France.

Subsequent events proved more in the Luftwaffe's favour. Earlier in the day 234 Squadron Spitfires had been bounced by Messerschmitts of III./JG 2, while during an afternoon sortie, 306 Squadron Hurricanes were also surprised by Bf 109s. This fateful patrol involved a formation of a dozen aircraft, as listed below:

F/O Nowak	Z3154/UZ-H	White section
Sgt Śmigielski	Z3162/UZ-M	White section
F/O S. Skalski	UZ-C	Red section
Sgt Wieprzkowicz	Z2968/UZ-D	Red section
P/O Rutkowski	Z3065/UZ-B	Yellow section
Sgt Jeka	Z3502/UZ-J	Yellow section
F/O Słoński	UZ-S	Blue section
Kpt. Studeny[84]	UZ-Y	Blue section
P/O Czapiewski	Z2456/UZ-W	Green section
Sgt Kroczyński	Z2965/UZ-K	Green section
P/O M. Skalski	Z2884/UZ-Z	Black section
Sgt Pietrzak	Z2959/UZ-T	Black section

The squadron, while over Maidstone at an altitude of 15,000 ft, received word of 'Three bandits ahead of you' and an order to fly north. When at 13,000 ft, another transmission advised: 'Turn left and look down'. At the same moment as they began a wide turn, the Polish pilots noticed three Messerschmitts diving out of the sun. S/Ldr Rolski later wrote in his report:

"The aircraft above were previously twice announced to the Squadron by Sgt Wieprzkowicz (4-5 Mes up sun some 4,000 ft above us). The news was not accepted by the Ops Room, while F/Lt Nowak took it only partly (he did not realise their numbers nor position). Already during the climb, when flying towards the patrol line, F/Lt Nowak felt slight play on the control stick when moving it sideways. Immediately before the Me attack the play increased so much that his ailerons would not react to the stick movements. Therefore, he reported this to the Ops Room and gave command to F/O Słoński. The attack took place exactly at

---

[84] Kpt. Antonin Studeny was the only Czech officer posted to the Polish Air Force as part of an official exchange of personnel, as opposed to a number of Czech NCOs, who volunteered from the outset to fly with 303 Squadron rather than their own national units (Sgt Josef František, Sgt Matej Pavlovic, P/O Miroslav Balejka).

the moment when the leader's section reformed. F/Lt Nowak had just turned back to the aerodrome, and F/O Słoński moved forward. As a result of the attack the Squadron scattered completely. Those shot down included Sgt Kroczyński (baled out, severely wounded, he is now in a hospital at Margate), P/O Czapiewski (no news at all). After the attack the Messerschmitts escaped. Some towards France, some into the clouds that reached 8,000 ft, with 8/10 cover.

"P/O Rutkowski sped towards two Me 109s that started climbing after the attack. At one moment at 22,000 ft he was unexpectedly attacked from behind and shot down. P/O Rutkowski baled out and landed at Ramsgate around 12.50 pm.

"F/O Słoński collected 5 aeroplanes, and returned with them, landing at 1.25 pm at Biggin Hill. Three aircraft separated from the whole formation returned individually to Northolt. Two landed at 1.20 pm and one at 1.40 pm.

"F/Lt Nowak forced landed in the field near Ewhurst at 1.30 pm."

Pilots of the attacking II./JG 52 reported the destruction of four RAF aircraft in this encounter. Olt. Johannes Steinhoff claimed two 'Spitfires', Fw. Adolf Glunz and Lt. Siegfried Simsch one each. Apart from the non-combat damage to F/Lt Nowak's aircraft, 306 Squadron lost three Hurricanes and two pilots, of which P/O Czapiewski was killed.

20 May 1941

Participation by 306 Squadron in a *Rhubarb* operation was cancelled, but in spite of this, the Polish unit suffered a loss. P/O Edward Jankowski crashed his Hurricane II Z3342/UZ-X during take-off from Northolt, when he retracted the undercarriage too soon; he escaped unhurt.

316 recorded in the Squadron chronicle:

"Hurricane I aeroplanes that the Sqn now uses, are about to end their meritorious lives. More and more often their engines fail due to so-called material fatigue. Well, the type of aeroplane has been in service since 1938 and has played its part with distinction. Also the squadron aircraft, in spite of the care of our fitters, fail more and more often, which is not a joy for the pilots, especially when it happens over sea.

"Today Sgt Władysław Kiedrzyński was forced to bale out when his engine ignited during a combat sortie over open sea. Fortunately, he only plunged into the sea some 80 metres from the coast and managed to reach it himself. Due to general shock and slight burns he had to be taken to a hospital."

Needless to say, his Hurricane V6873/SZ-M was written off. The chronicle continued to complain about the Hurricane Is:

"Squadron aeroplanes, after having worked their hours, are sent back in turns for a factory overhaul, and are replaced by others, brought from O.T.U. (schools). The state of these recent arrivals is often lamentable, and our fitters have to work hard to make them properly serviceable. The Sqn was promised that within four weeks new Hurricane II aeroplanes will be delivered, and the pilots await those eagerly."

Sgt Bernard Samp of 605 Squadron was killed on 20 May while force-landing in

Hurricane Z2319 near Ternhill airfield. He was flying in a section led by S/Ldr Edge, practising landing in section formation. Just before touching down, a Master unexpectedly crossed the runway in front of them. All three pilots pulled up and retracted their undercarriages but the engine of Samp's aircraft suddenly cut at some 50 ft. It was later found that he had not switched the fuel from the main tank at the right time.

During the month Polish pilots of 605 Squadron undertook patrols over the west coast of Wales, but soon they would all be transferred to newly established Polish units.

21 May 1941

The two Polish squadrons based at Northolt took part in *Circus* no. 18. 303 and 306 Squadrons were despatched ahead of the main force. Recorded the 303 Squadron chronicle:

> "the Wing's duty was to arrive over Berck aerodrome about the same time as the bombing formation of 18 Blenheims, escorted by three fighter squadrons, crossed the French coast on its way to the target . . ."

Thirteen Spitfires of 303 Squadron and a dozen Hurricanes of 306 strafed dispersal huts at Berck-sur-Mer airfield. On their way back they were followed by four Bf 109s, but were not attacked.

The main force of *Circus* 18 included another Polish unit, 302 Squadron, acting as the Blenheim bombers' close cover. The raid on the power station at Gosnay, east of Bethune, was well remembered by Władysław Gnyś, who described it in his memoirs *First Kill*[85]:

> "I was flying on the right side of the leader aircraft. Out task was to stay with the bombers and protect their safety at all times. Above us, towards the rear, were two more Hurricane squadrons[86] and above them, three Spitfire squadrons flying as top cover. Their purpose was itself to take the first impact of any attack by enemy fighters.
>
> "As we approached the French coastline, our ground control room informed the squadron leader of large numbers of enemy fighters above our formation. Moments later, our Spitfires were heavily engaged in combat with them, but were unable to prevent them from closing in on our bombers.
>
> "Flying at our bombers' sides, I saw this tremendous circus above our heads. Lots of aircraft, ours and the enemy's, were tangled in a vicious circle. Some aircraft were spiralling downwards, leaving black trails of smoke behind them.
>
> "Many pilots attached to their parachutes were floating towards the ground which added to the picture. Suddenly, we saw enemy fighters diving towards our bomber formations. We were the last ones now to stop the Messerschmitts from their attack. Unfortunately, because of the position of our Hurricanes' formation, we had not enough room to manoeuvre or gain speed. Both Hurricane squadrons

---

[85] Wladek Gnyś, *First Kill – A Fighter Pilot's Autobiography*, William Kimber, London, 1981.
[86] Apart from 302, the Blenheim cover included 1 and 258 Squadrons on Hurricanes.

were now under attack and had broken into loose formation; some individually, some in sections intercepting Messerschmitts diving down.

"It was a vicious dance. Our Hurricanes were holding well; traces of bullets were everywhere. I saw some Hurricanes smoking, turning and twisting constantly in combat. We were meeting the Messerschmitts in practically head-on collisions.

"Suddenly, I saw an enemy fighter diving rapidly at me, shooting furiously. I threw my plane to the right and managed to escape the deadly line of fire but received some bullet holes in my left wing. Instantaneously more enemy fighters appeared from nowhere. Some of the 'top cover' Hurricanes and Spitfires came down to give us a hand.

"We were fired upon and were firing back with frenzy. At the same time I was attacking a Messerschmitt I was also attacked by another German fighter. I saw him on my tail, but could not escape from his line of fire completely. My engine had been hit and became very hot and was smoking. It started to cough and lose speed. I looked around quickly for another enemy attack and saw the Messerschmitts disappearing into the horizon.

"My engine was now smoking badly and was shaking. I reduced my speed and turned towards home. The English coastline was still quite a way, and I was rather apprehensive that, without my engine, I would not be able to glide the distance, and would have to ditch in the sea. The bombers were now on their way home, successfully having deposited their bombs on target. There had been no losses.

"Two of my friends seeing my plight, joined me and while flying by my side kept a protective watch over me. They were waving and motioning from their cockpits, making movements of rocking back and forth in their cockpits in the pretence of helping my spluttering aircraft make its way over the rough aqua-green swell below.

"The gratifying sight of the white cliffs of Dover gave me the reassurance that, with lady luck on my side, I might be fortunate enough to make the aerodrome.

"The waves below me tipped with white crests, seemed only a short distance beneath me. My Spitfire[87] was spluttering and groaning, 'Come on baby . . . come on' . . . I glided over the cliffs, my engine was smoking very badly, I switched it off to avoid it catching fire. Then I saw the aerodrome in front of me and the landing strip. I was losing height rapidly, I knew I would not make the runway. I looked around . . . a large field was close . . . I guided her in cautiously. I did not want to damage my plane any more than necessary. I felt the wheels touch the ground. I patted the side of my plane, 'Good old girl, I knew you could make it!' My friends flew over me waving their wings in happy relief that I had landed on dry land safely.

"Our losses were only one Hurricane shot down. Fortunately, the pilot was able to parachute to safety and avoided capture by the Germans. After a few months, he arrived back to England via Spain."

The airman mentioned by Władek Gnyś, who was shot down over France was P/O Rytka. P/O Zbigniew Wróblewski and Sgt Marian Rytka were the only Polish pilots to be credited with victories over the Messerschmitts. The former claimed a Bf 109F probably destroyed, and the latter, after firing several bursts, had to abandon his Hurricane Z2423/WX-V. To his comrades' surprise, Rytka returned to the unit within a few months, and later described his adventures:

---

[87] In fact Gnyś flew a Hurricane, not a Spitfire.

"During this battle one of our aircraft was attacked from the rear by one Me 109F, and seeing this I attacked that enemy aircraft from the side trying to get in from the rear. After two bursts from a distance of about 150 yards the enemy aircraft turned to its right and the pilot baled out by parachute. I followed the enemy pilot until he reached the height of about 6000 ft and then seeing our Squadron flying towards the target, I started to join it having to fly 5/6 miles, the distance which separated me from my formation. I did not see any enemy aircraft around. Just at the moment when I was about to join our formation and was about 700 yards from my Squadron, I was attacked by four Messerschmitt Bf 109Fs. A fight took place and the engine and cockpit of my aircraft were hit by the enemy. The situation began to get critical, my aircraft started to smoke, but at that moment I made a half turn and then I attacked the middle enemy aircraft head on, giving it one long burst. After that I dived until having reached 2,000 ft and having no enemy around me I made for the English coast, but after a period of 4-5 minutes I noticed that the engine of my aircraft had seized up and I was obliged to force land in occupied France, about 7 miles from Boulogne.

"I was able to reach unoccupied France due to the help of the French population and from there to Spain and Gibraltar. From Gibraltar I arrived in Glasgow and then rejoined my Squadron after three months absence."

This report permitted him to claim the destruction of one Bf 109. Despite this, there is no evidence of any such aircraft being lost by the Luftwaffe that day in this part of France, or of a Luftwaffe pilot having to bale out. RAF casualties during this raid were in fact rather high – eight fighters[88] and two bombers lost, and three fighters damaged.

22 May 1941
601 Squadron, previously based with the two Polish units at Northolt, left this station on 2 May. The unit now moved to Manston, still retaining some Polish personnel. One of these, P/O Ryszard Malczewski, took off on 22 May with P/O Donald B. Ogilvie for a patrol at about noon. Both were ordered to Sweep over France in their Hurricane IIs, Ogilvie in Z3239 and Malczewski in Z3268/UF-M. While over France, they spotted a Junkers 52 in the Forêt d'Eperterques area and shot up the engines of the transport aircraft. Malczewski reported:

"Red One made two quick attacks on the Ju 52, stopping the centre engine dead, and causing an aileron or large panel to fall off. When Red One broke away I attacked the Ju 52 from port, above, firing a burst at 50 yards which caused the port engine to slow up and emit smoke. When last seen the e/a was at 250 feet over an area in which landing was impossible (forest) gradually loosing height after vainly trying to pull up into cloud. No return fire was experienced. I claim half a probable in the Ju 52."

The pair of Hurricanes were then attacked by a pair of III./JG 3 Bf 109s, and had to take evasive action, leaving the Junkers flying on one engine. In the ensuing engagement Ogilvie caught one of the Messerschmitts in his gunsight and shot it

---

[88] Two collided in the air.

down; this was a Bf 109F-2, "White 3", flown by Gefr. Hans-Günther Kärger. Both pilots then returned to Manston.

24 May 1941

P/O Eugeniusz Fiedorczuk of 315 Squadron again damaged a Hurricane whilst landing at Speke, this time in R4122/PK-S. However, he was not to blame on this occasion. According to the Composite Combat Report sent to HQ 9 Group, at about 2.50 pm P/O Fiedorczuk in R4122 and F/Lt Mickiewicz in V7660/PK-V were ordered to intercept a Junkers 88 approaching Chester. Both pilots spotted the German bomber somewhere over Ruthin, F/Lt Mickiewicz firing all his ammunition in one long burst and then breaking away. P/O Fiedorczuk made several attacks, firing short bursts, but no real effects of their fire was observed. The enemy gunner fired at the attacking Hurricanes and gained a hit on the port main plane and beneath the tail plane of Fiedorczuk's aircraft; the cockpit perspex was also damaged by bullets. The Junkers then banked to port and dived into cloud cover. P/O Fiedorczuk reported that he saw slight black smoke from the starboard engine of the enemy aircraft, but no claim was made.

315 Squadron pilots had almost certainly intercepted a Junkers 88A-5 of II./KG 77, which subsequently belly-landed at Le Culot airfield with two of the crew wounded. The German gunner reported the destruction of a 'Spitfire' which appears actually to have been Fiedorczuk's Hurricane.[89]

Thus, although not claimed by the Polish pilots, this was the first successful encounter of 315 Squadron, and would have been the first victory of this unit.

25 May 1941

On the way back from a training flight, Sgt Karaszewski of 317 Squadron crash-landed Hurricane R4192/JH-J at Whitchester.

26 May 1941

The 316 Squadron chronicle described an unusual accident which occured at Pembrey:

> "The month of May was less successful for the squadron than April in terms of crashes or damage to aircraft. This is a question of more and more frequent engine failures and pilots are then forced to land in unfavourable conditions. The only case of damaging an aeroplane is that of plut. Gallus. Namely, due to premature retraction of the undercarriage, his propeller blades hit the ground, and were cut evenly shorter by some 10 cm. The pilot failed to notice that, and performed a 90-minute sortie over sea. The surprise of the fitters, when they saw a machine land with a strangely reduced propeller, was enormous."

Sgt Paweł Gallus was flying the Hurricane I P3100/SZ-O on the occasion recorded.

---

[89] A recent publication linked the destruction of the Ju 88 of II./KG 77 with a combat by 87 Squadron pilots. However, S/Ldr Ian Gleed and Sgt Thorogood in fact claimed the destruction of a Do-18 flying boat, which crashed into the sea!

27 May 1941

F/O Jerzy Solak of 317 Squadron was scrambled to patrol over Ouston in Hurricane I W9170/JH-E. Five minutes later he was ordered to land and during this landing he hit a fire truck, damaging his aircraft. The pilot was unhurt.

28 May 1941

In the middle of February 1941 another group of Polish airmen had joined 43 Squadron. P/O Czajkowski, F/O Bernard Groszewski, P/O Malarowski and F/O Mickiewicz served in this unit for less than two months and then were sent to freshly formed Polish squadrons. P/O Czajkowski was the only one to stay longer, and he was the only successful Pole who had his share in a victory while flying FT-coded Hurricanes. He very often flew as a wingman to F/Lt DuVivier, and on 28 May 1941 Red Section comprising F/Lt DuVivier in Hurricane Z3031 and P/O Czajkowski in Z3079, was scrambled to intercept a Junkers 88 near Prestwick. Both saw the enemy aircraft flying in a southerly direction to the south west of Glasgow at 24,000 ft. The moment when they both set off to intercept the enemy, the oil system in the aircraft flown by Czajkowski began to leak. He had to force land at an abandoned airfield near Carlisle, the aircraft being slightly damaged.

F/Lt DuVivier continued his chase, attacked the enemy aircraft near Newcastletown (north east of Carlisle) and shot it down. Two of the crew of the Ju 88A Werk Nr. 0615, which was from 2./*Aufklärungsgruppe Oberbefehlshaber der Luftwaffe*, were captured and two others were killed. The rear gunner had aimed very well and DuVivier's aircraft, hit in the oil tank, was also forced to land at Acklington. Both Red Section fighters were back at their home base at Drem next morning.

On 28 May 302 Squadron moved from Kenley to Jurby and began intensive training, replacing the Hurricane IIs with older Mk Is, taken over from 312 (Czechoslovak) Squadron.

1 June 1941

308 Squadron, still equipped with Spitfire Is, moved from Baginton to Chilbolton near Andover, under the command of 10 Group.

2 June 1941

316 Squadron suffered the loss of its first victorious pilot, when at about 10.00 am F/O Nowierski took off from Pembrey in a Hurricane I, in order to deliver it to a repair depot. P/O Bohdan Anders followed in Magister R1838, to bring him back home. The weather was bad, but lack of serviceable aircraft had caused the 316 Squadron OC to send the old Hurricane away to obtain a replacement. Due to a deterioration in the weather, however, F/O Nowierski returned to Pembrey, meanwhile P/O Anders continued his flight to Hansworth. Trying to break through the clouds, he changed course and hit barrage balloons near Newport about 10.20. The pilot died in the burning aircraft.

One of the last Polish pilots to serve in 43 Squadron, P/O Czajkowski, ended his time with the Fighting Cock Squadron when he crash-landed two miles south of North Berwick. He was on patrol with his usual leader, F/Lt DuVivier, flying an all black Hurricane II Z2638. The injured Polish pilot was sent to a hospital, and after recovery was posted to a Polish squadron.

The second day of June proved to be a good one for 317 Squadron. That day the

Luftwaffe despatched about 50 bombers to harass convoys passing along the east coast of England. Pairs of Hurricanes undertook afternoon patrols in the Seaham and Blyth area, each patrol lasting approximately 70 minutes. Late in the afternoon the frequency of patrols was increased. The last pair (Black Section) were in the air about 10 pm, F/O Paweł Niemiec, flying V7123, leading Sgt Baranowski in W9183. After their return they reported shooting down a Ju 88 over the Tyne. Sgt Baranowski was the author of this first victory for the unit, the aircraft he claimed being a Ju 88A-5, Werk Nr. 3422, coded M2+DL, of 3./KüFlGr 506, with the crew of Ofw. Bernhard Winse. The Intelligence Combat Report reported:

"Black Section took off Ouston 22.00 hours to patrol convoy between Hartlepool and Tyne, but were vectored across Tyne gun zone to Raid 623 which had entered sector from Tees and was flying north along coast reported at 2000 ft. Section crossed coast south of Tynemouth and were vectored after raid and about 7 miles behind near Blyth e/a turned south and Black Section were vectored 180 at gate. At Seaham e/a turned north and section followed sighting e/a at 22.26 hours off Tyne. Throughout this approach R.O.C. provided a commentary on relative positions which greatly assisted Controller. Section approached in line astern below and climbed above, Black 1 attacking from port above and astern and Black 2 from starboard above and astern. Fire from upper rear position experienced which ceased during attack by Black 2. E/a then began to lose height and smoke appeared from both motors. Black 1 attacked again to make sure and e/a plunged into sea near a ship off Tyne. A/c quickly sank and none of the crew were seen to leave. During first attack e/a tried to escape climbing to cloud but although momentarily lost by Black 1 was engaged by Black 2. Casualty confirmed by 72 blue, some searchlight sites and police who saw e/a enter sea.

"E/a was Ju 88 camouflaged dark green, light bluish green undersurface. At first e/a appeared to be four engined because of bomb rack blisters under wings.

"Weather cloudy base 1000 ft to 2000 ft 6 to 10/10 varying in thickness. Visibility 1 to 3 miles.

"Black 1 F/O Niemiec (Polish)
"Black 2 Sgt Baranowski (Polish)"

Luck was with Sgt Baranowski not only in his action against the Ju 88, but also in a court of law at Newcastle-upon-Tyne. The superstitious pilot stole a goose from a country policeman who started an investigation. By chance he discovered his property being held and fed by Polish airmen, and even walked on a leash around the aerodrome. The case was settled in court:

"The defendant, when asked if he pled guilty, replied that before answering the question he would like to make a short explanation to the court. The judge permitted him to speak, and waited for what the Pole was going to say in his broken English. The sergeant, as befits a soldier, looked the judge straight in the eyes, and related briefly, as if reporting, the story of his fighter squadron, which had not even encountered the Germans, to say nothing about scoring a victory. At the same time British squadrons in the area were enjoying more luck. After researching the question in detail, he found that every other squadron had a mascot, while the Polish unit had none. One day, walking through the village, he saw a goose. He recalled the story of the geese in ancient Rome that saved the city. So he decided to steal a goose. At night, while everybody else was having a good time in the Sergeants' Mess, he accomplished his plan. That was all he had to say in his defence.

"'Well', asked the judge ironically, 'has a German aeroplane fallen into the hands of the defendant, too?'

"The counsel for the defence, a British officer, asked permission to speak, which was granted by the judge.

"'Two days after the goose was brought to the aerodrome', said the counsel, 'the defendant shot down a Dornier during a patrol . . .'

". . . On hearing this the policeman asked the court to close the case, paid several pound sterling in costs, and shook the Polish airman's hand, saying 'sorry'."[90]

On the date 317 Squadron gained its first victory, P/O Szumowski described in his diary some convoy escort sorties carried out by this unit. The boring convoy patrols frustrated him, and he wrote words that well described the nature of Polish fighter pilots:

"It is our Polish nature to be rash, impulsive – foolhardy even – and now yet again we must do mundane duties whilst excitement, exhilaration, the do-or-die glory of battles falls to others . . ."[91]

[90] Edward Kwolek, *Bomby w celu*, Brighton, 1984.
[91] Tadeusz Szumowski, *Through many skies* . . .

EPILOGUE

On 3 June 1941 W/Cdr John Kent took command of the Northolt Wing which by that time had become an all-Polish unit. This marked the end of the period during which Polish fighters were mostly employed in air defence duties. The Northolt-based squadrons, as with much of Fighter Command, were preparing for a large-scale offensive across the Channel.

At about the same time major Luftwaffe units moved east, in preparation for the invasion of the Soviet Union. Thus daylight air attacks against Britain would virtually come to an end. Although the night Blitz would continue at a reduced level, it is right to conclude that the defence of Britain was effectively at an end.

Appendix I

302 SQUADRON HURRICANES

August 1940 – April 1941

	WX-A	WX-B	WX-C	WX-D	WX-E	WX-F	WX-G	WX-H	WX-J	WX-K	WX-L	WX-M
1940												
VI	P3085	R2684	P3942	P3935	P3927 +.17.08 P2954	P3867	R2685	P3939	P3538	V6569	P3812	R4095
IX	P3085	R2684 +15.09	V6744	P3935	P3205	P3867		P3939 +6.09	P3538	V6734	P3812	R4095 +15.09
X	P3085	V6860	V6744	P3935	P3205	P3867	V6694	P2717	P3538	V6734	P3812 +15.10 V6865	V6735 +17.10
XI	V7045	V6860	V6744	P3335 V7046	P3205	P3867	V6694	P2717	P3538 +8.11	V6734	V6865	
XI	V7045	V6860	V6744	V7046	P3205	P3867		P2717		V6734	V6865	
1941												
I	V7047	V6860	V6744	V7046	P3204	P3867		P2717		V6734	V6865	
II	V7047	V6860	V6744	V7046	P3204	P3867 +14.02		P2717		V6734	V6865	
III	V7047 V3207	V6860	V6744	V7046	P3204²	V6742		P2717		V6865	/5.03	V7145³
Hurricane II	Z2806	Z2772	Z2386	Z2775	Z2667	Z2342	Z2523	Z2668		Z2814	Z2816	Z3091
IV	Z3098	Z3099	Z2386	Z2775	Z2806 +29.04	Z2342	Z2523	Z2668		Z2814 +26.04	Z2816	Z3091

1 Sometimes appeared under the erroreous number N2723.
2 Sometimes appeared under the erroreous number V3402.
3 Erroreous serial number in 302 Squadron ORB.

	WX-N	WX-Q	WX-R	WX-S	WX-T	WX-U	WX-V	WX-W	WX-X	WX-Y	WX-Z
1940											
VI		V6570 V6571	P2752		P3934 +24.08 V7417	P3923		P3120	P3930	P3924	P3086
IX		V6571	P2752		V7417	P3923	P3931	P3120 6.09/	P3930	P3924 +30.09	P3086 +18.09
X		V6571 +18.10	P2752 +15.10 P3872 +18.10 P3785	V6942	V7417 +17.10 P3877	V6923 (P3923)	P3931 +18.10 V7593 +25.10	/25.10 V6941	P3930 +18.10 R2687	P2918 +18.10 P2918	V6753
XI			P3785	V6942	P3877	/08.11 N2352	V7047	V6941	R2687	P2918	V6753
XI		V3751	P3785	V6942	P3877			V6941	R2687	P2918	V6753
1941											
I		V3751	P3785	V6942	P3877		V7045	V6941	R2687	P2918	V6753
II		V3751	P3785	V6942	P3877	N2423[1]	V7045	V6941	R2687 +20.02	P2918 +02.02	V6753
III		V3751	P3785	V6942	P3877		V7045	V6941		P2918	V7191
Hurricane II											
	Z3095		Z2629	Z2497	Z2773	Z2485	Z2423	Z235	Z2357	Z267	Z2681
IV	Z3095		Z2629	Z2497	Z2773	Z2485	Z2423	Z2350	Z2357	Z267 3	Z2681

Appendix II

303 SQUADRON HURRICANES

30 August 1940 – 10 February 1941

	RF-A	RF-B	RF-C	RF-D	RF-E	RF-F	RF-G	RF-H	RF-J	RF-K	RF-M	RF-N
1940 VIII	V7284	V7242	V7244	V7246	P3700	R2688	R4178	V7290	P3974		V7235	P3890
IX	V7284 +6.09 P3120	V7242 11.09/ /13.09 V6681	V7244	V7246 27.09/ /30.09 N2460	P3700 9.09/ /12.09 P3577 15.09/ /18.09 P3901	R2688 3.09/ /6.09 P3089 9.09/ /13.09 V6684	R4178 2.09/ /6.09 R2685 28.09/ L1770[1] /30.09 V7504[2]	V7290 6.09/[3] /7.09 P3939 15.0/ /18.09 P3544 26.09/ /29.09 P3663 30.09/	P3974 6.09/ /9.09 V6665 27.09/ /30.09 N2661	/9.09 V6667 11.09/	V7235	P3890 7.09/
X	P3120 /2.10 /10.10 V6808	V6681 /25.10 /26.10 V7624	V7244	N2460	P3901 /27.10	V6984	V7504		N2661		V7235 (V7234)[4]	
XI	V6808 /9.11 /14.11 V6982	V7624	V7244 /1.11 /3.11 P3585	N2460	P3901		V7504	/1.11 V7384	N2661		V7235	
XI	V6982 /29.12	V7624 /31.12	P3585 /23.12	N2460 /29.12	P3901 /29.12	V7130[8]	V7504 /29.12	V7384 /29.12	N2661 /29.12		V7235 /31.12	
1941 I	V7606	/5.01 V7608	/12.01 V6956	/16.01 V7499 /22.01	/12.01 V6757	/5.01 P3551 /16.01	/5.01 V6637	/5.01 V7727	/5.01 V7183		V7619	
II	V7606 /2.02	V7608 /1.02	V6956 /3.02		V6757 /2.02			V7727 /10.02	V7183 /10.02		V7619 2.02	

P2645 which crashed on 9 September 1940 does not appear in the table because its individual code letter is not known

1 Only one mission on 29 September. Aircraft borrowed from 229 Sqn.
2 Sometimes appear under erroreous number V7505.
3 V7290 sometimes appear after 6 September.
4 Sometimes appeared in October, but was crashed in September and went to a repair depot.

	RF-O	RF-P	RF-Q	RF-R	RF-S	RF-T	RF-U	RF-V	RF-W	RF-X	RF-Y	RF-Z
1940												
VI		V7243	R4179	R4175	V7289	R4173	P3975	R4217				P2985
	/11.09	V7243	R4179	R4175	V7289	R4173	P3975	R4217				P2985
	L2099	6.09/	6.09/		27.09/	11.09/	9.09/	7.09/				5.09/
		/11.09	/11.09		/29.09	/16.09	/11.09	/9.09				/13.09
		P3089	L2026		P3217	L1696	V6673	V7465				P2903
						27.09/	15.09/					15.09/
						/30.09	/16.09					
						P3383	P3975					
							20.09/					
							/29.09					
							V7503					
X	L2099	P3089	L2026	R4175	P3217	P3383	V7503	V7465	/8.10	V6577[5]		
		7.10/		8.10/	6.10/			5.10/	V7401	P3206[6]		
		/10.10			/9.10				27.10/			
		V6577			V6843							
XI	L2099	V6577	L2026	/6.11	V6843	P3383	V7503				/3.11	
				L1825							P3814	
				/9.11								
				(V6929)[7]								
XII	L2099	V6577	L2026		V6843	P3383	V7503				P3814	
	/23.12				/31.12						/31.12	
1941												
I	/5.01	V6577	L2026	/5.01	/5.01	P3383	V7503		/5.01		/5.01	/5.01
	R4081	/1.01	/3.01	V6533	V7466	/1.01	/3.01		W9129		V6815	V7644
				/10.1		/5.01	/5.01				/9.01	
						P3162	V7182					
II	R4081				V7466	P3162	V7182		W9129			V7644
	/6.02				/10.02	/2.02	/9.02		/10.02			/10.02

5 Appears in ORB only on 11 October.
6 Appears in ORB only on 15 and 29 October.
7 RF-R or RF-W to 3 January 1941.
8 Appeared incidentally on 31 December 1940.

Appendix III

POLISH AIR FORCE FLYING PERSONNEL IN
RAF FIGHTER UNITS (JUNE 1940 TO 2 JUNE 1941)

based on official *Ewidencja Lotnictwa Myśliwskiego* (Evidence of PAF Fighter Pilots)

Rank	Name	First name	Units
Sgt	Adamek	Mieczysław	57 OTU; 28.04.41 – 303 Sqn
Sgt	Adamiak	Jan	5 OTU; 06.01.41 – 302 Sqn; 24.01.41 – 315 Sqn
Sgt	Adamiecki	Mieczysław	15.10.40 – 307 Sqn
P/O	Alexandrowic	Antoni	31.10.40 – 307 Sqn
Sgt	Ambroziewicz	Aleksander	307 Sqn
P/O	Anders	Bohdan	Upavon OTU; 23.07.40 – 302 Sqn; 30.07.40 – CFS; 24.03.41 – 316 Sqn; 02.06.41 – †
Sgt	Andruszków	Tadeusz	21.08.40 – 303 Sqn; 5 OTU; 10.09.40 – 303 Sqn; 27.09.40 – †
F/O	Antolak	Eugeniusz	5 OTU; 21.11.40 – 302 Sqn; 25.04.41 – 32 Sqn
P/O	Antolak		Polish Depot; 07.01.41 – 302 Sqn
F/O	Antonowicz	Jerzy	15 OTU, 18 OTU, 24 OTU, 300 Sqn; 02.12.40 – 307 Sqn; 26.02.41 – 307 Sqn (F/Lt)
F/O	Arentowicz	Tadeusz	09.12.40 – 303 Sqn; 20.02.41 – 303 Sqn (F/Lt); 13.04.41 – 303 Sqn (S/Ldr)
Sgt	Armanowski	Józef	07.05.41 – 307 Sqn
P/O	Balejka	Josef	1 FTS; 02.04.41 – 317 Sqn; 07.04.41 – 57 OTU
Sgt	Bałucki	Józef	04.04.41 – 307 Sqn
Sgt	Banyś	Jan	10.09.40 – 307 Sqn
Sgt	Baranowski	Tadeusz	55 OTU; 16.04.41 – 317 Sqn
F/O	Barański	Wienczysław	25.08.40 – 5 OTU; 11.10.40 – 607 Sqn; 12.11.40 – 303 Sqn; 22.02.41 – 316 Sqn (F/Lt)
P/O	Barciszewski	Zygmunt	307 Sqn; CAACU; 25.05.41 – 24 Sqn
Sgt	Beda	Antoni	20.08.40 – 302 Sqn; 02.09.40 – 5 OTU; 26.09.40 – 302 Sqn
P/O	Befinger	Mieczysław	10.11.40 – 7 AACU
Sgt	Bełc	Marian	02.08.40 – 303 Sqn; ? – 21.05.41 – Cadet Officers' School
Sgt	Bełza	Mieczysław	17.03.41 – 316 Sqn; ??.05.41 – 303 Sqn
P/O	Bełza	Stanisław	57 OTU; 21.04.41 – 303 Sqn
S/L	Benz	Kazimierz	03.10.40 – 307 Sqn; 17.11.40 – RAF Jurby
P/O	Bernaś	Bronisław	6 OTU; 23.09.40 – 302 Sqn; 14.04.41 – 58 OTU
Sgt	Bernatowicz	Wacław	15.10.40 – 307 Sqn
P/O	Bettcher	Jerzy	504 Sqn
Sgt	Biel	Józef	??.10.40 – 3 Sqn; 24.02.41 – 317 Sqn; ??.04.41 – 72 Sqn
P/O	Bielkiewicz	Bohdan	04.09.40 – 306 Sqn; 13.02.41 – †
F/O	Bieńkowski	Zygmunt	55 OTU; 26.05.41 – 245 Sqn
Sgt	Bilau	Juliusz	13.10.40 – 307 Sqn
P/O	Blach	Tadeusz	??.05.41 – 55 OTU; 02.12.40 (?) – 504 Sqn
Sgt	Blachowski	Zygmunt	05.10.40 – 307 Sqn
F/O	Błaszczyk	Jan	25.02.41 – 307 Sqn
P/O	Blok	Stanisław	55 OTU; 14.05.41 – 56 Sqn
Sgt	Bocheński	Kazimierz	14.10.40 – 307 Sqn; 17.02.41 – †
P/O	Bochniak	Stanisław	56 OTU;10.03.41 – CFS Upavon;

Rank	Name	First name	Units
			24.03.41 – 317 Sqn
F/O	Bokowiec	Kazimierz	54 OTU; 255 Sqn; 04.03.41 – 151 Sqn;
			02.05.41 – 23 Sqn
P/O	Bondar	Józef	56 OTU; 02.06.41 – 303 Sqn
P/O	Borowski	Jan	5 OTU; 17.10.40 – 302 Sqn; 18.10.40 – †
Sgt	Borusiewicz	Zbigniew	05.05.41 – 316 Sqn
P/O	Bożek	Władysław	06.08.40 – 302 Sqn; 15.08.40 – Blackpool Depot;
			12.09.40 – 308 Sqn
Sgt	Broda	Jan	10.09.40 – 307 Sqn
Sgt	Brzeski	Stanisław	10.09.40 – 307 Sqn; 02.10.40 – 5 OTU;
			11.10.40 – 303 Sqn; 08.11.40 – 245 Sqn;
			??.12.40 – 249 Sqn; 25.02.41 – 317 Sqn
F/O	Brzezina	Stanisław	5 OTU; 05.08.40 – 74 Sqn;
			22.10.40 – 12 Group HQ (Liaison Officer);
			12.01.41 – 9 Group HQ; 26.02.41 – 317 Sqn (S/Ldr)
Sgt	Brzezowski	Michał	5 OTU; 21.08.40 – 303 Sqn; 15.09.40 – †
P/O	Buchwald	Bernard	55 OTU; 27.03.41 – 316 Sqn
P/O	Buczyński	Jan	16.10.40 – 307 Sqn
P/O	Budrewicz	Ryszard	55 OTU; 14.05.41 – 302 Sqn; 31.05.41 – 43 Sqn
P/O	Budziński	Jan	12.08.40 – 145 Sqn; 31.08.40 – 605 Sqn;
			27.04.41 – 302 Sqn
P/O	Bury-Burzymski	Jan	10.09.40 – 307 Sqn; 02.10.40 – 5 OTU;
			11.10.40 – 303 Sqn; 24.10.40 – †
F/O	Cebrzyński	Arsen	21.08.40 – 303 Sqn; 11.09.40 – †
F/O	Chałupa	Stanisław Józef	23.07.40 – 302 Sqn
P/O	Chciuk	Władysław	12.09.40 – 308 Sqn
P/O	Chełmecki	Marian	6 OTU; 31.08.40 – 56 Sqn;
			10.09.40 – 17 Sqn; 20.03.41 – 55 OTU
F/L	Chłopik	Tadeusz Paweł	6 OTU; 03.08.40 – 302 Sqn; 15.09.40 – †
P/O	Choms	Wiesław	Hucknall; 02.04.41 – 317 Sqn;
			08.04.41 – 55 OTU; 26.05.41 – 306 Sqn
Sgt	Ciepliński	Filip	307 Sqn
P/O	Cwynar	Michał	55 OTU; 15.04.41 – 315 Sqn
P/O	Czachowski	Józef	5 OTU; 09.12.40 – 303 Sqn; 22.01.41 – 315 Sqn
P/O	Czajkowski	Franciszek	08.40 – 151 Sqn; 16.02.41 – 43 Sqn
F/O	Czaykowski	Zbigniew	5 OTU; 09.12.40 – 303 Sqn; 24.01.41 – 315 Sqn
P/O	Czapiewski	Jan	04.09.40 – 306 Sqn; 19.05.41 – †
P/O	Czarnecki	Stanisław	56 OTU; 24.03.41 – 317 Sqn; 17.04.41 – 302 Sqn
P/O	Czerniak	Jerzy Michał	21.08.40 – 302 Sqn; 02.09.40 – 5 OTU;
			26.09.40 – 302 Sqn; 25.01.41 – 315 Sqn
F/L	Czerny	Jan Tadeusz	21.08.40 – 302 Sqn; 02.09.40 – 5 OTU;
			26.09.40 – 302 Sqn; 19.12.40 – 1 PFTS
F/L	Czerwiński	Tadeusz	23.07.40 – 302 Sqn; 13.12.40 – 302 Sqn (F/Lt);
			03.05.41 – 55 OTU
P/O	Czternastek	Stanisław	12.10.40 – 32 Sqn; 12.40 – 615 Sqn; 05.02.41 – †
P/O	Daszewski	Jan Kazimierz	02.08.40 – 303 Sqn
P/O	Damm	Adam	55 OTU; 11.06.41 – 303 Sqn
Sgt	Danielewski	Jerzy	05.10.40 – 307 Sqn; 07.11.40 – RAF Kirton-in-Lindsey
Sgt	Derma	Józef	09.10.40 – 308 Sqn; 29.12.40 – 5 BGS
Sgt	Dobrut-Dobrucki	Tadeusz	5 OTU; 15.09.40 – 607 Sqn; 26.03.41 – 316 Sqn
Sgt	Domagała	Marian	05.08.40 – 238 Sqn; 06.04.41 – 302 Sqn
P/O	Drecki	Władysław	56 OTU; 18.04.41 – 303 Sqn
P/O	Drobiński	Bolesław	7 OTU; 22.08.40 – 65 Sqn; 02.03.41 – 303 Sqn
F/O	Drybański	Zygmunt	55 OTU; 16.04.41 – 315 Sqn
Sgt	Dukszto	Witold	25.10.40 – 307 Sqn; 09.05.41 – Ferry Pool
F/O	Duryasz	Marian	17.08.40 – 213 Sqn; 20.11.40 – 302 Sqn
Sgt	Duszyński	Stanisław	02.09.40 – 238 Sqn; 11.09.40 – †
F/O	Dyrgałła	Ryszard	04.10.40 – PRU; 01.02.41 – 5 AOS
Sgt	Erdt	Józef	54 OTU; 01.04.41 – 255 Sqn
F/O	Ebenrytter	Eugeniusz	15.12.40 – 307 Sqn; 16.04.41 – 6 BGS
P/O	Falkowski	Jan	12.09.40 – 32 Sqn
P/O	Ferić	Mirosław	02.08.40 – 303 Sqn
Sgt	Feruga	Józef	54 OTU; 01.04.41 – 255 Sqn
P/O	Fiedorczuk	Eugeniusz	5 OTU; 05.11.40 – 303 Sqn; 22.01.41 – 315 Sqn
F/O	Filipowicz	Józef	13.10.40 – 307 Sqn (F/Lt);
			04.11.40 – 4 FPP; 01.04.41 – 308 Sqn
Sgt	Franczak	Aleksander	55 OTU; 258 Sqn; 11.06.41 – 306 Sqn
Sgt	Frantisek	Josef	02.08.40 – 303 Sqn; 08.10.40 – †
Sgt	Frąckiewicz	Kazimierz	10.09.40 – 307 Sqn; 17.02.41 – †
F/O	Frey	Juliusz	20.09.40 – 5 OTU; 11.10.40 – 607 Sqn;
			13.11.40 – 303 Sqn (F/Lt); 22.02.41 – 316 Sqn (S/Ldr)

Rank	Name	First name	Units
Sgt	Frychel	Maksymilian	307 Sqn; 10.04.41 – †
P/O	Gabszewicz	Aleksander	5 OTU; 11.10.40 – 607 Sqn;
			13.11.40 – 303 Sqn; 22.02.41 – 316 Sqn
Sgt	Gadus	Romuald	5 OTU; 08.10.40 – 607 Sqn;
			24.11.40 – 501 Sqn; 26.02.41 – 316 Sqn
Sgt	Gallus	Paweł	02.08.40 – 303 Sqn; 02.09.40 – 5 OTU;
			27.09.40 – 3 Sqn; 27.03.41 – 316 Sqn
Sgt	Gandurski	Wiktor	10.09.40 – 307 Sqn; 10.01.41 – †
F/O	Gauze	Czeslaw	56 OTU; 01.10.40 – 85 Sqn;
			26.10.40 – 605 Sqn; 15.11.40 – †
P/O	Gayzler	Witold	307 Sqn
Sgt	Giermer	Wacław	10.09.40 – 307 Sqn; 02.10.40 – 5 OTU;
			11.10.40 – 303 Sqn; 08.11.40 – 43 Sqn;
			15.03.41 – 303 Sqn
P/O	Gil	Józef	27.09.40 – 43 Sqn; 25.10.40 – 229 Sqn;
			12.03.41 – 53 OTU; 13.04.41 – 315 Sqn
P/O	Gładych	Bolesław	57 OTU; 21.04.41 – 303 Sqn
Sgt	Głowacki	Antoni	6 OTU; 04.08.40 – 501 Sqn; ??.02.41 – 55 OTU
P/O	Głowacki	Witold Józef	12.08.40 – 145 Sqn; 31.08.40 – 605 Sqn; 24.09.40 – †
P/O	Główczyński	Czeslaw	31.07.40 – 302 Sqn
Sgt	Gmitrowicz	Władysław	24.09.40 – 306 Sqn
Sgt	Gmur	Feliks	21.08.40 – 151 Sqn; 30.08.40 – †
P/O	Gnyś	Władysław	28.07.40 – 302 Sqn; 5 OTU; 26.09.40 – 302 Sqn
P/O	Godlewski	Jerzy	74 Sqn
F/O	Goettel	Władyslaw	5 OTU; 19.10.40 – 302 Sqn; 08.12.40 – 1 AACU
F/O	Gorzula	Mieczysław	5 OTU; 229 Sqn; 607 Sqn; 12.40 – 615 Sqn;
			16.05.41 – 302 Sqn
Sgt	Gottowt	Eugeniusz	5 OTU; 15.11.40 – 607 Sqn; 26.03.41 – 316 Sqn
P/O	Gozdecki	Dariusz	5 OTU, 55 OTU; 26.03.41 – 316 Sqn
P/O	Górski	Józef	55 OTU; 303 Sqn; 16.04.41 – 316 Sqn
Sgt	Górski	Zygmunt	10.09.40 – 307 Sqn; 07.11.40 – Kirton-in-Lindsey
Sgt	Grobelny	Jan	19.03.41 – 317 Sqn
S/L	Grodzicki	Stanisław	5 OTU; 20.10.40 – 307 Sqn
Sgt	Grondowski	Stanisław	18.09.40 – 307 Sqn
F/O	Groszewski	Bernard	10.09.40 – 307 Sqn; 28.10.40 – 43 Sqn;
			21.01.41 – 315 Sqn; 21.02.41 – 43 Sqn
P/O	Grudziński	Władysław	17.10.40 – 308 Sqn;
		Mieczyslaw	??.12.40 – 615 Sqn; 22.01.41 – 315 Sqn
F/O	Gruszka	Franciszek	07.08.40 – 65 Sqn; 18.08.40 – †
F/O	Grzeszczak	Bogdan	21.08.40 – 303 Sqn; 21.04.41 – 58 OTU
P/O	Hegenbarth	Tadeusz	12.09.40 – 308 Sqn
F/O	Henneberg	Zdzisław Karol	02.08.40 – 303 Sqn; 07.09.40 – 303 Sqn (F/Lt);
			20.02.41 – 303 Sqn (S/Ldr); 12.04.41 – †
P/O	Hoyden	Tadeusz	21.09.40 – 308 Sqn; 21.01.41 – 315 Sqn;
			27.03.41 – †
Sgt	Horn	Zdzisław	24.03.41 – 303 Sqn; 02.06.41 – 58 OTU
Sgt	Illaszewicz	Władysław	54 OTU; 07.05.41 – 307 Sqn
F/L	Jakszewicz	Mieczysław	27.11.40 – 307 Sqn; 55 OTU; 7.06.41 – 32 Sqn
P/O	Jander	Witold	30.07.40 – 302 Sqn; 03.08.40 – Blackpool Depot
P/O	Janicki	Zbigniew	5 OTU; 12.10.40 – 32 Sqn; 28.11.40 – 46 Sqn;
			15.01.41 – 213 Sqn; 17.04.41 – 17 Sqn;
			23.04.41 – 307 Sqn; 03.05.41 – 302 Sqn
F/O	Jankiewicz	Jerzy	6 OTU; 18.08.40 – 601 Sqn; 22.10.40 – 303 Sqn;
			08.02.41 – 303 Sqn (Ops Room);
			13.04.41 – 303 Sqn (F/Lt)
Sgt	Jankowiak	Franciszek	02.12.40 – 307 Sqn
P/O	Jankowski	Edward	04.09.40 – 306 Sqn
F/O	Janus	Stefan	12.09.40 – 308 Sqn
F/O	Januszewicz	Wojciech	02.08.40 – 303 Sqn; 05.10.40 – †
Sgt	Jarzembowski	Stanisław	05.10.40 – 307 Sqn
Sgt	Jasiński	Wawrzyniec	23.10.41 – 306 Sqn
F/O	Jasionowski	Walerian	17.10.40 – 308 Sqn;
			12.12.40 – Kemble;
			21.04.41 – 315 Sqn (Ops Room)
P/O	Jastrzębski	Franciszek	26.07.40 – 302 Sqn; 25.10.40 – †
P/O	Jaworski	Edward	55 OTU; 07.05.41 – 605 Sqn
Sgt	Jeka	Józef	02.09.40 – 238 Sqn; 25.04.41 – 306 Sqn
F/O	Jereczek	Edmund	6 OTU; 05.09.40 – 43 Sqn;
			16?.10.40 – 229 Sqn; 08.01.41 – 25 PFTS
Sgt	Joda	Antoni	18.09.40 – 307 Sqn; 10.01.41 – †
P/O	Juszczak	Stanisław	CFS Upavon; 24.03.41 – 317 Sqn; 19.03.41 – 303 Sqn

250

Rank	Name	First name	Units
P/O	Kaczmarek	Bolesław	55 OTU; 26.05.41 – 306 Sqn
Sgt	Kaliszewski	Stanisław	10.09.40 – 307 Sqn
P/O	Kamiński	Władysław	5 OTU; 05.11.40 – 303 Sqn; 30.12.40 – 302 Sqn
Sgt	Kania	Józef	22.08.40 – 303 Sqn; 16.09.40 – 6 OTU; 06.10.40 – 303 Sqn; 22.01.41 – 315 Sqn; 22.04.41 – 4 Ferry Pool
Sgt	Karais	Jerzy	10.09.40 – 307 Sqn
Sgt	Karaszewski	Kazimierz	55 OTU; 07.05.41 – 317 Sqn
Sgt	Karubin	Stanisław	02.08.40 – 303 Sqn; 07.03.41 – 58 OTU; 55 OTU
P/O	Karwowski	Włodzimierz	302 Sqn; 317 Sqn
F/O	Karwowski	Lech	10.09.40 – 307 Sqn
P/O	Kawalecki	Tadeusz	151 Sqn; ??.??.41 – 1 AACU
P/O	Kawnik	Erwin	31.09.40 – 308 Sqn
F/O	Kawczyński	Olech Antoni	14.10.40 – 32 Sqn; 08.05.41 – †
P/O	Kazimierczuk	Kazimierz	18.10.40 – 307 Sqn; 16.02.41 – Kirton-in-Lindsey
P/O	Kędzierski	Stanisław	605 Sqn; 05.07.41 – 302 Sqn
Sgt	Kiedrzyński	Władysław	01.03.41 – Upavon OTU; 24.03.41 – 316 Sqn
P/O	Kinel	Zygmunt	5 OTU; 29.10.40 – 607 Sqn; 17.03.41 – 302 Sqn; 08.05.41 – †
Sgt	Kita	Szymon	12.09.40 – 85 Sqn; 30.09.40 – 253 Sqn
P/O	Klawe	Włodzimierz	24.09.40 – 55 OTU; 303 Sqn; 16.04.41 – 316 Sqn
P/O	Kleczkowski	Stefan	6 OTU; 23.09.40 – 302 Sqn; 09.02.41 – 10 BGS
Sgt	Klein	Zygmunt	06.08.40 – 234 Sqn; 05.10.40 – 152 Sqn; 28.11.40 – †
P/O	Kleniewski	Zbigniew	6 OTU; 23.09.40 – 302 Sqn; 05.11.40 – 1 AACU
Sgt	Kleniewski	Alfred	307 Sqn
P/O	Klozinski	Władysław	02.06.40 – 54 Sqn
P/O	Kłosin	Bronisław	57 OTU; 21.04.41 – 303 Sqn
P/O	Koc	Tadeusz	18.09.40 – 307 Sqn; 02.10.40 – 5 OTU; 11.10.40 – 303 Sqn; 08.11.40 – 245 Sqn; 13.03.41 – 317 Sqn
P/O	Koczor	Ryszard	12.09.40 – 308 Sqn; 04.12.40 – †
P/O	Kolubiński	Antoni Michał	55 OTU; 15.04.41 – 32 Sqn
F/O	Kołaczkowski	Wojciech	09.12.40 – 303 Sqn
P/O	Kołecki	Tadeusz Marian	55 OTU; 05.05.41 – 306 Sqn
Sgt	Kondras	Stanisław	10.09.40 – 307 Sqn
P/O	Kornicki	Franciszek	10.09.40 – 307 Sqn; 02.10.40 – 5 OTU; 11.10.40 – 303 Sqn; 12.40 – 615 Sqn; 22.01.41 – 315 Sqn
Sgt	Kosarz	Wihelm	20.08.40 – 302 Sqn; 02.09.40 – 5 OTU; 26.09.40 – 302 Sqn; 08.11.40 – †
F/O	Kosiński	Bronisław Kazimierz	10.09.40 – 307 Sqn; 09.10.40 – 1 SAC Old Sarum; 10.10.40 – 32 Sqn; 25.10.40 – 229 Sqn; 22.12.40 – 308 Sqn (F/Lt)
P/O	Kosmowski	Janusz	01.41 – 32 Sqn; 03.04.41 – 306 Sqn
Sgt	Kosmowski	Leon	55 OTU; 306 Sqn
Sgt	Kościk	Bronisław	11.10.40 – 303 Sqn; 08.11.40 – 245 Sqn; 13.02.41 – 317 Sqn
F/O	Koterla	Marian	31.10.40 – 307 Sqn; ??.02.41 – 229 Sqn
Sgt	Kowala	Paweł	12.09.40 – 308 Sqn
F/O	Kowalczyk	Adam	11.10.40 – 607 Sqn; 07.11.40 – 303 Sqn; 01.03.41 – 317 Sqn
Sgt	Kowalski	Jan	21.08.40 – 303 Sqn; 22.01.41 – 315 Sqn
Sgt	Kowalski	Henryk	504 Sqn
F/O	Kowalski	Julian	31.12.40 – 302 Sqn; 14.05.41 – 302 Sqn (F/Lt)
P/O	Kozłowski	Franciszek	04.07.40 – 5 OTU; 05.08.40 – 501 Sqn; 25.02.41 – 316 Sqn
S/L	Krasnodębski	Zdzisław	03.08.40 – 303 Sqn
P/O	Kratke	Tadeusz	CFS Upavon; 24.03.41 – 317 Sqn
Sgt	Krawczyński	Karol	02.08.40 – 303 Sqn; 14.10.40 – Blackpool Polish Depot; 01.06.41 – 2 CFS Cranwell
Sgt	Kremski	Jan	12.09.40 – 308 Sqn
P/O	Krepski	Walenty	7 OTU; 22.08.40 – 54 Sqn; 07.09.40 – †
Sgt	Krieger	Tadeusz	18.09.40 – 308 Sqn; 21.01.41 – 315 Sqn
Sgt	Kroczyński	Bruno	306 Sqn
Sgt	Kropiwnicki	Eugeniusz	258 Sqn
P/O	Król	Wacław	21.08.40 – 302 Sqn; 02.09.40 – 5 OTU; 26.09.40 – 302 Sqn
Sgt	Krzystyniak	Marian	05.10.40 – 307 Sqn
P/O	Krzyżanowski	Jan	15.10.40 – 307 Sqn; 54 OTU – 15.01.41
P/O	Kudrewicz	Bruno	5 OTU; 151 Sqn; 23.10.40 – 303 Sqn; 02.12.40 – 308 Sqn

251

Rank	Name	First name	Units
Sgt	Kubiak		17.05.41 – 56 Sqn
P/O	Kumiega	Tadeusz	6 OTU; 01.09.40 – 17 Sqn; 25.02.41 – 317 Sqn
F/O	Kustrzyński	Zbigniew	5 OTU; 31.08.40 – 111 Sqn; 01.09.40 – 607 Sqn; 12.11.40 – 303 Sqn
Sgt	Kwieciński	Józef	5 OTU; 04.08.40 – 145 Sqn; 12.08.40 – †
P/O	Langhamer	Zdzisław	19.09.40 – 306 Sqn
Sgt	Laskowski	Jan	05.10.40 – 307 Sqn
F/O	Lewandowski	Maksymilian	PRU; 19.10.40 – 307 Sqn
Sgt	Lipiński	Józef	05.10.40 – 307 Sqn
F/L	Łaguna	Piotr	26.07.40 – 302 Sqn; 27.05.41 – Northolt Wing (W/Cdr)
P/O	Łapka	Stanisław	6 OTU; 17.07.40 – 302 Sqn
F/O	Łapkowski	Wacław	02.08.40 – 303 Sqn; 20.02.41 – 303 Sqn (F/Lt)
S/L	Łaszkiewicz	Stefan	12.09.40 – 308 Sqn; 10.11.40 – 245 Sqn (F/O); 23.02.41 – 315 Sqn
F/O	Łazarowicz	Jerzy	28.08.40 – 307 Sqn
F/O	Łazoryk	Włodzimierz	09.10.40 – 607 Sqn; ??.12.40 – 46 Sqn; 12.40 – 257 Sqn; 15.02.41 – 308 Sqn
Sgt	Łewczyński	Ryszard	18.09.40 – 307 Sqn
P/O	Łokuciewski	Witold	02.08.40 – 303 Sqn
P/O	Łukaszewicz	Marian	23.07.40 – 302 Sqn; 30.07.40 – Blackpool; 18.09.40 – 307 Sqn; 10.10.40 – 5 OTU; 12.10.40 – 303 Sqn; 08.11.40 – 616 Sqn; 21.01.41 – 315 Sqn
P/O	Łukaszewicz	Kazimierz	6 OTU; 26.07.40 – 303 Sqn; 07.08.40 – 501 Sqn; 12.08.40 – †
P/O	Łukaszewicz	Stanisław	55 OTU; 26.03.41 – 317 Sqn
Sgt	Łydka	Mieczysław	10.09.40 – 307 Sqn
Sgt	Łysek	Antoni	20.08.40 – 302 Sqn; 02.09.40 – 5 OTU; 26.09.40 – 302 Sqn
Sgt	Machowiak	Marcin	19.09.40 – 306 Sqn
Sgt	Maciejowski	Mirosław Michał	14.09.40 – 111 Sqn; 26.09.40 – 229 Sqn; ??.10.40 – 249 Sqn; 25.02.41 – 317 Sqn
P/O	Maciński	Janusz	31.08.40 – 111 Sqn; 04.09.40 – †
Sgt	Majchrzyk	Władysław	12.09.40 – 308 Sqn
P/O	Malarowski	Andrzej	10.09.40 – 307 Sqn; 02.10.40 – 5 OTU; 11.10.40 – 303 Sqn; 08.11.40 – 43 Sqn; 25.02.41 – 317 Sqn
P/O	Malczewski	Eugeniusz	55 OTU; 07.05.41 – 605 Sqn
P/O	Malczewski	Ryszard	03.05.41 – 601 Sqn
P/O	Malinowski	Bronisław	10.09.40 – 307 Sqn; 09.10.40 – 5 OTU; 25.10.40 – 43 Sqn; ??.12.40 – 501 Sqn; 11.04.41 – 302 Sqn
Sgt	Malinowski	Jan	58 OTU; 27.03.41 – 317 Sqn
Sgt	Malinowski	Jerzy	30.10.40 – 307 Sqn
P/O	Maliński	Jan Leonard	21.08.40 – 302 Sqn; 02.09.40 – 5 OTU; 26.09.40 – 302 Sqn
P/O	Maras	Jan Kazimierz	05.41 – 601 Sqn
P/O	Marciniak	Janusz	55 OTU; 15.04.41 – 32 Sqn
Sgt	Marcinkowski	Mieczysław	151 Sqn; ??.10.40 – 501 Sqn; 01.11.40 – †
Sgt	Markiewicz	Antoni	06.08.40 – 302 Sqn; 02.02.41 – 1 Delivery Flight Croydon
P/O	Martel	Ludwik	7 OTU; 10.08.40 – 54 Sqn; 28.08.40 – 603 Sqn; 19.03.41 – 317 Sqn
F/O	Mickiewicz	Bronisław	10.09.40 – 307 Sqn; 02.10.40 – 5 OTU; 11.10.40 – 303 Sqn; 08.11.40 – 43 Sqn; 25.02.41 – 316 Sqn; 14.04.41 – 315 Sqn (F/Lt)
P/O	Mierzwa	Bogusław	21.08.40 – 303 Sqn; 02.09.40 – 5 OTU; 27.09.40 – 303 Sqn; 16.04.41 – †
P/O	Miksa	Włodzimierz	5 OTU; 23.10.40 – 303 Sqn; 22.01.41 – 315 Sqn
Sgt	Mikszo	Jan	22.11.40 – 307 Sqn; 12.02.41 – Bramcote
Sgt	Mirończuk	Ludwik	24.10.40 – 307 Sqn; 15.04.41 – 8 BGS
P/O	Moszyński	Zbigniew	21.09.40 – 308 Sqn
Sgt	Muchowski	Konrad	5 OTU; 10.09.40 – 85 Sqn; 23.10.40 – 501 Sqn; 09.03.41 – 308 Sqn
Sgt	Mudry	Włodzimierz	17.08.40 – 5 OTU; 11.09.40 – 79 Sqn; 01.12.40 – 87 Sqn; 20.12.40 – 79 Sqn; 23.02.41 – 316 Sqn
S/L	Mümler	Mieczysław	23.07.40 – 302 Sqn; 15.12.40 – CFS Upavon;

Rank	Name	First name	Units
			24.02.41 – 58 OTU
P/O	Muth	Bogdan	308 Sqn
F/O	Nartowicz	Roman	5 OTU; 01.10.40 – 607 Sqn; 21.03.41 – 316 Sqn
P/O	Narucki	Aleksander Ryszard	09.10.40 – 607 Sqn; 13.11.40 – 302 Sqn; 11.05.41 – †
Sgt	Nastorowicz	Tadeusz	6 OTU; 03.12.40 – 302 Sqn; 26.04.41 – †
P/O	Neyder	Marceli	5 OTU; 25.10.40 – 303 Sqn; 03.12.40 – 302 Sqn
F/O	Niemiec	Paweł	6 OTU; 01.09.40 – 17 Sqn; 24.02.41 – 317 Sqn
Sgt	Niewiara	Andrzej	55 OTU; 18.04.41 – 315 Sqn
Sgt	Niewolski	Marian	10.09.40 – 307 Sqn
F/L	Nikonow	Witalis	28.12.40 – 308; 11.01.41 – †
F/O	Nosowicz	Zbigniew	5 OTU; 31.08.40 – 56 Sqn; 23.02.41 – 316 Sqn
P/O	Nowak	Tadeusz	6 OTU; 10.07.40 – 253 Sqn; 13.11.40 – 303 Sqn; 24.01.41 – 315 Sqn
F/O	Nowak	Władysław	04.09.40 – 306 Sqn; 13.05.41 – 306 Sqn (F/Lt)
Sgt	Nowakiewicz	Eugeniusz Jan	20.08.40 – 302 Sqn; 02.09.40 – 5 OTU; 23.10.40 – 302 Sqn
F/O	Nowierski	Tadeusz	05.08.40 – 609 Sqn; 21.03.41 – 316 Sqn
F/O	Oleński	Zbigniew	14.08.40 – 234 Sqn; 24.08.40 – 609 Sqn; 23.03.41 – RAE Farnborough
Sgt	Olewiński	Bolesław	229 Sqn; 43 Sqn; 10.10.40 – 111 Sqn; 03.11.40 – †
F/L	Opulski	Tadeusz	02.08.40 – 303; 07.09.40 – Blackpool Polish Depot
F/O	Orzechowski	Jerzy	5 OTU; 16.09.40 – 303 Sqn; 21.09.40 – 6 OTU; 03.10.40 – 615 Sqn; 10.10.40 – 607 Sqn; 22.10.40 – 306 Sqn (S/Ldr); 15.11.40 – 245 Sqn; 29.11.40 – 615 Sqn; 07.12.40 – 308 Sqn (S/Ldr)
P/O	Orzechowski	Mirosław	5 OTU; 12.40 – 607 Sqn; 02.03.41 – 56 Sqn; 11.07.41 – 308 Sqn
Sgt	Osieleniec	Kazimierz	19.10.40 – 307 Sqn
F/O	Ostaszewski-Ostoja	Piotr	5 OTU; 05.08.40 – 609; 08.03.41 – 317 Sqn
Sgt	Ostolski	Stefan	05.10.40 – 307 Sqn
P/O	Ostowicz	Antoni	16.07.40 – 145 Sqn; 11.08.40 – †
Sgt	Ostrowski	Henryk	10.09.40 – 307 Sqn
F/L	Ozyra	Piotr	55 OTU; 15.04.41 – 317 Sqn
Sgt	Pacut	Kazimierz	307 Sqn
P/O	Paderewski	Stefan	258 Sqn; 25.03.41 – 303 Sqn
Sgt	Palak	Jan	24.07.40 – 302 Sqn; 23.09.40 – 303 Sqn
P/O	Paley	Boleslaw	55 OTU; 20.05.41 – 315 Sqn; 26.05.41 – 245 Sqn
F/O	Palusinski	Jerzy Hipolit	27.09.40 – 303 Sqn
F/L	Pankratz	Wilhelm	16.07.40 – 145 Sqn; 12.08.40 – †
Sgt	Parafinski	Mieczyslaw	12.09.40 – 308 Sqn; 26.02.41 – †
F/O	Paszkiewicz	Ludwik Witold	02.08.40 – 303 Sqn; 27.09.40 – †
Sgt	Paterek	Edward	23.07.40 – 302 Sqn; 23.09.40 – 303 Sqn; 24.01.41 – 315 Sqn; 27.03.41 – †
Sgt	Pavlovič (Czech)	Matěj	22.10.40 – 303 Sqn
Sgt	Pelik	Czesław ·	07.05.41 – 307 Sqn
F/L	Pentz	Jan	12.40 – 257 Sqn; 20.02.41 – 306 Sqn (Ops Room)
P/O	Pfeiffer	Jan	16 SFTS; 18.08.40 – 32 Sqn; 16.09.40 – 257 Sqn; 28.09.40 – 5 BGS
P/O	Piątkowski	Stanisław	11.09.40 – 79 Sqn; 25.10.40 – †
Sgt	Piątkowski	Stanisław	21.09.40 – 308 Sqn
Sgt	Pietniunas	Stanisław	14.10.40 – 307 Sqn; 23.02.41 – †
F/L	Pietraszkiew	Stanislaw	21.08.40 – 303 Sqn; 10.09.40 – 307 Sqn; 25.10.40 – 303 Sqn; 08.11.40 – 616 Sqn; 21.01.41 – 315 Sqn (S/Ldr)
P/O	Petruszka	Aleksander	56 OTU; 5 OTU; 01.11.40 – 306 Sqn; 10.03.41 – 60 OTU
Sgt	Pietrzak	Henryk	306 Sqn
P/O	Pilch	Roman	6 OTU; 17.07.40 – 302 Sqn; 20.02.41 – †
F/O	Pisarek	Marian	21.08.40 – 303 Sqn; 28.09.40 – 303 Sqn (F/Lt); 21.01.41 – 315 Sqn; 30.03.41 – 308 (F/Lt)
P/O	Pisuliński	Ignacy Stanisław	27.10.40 – AACU; 03.11.40 – 8 AACU
Sgt	Piwko	Mieczysław	30.10.40 – 307 Sqn; 15.04.41 – 8 BGS
F/O	Pniak	Karol	6 OTU; 08.08.40 – 32 Sqn; 16.09.40 – 257 Sqn; 25.11.40 – 306 Sqn; 18.04.41 – AFDU
Sgt	Podgajny	Edward	05.10.40 – 307 Sqn
Sgt	Popek	Mieczysław	10.09.40 – 307 Sqn; 09.10.40 – 5 OTU; 09.10.40 – 249 Sqn; 28.02.41 – 303 Sqn

Rank	Name	First name	Units
P/O	Popławski	Jerzy	5 OTU; 30.07.40 – 302 Sqn; 10.09.40 – 111 Sqn; 26.09.40 – 229 Sqn; 17.03.41 – 308 Sqn
Sgt	Popławski	Aleksander	607 Sqn; 11.04.41 – †
Sgt	Prętkiewicz	Franciszek	23.09.40 – 307 Sqn; 02.10.40 – 1 SAC Old Sarum; 11.10.40 – 303 Sqn; 08.11.40 – 245 Sqn; 30.11.40 – †
P/O	Przysiecki	Eugeniusz	26.11.40 – 307 Sqn
Sgt	Pudrycki	Otto	19.09.40 – 306 Sqn
Sgt	Putz	Tadeusz	10.09.40 – 307 Sqn
Sgt	Pytlak	Tadeusz	607 Sqn; 05.07.41 – 302 Sqn
P/O	Radomski	Jerzy	21.08.40 – 303 Sqn; 02.09.40 – 5 OTU; 27.09.40 – 303 Sqn; 14.04.41 – 58 OTU
P/O	Radwański	Gustaw	151 Sqn; 607 Sqn; 14.10.40 – 56 Sqn; 21.05.41 – 302 Sqn
P/O	Ranoszek	Gerard	08.12.40 – 32 Sqn; 24.04.41 – 306 Sqn
P/O	Reymer-Krzywicki	Stanisław	54 OTU; 03.41 – 151 Sqn; 10.06.41 – 23 Sqn
P/O	Retinger	Witold	5 OTU; 55 OTU; 10.12.40 – 308 Sqn
Sgt	Rogowski	Jan Aleksander	13.08.40 – 303 Sqn; 91 Sqn; 02.02.41 – 74 Sqn
F/L	Rolski	Tadeusz Henryk	22.10.40 – 306 Sqn
P/O	Rozwadowski	Mieczysław	08.08.40 – 151 Sqn; 15.08.40 – †
Sgt	Rozworski	Zdzisław	31.05.41 – 43 Sqn
P/O	Różycki	Władysław	6 OTU; 17.08.40 – 238 Sqn; 20.11.40 – 306 Sqn; 03.05.41 – 23 Sqn
Sgt	Rudel	Andrzej	04.04.41 – 307 Sqn
P/O	Rutkowski	Kazimierz	19.09.40 – 306 Sqn
Sgt	Rybacki	Tadeusz	54 OTU; 07.05.41 – 307 Sqn
P/O	Rychlicki	Bolesław	5 OTU; 55 OTU; 27.03.41 – 316 Sqn
F/O	Ryciak	Edward	03.04.41 – 23 Sqn
Sgt	Rygiel	Edmund	307 Sqn
Sgt	Rytka	Marian	5 OTU; 17.10.40 – 303 Sqn; 23.10.40 – 302 Sqn
P/O	Rzyski	Tomasz	55 OTU; 01.05.41 – 32 Sqn
Sgt	Sadawa	Stanisław	05.10.40 – 307 Sqn
P/O	Samolinski	Włodzimierz Michał	6 OTU; 16.07.40 – 253 Sqn; 26.09.40 – †
P/O	Samp	Bernard	55 OTU; 07.05.41 – 605 Sqn; 20.05.41 – †
Sgt	Sanetra	Edward	29.8.40 – 285 Sqn; 02.12.40 – 307 Sqn
Sgt	Sasak	Wilhelm	6 OTU; ??.09.40 – 32 Sqn; 145 Sqn; 30.11.40 – †
F/O	Sawicz	Tadeusz	5 OTU; 20.10.40 – 303 Sqn; 22.02.41 – 316 Sqn
Sgt	Serafin	Władysław	54 OTU; 01.04.41 – 255 Sqn; 03.06.41 – 307 Sqn
P/O	Seredyn	Antoni	12.11.40 – 32 Sqn; 13 Group HQ; 02.06.41 – 285 Sqn
P/O	Schiele	Tadeusz	58 OTU; 02.06.41 – 122 Sqn
P/O	Sikorski	Marian	55 OTU; 26.03.41 – 317 Sqn
Sgt	Siudak	Antoni	23.07.40 – 302 Sqn; 23.09.40 – 303 Sqn; 06.10.40 – †
P/O	Skalski	Stanisław	6 OTU; 03.08.40 – 302 Sqn; 12.08.40 – 501 Sqn; 25.02.41 – 306 Sqn
P/O	Skalski	Marian Janusz	55 OTU; 09.12.40 – 306 Sqn
F/O	Skalski	Henryk	46 Sqn 05.12.40 – 249 Sqn; 242 Sqn; 25.02.41 – 306 Sqn; 03.03.41 – 72 Sqn
Sgt	Skiba	Antoni	258 Sqn; 23.02.41 – 307 Sqn
F/L	Skiba	Franciszek	04.09.40 – 306 Sqn; 08.03.41 – Air Ministry
Sgt	Skibiński	Karol	307 Sqn
P/O	Skibiński	Bronisław	21.09.40 – 308 Sqn
Sgt	Skowron	Henryk	23.10.40 – 303 Sqn; 01.02.41 – 151 Sqn; 10 BGS
F/O	Słoński	Jerzy	04.09.40 – 306 Sqn
Sgt	Słoński-Ostoja	Marek	04.09.40 – 306 Sqn; 10.02.41 – 315 Sqn
F/O	Smok	Roman	14.10.40 – 307 Sqn; 23.02.41 – 307 Sqn (F/Lt); 28.05.41 – 307 Sqn (Ops Room)
P/O	Solak	Jerzy	28.08.40 – 151 Sqn; 27.09.40 – 249 Sqn; 24.02.41 – 317 Sqn
P/O	Sologub	Grzegorz	55 OTU; 02.04.41 – 307 Sqn
Sgt	Sosiński	Walerian	307 Sqn
F/O	Sporny	Kazimierz	5 OTU; 19.10.40 – 302 Sqn; 15.11.40 – 213 Sqn; ??.03.41 – ?
Sgt	Sroka	Wiktor	54 OTU; 07.05.41 – 307 Sqn
P/O	Stabrowski	Tadeusz	258 Sqn; 19.03.41 – 317 Sqn
Sgt	Staliński	Marian	607 Sqn; 15.04.41 – 315 Sqn
Sgt	Starosta	Józef	19.09.40 – 307 Sqn
P/O	Stegman	Stefan	5 OTU; 10.09.40 – 111 Sqn; 26.09.40 – 229 Sqn; 26.03.41 – 316 Sqn
F/O	Stęborowski	Michał	5 OTU; 05.08.40 – 238 Sqn; 11.08.40 – †

Rank	Name	First name	Units
Sgt	Stengierski	Jan	10.09.40 – 307 Sqn
F/O	Strasburger	Andrzej	17.05.41 – 23 Sqn
P/O	Strzembosz	Wiktor	55 OTU; 09.12.40 – 303 Sqn
Sgt	Sumara	Karol	Ferry Pool, 55 OTU; 28.03.41 – 316 Sqn
P/O	Surma	Franciszek	??.08.40 – 151 Sqn; 11.09.40 – 607 Sqn; 20.10.40 – 257 Sqn; 12.12.40 – 242 Sqn; 13.03.41 – 308 Sqn
P/O	Suryn	Leon	08.12.40 – 307 Sqn; 01.05.41 – Ferry Pool
Sgt	Suczyński	Aleksander	307 Sqn
P/O	Suszyński	Edward	17.10.40 – 306 Sqn; 30.11.40 – 4 FPP
P/O	Szabłowski	Stanisław	24.10.40 – 307 Sqn
P/O	Szafraniec	Wilhelm	12.09.40 – 151 Sqn; 29.09.40 – 607 Sqn; 14.10.40 – 56 Sqn; 23.11.40 – †
F/O	Szalewicz	Marian	303 Sqn; 02.06.41 – 316 Sqn
Sgt	Szaposznikow	Eugeniusz	02.08.40 – 303 Sqn; 14.05.41 – 8 SFTS
Sgt	Szczepański	Stanisław	307 Sqn
F/O	Szczęsny	Henryk	5 OTU; 01.08.40 – 74 Sqn; 10.12.40 – 257 Sqn; 19.12.40 – 302 Sqn; 23.02.41 – 317 Sqn (F/Lt)
F/O	Szczęśniewsk	Władysław	10.09.40 – 307 Sqn; 02.10.40 – 5 OTU; 11.10.40 – 303 Sqn; 08.11.40 – 245 Sqn; 24.01.41 – 315 Sqn (F/Lt)
Sgt	Szempliński	Lucjan	18.09.40 – 307 Sqn
Sgt	Szlagowski	Jan	5 OTU; 03.08.40 – 234 Sqn; 21.10.40 – 152 Sqn; 04.03.41 – 303 Sqn
P/O	Szmejl	Stanisław	5 OTU; 09.12.40 – 32 Sqn; 26.03.41 – 316 Sqn
F/O	Szkop	Stanisław	26.08.40 – 307 Sqn
Sgt	Szope	Henryk	55 OTU; 27.05.41 – 302 Sqn
Sgt	Sztramko	Kazimierz	55 OTU; 16.04.41 – 317 Sqn
F/L	Szulkowski	Władysław	5 OTU; 05.08.40 – 65 Sqn; 21.01.41 – 315 Sqn; 27.03.41 – †
P/O	Szumowski	Tadeusz	04.03.41 – CFS Upavon; 29.03.41 – 58 OTU; 12.04.41 – 317 Sqn
P/O	Szymankiewic	Jerzy	55 OTU; 27.03.41 – 316 Sqn
P/O	Szyszka	Feliks	12.09.40 – 308 Sqn
Sgt	Śmigielski	Jan	04.09.40 – 306 Sqn
P/O	Śniechowski	Wilhelm	10.09.40 – 307 Sqn; 09.10.40 – 310 Sqn; 02.41 – 32 Sqn
P/O	Śnieć	Czesław	1 FTS; 02.04.41 – 317 Sqn; 07.04.41 – 55 OTU; 27.05.41 – 302 Sqn
Sgt	Świton	Leon	5 OTU; 03.08.40 – 54 Sqn; 16.08.40 – 303 Sqn; 27.10.40 – 1 FTS; 03.3.41 – 8 SFTS
F/L	Tański	Józef	13.10.40 – 307 Sqn
Sgt	Talkowski	Julian	307 Sqn
P/O	Tarkowski	Czesław	56 OTU; 01.10.40 – 85 Sqn; 26.10.40 – 605 Sqn
Sgt	Thiesler	Kazimierz	54 OTU; 01.04.41 – 255 Sqn; 03.05.41 – 307 Sqn
P/O	Topolnicki	Juliusz	18.08.40 – 601 Sqn; 21.09.40 – †
Sgt	Trawicki	Maksymilian	10.09.40 – 307 Sqn
F/O	Trzebiński	Marian	55 OTU; 28.03.41 – 317 Sqn
Sgt	Turżański	Bolesław	04.09.40 – 306 Sqn; 10.02.41 – 315 Sqn; 601 Sqn
Sgt	Uher	Władysław	10.09.40 – 307 Sqn; 09.10.40 – 1 SAC Old Sarum – 257 Sqn
F/O	Urbanowicz	Witold	601 Sqn; 145 Sqn; 21.08.40 – 303 Sqn (F/Lt); 07.09.41 – 303 Sqn (acting S/Ldr); 20.10.40 – 43 Sqn; 22.10.40 – Liaison Officer; 01.04.41 – Northolt Wing HQ
P/O	Wandzilak	Stanisław	21.09.40 – 308 Sqn; 12.05.41 – 25 Group HQ
P/O	Wapniarek	Stefan	30.07.40 – 302 Sqn; 18.10.40 – †
Sgt	Waśkiewicz	Kazimierz	24.09.40 – 306 Sqn; 30.11.40 – 4 FPP; ??.12.40 – 32 Sqn
P/O	Waszkiewicz	Mieczysław	18.09.40 – 307 Sqn; 09.10.40 – 32 Sqn; 26.03.41 – 303 Sqn; 16.04.41 – †
P/O	Waltoś	Antoni	5 BGS; 02.12.40 – 307 Sqn
Sgt	Watolski	Ernest	12.09.40 – 308 Sqn
F/O	Wczelik	Antoni	20.08.40 – 302 Sqn; 02.09.40 – 5 OTU; 26.09.40 – 302 Sqn; 07.10.40 – 303 Sqn; 13.10.40 – 302 Sqn; 06.03.41 – 317 Sqn (F/Lt)
F/O	Wesołowski	Marian	5 OTU; 29.10.40 – 607 Sqn; ??.02.41 – 56 Sqn
Sgt	Wędzik	Marian	23.07.40 – 302 Sqn
Sgt	Widlarz	Stanisław	21.09.40 – 308 Sqn
P/O	Wielgus	Stanisław	12.09.40 – 308 Sqn
Sgt	Wieprzkowicz	Stanisław	24.09.40 – 306 Sqn

Rank	Name	First name	Units
P/O	Wieraszka	Władysław	5 OTU; 17.11.40 – 302 Sqn; 02.12.40 – 303 Sqn; 01.02.41 – Blackpool
F/O	Wilczewski	Wacław	15.09.40 – 5 OTU; 10.10.40 – 607 Sqn; 27.11.40 – 145 Sqn; 07.12.40 – 501 Sqn; 22.12.40 – 308 Sqn; 24.02.41 – 316 Sqn (F/Lt)
F/L	Wiórkiewicz	Mieczysław	12.09.40 – 308 Sqn; 01.04.41 – HQ FC
Sgt	Wisthal	Jan	10.09.40 – 307 Sqn
F/O	Wiśniewski	Jan	18.09.40 – 307 Sqn (F/Lt); 22.10.40 – 245 Sqn; 13.03.41 – 317 Sqn
F/O	Witorzeńć	Stefan	05.08.40 – 501 Sqn; 22.11.40 – 306 Sqn (F/Lt); 14.05.41 – 302 Sqn (F/Lt); 29.05.41 – 302 Sqn (S/Ldr)
P/O	Własnowolski	Bolesław	08.08.40 – 32 Sqn; 13.09.40 – 607 Sqn; 17.09.40 – 213 Sqn; 01.11.40 – †
Sgt	Wojciechowsk	Mirosław	13.08.40 – 303 Sqn
F/O	Woliński	Kazimierz	04.09.40 – 306 Sqn; 10.02.41 – 315 Sqn
P/O	Wolski	Jerzy	21.09.40 – 308 Sqn; 11.01.41 – †
Sgt	Woźny	Jan	10.09.40 – 307 Sqn
Sgt	Wójcicki	Antoni	19.08.40 – 213 Sqn; 11.09.40 – †
P/O	Wójcik	Karol	55 OTU; 26.03.41 – 317 Sqn
Sgt	Wójcik	Stefan	17.10.40 – 307 Sqn; 22.12.40 – Hucknall
Sgt	Wójtowicz	Stefan	02.08.40 – 303 Sqn; 11.09.40 – †
P/O	Wróblewski	Zbigniew	24.08.40 – 302 Sqn; 02.09.40 – 5 OTU; 26.09.40 – 302 Sqn; 501 Sqn
F/O	Wróblewski	Aleksander	57 OTU; 21.04.41 – 303 Sqn
Sgt	Wünsche	Kazimierz	02.08.40 – 303 Sqn
P/O	Wydrowski	Bronislaw	??.09.40 – 615 Sqn; 09.10.40 – 607 Sqn; ??.11.40 – 229 Sqn; ??.??.?? – 615 Sqn; 16.05.41 – 302 Sqn
F/O	Zadroziński	Zdzisław	02.10.40 – 307 Sqn; 09.10.40 – 5 OTU; 11.10.40 – 303 Sqn
Sgt	Zakrocki	Mieczysław	10.09.40 – 307 Sqn
P/O	Załuski	Jerzy Sergiusz	6 OTU; 23.09.40 – 302 Sqn; 17.10.40 – †
Sgt	Zaniewski	Piotr	21.09.40 – 308 Sqn; 21.01.41 – 315 Sqn; 22.01.41 – 601 Sqn
F/L	Zaremba	Jerzy	04.09.40 – 306 Sqn
P/O	Zenker	Paweł	5 OTU; 07.08.40 – 501 Sqn; 24.08.40 – †
F/O	Zieliński	Benedykt	151 Sqn; 23.10.40 – 303 Sqn; 20.12.40 – 306 Sqn
F/O	Zieliński	Stanisław	19.09.40 – 306 Sqn
P/O	Zumbach	Jan Eugeniusz	02.08.40 – 303 Sqn
P/O	Zwoliński	Ryszard	07.05.41 – 307 Sqn
F/O	Żak	Walerian	21.08.40 – 303 Sqn
P/O	Żukowski	Aleksiej	21.08.40 – 302 Sqn; 02.09.40 – 5 OTU; 26.09.40 – 302 Sqn; 18.10.40 – †
P/O	Żulikowski	Józef	19.09.40 – 306 Sqn
P/O	Żurakowski	Janusz	5 OTU; 05.08.40 – 152 Sqn; 12.08.40 – 234 Sqn; 06.10.40 – 609 Sqn; 21.03.41 – 57 OTU; 15.04.41 – 55 OTU; 16.04.41 – 56 OTU; 22.04.41 – 55 OTU

Appendix IV

LIST OF COMBAT CLAIMS BY POLISH PILOTS

19 July 1940 – 2 June 1941

italic – claims against aircraft on the ground   **bold italic** – friendly aircraft   **bold** – not claimed officially

Date	Rank	First name	Name	Unit	A/C type	Serial numbers	Code letters	Time	Claim	Place
1940										
19 July	F/O	Antoni	Ostowicz	145	Hurricane I	N2496	SO-	17.55	He 111	dest 1/2	Shoreham
31 July	F/O	Antoni	Ostowicz	145	Hurricane I		SO-		"Do 215"	dam	
8 August	F/O	Antoni	Ostowicz	145	Hurricane I	P3391	SO-	09.10	Bf 109	dest	Isle of Wight (Peewit convoy)
8 August	Sgt	Marian	Domagała	238	Hurricane I	P2989	VK-	12.30	Bf 109	dest	Isle of Wight (Peewit convoy)
8 August	Sgt	Marian	Domagała	238	Hurricane I	P2989	VK-	12.30	Bf 110	dest	Isle of Wight (Peewit convoy)
8 August	F/O	Michał	Stęborowski	238	Hurricane I	P3819	VK-	12.30	Bf 110	dest	Isle of Wight (Peewit convoy)
8 August	F/O	Antoni	Ostowicz	145	Hurricane I	N2496	SO-	16.00-16.30	Bf 109	dam	Isle of Wight (Peewit convoy)
8 August	Sgt	Józef	Kwieciński	145	Hurricane I		SO-		"He 113"	dest	
8 August	F/O	Witold	Urbanowicz	601	Hurricane I	L1819			Bf 110	dest	
9 August	Sgt	Józef	Szlagowski	234	Spitfire I	R6985	AZ-	16.30?	"Do 215" Do 17	dam	
11 August	**Sgt**	**Marian**	**Domagała**	**238**	**Hurricane I**	**P2989**	**VK-**	**10.40**	**Hurricane** [1]	**dest**	**Weymouth**
11 August	Sgt	Marian	Domagała	238	Hurricane I	P2989	VK-	10.45	Bf 109	dest	Weymouth
12 August	**Sgt**	**Józef**	**Kwieciński**	**145**	**Hurricane I**	**P3391**	**SO-**	**12.20**	**Bf 110**	**dest 1/3**	**Isle of Wight**
12 August	**F/Lt**	**Wilhelm**	**Pankratz**	**145**	**Hurricane I**	**R4176**	**SO-**	**12.20**	**Bf 110**	**dest 1/3**	**Isle of Wight**
12 August	**F/Lt**	**Wilhelm**	**Pankratz**	**145**	**Hurricane I**	**R4176**	**SO-**	**12.30**	**Bf 109**	**dam**	**Isle of Wight**
12 August	P/O	Stefan	Witorzeńć	501	Hurricane I	V7230	SD-H	12.40	Bf 110	dam	Manston
12 August	P/O	Paweł	Zenker	501	Hurricane I	P3397	SD-	11.30	Ju 87	dest	Ramsgate
12 August	F/O	Witold	Urbanowicz	145	Hurricane I	R4177	SO-	12.12	Ju 88	dest	Ventnor
12 August	P/O	Karol	Pniak	32	Hurricane I	R4106	GZ-	17.20	Bf 109	dest	Dover
12 August	Sgt	Wojciech	Kloziński	54	Spitfire I	L1042	KL-	11.55	Bf 109	dest	Dover
12 August	Sgt	Wojciech	Kloziński	54	Spitfire I	L1042	KL-	17.15-18.25	Bf 109	prob	Dover

Date	Rank	First name	Name	Unit	A/C type	Serial numbers	Code letters	Time	Claim		Place
13 August	F/O	Stanisław	Brzezina	74	Spitfire I	N3091	ZP-	07.00	"Do 215" / Do 17	dest	Thames Estuary
13 August	F/O	Stanisław	Brzezina	74	Spitfire I	N3091	ZP-	07.00	"Do 215" / Do 17	dam / [dest]	Whitstable
13 August	F/O	Tadeusz	Nowierski	609	Spitfire I	L1082	PR-A?	16.00	Bf 109	dest	Weymouth
13 August	F/O	Tadeusz	Nowierski	609	Spitfire I	L1082	PR-A?	16.00	Bf 109	dam	Weymouth
13 August	**F/O**	**Piotr**	**Ostaszewski-Ostoja**	**609**	**Spitfire I**	**R6915**	**PR-**	**16.10**	**Ju 87**	**2 prob**	**Weymouth**
13 August	F/O	Henryk	Szczęsny	74	Spitfire I	K9871	ZP-O	07.00	Do 17	dest	Thames Estuary / E of Isle of Sheppey
15 August	P/O	Stefan	Witorzeńć	501	Hurricane I	V7230	SD-H	11.30	Ju 87	dest2	Hawkinge
15 August	Sgt	Antoni	Głowacki	501	Hurricane I	V7234	SD-A	11.40	Ju 87	dest	Folkestone ?
15 August	Sgt	Antoni	Głowacki	501	Hurricane I	V7234	SD-A	11.40	Do 215	dam	Hawkinge / Folkestone ? Kent
15 August	P/O	Mieczysław	Rozwadowski	151	Hurricane I	V7410	DZ-	14.50	Bf 109	dest 1/2	Dover
15 August	P/O	Bolesław	Własnowolski	32	Hurricane I	N2671	GZ-	15.30	Bf 109	dest	off Harwich
15 August	P/O	Karol	Pniak	32	Hurricane I	N2524	GZ-	17.45	Do 17	prob	Croydon
15 August	P/O	Karol	Pniak	32	Hurricane I	N2524	GZ-	17.45	Bf 109E	dam	Croydon
15 August	F/O	Piotr	Ostaszewski-Ostoja	609	Spitfire I	L1065	PR-E	18.06	Bf 110	dest	Portland
15 August	P/O	Janusz	Żurakowski	234	Spitfire I	X4016	AZ-	18.00	Bf 110	dest	Portland ? / Middle Wallop - Isle of Wight
16 August	Sgt	Zygmunt	Klein	234	Spitfire I	P9466	AZ-	17.10	Bf 109	dest	Isle of Wight
18 August	P/O	Paweł	Zenker	501	Hurricane I		SD-	09.00~	Bf 109	dam	Whitstable
18 August	P/O	Bolesław	Własnowolski	32	Hurricane I	P3679	GZ-	13.20	"Do 215" / Do 17	dest	6m S of Biggin Hill
18 August	P/O	Karol	Pniak	32	Hurricane I	N2524	GZ-	17.30	Bf 109	dest	Canterbury
18 August	P/O	Karol	Pniak	32	Hurricane I	N2524	GZ-	17.30	Bf 109	dest	Canterbury
18 August	P/O	Bolesław	Własnowolski	32	Hurricane I	P3679	GZ-	17.30	Bf 109	dest	Chatham
18 August	P/O	Stefan	Witorzeńć	501	Hurricane I	L1868	SD-D	17.35	Bf 109	*dest1/2	Whitstable / N Goodwin Sands
18 August	P/O	Paweł	Zenker	501	Hurricane I	R4103	SD-	17.35	Bf 109	dest	Whitstable
18 August	P/O	Franciszek	Czajkowski	151	Hurricane I	P3320	DZ-Y	17.40	Bf 110	dest	Thames Estuary
18 August	**F/O**	**Franciszek**	**Gruszka**	**65**	Spitfire I	**R6713**	YT-	**13.30**	**Bf 109**	**dest**	**Preston**
20 August	S/Ldr	William Arthur John	Satchell	302	Hurricane I	P3812	WX-L	19.10	Ju 88	dest	6m SW Whiternsea

258

Date	Rank	First name	Name	Unit	A/C type	Serial numbers	Code letters	Time	Claim		Place
21 August	P/O	Stanisław	Chałupa	302	Hurricane I	P3934	WX-T	15.50	Ju 88	prob	2m E Bridglinton
21 August	F/Lt	William	Riley	302	Hurricane I			15.50	Ju 88	prob	2m E Bridglinton
22 August	P/O	Karol	Pniak	32	Hurricane I	V6546	GZ-	19.20	Do 17	dam1/2	Dover
22 August	P/O	Władysław	Szulkowski	65	Spitfire I	R6712	YT-	13.00	Bf 109	dest	Ramsgate
24 August	P/O	Stefan	Witorzeńć	501	Hurricane I	P3803	SD-Z	10.30	Ju 88	dam	Dover
24 August	Sgt	Antoni	Głowacki	501	Hurricane I	V7234	SD-A	11.30	Bf 109	dest	Ramsgate
24 August	P/O	Franciszek	Czajkowski	151	Hurricane I	V6537	DZ	13.00	Bf 109	dest	Ramsgate
24 August	Sgt	Antoni	Głowacki	501	Hurricane I	V7234	SD-A	13.00	Bf 109	prob	Ramsgate
24 August	Sgt	Antoni	Głowacki	501	Hurricane I	V7234	SD-A	15.08	Ju 88	dest	Kent coast
24 August	P/O	Karol	Pniak	32	Hurricane I	V6572	GZ-	15.40	Bf 109E	prob	Manston
24 August	Sgt	Antoni	Głowacki	501	Hurricane I	V7234	SD-A	15.40	Bf 109	dest	nr Chatham
24 August	Sgt	Antoni	Głowacki	501	Hurricane I	V7234	SD-A	16.50	Ju 88	dest	Isle of Wight
24 August	F/O	Zbigniew	Oleński	234	Spitfire I	N3279	AZ-	16.50	Bf 110	prob	mid-Channel
28 August	Sgt	Antoni	Głowacki	501	Hurricane I	P5193	SD-O	09.35	Bf 109	dest	
30 August	Sgt	Antoni	Głowacki	501	Hurricane I	P3820	SD-	16.50.	He 111	dam	
30 August	P/O	Stanisław	Skalski	501	Hurricane I	P2760	SD-B		He 111	dam	N Herne Bay
30 August	P/O	Tadeusz II	Nowak	253	Hurricane I	P2883	SW-	11.10	Do 215	prob	Gatwick
30 August	P/O	Włodzimierz	Samoliński	253	Hurricane I	P3717	SW-	11.15	Bf 110	dest	Redhill
30 August	P/O	Franciszek	Surma	151	Hurricane I		DZ-	16.20	He 111	prob	Radlett
30 August	F/O	Ludwik	Paszkiewicz	303	Hurricane I	R4217	RF-V	16.35	"Do 215" (Bf 110)	dest	St Albans
30 August	P/O	Stanisław	Skalski	501	Hurricane I	P2760	SD-B	16.50	He 111	dest	Dungeness ? N Herne Bay
31 August	F/O	Jerzy	Jankiewicz	601	Hurricane I	R4214	UF-	08.40~	Bf 109	dam	
31 August	P/O	Franciszek	Czajkowski	151	Hurricane I	P3301	DZ-	10.25	Bf 109	prob	Thames Estuary
31 August	Sgt	Antoni	Głowacki	501	Hurricane I	V6540	SD-P	13.00	Do 17	dest	Gravesend
31 August	P/O	Tadeusz II	Nowak	253	Hurricane I	P2883	SW-	13.00	He 111	dest	Biggin Hill
31 August	P/O	Stanisław	Skalski	501	Hurricane I	P5194	SD-J	13.15	Bf 109	dest	Gravesend ? Hornchurch
31 August	P/O	Mirosław	Ferić	303	Hurricane I	P3974	RF-J	18.25	Bf 109	dest	E Biggin Hill
31 August		Zdzisław	Henneberg	303	Hurricane I	V7290	RF-H	18.25	Bf 109	dest	E Biggin Hill
31 August	Sgt	Stanisław	Karubin	303	Hurricane I	R2688	RF-F	18.25	Bf 109	dest	E Biggin Hill
31 August	S/Ldr	Ronald Gustave	Kellett	303	Hurricane I	R4178	RF-G	18.25	Bf 109	dest	E Biggin Hill
31 August	Sgt	Eugeniusz	Szaposznikow	303	Hurricane I	V7242	RF-B	18.25	Bf 109	dest	E Biggin Hill
31 August		Kazimierz	Wünsche	303	Hurricane I	V7244	RF-C	18.25	Bf 109	dest	E Biggin Hill
1 September	Sgt	Stanisław	Skalski	501	Hurricane I	P2329	SD-	07.30	Ju 88 ?	dam	Tunbridge Wells
2 September	P/O	Stefan	Witorzeńć	501	Hurricane I	L1868	SD-D	07.30	Do 17	dest	North Kent ? nr Newchurch

Date	Rank	First name	Name	Unit	A/C type	Serial numbers	Code letters	Time	Claim		Place
2 September	P/O	Mirosław	Ferić	303	Hurricane I	R4178	RF-G	17.50	Bf 109	prob	nr Dover -> FC
2 September	Sgt	Josef	František	303	Hurricane I	P3975	RF-U	17.50	Bf 109	dest	nr Dover 2/3m from sea
2 September	F/O	Zdzisław	Henneberg	303	Hurricane I	V7246	RF-D	17.50	Bf 109	dam	nr Dover 8m ins F
2 September	Sgt	Jan	Rogowski	303	Hurricane I	R4217	RF-V	17.50	Bf 109	dest	nr Dover 10m from FC
2 September	P/O	Stanisław	Skalski	501	Hurricane I	V7230	SD-F/H	17.50	Bf 109	2 dest	North Kent ? Maidstone-Ashford
3 September	Sgt	Josef	František	303	Hurricane I	P3975	RF-U	15.40	"He 113" (Bf 109)	dest	mid Channel from Dover
4 September	P/O	Tadeusz II	Nowak	253	Hurricane I	P2883	SW-	13.30	Bf 110	dest	Brooklands
4 September	P/O	Włodzimierz	Samoliński	253	Hurricane I		SW-	13.30	Bf 110	dest	S of Brooklands
4 September	P/O	Jerzy	Jankiewicz	601	Hurricane I	R4214	UF-	14.00	Bf 110	dam	Worthing
4 September	Sgt	Zygmunt	Klein	234	Spitfire I	R6896	AZ-	13.30	Bf 110	dest	Haslemere
4 September	F/O	Zbigniew	Oleński	234	Spitfire I	X4182	AZ-	13.20	Bf 110	dest	Haslemere
4 September	Sgt	Józef	Szlagowski	234	Spitfire I	X4251	AZ-	13.20	Bf 110	dest	Haslemere
4 September	Sgt	Józef	Szlagowski	234	Spitfire I	X4251	AZ-	13.20	Do 17	dest?	Haslemere
5 September	**P/O**	**Stanisław**	**Skalski**	**501**	**Hurricane I**	**V6644**	**SD-B**	15.05	**He 111**	**dest?**	**nr Channel**
5 September	**P/O**	**Stanisław**	**Skalski**	**501**	**Hurricane I**	**V6644**	**SD-B**	15.05	**Bf 109E**	**dest?**	**nr Channel**
5 September	**P/O**	**Stanisław**	**Skalski**	**501**	**Hurricane I**	**V6644**	**SD-B**		**Bf 109E**		
5 September	F/Lt	Athol Stanhope	Forbes	303	Hurricane I	R4217	RF-V	15.05	Ju 88	dest	Thames Haven
5 September	Sgt	Josef	František	303	Hurricane I	R4175	RF-R	15.05	Ju 88	dest	Thames Haven
5 September	Sgt	Stanisław	Karubin	303	Hurricane I	R4175	RF-R	15.05	Bf 109E	dest	Thames Haven
5 September	Sgt	Stanisław	Karubin	303	Hurricane I	P3975	RF-U	15.05	Bf 109E	dest	Thames Haven
5 September	S/Ldr	Ronald Gustave	Kellett	303	Hurricane I	P3975	RF-U	15.05	Bf 109E	dest	Thames Haven
5 September	S/Ldr	Ronald Gustave	Kellett	303	Hurricane I	V7284	RF-A	15.05	Bf 109	dest	Thames Haven
5 September	F/O	Wacław	Łapkowski	303	Hurricane I	V7284	RF-A	15.05	Bf 109	prob	Thames Haven
5 September	Sgt	Kazimierz	Wünsche	303	Hurricane I	P2985	RF-Z	15.05	Ju 88	dest	Thames Haven
5 September	P/O	Janusz	Żurakowski	234	Spitfire I	V7289	RF-S	15.05	Bf 109	dest	Isle of Sheppey
						N3279	AZ-	15.38	Bf 109	dest	- Hastings
6 September	P/O	Mirosław	Ferić	303	Hurricane I	P3700	RF-E	09.00	Bf 109	dest	Sevenoaks
6 September	F/Lt	Athol Stanhope	Forbes	303	Hurricane I	R4179	RF-Q	09.00	Bf 109	dest	Sevenoaks
6 September	F/Lt	Athol Stanhope	Forbes	303	Hurricane I	R4179	RF-Q	09.00	Bf 109	prob	Sevenoaks
6 September	Sgt	Josef	František	303	Hurricane I	R4175	RF-R	09.00	Bf 109	dest	Sevenoaks
6 September	Sgt	Stanisław	Karubin	303	Hurricane I	V7290	RF-H	09.00	He 111	dest	Sevenoaks
6 September	S/Ldr	Ronald Gustave	Kellett	303	Hurricane I	V7284	RF-A	09.00	Do 215	dest	Sevenoaks
6 September	F/O	Witold	Urbanowicz	303	Hurricane I	V7242	RF-B	09.00	Bf 109	dest	Sevenoaks
6 September	Sgt	Kazimierz	Wünsche	303	Hurricane I	V7289	RF-S	09.00	Bf 109	dest	Sevenoaks

Date	Rank	First name	Name	Unit	A/C type	Serial numbers	Code letters	Time	Claim		Place
6 September	Sgt	Kazimierz	Wünsche	303	Hurricane I	V7289	RF-S	09.00	Bf 109	prob	Sevenoaks
6 September	F/O	Juliusz	Topolnicki	601	Hurricane I	P3382	UF-	09.30	Bf 109	dest1/2	Mayfield
6 September	F/O	Janusz	Topolnicki	601	Hurricane I	P3382	UF-	09.30	Bf 109	prob	Sutton Valence
6 September	P/O	Janusz	Żurakowski	234	Spitfire I	N3279	AZ-	09.40	Bf 109	dest	N Beachy Head
6 September	**F/O**	**Wojciech**	**Januszewicz**	**303**	**Hurricane I**	**P3089**	**RE-F**	**15.45-**	**Bf 110**	**prob**	
7 September	P/O	Jan Kazimierz	Daszewski	303	Hurricane I	P3890	RF-N	17.00	Do 215	dest	Canterbury Gate
7 September	P/O	Jan Kazimierz	Daszewski	303	Hurricane I	P3890	RF-N	17.00	Do 215	prob	Canterbury Gate
7 September	F/Lt	Athol Stanhope	Forbes	303	Hurricane I	R4217	RF-V	17.00	Do 215	dest	Essex
7 September	F/O	Zdzisław	Henneberg	303	Hurricane I	V6605	YO-N	17.00	Bf 109	prob	Essex
7 September	F/O	Zdzisław	Henneberg	303	Hurricane I	V6605	YO-N	17.00	Bf 109	dest	Essex
7 September	P/O	Witold	Łokuciewski	303	Hurricane I	P3975	RF-U	17.00	Do 215	dest	Essex
7 September	P/O	Witold	Łokuciewski	303	Hurricane I	P3975	RF-U	17.00	Do 215	prob	Essex
7 September	F/O	Ludwik	Paszkiewicz	303	Hurricane I	V7235	RF-M	17.00	Do 215	dest	Essex
7 September	F/O	Ludwik	Paszkiewicz	303	Hurricane I	V7235	RF-M	17.00	Do 215	dest	Essex
7 September	F/O	Marian	Pisarek	303	Hurricane I	R4173	RF-T	17.00	Bf 109	dest	Essex
7 September	Sgt	Eugeniusz	Szaposznikow	303	Hurricane I	V7244	RF-C	17.00	Do 215	dest	Essex
7 September	Sgt	Eugeniusz	Szaposznikow	303	Hurricane I	V7244	RF-C	17.00	Bf 109	dest	Essex
7 September	F/O	Witold	Urbanowicz	303	Hurricane I	R2685	RF-G	17.00	Do 215	dest	Essex
7 September	F/O	Witold	Urbanowicz	303	Hurricane I	R2685	RF-G	17.00	Bf 109	prob	Essex
7 September	Sgt	Stefan	Wójtowicz	303	Hurricane I	V7290	RF-H	17.00	Do 215	dest	Essex
7 September	Sgt	Stefan	Wójtowicz	303	Hurricane I	V7290	RF-H	17.00	Do 215	dest	Essex
7 September	P/O	Jan	Zumbach	303	Hurricane I	V7242	RF-B	17.00	Do 215	dest	Essex
7 September	Sgt	Jan	Zumbach	303	Hurricane I	V7242	RF-B	17.00	Do 215	dest	SE London
7 September	Sgt	Zygmunt	Klein	234	Spitfire I	R6896	AZ-	18.15	Do 17	prob	Essex
7 September	F/O	Tadeusz	Nowierski	609	Spitfire I	R6922	PR-	17.30	Do 17	prob	
9 September	Sgt	Josef	František	303	Hurricane I	P3975	RF-U	18.00	Bf 109	dest	Horsham ar
9 September	Sgt	Josef	František	303	Hurricane I	P3975	RF-U	18.00	He 111	dest	nr Beachy Head
9 September	F/Lt	John Alexander	Kent	303	Hurricane I	V6665	RF-J	18.00	Bf 110	dest	Horsham ar
9 September	F/Lt	John Alexander	Kent	303	Hurricane I	V6665	RF-J	18.00	Ju 88	prob	nr Beachy Head
9 September	P/O	Jan	Zumbach	303	Hurricane I	R2685	RF-G	18.00	Bf 109	dest	Horsham ar
9 September	P/O	Jan	Zumbach	303	Hurricane I	R2685	RF-G	18.30	Bf 109	prob	nr Beachy Head
11 September	F/O	Marian	Duryasz	213	Hurricane I	P3618	AK-A	16.30	Bf 110	dest	Selsey Bill
11 September	P/O	Władysław	Różycki	238	Hurricane I	V7242	VK-	15.45	He 111	dest	Lingfield
11 September	Sgt	Stefan	Wójtowicz	303	Hurricane I	V7242	RF-B	16.00	Bf 110	dest	Horsham ar
11 September	Sgt	Stefan	Wójtowicz	303	Hurricane I	V7242	RF-B	16.00	Bf 110	prob	Horsham ar
11 September	Sgt	Michał	Brzezowski	303	Hurricane I	V6667	RF-K	16.00	He 111	dest	Horsham ar
11 September	Sgt	Michał	Brzezowski	303	Hurricane I	V6667	RF-K	16.00	He 111	dest	Horsham ar
11 September	F/Lt	Athol Stanhope	Forbes	303	Hurricane I	V7465	RF-V	16.00	Do 215	dest	Horsham ar
11 September	F/Lt	Athol Stanhope	Forbes	303	Hurricane I	V7465	RF-V	16.00	Do 215	dest	Horsham ar

Date	Rank	First name	Name	Unit	A/C type	Serial numbers	Code letters	Time	Claim		Place
11 September	Sgt	Josef	František	303	Hurricane I	V7289	RF-S	16.00	Bf 109	dest	Horsham ar
11 September	Sgt	Josef	František	303	Hurricane I	V7289	RF-S	16.00	Bf 109	dest	Horsham ar
11 September	Sgt	Josef	František	303	Hurricane I	V7289	RF-S	16.00	He 111	dest	Horsham ar
11 September	F/O	Zdzisław	Henneberg	303	Hurricane I	P3939	RF-H	16.00	Bf 109	dest	Horsham ar
11 September	F/O	Zdzisław	Henneberg	303	Hurricane I	P3939	RF-H	16.00	He 111	dest	Horsham ar
11 September	P/O	Witold	Łokuciewski	303	Hurricane I	L2099	RF-O	16.00	Do 215	dest	Horsham ar
11 September	P/O	Witold	Łokuciewski	303	Hurricane I	L2099	RF-O	16.00	Bf 109	dest	Horsham ar
11 September	F/O	Ludwik	Paszkiewicz	303	Hurricane I	V7235	RF-M	16.00	Bf 110	dest	Horsham ar
11 September	Sgt	Eugeniusz	Szaposznikow	303	Hurricane I	V7244	RF-C	16.00	Bf 110	dest	Horsham ar
11 September	Sgt	Eugeniusz	Szaposznikow	303	Hurricane I	V7244	RF-C	16.00	Bf 110	dest	Horsham ar
11 September	P/O	Jan	Zumbach	303	Hurricane I	R2685	RF-G	16.00	Bf 109	dest	Horsham ar
11 September	P/O	Stefan	Witorzeńć	501	Hurricane I	P5194	SD-	16.00	Do 215	dest1/2 ?	Maidstone ?
										dest1/5	Thames Estuary
11 September	Sgt	Jan	Budziński	605	Hurricane I		UP-	16.00	Bf 109	dest	Wrotham
11 September	P/O	Witold	Głowacki	605	Hurricane I		UP-	16.00	Bf 110	dest	Lingfield
11 September	F/O	Henryk	Szczęsny	74	Spitfire I	X4167	ZP-	16.00	Bf 110	dest	Thames Estuary ?
13 September	P/O	Tadeusz II	Nowak	253	Hurricane I	N2455	SW-	15.40-16.00	He 111	dam	London ar
13 September	**F/O**	**Marian**	**Duryasz**	**213**	**Hurricane I**	**V6866**	**AK-D**	**16.10-**	**balloon**	**dest**	Hastings area
15 September	F/O	Marian	Duryasz	213	Hurricane I	P3174	AK-G	12.30	Do 17	dest	Edenbridge
15 September	P/O	Paweł	Niemiec	17	Hurricane I	P3788	YB-	14.00~	Do 17	dam	
15 September	P/O	Władysław	Różycki	238	Hurricane I	P3618	VK-		He 111	dam	
15 September	Sgt	Tadeusz	Andruszków	303	Hurricane I	P3939	RF-H	12.00	Do 215	dest1/2	
15 September	P/O	Mirosław	Ferić	303	Hurricane I	R2685	RF-G	12.00	Bf 109	dest	S London to Hastings
15 September	Sgt	Josef	František	303	Hurricane I	P3089	RF-P	12.00	Bf 110	dest	S London to Hastings
15 September	F/O	Zdzisław	Henneberg	303	Hurricane I	P3120	RF-A	12.00	Do 215	dest	S London to Hastings
15 September	F/O	Zdzisław	Henneberg	303	Hurricane I	P3120	RF-A	12.00	Bf 109	dest	S London to Hastings
15 September	P/O	Witold	Łokuciewski	303	Hurricane I	P2903	RF-Z	12.00	Bf 109	dest	S London to Hastings
15 September	F/O	Ludwik	Paszkiewicz	303	Hurricane I	V7235	RF-M	12.00	Bf 109	dest	S London to Hastings
15 September	F/O	Marian	Pisarek	303	Hurricane I	V7465	RF-V	12.00	Bf 109	dest	S London to Hastings

Date	Rank	First name	Name	Unit	A/C type	Serial numbers	Code letters	Time	Claim	Place
15 September	Sgt	Miroslaw	Wojciechowski	303	Hurricane I	V6673	RF-U	12.00	Do 215	S London to Hastings
15 September	Sgt	Miroslaw	Wojciechowski	303	Hurricane I	V6673	RF-U	12.00	Bf 109	S London to Hastings
15 September	P/O	Jan	Zumbach	303	Hurricane I	P3577	RF-E	12.00	Bf 109	S London to Hastings
15 September	P/O	Stanisław	Chałupa	302	Hurricane I	P3923	WX-U	12.10	Do 17	SE London
15 September	P/O	Stanisław	Chałupa	302	Hurricane I	P3923	WX-U	12.10	Do 215	SE London
15 September	F/Lt	Tadeusz	Chłopik	302	Hurricane I	P2954	WX-E	12.10	Do 215	SE London
15 September	F/Lt	Tadeusz	Chłopik	302	Hurricane I	P2954	WX-E	12.10	Do 17	SE London
15 September	F/O	Tadeusz	Czerwiński	302	Hurricane I	V6571	WX-Q	12.10	Do 17	SE London
15 September	F/Lt	Franciszek	Jastrzębski	302	Hurricane I	R2684	WX-B	12.10	Do 17	SE London
15 September	F/O	Julian	Kowalski	302	Hurricane I	P3935	WX-D	12.10	"Do 215"	SE London
15 September	P/O	Stanisław	Łapka	302	Hurricane I	V6569	WX-K	12.10	Do 17	SE London
15 September	Sgt	Jan	Palak	302	Hurricane I	V7417	WX-T	12.10	Bf 109	SE London
15 September	Sgt	Jan	Palak	302	Hurricane I	V7417	WX-T	12.10	Do 17	SE London
15 September	Sgt	Edward	Paterek	302	Hurricane I	P3086	WX-Z	12.10	He 111	SE London
15 September	S/Ldr	William Arthur John	Satchell	302	Hurricane I	P3812	WX-L	12.10	Do 215	SE London
15 September	S/Ldr	William Arthur John	Satchell	302	Hurricane I	P3812	WX-L	12.10	Do 17	London
15 September	Sgt	Antoni	Siudak	302	Hurricane I	P3867	WX-F	12.10	Do 17	London
15 September	Sgt	Marian	Wędzik	302	Hurricane I	P2752	WX-R	12.10	Do 17	SE London
15 September	F/O	Julian	Kowalski	302	Hurricane I	P3935	WX-D	14.25	Do 17	SE London
15 September	F/O	Julian	Kowalski	302	Hurricane I	P3935	WX-D	14.25	Do 17	N London
15 September	**P/O**	**Edward**	**Pilch**	**302**	**Hurricane I**	**P3086**	**WX-Z**	**14.45**	**Do 17**	**N London**
15 September	P/O	Edward	Pilch	302	Hurricane I	P3086	WX-Z	14.45	Do 215	
15 September	S/Ldr	William Arthur John	Satchell	302	Hurricane I	P2752	WX-R	14.45	Bf 109	
15 September	P/O	Miroslaw	Ferić	303	Hurricane I	R2685	RF-G	15.00	Bf 110	London
15 September	Sgt	Józef	Jeka	238	Hurricane I	P3219	VK-	15.00	Bf 110	Gravesend
15 September	**Sgt**	**Józef**	**Jeka**	**238**	**Hurricane I**	**P3219**	**VK-**	**15.00**	**unident**	**S London**
15 September	S/Ldr	Ronald Gustave	Kellett	303	Hurricane I	V7465	RF-V	15.00	Do 215	Gravesend
15 September	S/Ldr	Ronald Gustave	Kellett	303	Hurricane I	V7465	RF-V	15.00	Bf 110	Gravesend
15 September	F/O	Witold	Urbanowicz	303	Hurricane I	V6684	RF-F	15.00	Do 215	Gravesend
15 September	F/O	Witold	Urbanowicz	303	Hurricane I	V6684	RF-F	15.00	Do 215	Gravesend
15 September	P/O	Boleslaw	Własnowolski	607	Hurricane I		AF-	15.00	Do 17	near Poole
15 September	Sgt	Miroslaw	Wojciechowski	303	Hurricane I	V6673	RF-U	15.00	Bf 109	Gravesend
15 September	F/O	Walerian	Żak	303	Hurricane I	L2099	RF-O	15.00	Do 215	Gravesend
17 September	Sgt	Miroslaw	Wojciechowski	303	Hurricane I	P3975	RF-U	16.00	Bf 109	Thames Estuary

263

Date	Rank	First name	Name	Unit	A/C type	Serial numbers	Code letters	Time	Claim		Place
18 September	Sgt		8 pilots	303	Hurricane I		RF-	13.15	Do 215	dest	Yalding
18 September	Sgt	Josef	František	303	Hurricane I	V7465	RF-V	13.15	Bf 109	dest	West Malling
18 September	F/O	Antoni	Głowacki	501	Hurricane I	P5193	SD-	13.15	Bf 109	prob	Maidstone
18 September	F/Lt	Julian	Kowalski	302	Hurricane I	P3935	WX-D	17.15	"Do 215"	prob	S London
18 September	F/Lt	James Nigel Watts	Farmer	302	Hurricane I	V6734	WX-K	17.20	Ju 88	dam	Thames Estuary
18 September	F/Lt	Franciszek	Jastrzębski	302	Hurricane I	P3930	WX-X	17.20	Do 17	prob	Thames Estuary
18 September	W/Cdr	Mieczysław	Mümler	302	Hurricane I	P3538	WX-Z	17.20	Do 17	dest	Thames Estuary
18 September	Sgt	Edward	Paterek	302	Hurricane I	P3086	WX-J	17.20	Ju 88	dest	near Romford
18 September	S/Ldr	William Arthur John	Satchell	302	Hurricane I	P3812	WX-L	17.20	Do 215	dest	Thames Estuary
18 September	P/O	Stefan	Wapniarek	302	Hurricane I	P3924	WX-V	17.20	Ju 88	dest	Thames Estuary
18 September	P/O	Włodzimerz	Karwowski	302	Hurricane I	P3085	WX-A	17.23	Ju 88	dest	Thames Estuary
18 September	P/O	Edward	Pilch	302	Hurricane I	V7417	WX-T	17.23	Ju 88	dest	Thames Estuary
18 September	F/Lt	William	Riley	302	Hurricane I	V6735	WX-M	17.30	Ju 88	dest	Thames Estuary
18 September	F/O	William	Riley	302	Hurricane I	V6735	WX-M	17.30	Ju 88	prob	Mildenhall
19 September	F/Lt	Julian	Kowalski	302	Hurricane I	P3935	WX-D	11.00	Ju 88	dest	Thames Estuary
23 September	F/Lt	John Alexander	Kent	303	Hurricane I	V6681	RF-B	10.00	Bf 109	dest	to Calais
23 September	F/Lt	John Alexander	Kent	303	Hurricane I	V6681	RF-B	10.00	Fw 58 [2]	dam	Channel
23 September	Sgt	Eugeniusz	Szaposznikow	303	Hurricane I	V7244	RF-C	10.00	Bf 109	dest	mid-Channel
23 September	P/O	Witold	Głowacki	605	Hurricane I	P3583	UP-		Bf 109	dam	near Tunbridge Wells
24 September	P/O	Witold	Głowacki	605	Hurricane I	P3832	UP-P	16.50	Do 17	dest1/2	Boulogne
25 September	P/O	Jerzy	Jankiewicz	601	Hurricane I	V6666	UF-J	11.20-12.30	Bf 110	dest	Yeovil
25 September	P/O	Władysław	Różycki	238	Hurricane I	P3618	VK-	12.00	He 111	dest	S Yeovil
25 September	**F/O**	**Tadeusz**	**Nowierski**	**609**	**Spitfire I**	**N3223**	**PR-M**	**11.30**	**He 111**	**dest**	**Bristol**
26 September	F/O	Marian	Duryasz	213	Hurricane I	V6541	AK-I	16.30	He 111	prob	Isle of Wight
26 September	P/O	Franciszek	Surma	607	Hurricane I		AF-	16.10	Bf 109	dest	15-20m SE of St. Catherine's Point
26 September	Sgt	Józef	Jeka	238	Hurricane I	L1998	VK-	16.30	He 111	dest	Isle of Wight
26 September	Sgt	Józef	Jeka	238	Hurricane I	L1998	VK-	16.30	He 111	dest	Isle of Wight
26 September	Sgt	Tadeusz	Andruszkow	303	Hurricane I	V6665	RF-J	16.30	Bf 109	dest	Portsmouth
26 September	Sgt	Marian	Belc	303	Hurricane I	V6673	RF-U	16.30	He 111	dest	Portsmouth
26 September	F/Lt	Athol Stanhope	Forbes	303	Hurricane I	V7465	RF-V	16.30	He 111	dest	Portsmouth
26 September	Sgt	Josef	František	303	Hurricane I	R4175	RF-R	16.30	He 111	dest	Portsmouth
26 September	Sgt	Josef	František	303	Hurricane I	R4175	RF-R	16.30	He 111	dest	Portsmouth
26 September	S/Ldr	Ronald Gustave	Kellett	303	Hurricane I	V6681	RF-B	16.30	Bf 109	dest	Portsmouth
26 September	Sgt	Jan	Kowalski	303	Hurricane I	P3089	RF-P	16.30	Bf 109	dest	Portsmouth

Date	Rank	First name	Name	Unit	A/C type	Serial numbers	Code letters	Time	Claim	Place
26 September	F/O	Ludwik	Paszkiewicz	303	Hurricane I	V7235	RF-M	16.30	He 111	dest	Portsmouth
26 September	F/O	Witold	Urbanowicz	303	Hurricane I	P3901	RF-E	16.30	He 111	dest	Portsmouth
26 September	P/O	Jan	Zumbach	303	Hurricane I	V6684	RF-F	16.30	He 111	dest	Portsmouth
26 September	P/O	Jan	Zumbach	303	Hurricane I	V6684	RF-F	16.30	Bf 109	dest	Portsmouth
26 September	F/O	Walerian	Żak	303	Hurricane I	V7289	RF-S	16.30	He 111	dest	Portsmouth
26 September	F/O	Walerian	Żak	303	Hurricane I	V7289	RF-S	16.30	He 111	dam	Portsmouth
26 September	**F/O**	**Walerian**	**Żak**	**303**	**Hurricane I**	**V7289**	**RF-S**	**16.30**	**He 111**	**dest**	**Horsham**
26 September	P/O	Bogdan	Grzeszczak	303	Hurricane I	P3120	RF-A	16.40	He 111	dest	S Portsmouth
27 September	Sgt	Józef	Jeka	238	Hurricane I	P3836	VK-		Bf 110	dest1/2	S Bristol
27 September	P/O	Mirosław	Ferić	303	Hurricane I	V6681	RF-B	09.20	Bf 109	dest	Horsham
27 September	P/O	Mirosław	Ferić	303	Hurricane I	V6681	RF-B	09.20	He 111	dest	between Croydon and Gatwick
27 September	F/Lt	Athol Stanhope	Forbes	303	Hurricane I	L2099	RF-O	09.20	He 111	dest	Horsham
27 September	Sgt	Josef	František	303	Hurricane I	R4175	RF-R	09.20	He 111	dest	Horsham
27 September	Sgt	Josef	František	303	Hurricane I	R4175	RF-R	09.20	Bf 110	dest	Gatwick
27 September	P/O	Bogdan	Grzeszczak	303	Hurricane I	V7244	RF-C	09.20	Bf 109	dest	Horsham
27 September	P/O	Zdzisław	Henneberg	303	Hurricane I	V7246	RF-D	09.20	Bf 109	dest	Horsham
27 September	Sgt	Jan	Kowalski	303	Hurricane I	P3089	RF-P	09.20	He 111	dam	Horsham ar
27 September	F/O	Witold	Urbanowicz	303	Hurricane I	P3901	RF-E	09.20	"Do 17"	dest	Horsham ar 35m S London
27 September	F/O	Witold	Urbanowicz	303	Hurricane I	P3901	RF-E	09.20	Bf 110	dest	Horsham ar
27 September	P/O	Jan	Zumbach	303	Hurricane I	V6684	RF-F	09.20	Bf 109	dest	Horsham
27 September	Sgt	Jan	Budziński	605	Hurricane I		UP-	09.30	Bf 110	dest	Oxted
27 September	F/Lt	John Alexander	Kent	303	Hurricane I	V6684	RF-F	15.25	Ju 88	dest	London ->
27 September	Sgt	Eugeniusz	Szaposznikow	303	Hurricane I	V7244	RF-C	15.25	Bf 109	dest	London -> Hastings
27 September	F/O	Witold	Urbanowicz	303	Hurricane I	P3901	RF-E	15.25	Ju 88	dest	London -> Hastings
27 September	F/O	Witold	Urbanowicz	303	Hurricane I	P3901	RF-E	15.25	Ju 88	dest	London -> Hastings
27 September	F/O	Tadeusz	Nowierski	609	Spitfire I	N3223	PR-M	11.00	Bf 110	dam	Portland
28 September	P/O	Władysław	Różycki	238	Hurricane I	P3618	VK-	14.40	Bf 109	dest	Isle of Wight
29 September	F/O	Janusz	Żurakowski	234	Spitfire I	N3191	AZ-	13.45	Bf 110	prob1/2	5m S Exmouth
30 September	Sgt	Józef	Jeka	238	Hurricane I	P3219	VK-		Bf 110	dam	20m S Portland
30 September	F/O	Witold	Urbanowicz	303	Hurricane I	P3901	RF-E	13.35	Bf 109	dest	S coast - Channel
30 September	F/O	Witold	Urbanowicz	303	Hurricane I	P3901	RF-E	13.35	Bf 109	dest	S coast - Channel
30 September	F/O	Witold	Urbanowicz	303	Hurricane I	P3901	RF-E	13.35	Do 215	dest	S coast - Channel
30 September	Sgt	Stanisław	Karubin	303	Hurricane I	V7504	RF-G	14.00	Bf 109	dest	SE London & Channel

Date	Rank	First name	Name	Unit	A/C type	Serial numbers	Code letters	Time	Claim	Place
30 September	P/O	Jerzy	Radomski	303	Hurricane I	P3663	RF-H	14.00	Do 215	dest1/2	Dungeness & Channel
30 September	F/O	Witold	Urbanowicz	303	Hurricane I	P3901	RF-E	16.35	Bf 109	dest	S London
30 September	Sgt	Josef	František	303	Hurricane I	L2099	RF-O	16.50	Bf 109	dest	Brooklands
30 September	Sgt	Josef	František	303	Hurricane I	L2099	RF-O	16.50	Bf 109	prob	Brooklands
30 September	F/O	Tadeusz	Nowierski	609	Spitfire I	R6961	PR-P	17.15	Bf 109	dest	Warmwell
30 September	F/O	Tadeusz	Nowierski	609	Spitfire I	R6961	PR-P	17.15	Bf 109	dam	Warmwell
1 October	F/Lt	John Alexander	Kent	303	Hurricane I	V6681	RF-B	14.00	Bf 109	dest	North Foreland
1 October	F/Lt	John Alexander	Kent	303	Hurricane I	V6681	RF-B	14.00	Bf 109	prob	North Foreland
2 October	P/O	Ludwik	Martel	603	Spitfire	X4274	XT-P	9.20-10.37	Bf 109	dam	
5 October	Sgt	Marian	Belc	303	Hurricane I	V7235	RF-M	11.40	Bf 110	dest	Rochester to Channel
5 October	P/O	Mirosław	Ferič	303	Hurricane I	V6681	RF-B	11.40	Bf 110	dest	nr Lympne Rochester to Channel
5 October	F/O	Zdzisław	Henneberg	303	Hurricane I	V6684	RF-F	11.40	Bf 110	dest	Rochester
5 October	Sgt	Stanisław	Karubin	303	Hurricane I	P3901	RF-E	11.40	Bf 109	dest	Rochester
5 October	S/Ldr	Ronald Gustave	Kellett	303	Hurricane I	V7504	RF-G	11.40	Bf 109E	dam	Rochester
5 October	Sgt	Jan	Palak	303	Hurricane I	P3217	RF-S	11.40	Bf 109	dest	Rochester
5 October	Sgt	Jan	Palak	303	Hurricane I	P3217	RF-S	11.40	Bf 110	dam	Rochester
5 October	F/O	Marian	Pisarek	303	Hurricane I	V7503	RF-U	11.40	Bf 110	dest	Rochester
5 October	F/O	Marian	Pisarek	303	Hurricane I	V7503	RF-U	11.40	Bf 110	dam	Rochester
5 October	Sgt	Antoni	Siudak	303	Hurricane I	N2460	RF-D	11.40	Bf 110	dest1/2	nr Ashford
5 October	Sgt	Antoni	Siudak	303	Hurricane I	N2460	RF-D	11.40	Bf 109	dest	nr Ashford
5 October	Sgt	Antoni	Siudak	303	Hurricane I	N2460	RF-D	11.40	Bf 109	dest	off Littlestone
5 October	P/O	Ludwik	Martel	603	Spitfire	X4348	XT-R	11.50	Bf 109	dest	Dover
5 October	F/O	Henryk	Szczęsny	74	Spitfire II	P7363	ZP-	14.05	Do 17	dest1/3	30m E Harwich
7 October	P/O	Jerzy	Palusiński	303	Hurricane	N2661	RF-J	13.50	Bf 109	dest?	SW of Redhill
7 October	Sgt	Marian	Belc	303	Hurricane I	L2099	RF-O	13.50	Bf 109	dest	off Kent coast
7 October	F/O	Marian	Pisarek	303	Hurricane I	V7503	RF-U	13.50	Bf 109	dest	off Brighton
7 October	Sgt	Eugeniusz	Szaposznikow	303	Hurricane I	V7244	RF-C	13.50	Bf 109	dest	S London
7 October	Sgt	Eugeniusz	Szaposznikow	303	Hurricane I	V7244	RF-C	13.50	Bf 109	dam	(East Sussex)
7 October	P/O	Zbigniew	Nosowicz	56	Hurricane I	V7605	US-	16.00	Do 17	prob	Yeovil
7 October	P/O	Zbigniew	Nosowicz	56	Hurricane I	V7605	US-	16.00	Bf 110	dam	Cranbrook
7 October	Sgt	Jan	Budziński	605	Hurricane I	P3965	UP-	16.30	Bf 109	dest1/2	Yeovil ? N
7 October	Sgt	Józef	Jeka	238	Hurricane I	L1889	VK-	16.30	Ju 88	dest	Portland

266

Date	Rank	First name	Name	Unit	A/C type	Serial numbers	Code letters	Time	Claim		Place
7 October	Sgt	Zygmunt	Klein	152	Spitfire I	P9386	UM-	15.45	Bf 110	dam	5m W Swanage
10 October	P/O	Władysław	Różycki	238	Hurricane I	P3618	VK-		Bf 109	dam	
15 October	F/Lt	William	Riley	302	Hurricane I	P3923	WX-U	10.15	Bf 109	dest	Canterbury
15 October	P/O	Wacław	Król	302	Hurricane I	P3931	WX-V	10.15	Bf 109	dest	Maidstone
15 October	P/O	Bolesław	Własnowolski	213	Hurricane I	P3641	AK-P	12.30	Bf 109	dest	Centre of Isle of Wight
15 October	F/O	Tadeusz	Nowierski	609	Spitfire I	R6961	PR-P	12.30-12.45	Bf 109	dest	Christchurch
18 October	Sgt	Eugeniusz	Nowakiewicz	302	Hurricane I	P3205	WX-E	17.05	Ju 88	prob	South coast
26 October	Sgt	Antoni	Markiewicz	302	Hurricane I	V6942	WX-S	11.30	Bf 109	prob	Boulogne
26 October	S/Ldr	William Arthur John	Satchell	302	Hurricane I	V6865	WX-L	11.30	Bf 109	prob	Boulogne
27 October	P/O	Paweł	Niemiec	17	Hurricane I	P2794	YB-E		Do 17	dam1/2	
27 October	**F/O**	**Piotr**	**Ostaszewski-Ostoja**	**609**	**Spitfire I**	**X4165**	**PR-**		**Ju 88**	**dest?**	**near Andover**
28 October	P/O	Franciszek	Surma	257	Hurricane I	P3893	DT-	10.40-11.00	He 111	dam	Romney-Folkestone area
29 October	**P/O**	**Jerzy**	**Solak**	**249**	**Hurricane**	V6743	**GN-**	**17.00**	**Bf 109**	**dest?**	Foulness
29 October	P/O	Tadeusz	Kumięga	17	Hurricane I	P3463	YB-	17.00	Bf 109	dest1/2	North Weald ?
29 October	Sgt	Michał Mirosław	Maciejowski	249	Hurricane I		GN-L	17.00	Bf 109	dest	Maldon area
29 October	P/O	Tadeusz II	Nowak	253	Hurricane I	V6637	SW-	17.15-17.25	Do 17	dest	Rye
3 November	**Sgt**	**Bolesław**	**Olewinski**	**111**	**Hurricane**	**V6560**	**JU-**	12.45	**He 111**	**dest1/3**	**Moray Firth**
7 November	Sgt	Michał Mirosław	Maciejowski	249	Hurricane I	V6534	GN-		Bf 109E	dest	8m NW of Margate
8 November	P/O	Marian	Chełmecki	17	Hurricane I	P2794	YB-E	16.00-1700	Ju 87	dest	
8 November	P/O	Paweł	Niemiec	17	Hurricane I	V6759	YB-	16.00-17.00	Ju 87	dest	
8 November	P/O	Stanisław	Skalski	501	Hurricane I	V6723	SD-	13.40	Bf 109	dest1/3	
8 November	P/O	Stanisław	Skalski	501	Hurricane I	V6723	SD-	13.40	Bf 109	dest1/3	
9 November	P/O	Marian	Chełmecki	17	Hurricane I	P2794	YB-E	15.30	Do 17	dam1/2	
11 November	P/O	Marian	Chełmecki	17	Hurricane I	V6553	YB-J		Bf 109	dest	
11 November		Karol	Pniak	257	Hurricane I	V7296	DT-Z	13.30	BR.20	dest1/3	10m E Harwich nr Woodbridge
11 November		Karol	Pniak	257	Hurricane I	V7296	DT-Z	13.30	BR.20	dest1/2	
13 November	P/O	Bohdan	Bielkiewicz	306	Hurricane I	V6950	UZ-T	16.45	He 111	prob1/3	10 m W Worcester
13 November	P/O	Edward	Jankowski	306	Hurricane I		UZ-	16.45	He 111	prob1/3	10 m W Worcester

Date	Rank	First name	Name	Unit	A/C type	Serial numbers	Code letters	Time	Claim		Place
13 November	F/Lt	Hugh Charles	Kennard	306	Hurricane I		UZ-	16.45	He 111	prob1/3	10 m W Worcester
17 November	Sgt	Paweł	Niemiec	17	Hurricane I	V6759	YB-	09.15	Bf 110C	dest1/2	Baginton ar
24 November	Sgt	Mieczysław	Parafiński	308	Hurricane I		ZF-	16.00~	Ju 88	dest	
28 November	**Sgt**	**Michał Mirosław**	**Maciejowski**	**249**	**Hurricane I**	**V6855**	**GN-**		**Bf 109E**	**prob?**	**Maidstone ar**
28 November	**Sgt**	**Zygmunt**	**Klein**	**152**	**Spitfire I**	**P9427**	**UM-**	**15.25**	**Bf 109**	**dest?**	**5-10m S Dover**
1 December	**Sgt**	**Szymon**	**Kita**	**253**	**Hurricane**	**P3678**	**SW-**		**Bf 109E**	**dest?**	**5m S Southampton**
2 December	F/O	Henryk	Szczęsny	74	Spitfire II	P7363	ZP-	11.40	Bf 109E	dam1/2	Dungeness-Dover ar
2 December	F/O	Tadeusz	Nowierski	609	Spitfire I	X4471	PR-R	12.00	Do 17	dam	over Wallard Marsh
2 December	F/O	Henryk	Szczęsny	74	Spitfire II	P7363	ZP-	11.00-11.15	Bf 109E	dest	Channel
5 December	Sgt	Michał Mirosław	Maciejowski	249	Hurricane I	V6614	GN-B	15.30	Bf 109E	dest	
5 December	F/O	Henryk	Szczęsny	74	Spitfire II	P7363	ZP-	10.05	Bf 109E		
10 December	F/Lt	John F.	Finnis	302	Hurricane I	V7045	WX-A		Ju 88	prob	10m S Bognor
1941											
10 January	**Sgt**	**Michał Mirosław**	**Maciejowski**	**249**	**Hurricane I**	**V6614**	**GN-B**	**13.00**	**Bf 109E**	**dest[3]**	**nr Guines-La Plage a/f**
16 January	F/O	Jan	Falkowski	32	Hurricane II	Z2984	GZ-	19.40	He 111	dest	Bristol ar
22 January	*F/O*	*Wacław*	*Łapkowski*	*303*	*Hurricane I*	*W9129*	*RF-W*		*Bf 109*	*dam on the ground*	*Auxi-le-Chateau Crecy (Abbeville)*
22 January	*P/O*	*Wiktor*	*Strzembosz*	*303*	*Hurricane I*	*R4081*	*RF-O*	*11.45*	*Bf 109*	*dest*	*Gravelines-Dunkirk*
10 February	Sgt	Stanisław	Brzeski	249	Hurricane I	R4178	GN-	12.50	Bf 109E	dest	Dunkirk-Gravelines
10 February	Sgt	Michał Mirosław	Maciejowski	249	Hurricane I	V6614	GN-B		Bf 109E		10m SE
13 February	F/O	Tadeusz	Nowierski	609	Spitfire I	X4773	PR-	17.00-1703	Ju 88	dam	Isle of Wight
16 February	P/O	Edward	Pilch	302	Hurricane I	P3877	WX-T	12.10	Ju 88	dest1/2	over Bognor
16 February	Sgt	Marian	Wędzik	302	Hurricane I	P2918	WX-Y	12.10	Ju 88	dest1/2	15m S Ford
18 February	*Sgt*	*Stanisław*	*Brzęski*	*249*	*Hurricane I*		*GN-*		*Bf 109*	*dest on the ground*	
4 March	F/Lt	Julian	Kowalski	302	Hurricane I	V6744	WX-C	11.10	Ju 88	dam 1/3	S St Catherines Pt
4 March	Sgt	Antoni	Łysek	302	Hurricane I	V3207	WX-A	11.10	Ju 88	dam 1/3	S St Catherines Pt
4 March	P/O	Jan	Maliński	302	Hurricane I	V6860	WX-B	11.10	Ju 88	dam 1/3	S St Catherines Pt

Date	Rank	First name	Name	Unit	A/C type	Serial numbers	Code letters	Time	Claim		Place
11 March	**F/O**	**Tadeusz**	**Arentowicz**	**303**	**Spitfire II**	**P7786**	**RF-C**	**12.30-13.20**	**Whitley**	**dest1/2**	
11 March	**Sgt**	**Mieczysław**	**Popek**	**303**	**Spitfire II**	**P7858**	**RF-H**	**12.30-13.20**	**Whitley**	**dest1/2**	
12 March	Sgt (Sgt	Kazimierz Jerzy	Jankowiak (Karaís)	307	Defiant	N3439	EW-E?	21.50-	He 111	dam	Garn
13 March	**Sgt**	**Eugeniusz**	**Nowakiewicz**	**302**	**Hurricane I**	**Z2523**	**WX-G**	**15.20-**	**Ju 88**	**dam1/2?**	**Selsey Bill**
13 March	**F/O**	**Włodzimierz**	**Karwowski**	**302**	**Hurricane II**	**Z2386**	**WX-C**	**15.20-**	**Ju 88**	**dam1/2?**	**Selsey Bill**
13 March	P/O	Bronisław	Bernaś	302	Hurricane II	Z2350	WX-W	16.40	Ju 88	dam1/3	Selsey Bill
13 March	P/O	Wacław	Król	302	Hurricane II	Z2485	WX-U	16.40	Ju 88	dam1/3	Selsey Bill
13 March	P/O	Marceli	Neyder	302	Hurricane II	Z2423	WX-V	16.40	Ju 88	dam1/3	above coast line W Patrol Point
14 March	F/O (Sgt	Maksymilian Marian	Lewandowski Niewolski)	307	Defiant	N3439	EW-E?	00.50	twin engine	dam	George
26 March	P/O	Władysław	Bożek	308	Hurricane I	V7177	ZF-	12.00	Ju 88	prob1/3	2m E Kenilworth
26 March	Sgt	Jan	Kremski	308	Hurricane I	P2855	ZF-	12.00	Ju 88	prob1/3	2m E Kenilworth
26 March	P/O	Franciszek	Surma	308	Hurricane I	V6999	ZF-	12.00	Ju 88	prob1/3	2m E Kenilworth
28 March	P/O	Władysław	Kamiński	302	Hurricane II	Z2342	WX-F	12.35	Ju 88	dest1/3	5-7 m SSW St Catherine's Point
28 March	P/O	Stanisław	Łapka	302	Hurricane II	Z2668	WX-H	12.35	Ju 88	dest1/3	5-7 m SSW St Catherine's Point
28 March	Sgt	Antoni	Łysek	302	Hurricane II	Z2806	WX-A	12.35	Ju 88	dest1/3	5-7 m SSW St Catherine's Point
1 April	P/O	Bohdan	Anders	316	Hurricane I	V6635	SZ-X	18.05	He 111	dest1/2	Linney Head
1 April	F/O	Aleksander	Gabszewicz	316	Hurricane I	V7000	SZ-S	18.05	He 111	dest1/2	Linney Head
2 April	F/Lt	John R.	Young	317	Hurricane I	V6552	JH-	14.20	Ju 88	dam	3m S Ahnmouth
6 April	F/Lt	Gustaw	Radwański	56	Hurricane II	Z2636	US-U		Do 17	dam	
7 April	Sgt	Jan	Rogowski	74	Spitfire II	P8199	ZP-	09.25-10.25	Bf 109	dest	off Cap Gris Nez
9 April	F/O	Tadeusz	Sawicz	316	Hurricane I	P3926	SZ-P	09.50	He 111	dest	3m W St Ann's Head
12 April	Sgt (Sgt	Kazimierz Józef	Jankowiak Lipiński)	307	Defiant	N3315	EW-C	01.35	He 111	dest	20m S Bristol
16 April	F/O (Sgt	Maksymilian Mieczysław	Lewandowski Zakrocki)	307	Defiant	N3490	EW-	01.10-01.20	He 111	dam	Taunton Chard

269

Date	Rank	First name	Name	Unit	A/C type	Serial numbers	Code letters	Time	Claim		Place
20 April	P/O	Jan Kazimierz	Daszewski	303	Spitfire II	P8041	RF-E	11.00	Bf 109	prob	Le Touquet area
20 April	P/O	Witold	Lokuciewski	303	Spitfire II	P7546	RF-T	11.10	Bf 109	dest	Le Touquet area
20 April	Sgt	Jan	Palak	303	Spitfire II	P8079	RF-M	11.20	Ju 88	dam	over Channel
5 May	P/O	Jerzy	Godlewski	72	Spitfire II	P7376	RN-		Ju 88	dam1/2	Ashford-Tenterden area
8 May	F/O	Zygmunt	Kinel	302	Hurricane II	Z3095	WX-N	12.15	Bf 109F	dest	Ashford-Tenterden area
8 May	P/O	Wacław	Król	302	Hurricane II		WX-	12.15	Bf 109F	dest	Ashford-Tenterden area
8 May	Sgt	Marian	**Rytka**	302	Hurricane II		WX-	12.15	Bf 109	prob	5m NE Dover
8 May	F/O	Eugeniusz	Nowakiewicz	302	Hurricane II		WX-	13.00	Bf 109	dest	appr. Sevenoaks
8 May	Sgt	Zbigniew	Wróblewski	302	Hurricane II	Z2806	WX-E	19.00	Bf 109	prob	nr Ashford
10 May	P/O	Marceli	Neyder	302	Hurricane IIB		WX-	19.20	Bf 109	dam	N London -> nr S coast
11 May	F/O	Władysław	Nowak	306	Hurricane II	Z2969	UZ-F	01.15	He 111	dest	NE London
11 May	F/O	Gerard K.	Ranoszek	306	Hurricane II	Z2968	UZ-D	02.00-02.30	Ju 88	dam	
12 May	Sgt (Sgt	Jerzy Stanisław	Malinowski Jarzembowski)	307	Defiant 03.35	N3404	EW-	03.25-	He 111	dest	4m S Exmouth
15 May	*Sgt*	*Marian*	*Bełc*	*303*	*Spitfire II*	*P8099*	*RF-V*	*12.15-13.25*	*Ju 52*	*dam 1/2 on the ground*	*St Inglevert*
15 May	*Sgt*	*Marian*	*Bełc*	*303*	*Spitfire II*	*P8099*	*RF-V*	*12.15-13.25*	*vessel*	*dam*	
15 May	*Sgt*	*Marian*	*Bełc*	*303*	*Spitfire II*	*P8099*	*RF-V*	*12.15-13.25*	*vessel*	*dam*	
15 May	*P/O*	*Bolesław*	*Drobiński*	*303*	*Spitfire II*	*P8038*	*RF-D*	*12.15-13.25*	*Ju 52*	*dam 1/2 on the ground*	*St Inglevert*
15 May	*P/O*	*Bolesław*	*Drobiński*	*303*	*Spitfire II*	*P8038*	*RF-D*	*12.15-13.25*	*vessel*	*start fire*	
15 May	Sgt	Wacław	Giermer	303	Spitfire II	P7786	RF-C	12.45	Ju 52	dest1/2	S St Omer
15 May	F/Lt	Jerzy	Jankiewicz	303	Spitfire II	P8130	RF-T	12.45	Ju 52	dest1/2	S St Omer
15 May	*P/O*	*Stefan*	*Paderewski*	*303*	*Spitfire II*	*P8360*	*RF-*	*12.15-13.25*	*Bf 109*	*damaged on the ground*	*S St. Omer*
15 May	*Sgt*	*Mieczysław*	*Popek*	*303*	*Spitfire II*	*P8085*	*RF-J*	*12.15-13.25*	*bowser*	*damaged on the ground*	*S St. Omer*
21 May	P/O	Marian	Rytka	302	Hurricane II	Z2423	WX-V	17.35	Bf 109F	dest	Bethune
21 May	P/O	Zbigniew	Wróblewski	302	Hurricane II		WX-		Bf 109	prob	St Pol area
22 May	P/O	Ryszard	Malczewski	601	Hurricane II	Z3268	UF-M	12.10	Ju 52	prob1/2	Foret d'Eperterques
24 May	**P/O**	**Eugeniusz**	**Fiedorczuk**	**315**	**Hurricane I**	**R4122**	**PK-S**	**14.50**	**Ju 88 1/2**	**dest**	**over Chester**
24 May	**F/Lt**	**Bronisław**	**Mickiewicz**	**315**	**Hurricane I**	**V7660**	**PK-V**	**14.50**	**Ju 88 1/2**	**dest**	**over Chester**
2 June	Sgt	Tadeusz	Baranowski	317	Hurricane I	W9183	JH-	22.29	Ju 88	dest1/2	4-5m ENE Tynemouth
2 June	F/O	Paweł	Niemiec	317	Hurricane I	V7123	JH-	22.29	Ju 88	dest1/2	4-5m ENE Tynemouth

1 One of four 238 Sqn Hurricanes lost in combat: F/Lt S. C. Walch, P3819 F/O Michał Steborowski, P/O F. N. Cawse, Sgt G. Gledhill.
2 Reported as 'Potez'.
3 Qualified as Me 109 destroyed on land.

Appendix 5

POLISH AIR FORCE RANKS

Polish Air Force ranks were identical to those of the army. Flying personnel were identified by adding (after the rank) the word *pilot* (abbreviated *pil.*) or *obserwator* (*obs.*) for pilots or navigators respectively. For the sake of simplicity the *pil.* suffixes are omitted in this book, although in fact every fighter pilot's rank carried it. In the PAF one had to be a commissioned officer to become an "observer" (i. e. navigator), but even a private could be a pilot. Some of the aces mentioned in this book claimed their first victories at this modest rank.

Polish airmen in France in 1940 used an unchanged PAF rank system.

Things got complicated in Britain. Polish personnel there had two parallel ranks: Polish and British. In this book only RAF ranks are quoted (official documents typically used only one of these), and it has to be kept in mind that these were not equivalent! Pilots in the ranks from *szeregowy* up to *plutonowy* were all RAF Sergeants, as were usually Polish NCOs with the rank of *sierżant*. At higher levels too, Polish ranks were often lower than the RAF ones. For example, when in September 1940 Witold Urbanowicz assumed command of 303 Sqn, becoming a Squadron Leader, he continued as Polish *porucznik*. Or precisely *porucznik pilot obserwator* (*por. pil. obs.*), as he had completed officers' training in both functions.

rank	abbr.	translation	RAF equivalent
szeregowy	szer.	private	Aircraftsman
starszy szeregowy	st. szer.	senior private	Leading Aircraftsman
kapral	kpr.	corporal	Senior Aircraftsman
plutonowy	plut.	platoon commander	Corporal
sierżant	sierż.	sergeant	Sergeant
starszy sierżant	st. sierż.	senior sergeant	Flight Sergeant
chorąży	chor.	warrant officer	Warrant Officer
podporucznik	ppor.	sublieutenant	Pilot Officer
porucznik	por.	lieutenant	Flying Officer
kapitan	kpt.	captain	Flight Lieutenant
major	mjr	major	Squadron Leader
podpułkownik	ppłk	subcolonel	Wing Commander
pułkownik	płk	colonel	Group Captain
generał brygady	gen. bryg.	brigadier general	Air Commodore
generał dywizji	gen. dyw.	divisional general	Air Vice-Marshal
generał broni	gen. broni	service general	Air Marshal
(generał lotnictwa)	(gen. lotn.)	(air force general)	
generał armii	gen. armii	army general	Air Chief Marshal

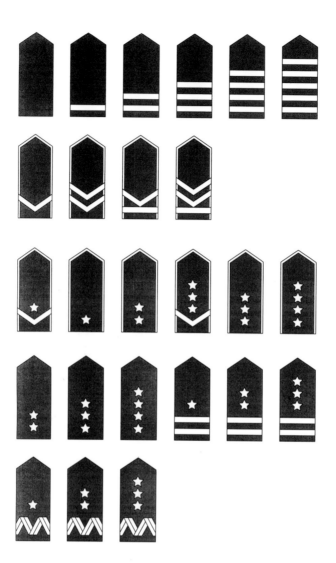

First row
1 szeregowy
2 starszy szeregowy
3 kapral
4 starszy kapral
5 plutonowy
6 starszy plutonowy

Second row
7 sierżant
8 starszy sierżant
9 sierżant sztabowy
10 starszy sierżant sztabowy

Third row
11 młodszy chorąży
12 chorąży
13 starszy chorąży
14 młodszy chorąży sztabowy
15 chorąży sztabowy
16 starszy chorąży sztabowy

Fourth row
17 podporucznik
18 porucznik
19 kapitan
20 major
21 podpułkownik
22 pułkownik

Fifth row
23 generał bygady
24 generał dywizji
25 generał broni

Appendix VI

ROLL OF HONOUR
LIST OF POLISH PILOTS KILLED 29 JULY 1940 – 2 JUNE 1941

(including pilots trained at OTU's)

1940

Date	Rank	First name	Surname	Unit	Aircraft	Serial	Code
29 July	P/O	Kazimierz	Olewiński	6 OTU	Hurricane I	L1714	
11 August	F/O	Antoni	Ostowicz	145	Hurricane I	V7294	SO-
11 August	F/O	Michał Jan	Stęborowski	238	Hurricane I	P3819	VK-
12 August	Sgt	Józef	Kwieciński	145	Hurricane I	P3391	SO-
12 August	F/O	Kazimierz	Łukaszewicz	501	Hurricane I	P3803	SD-Z
12 August	F/Lt	Wilhelm	Pankratz	145	Hurricane I	R4176	SO-
15 August	F/O	Mieczyslaw	Rozwadowski	151	Hurricane I	V7410	DZ-
18 August	F/O	Franciszek	Gruszka	65	Spitfire I	R6713	YT-
18 August	F/O	Kazimierz	Niedźwiecki	6 OTU	Hurricane I	324[1]	
24 August	F/O	Paweł	Zenker	501	Hurricane I	P3141	SD-W
30 August	Sgt	Feliks	Gmur	151	Hurricane I	R4213	DZ-
4 September	F/O	Janusz	Maciński	111	Hurricane II	Z2309	JU-
7 September	F/O	Walenty	Krepski	54	Spitfire I	R6901	KL-
11 September	F/O	Arsen	Cebrzyński	303	Hurricane I	V6667	RF-K
11 September	Sgt	Stanisław	Duszyński	238	Hurricane I	R2682	VK-
11 September	Sgt	Antoni	Wójcicki	213	Hurricane I	W6667	AK-P
11 September	Sgt	Stefan	Wójtowicz	303	Hurricane I	V7242	RF-B
15 September	Sgt	Michał	Brzezowski	303	Hurricane I	P3577	RF-E
15 September	F/Lt	Tadeusz	Chłopik	302	Hurricane I	P2954	WX-E
21 September	F/O	Juliusz	Topolnicki	601	Hurricane I	L1894	UF-
24 September	P/O	Witold Józef	Głowacki	605	Hurricane I	P3832	UP-P
26 September	P/O	Włodzimierz	Samoliński	253	Hurricane I	V7470	SW-
27 September	Sgt	Tadeusz	Andruszków	303	Hurricane I	V6665	RF-J
27 September	F/Lt	Ludwik Witold	Paszkiewicz	303	Hurricane I	L1696	RF-T
5 October	F/O	Wojciech	Januszewicz	303	Hurricane I	P3892	RF-V
6 October	Sgt	Antoni	Siudak	303	Hurricane I	P3120	RF-A
8 October	Sgt	Josef	František (Czech)	303	Hurricane I	R4175	RF-R
17 October	Sgt	Jerzy Sergiusz	Załuski	302	Hurricane I	V7417	WX-T
18 October	F/O	Jan	Borowski	302	Hurricane I	P3930	WX-X
18 October	F/O	Edward	Carter	302	Hurricane I	P3931	WX-V
18 October	P/O	Stefan	Wapniarek	302	Hurricane I	P3872	WX-R
18 October	F/O	Aleksiej	Żukowski	302	Hurricane I	V6571	WX-Q
24 October	F/O	Jan	Bury-Burzymski	303	Hurricane I	V6807	RF-R
25 October	F/Lt	Franciszek	Jastrzębski	302	Hurricane I	V7593	WX-V
25 October	F/O	Stanisław	Piątkowski	79	Hurricane I	N2708	NV-
1 November	Sgt	Mieczysław	Marcinkowski	501	Hurricane I	V7405	SD-
1 November	P/O	Bolesław Andrzej	Własnowolski	213	Hurricane I	N2608	AK-V
3 November	Sgt	Bolesław	Olewiński	111	Hurricane I	V6560	JU-
8 November	Sgt	Wilhelm	Kosarz	302	Hurricane I	P3538	WX-J
15 November	F/O	Czesław	Gauze	605	Hurricane I	V6951	UP-
23 November	P/O	Wilhelm	Szafraniec	56	Hurricane I	V7569	US-
28 November	Sgt	Zygmunt	Klein	152	Spitfire I	P9427	UM-
30 November	Sgt	Franciszek	Prętkiewicz	245	Hurricane I	R4079	DX-
30 November	Sgt	Wilhelm	Sasak	145	Hurricane I	P3704	SO-
4 December	F/O	Ryszard	Koczor	308	Hurricane I	V7071	ZF-

1941

Date	Rank	First name	Surname	Unit	Aircraft	Serial	Code
10 January	Sgt	Antoni	Joda	307	Defiant	N3401	EW-
10 January	Sgt	Wiktor	Gandurski	307	Defiant	N3401	EW-
11 January	F/O	Witalis	Nikonow	308	Master I	N7955	
11 January	P/O	Jerzy	Wolski	308	Master I	N7955	
5 February	F/O	Stanisław	Czternastek	615	Hurricane I	V7598	KW-U
13 February	F/O	Bogdan	Bielkiewicz	306	Hurricane I	P3069	UZ-Y
17 February	Sgt	Kazimierz	Bocheński	307	Defiant	N3314	EW-
17 February	Sgt	Kazimierz	Frąckiewicz	307	Defiant	N3314	EW-
20 February	F/O	Edward Roman	Pilch	302	Hurricane I	R2687	WX-X
26 February	Sgt	Mieczyslaw Jan	Parafiński	308	Hurricane I	V7073	ZF-
27 March	F/O	Tadeusz	Hoyden	315	Hurricane I	V7656	PK-V
27 March	Sgt	Edward	Paterek	315	Hurricane I	V7187	PK-W
27 March	F/O	Władysław	Szulkowski	315	Hurricane I	V7188	PK-X
10 April	Sgt	Maksymilian	Frychel	307	Defiant	N3390	EW-
10 April	Sgt	Jan Edward	Dziubek	307	Defiant	N3390	EW-
10 April	P/O	Jerzy	Niżyński	55 OTU	Hurricane I	N2337	
11 April	Sgt	Aleksander	Popławski	607	Hurricane I	P3425	AF-
12 April	S/Ldr	Zdzisław	Henneberg	303	Spitfire II	P8029	RF-P
16 April	F/O	Bogusław	Mierzwa	303	Spitfire IIA	P7819	RF-S
16 April	F/O	Mieczysław	Waszkiewicz	303	Spitfire II	P8039	RF-R
20 April	P/O	Matej	Pavlovic (Czech)	303	Spitfire II	P7859	RF-V
26 April	Sgt	Tadeusz	Nastorowicz	302	Hurricane IIA	Z2814	WX-K
08 May	F/O	Olech Antoni	Kawczyński	32	Hurricane II	Z2324	GZ-
08 May	F/O	Zygmunt	Kinel	302	Hurricane IIB	Z3095	WX-N
11 May	P/O	Aleksander Ryszard	Narucki	302	Hurricane IIB	Z3435	WX-B
15 May	Sgt	Tadeusz Henryk	Koch	58 OTU	Spitfire I	L1018	
19 May	F/O	Jan Artur	Czapiewski	306	Hurricane IIB	Z2456	UZ-W
20 May	P/O	Bernard	Samp	605	Hurricane II	Z2319	UP-
2 June	P/O	Bohdan	Anders	316	Magister	R1838	

1 ex-Canadian Mk I with three digit number.

SELECT BIBLIOGRAPHY AND SOURCES

Primary Sources

17 Squadron Combat Reports, AIR 50/9
17 Squadron ORB, PRO, AIR 27/234-235
32 Squadron Combat Reports, AIR 50/16
32 Squadron ORB, PRO, AIR 27/360-361
43 Squadron ORB, PRO, AIR 27/441-443
46 Squadron ORB, PRO, AIR 27/460
54 Squadron Combat Reports, AIR 50/20
54 Squadron ORB, PRO, AIR 27/511
56 Squadron Combat Reports, AIR 50/22
56 Squadron ORB, PRO, AIR 27/528-529
65 Squadron Combat Reports, AIR 50/25
65 Squadron ORB, PRO, AIR 27/592
72 Squadron Combat Reports, AIR 50/30
74 Squadron Combat Reports, AIR 50/32
74 Squadron ORB, PRO, AIR 27/640
85 Squadron Combat Reports, AIR 50/36
111 Squadron Combat Reports, AIR 50/43
111 Squadron ORB, PRO, AIR 27/866
145 Squadron Combat Reports, AIR 50/62
145 Squadron ORB, PRO, AIR 27/984
151 Squadron Combat Reports, AIR 50/63
151 Squadron ORB, PRO, AIR 27/1018
152 Squadron Combat Reports, AIR 50/64
152 Squadron ORB, PRO, AIR 27/1025
213 Squadron Combat Reports, AIR 50/83
213 Squadron ORB, PRO, AIR 27/1315
229 Squadron ORB, PRO, AIR 27/1418
234 Squadron Combat Reports, AIR 50/89
234 Squadron ORB, PRO, AIR 27/1439
238 Squadron Combat Reports, AIR 50/91
238 Squadron ORB, PRO, AIR 27/1453
245 Squadron ORB, PRO, AIR 27/
249 Squadron ORB, PRO, AIR 27/1498

253 Squadron Combat Reports, AIR 50/97
253 Squadron ORB, PRO, AIR 27/1511
257 Squadron Combat Reports, AIR 50/100
257 Squadron ORB, PRO, AIR 27/1526
302 Squadron Combat Reports, AIR 50/116
302 Squadron ORB, PRO, AIR 27/
303 Squadron Combat Reports, AIR 50/117
303 Squadron ORB, PRO, AIR 27/
306 Squadron Combat Reports, AIR 50/118
306 Squadron ORB, PRO, AIR 27/
307 Squadron Combat Reports, AIR 50/119
307 Squadron ORB, PRO, AIR 27/
308 Squadron Combat Reports, AIR 50/120
308 Squadron ORB, PRO, AIR 27/
315 Squadron Combat Reports, AIR 50/125
315 Squadron ORB, PRO, AIR 27/
316 Squadron Combat Reports, AIR 50/126
316 Squadron ORB, PRO, AIR 27/1705
317 Squadron Combat Reports, AIR 50/127
317 Squadron ORB, PRO, AIR 27/1706
501 Squadron Combat Reports, AIR 50/162
501 Squadron ORB, PRO, AIR 27/1949-1950
601 Squadron Combat Reports, AIR 50/165
601 Squadron ORB, PRO, AIR 27/2068
603 Squadron Combat Reports, AIR 50/167
605 Squadron Combat Reports, AIR 50/169
605 Squadron ORB, PRO, AIR 27/2088-2089
607 Squadron Combat Reports, AIR 50/170
609 Squadron Combat Reports, AIR 50/171
609 Squadron ORB, PRO, AIR 27/2102
615 Squadron Combat Reports, AIR 50/175
615 Squadron ORB, PRO, AIR 27/

Various combat reports, Polish Institute and Sikorski Museum, LOT A.V.44/11, LOT A.V.44/3G
302 Squadron Chronicle, Polish Institute and Sikorski Museum, LOT A.V.48/59
303 Squadron Chronicle, Polish Institute and Sikorski Museum
308 Squadron Monthly Reports, Polish Institute and Sikorski Museum, LOT A.V.52/4
308 Squadron Chronicle, Polish Institute and Sikorski Museum, LOT A.V.52/23
316 Squadron Chronicle, Polish Institute and Sikorski Museum, LOT A.V.54/10

Log books
George Barclay, Bernard Buchwald, Marian Chełmecki, Władysław Drecki, Aleksander Gabszewicz, Antoni Głowacki, Czesław Główczyński, Zbigniew Janicki, Walerian Jasionowski, Edward Jaworski, Józef Jeka, John Alexander Kent, Jan Kowalski, Władysław Majchrzyk, Eugeniusz Malczewski, Ludwik Martel, Włodzimierz Miksa, Mieczysław Mümler, Władusław Różycki, Stanisław Wandzilak, Kazimierz Wünsche, Walerian Żak.

Published sources
Baxter, G.G., Owen, K.A., Baldock, P., *Aircraft Casualties in Kent, Part I: 1939 to 1940*, Meresborough Books, Rainham 1990;
Bickers, Richard T. *The Battle of Britain*, Salamander Books, London 1990;
Bracken, Robert, *Spitfire: the Canadians*, Boston Mills Press, Ontario 1995;

Brew, Alec, *The Defiant File*, Air Britain (Historians) Ltd, Tunbridge Wells 1996;
Caldwell, Donald, *The JG 26 War Diary, Volume 1, 1939-1942*, Grub Street, London 1996;
Cull, Brian, *249 at War*, Grub Street, London 1997;
Crook, F/Lt D. M., *Spitfire Pilot*, Faber & Faber 1942;
Cynk, Jerzy B., *The Polish Air Force at War – The Official History 1939-1943*, Schiffer Military History, Atglen PA 1998;
Cynk, Jerzy B., *The Polish Air Force at War – The Official History 1943-1945*, Schiffer Military History, Atglen PA 1998;
Dreja, Alojzy (ed.), *Czyż mogli dać więcej. Dzieje 13 Promocji Szkoły Podchorążych Lotnictwa w Dęblinie*, London 1989, (in Polish);
Ejbich, Bohdan, *Gdzie niebo się kończy*, Bellona, Warszawa 1997, (in Polish);
Foreman, John, *The Fighter Command War Diaries, Volume 1, September 1939 to September 1940*, Air Research Publications, 1996;
Foreman, John, *The Fighter Command War Diaries, Volume 2, September 1940 to December 1941*, Air Research Publications, 1998;
Foreman, John, *Battle of Britain – The Forgotten Months, November and December 1940*, Air Research Publications, 1988;
Foreman, John, *Air War 1941 – The Turning Point, Part 1, From the Battle of Britain to the Blitz*, Air Research Publications, 1993;
Foreman, John, *Air War 1941 – The Turning Point, Part 2, From the Blitz to the Non-Stop Offensive*, Air Research Publications, 1994;
Giermer, F/Lt Wacław, *Jeden z Dywizjonu 303*, Nottingham 1994, (in Polish);
Gnyś, S/Ldr Wladek, *First Kill – A Fighter Pilot's Autobiography*, William Kimber, London 1981;
Gretzyngier, Robert and Matusiak Wojtek, *Polish Aces of World War 2*, Osprey Publishing, 1998;
Halley, James J., *Royal Air Force Aircraft L1000-N9999*, Air Britain (Historians) Ltd, Tunbridge Wells 1996;
Halley, James J., *Royal Air Force Aircraft P1000-R9999*, Air Britain (Historians) Ltd, Tunbridge Wells 1996;
Halley, James J., *Royal Air Force Aircraft W1000-Z9999*, Air Britain (Historians) Ltd, Tunbridge Wells 1998;
Halley, James J., *Royal Air Force Aircraft BA100-BZ999*, Air Britain (Historians) Ltd, Tunbridge Wells 1986;
Janczak, Andrzej R., *Przez ciemnię nocy. Dzieje 307 Nocnego Dywizjonu Myśliwskiego Lwowskiego 1940-1947*, Redakcja Przegladu Wojsk Lotniczych i Obrony Powietrznej, Poznan 1997, (in Polish);
Jokiel, F/O Jan, *Udział Polaków w Bitwie o Anglię*, PAX, Warszawa 1968, (in Polish);
Kelly, Terence, *Hurricane and Spitfire Pilots at War*, Kimber, London 1986;
Kent, G/Cpt John Alexander, *One of the Few*, Kimber, London 1971;
Król, S/Ldr Wacław, *Polskie Dywizjony Lotnicze w Wielkiej Brytanii*, Wydawnictwo MON, Warszawa 1982, (in Polish);
Kwolek, Edward, *Bomby w Celu*, Brighton 1984, (in Polish);
Mackenzie, W/Cdr Ken W., *Hurricane Combat – The Nine Lives of a Fighter Pilot*, Grenville Publishing Co. Ltd, London 1990;
Mason, Francis K., *Battle over Britain*, McWhirter Twins, London 1969;
Mason, Francis K., *The Hawker Hurricane*, Macdonald, London 1962;
McIntosh, Dave, *High Blue Battle – the War Diary of No. 1(401) Fighter Squadron RCAF*, Spa Books, Stevenage 1990;
Price, Alfred, *Battle of Britain Day – 15 September 1940*, Sidgwick & Jackson, London 1990;
Price, Alfred, *The Hardest Day – 18 August 1940*, Arms & Armour Press, London 1988;
Quill, Jeffrey, *Spitfire: a Test Pilot's Story*, Arrow Books, London 1986;
Ramsey, Winston G. (ed.), *The Battle of Britain then and now*, After the Battle, London 1989;
Ramsey, Winston G. (ed.), *The Blitz then and now, Volume 1*, After the Battle, London 1987;
Ramsey, Winston G. (ed.), *The Blitz then and now, Volume 2*, After the Battle, London 1988;
Ramsey, Winston G. (ed.), *The Blitz then and now, Volume 3*, After the Battle, London 1990;
Rawlings, John, *Fighter Squadrons of the RAF and their aircraft*, Macdonald, 1969;
Robinson, Anthony, *RAF Fighter Squadrons in the Battle of Britain*, Brockhampton Press, London 1999;
Rolski, W/Cdr Tadeusz, *Uwaga, wszystkie samoloty*, PAX, Warszawa 1959, (in Polish);
Sarkar, Dilip, *Missing in Action: Resting in Peace?*, Ramrod Publications, Worcester 1998;
Sarkar, Dilip, *Angriff Westland*, Ramrod Publications, Worcester 1994;
Shores, Christopher and Williams C, *Aces High*, Grub Street 1994;
Stokes, Dough, *Wings Aflame – The Biography of G/Cpt Victor Beamish*, Crecy Publishing Ltd., Manchester 1998;
Stones, Donald, *Dimsie, Memoirs of a Pilot from Air to Ground – A trilogy*, Wingham Press, Canterbury 1991;
Szumowski, S/Ldr Tadeusz, *Through Many Skies – The Flying Days of One Polish Pilot*, Highgate Publications (Beverley) Ltd., Beverley 1993;
Urbanowicz, G/Cpt Witold, *Początek Jutra*, Znak, Kraków 1966, (in Polish);
Urbanowicz, G/Cpt Witold, *Świt Zwycięstwa*, Znak, Kraków 1971, (in Polish);
Vraný, Jiří and Hurt Zdeněk, *Ilustrovaná Historie Letectví, Edice Triada, Hawker Hurricane Mk. I*, Naše Vojsko, Praha 1989;
Wakefield, Kenneth, *Target Filton, The two Luftwaffe attacks in September 1940*, Redcliffe, Bristol 1979;
Węgrzecki, Kazimierz (ed.), *Kosynierzy Warszawscy – Historia 303 Dywizjonu Myśliwskiego Warszawskiego imienia Tadeusz Kościuszki*, London 1968, (in Polish);

Węgrzecki, Kazimierz (ed.), *Kosynierzy Warszawscy – Historia 303 Dywizjonu Myśliwskiego Warszawskiego imienia Tadeusz Kościuszki*, (manuscript in Polish);

Wynn, Humphrey (ed.), *Fighter Pilot: A Self-Portrait by George Barclay*, Kimber, London 1976;

Wynn, Kenneth G., *Men of the Battle of Britain*, Gliddon Books, Norwich 1989;

Zieliński, Józef, *Lotnicy Polscy w Bitwie o Wielk Brytanię/Polish Airmen in the Battle of Britain*, Oficzyna Wydawnicza "MH", Warszawa 1999;

Zumbach, W/Cdr Jan, *On wings of war – My Life as a Pilot Adventurer*, Corgi Books, London 1977;

Destiny Can Wait, The Polish Air Force in the Second World War, The Battery Press, Nashville 1988;

Wspomnienia – Ostatni mohikanie szkół podchorążych lotnictwa przedwojennej Polski, London 1994, (in Polish);

Newspapers and Magazines

Aeroplan (Polish)

Aero-technika lotnicza (Polish)

Aircraft Illustrated

Air Enthusiast

The Aeroplane Monthly

Air Pictorial

Aviation News

Flight

Letectví+Kosmonautika (Czechoslovak)

Scale Aircraft Modelling

Skrzydła – Wiadomości ze świata (Polish)

Skrzydlata Polska (Polish)

INDEX

General Index, Places and Names

278

283

Air Force Units Index

Aircraft Index

Do 17Z, Werk Nr. 3317, F1+GK 108
Do 17Z-3, Werk Nr. 2891 160
Do 17, Werk.Nr.3618, 7T+KL, KÄFlGr 606 170
Do 215, Werk Nr.0038, G2+KH 102

Fairey Battle R7411 153

Heinkel
He 111, G1+GS, III./KG 55 199
He 111, G1+HA, Stab./KG 55 199
He 111H-2, Werk Nr. 3305, V4+HV 43
He 111H-2, Werk Nr. 2710, 5./KG 53 180
He 111H-3, V4+OK 86
He 111H-3, Werk Nr. 3171, I./KG 26 154
He 111H-3, Werk Nr. 3328, V4+CH, III./KG 40 211
He 111H-3, Werk Nr. 6937, 6N+MH, 1./KGr 100 216
He 111H-3, Werk Nr. 3157, 1H+ML, 3./KG 26 83
He 111H-5, 1G+LH 205
He 111P-4, Werk Nr. 2994, 5./KG 55 162
He 111P, G1+AR,7./KG 55 8
He 111P-2, Werk Nr. 2002, 1G+HT, 9./KG 27 213

Hawker Hurricane
311 194
324 273
L1696/RF-T 86, 114, 247, 273
L1714 273
L1717 146, 167
L1750 30
L1770 246
L1771 145
L1819 12, 257
L1825 247
L1868/SD-D 29, 35, 53, 258, 259
L1889 135, 266
L1894 106, 273
L1975 24
L1998 111, 264
L2005/DZ-D 30
L2014 135
L2026/RF-Q 80, 118, 120, 127, 247
L2089 99
L2092 152
L2099/RF-O 80, 96, 99, 101, 106, 114, 120, 122, 132, 164,
    247, 262, 263, 265-266
N2329/SD-K 35
N2337 274
N2352 245
N2386/US-U 134
N2423 245
N2455 86
N2460/RF-D 120, 122, 124, 127, 131-132, 246, 266
N2496 8, 11, 257
N2524 24, 258
N2542 28
N2557 107
N2594 175
N2602 12
N2607 145
N2608/AK-V 154, 273
N2616 8
N2646/UP-O 159
N2661/RF-J 124, 132, 246, 266
N2668 46
N2671 23, 258
N2708 146, 273
N2712/US-M 134
N3390 212
P2270 8
P2329 259
P2565 160
P2645 246
P2717/WX-H 146, 173, 244
P2718 40
P2752/WX-R 88, 94, 103, 105, 139, 245, 263
P2760/SD-B 43, 53, 259
P2792 157
P2794/YB-E 148, 160-161, 267, 267
P2795 34
P2826 48
P2836 98

P2855 201, 269
P2883 48, 259, 260
P2903/RF-Z 90, 247, 262
P2906 163
P2910 165
P2918/WX-Y 142, 146, 189, 245, 268
P2949 108
P2954/WX-E 88, 94, 244, 263, 273
P2957 11
P2972 148, 160, 161
P2974 209
P2979 154
P2985/RF-Z 50, 54, 62, 247, 260
P2989 10, 14, 257
P3022 135
P3023 173
P3032 48
P3055/US-P 134
P3061 151, 156
P3065 24
P3069/UZ-Y 187, 274
P3085/WX-A 88, 106, 138, 142, 152, 244, 264
P3086/WX-Z 88, 94, 103, 245, 263, 264
P3089 133
P3089/RE-F 70, 261
P3089/RF-P 76, 90, 99, 101, 106, 111, 114, 118, 120, 122,
    124, 127, 132, 246, 247, 262, 264, 265
P3100/SZ-O 239
P3102 35
P3115 48
P3120/RF-A 90, 96, 99, 101, 111, 122, 124, 131, 245-246,
    262, 265, 273
P3141/SD-W 35, 273
P3155 8
P3161 184
P3162/RF-T 247
P3174/AK-G 94, 262
P3176 161
P3183 48
P3204/WX-E 192, 244
P3205 34
P3205/WX-E 138, 142, 244, 267
P3206/RF-X 152, 247
P3217 8
P3217/RF-S 120, 122, 124, 127, 131, 247, 266
P3219 99, 126, 263, 265
P3230 135
P3301 48, 259
P3306 30
P3308 135
P3309 24
P3312 30
P3319 9
P3320 30, 258
P3337 49
P3351 49, 154
P3382 261
P3383/RF-T 132, 247
P3385 163
P3391 15, 257, 273
P3397 35, 43, 53, 257
P3399 141
P3425 212, 274
P3452 144
P3460 155
P3462 99
P3463/GN-L 150, 155, 267
P3471 8
P3514 134
P3521 11, 12
P3527 166
P3538/WX-J 102, 142, 146, 157, 244, 264, 273
P3544/RF-H 106, 111, 112, 246
P3551/RF-F 246
P3577/RF-E 90, 96, 246, 263, 273
P3579/GN-Y 155
P3583 107, 264
P3585/RF-C 246
P3598 179
P3618 83, 99, 108, 136, 163, 261-262, 264-265, 267
P3623 157

V6681/RF-B 99, 101, 106, 111, 115, 120, 122, 124, 127, 132, 146, 246, 264-266
V6684/RF-F 96, 101, 106, 111, 115, 117, 120, 124, 127, 132, 175, 246, 263, 265
V6685 153
V6692/GN-O 145, 156, 172
V6694/WX-G 157, 163, 244
V6695/JH-J 234
V6699 107
V6722 106
V6723 159, 267
V6728/GN-Z 137, 172, 186
V6733/PK-P 202
V6734/WX-K 102, 156, 244, 264
V6735/SZ-B 207
V6735/WX-M 103, 105, 142, 244, 264
V6742/WX-F 244
V6743 148, 151, 267
V6744/WX-C 138, 146, 157, 192, 244, 268
V6751 156
V6753/WX-Z 142, 183, 245
V6755 135
V6757 246
V6759 147, 150, 157, 161, 164, 267, 268
V6783 135
V6786 135
V6791 148, 161
V6798 155, 172
V6807/RF-R 144, 273
V6808/RF-A 131, 246
V6812 196
V6815 151
V6815/RF-J 176, 247
V6817 186
V6843/RF-S 247
V6854/GN-F 172, 186
V6855 155, 167, 268
V6858 199
V6859 142
V6860/WX-B 142, 146, 157, 192, 244, 268
V6861 185
V6865/WX-L 142, 146, 157, 244, 267
V6866/AK-D 86, 153, 262
V6873/SZ-M 235
V6914 145
V6923/WX-U 146, 152, 245
V6927 178
V6929 247
V6936 165
V6939 185
V6941/WX-W 146, 158, 245
V6942/WX-S 146, 157, 245, 267
V6945 186
V6946/UZ-Q 187
V6948/UZ-R 192
V6950/UZ-F 200
V6950/UZ-T 162, 267
V6951 163, 273
V6956 246
V6958/GN-D 155, 171
V6962 193
V6982 246
V6984 246
V6986/UZ-Z 183
V6990 218
V6992 175
V6999 201, 269
V7000/SZ-S 269
V7019/AK-S 200
V7025 166
V7027 187
V7042 193
V7045/WX-A 173, 244-245, 268
V7046/WX-D 244
V7047 245
V7047/WX-A 192, 244
V7048 174
V7049 201
V7052 173
V7053 192, 212
V7064 223

V7071 171, 274
V7073 192, 274
V7115 167
V7119 225
V7123 241, 270
V7130 246
V7145 244
V7165/UZ-W 178
V7171 186
V7177 201, 269
V7182/RF-U 182, 247
V7183/RF-J 182, 246
V7187/PK-W 202, 274
V7188/PK-X 193, 199, 202, 274
V7191 245
V7205 9
V7223 19, 166
V7226 53
V7230 175
V7230/SD-H 15, 20, 53, 257, 258, 260
V7234/SD-A 35, 43, 49, 53, 258, 259
V7235/RF-M 13, 54, 71, 76, 80, 90, 96, 99, 101, 106, 111, 114, 120, 122, 124, 127, 246, 261-262, 265-266
V7236 108
V7237 154
V7241 148, 151, 161
V7242/RF-B 50, 54, 61, 64, 71, 76, 79, 246, 259, 260, 261, 273
V7243/RF-P 45, 50, 61, 64, 68, 247
V7244/RF-C 50, 71, 80, 90, 99, 101, 106, 115, 117, 127, 132, 246, 259, 261-262, 264-266
V7246/RF-D 54, 56, 99, 106, 115, 246, 260, 265
V7251 12
V7284/RF-A 45 ,61, 64, 246, 260
V7289/RF-S 61, 64, 71, 76, 80, 90, 101, 106, 111, 114, 247, 260-262, 265
V7290/RF-H 50, 64-65, 71, 76, 79, 246, 259, 260, 261
V7294 14, 273
V7296/DT-Z 161, 267
V7301 151
V7316 190
V7339 176
V7357/SD-G 35, 43, 53
V7384 48
V7384/RF-H 144, 246
V7401/RF-G 148, 247
V7402/SD-L 53
V7403/SD-N 54, 88
V7405 154, 273
V7408 148, 157
V7410 24, 258, 273
V7411 24, 30
V7417/WX-T 88, 103, 105, 139, 142, 245, 263-264, 273
V7465/RF-V 76, 80, 90, 96, 101, 106, 111, 247, 261-264
V7466 (253 Sqn) 86, 151
V7466/RF-S 182, 247
V7468 135
V7470 273
V7499 151
V7499/RF-D 182, 246
V7500/YB-D 148, 151, 157, 160-161
V7502 184
V7503/RF-U 120, 122, 124, 127, 132, 247, 266
V7504/RF-G 120, 122, 124, 127, 132, 246, 265-266
V7505 134, 120
V7506 135
V7507/GN-B 156
V7508/US-N 134
V7509/US-S 134
V7510 134, 173
V7533 166
V7535 155
V7538/GN-T 155, 172, 186
V7542 156
V7569 165, 273
V7570 147, 151, 157, 161
V7593/WX-V 145, 245, 273
V7598/KW-U 185, 274
V7600/GN-C 155, 172, 186
V7605 266
V7606 (253 Sqn) 151

Bf 109F-2, III./JG 3, white 3 239
Bf 110C, Werk Nr. 3615, M8+MM 46
Bf 110C, M8+BP, 6./ZG76 25
Bf 110C-2, Werk Nr. 3533, L1+LL, 15./LG 1 114
Bf 110D-0, Werk.Nr. 3390, S9+AB 59

Supermarine Spitfire
L1018 274
Spitfire N3223/PR-M 130
K9871/ZP-O 18, 258
K9882 133
L1042 257
L1048 133, 167
L1065/PR-E 258
L1082/PR-A 18, 258
N3057 58, 64
N3061 63
N3091 17, 64, 120, 258
N3108/RF-P 191
N3122/RF-Y 192
N3191 265
N3223/PR-M 117, 264-265
N3239 37
N3277/AZ-H 9, 25
N3278 9
N3279 261
N3279 37, 64, 69, 259, 260
N3283 9, 26
N3285/RF-J 192
P7325/XT-W 145
P7363 130, 170-172, 266, 268
P7376 225, 270
P7385/RF-P 217, 218
P7524/RF-G 194, 218
P7546/RF-T 218, 219, 270
P7559 191
P7567 215
P7590/RF-F 200
P7600 200
P7746/RF-B 213, 217-218
P7786/RF-C 194, 217, 232, 269, 270
P7819/RF-S 217, 218, 274
P7821/RF-A 194
P7829 188
P7830 200
P7835 198
P7858/RF-H 194, 213, 217, 219, 269
P7859/RF-V 213, 219, 274
P7962/RF-A 213, 218, 227
P7989/RF-U 207
P8029/RF-P 213, 274
P8038/RF-D 232, 270
P8038/RF-W 218, 219, 227, 200
P8039/RF-R 217, 218, 274
P8040/RF-D 194, 217
P8041/RF-E 219, 221, 227, 270
P8073/RF-Z 218
P8079/RF-M 213, 215, 219, 230, 270
P8085/RF-H 217
P8085/RF-J 227, 231, 232, 270
P8099/RF-V 227, 232, 270
P8130/RF-T 232, 270
P8164 223
P8174 223
P8199 210, 269
P8325/RF-K 234
P8360 227, 232, 270
P9363 25
P9386 133, 267
P9391 133
P9427 168, 268, 274
P9454 166
P9460 26
P9466 37, 63, 258
P9494 37
P9508 58, 63
P9519/RF-M 192, 192
P9555/RF-D 191
R6607 133
R6608 133
R6631/PR-Q 38
R6643 133

R6644/ZF-H 230
R6700/RF-X 188
R6712 34, 259
R6713 28, 258, 273
R6763 133
R6763/RF-B 191
R6896 26, 58, 75, 260, 261
R6901 75, 273
R6915 258
R6922 261
R6957 37, 58
R6959 58, 64
R6961/PR-P 123, 124, 141, 266-267
R6963 224
R6964 133
R6968 133
R6972/RF-N 191
R6975/RF-A 191
R6977/RF-C 190
R6985 257
R6986/PR-S 39
R6987 166
R6996/RF-E 191
R7015 20
X4009 37, 58, 63
X4010 37, 58
X4016 25, 258
X4023 37
X4035 37, 63
X4036 58, 63
X4165 169, 267
X4167 85, 262
X4172 218, 224
X4174 223
X4182 37, 58, 260
X4183 58, 64
X4184 221
X4233 166
X4251 37, 58, 63, 260
X4272 126
X4274/XT-P 126, 266
X4279 58
X4344/RF-R 191
X4348/XT-R 129, 266
X4381 133
X4388 208
X4424 120
X4471/PR-R 188, 268
X4477 225
X4481/RF-G 191
X4539 141
X4550 133
X4560/PR-H 160
X4617 227
X4770/RF-H 191
X4773 188, 268
X4859 224